the
mother of all
battles

the
mother of all
battles

SADDAM HUSSEIN'S STRATEGIC PLAN FOR THE PERSIAN GULF WAR

Kevin M. Woods

NAVAL INSTITUTE PRESS
Annapolis, Maryland

Naval Institute Press
291 Wood Road
Annapolis, MD 21402

Library of Congress Cataloging-in-Publication Data
Woods, Kevin M.
  The mother of all battles : Saddam Hussein's strategic plan for the Gulf War / Kevin M. Woods.
    p. cm.
  Includes bibliographical references and index.
  ISBN 978-1-59114-942-2 (alk. paper)
  1. Persian Gulf War, 1991—Iraq. 2. Iraq—History, Military—20th century. 3. Iraq—Politics and government—1979-1991. 4. Hussein, Saddam, 1937-2006. I. Title.
  DS79.724.I72W66 2008
  956.7044'2--dc22
                          2008023329

Printed in the United States of America on acid-free paper

14 13 12 11 10 09 08   9 8 7 6 5 4 3 2
First printing

Contents

List of Figures and Tables ix

Foreword xi

Preface xiii

A Note on Sources xv

    Notes xvii

Introduction xix

    Purposes of This Study xxi

    Notes xxiv

Chapter I. An Overview of the Gulf War from the U.S. Perspective 1

    The Diplomatic Background 1

    The Air War 3

    The Ground War 5

    Notes 11

Chapter II. The "Victory" at al-Khafji 14

    Notes 27

Chapter III. The Beginning: Saddam's Narrative 31

    A Long View 31

    The Iran-Iraq War as Precursor 36

    The Coming War of the Elephant 40

    Notes 43

Chapter IV. Saddam's Strategic Calculations 47

    Kuwait 47

    Notes 57

Chapter V. Restoring the Branch to the Tree 60

    Planning an Invasion 60

Yum al-Nida (Day of the Great Call)—The Invasion 73

The Republican Guard's Blitzkrieg 81

Notes 88

Chapter VI. Occupation and Consolidation 93

A New Historical Juncture 93

Extending Ba'ath Control 96

Reaction and Iraqi Counteraction 103

The Americans 114

Notes 118

Chapter VII. The Iraqi Plan for the Defense of Kuwait 124

Assessing the Coalition Threat 126

Preparing a Naval Defense 134

Notes 163

Chapter VIII. Um Al-Ma'arik (The Mother of All Battles) 172

The End-of-the-Epic Duel 227

Notes 250

Chapter IX. Iraqi Lessons Learned 262

Selected Iraqi Military Lessons 268

Notes 293

Chapter X. Saddam's Strategic Lessons of the War 299

Saddam's Analysis of His Adversary 304

Notes 305

Epilogue: Insights from the Iraqi Perspective 307

Notes 309

Appendix A: Timeline 311

Appendix B: Key Personalities 319

Acronyms and Abbreviations 323

References..325

    Books, Periodicals, Reports, Web sites..325

    U.S. Government Publications..331

    Harmony Media Files 332

    Harmony Document Folders 336

Index...345

Figures and Tables

Figures

1. Saddam Hussein, circa 1991 — xx
2. Iraq and its neighbors — 2
3. Operation Desert Storm Ground Offensive — 8
4. Iraqi Regular Army conducting a multi-division-size raid into northeastern Saudi Arabia — 10
5. Saudi port of al-Khafji — 15
6. Iraqi concept sketch for attack into al-Khafji — 19
7. Legend of al-Khafji map translated — 20
8. Map of Kuwait — 48
9. U.S. ambassador April Glaspie and Saddam Hussein — 49
10. Saddam and Yasser Arafat — 50
11. Invasion of Kuwait: Phase I — 67
12. Annotated pre-invasion aerial photograph of military objectives in Kuwait City — 68
13. Naval battlespace — 74
14. Iraqi reconnaissance photograph of Kuwait International Airport — 85
15. Saddam and the Kuwaiti Quisling — 94
16. U.S. chargé d'affaires Joseph Wilson and Saddam Hussein — 95
17. Saddam supervised the details of the Kuwait occupation — 99
18. United Nations Security Council Resolution 660 of 2 August 1990 — 103
19. Iraqi enemy situation map — 130
20. Legend to Iraqi enemy situation map — 131
21. Saddam inspecting naval mines — 135
22. Wargaming Coalition options, August 1990 — 139
23. Saddam meeting with Republican Guard officers — 143
24. General disposition of forces — 173
25. Saddam coordinating the defense of Iraq — 177
26. Coalition damage to Iraqi airfield — 186
27. The Coalition moves to the west — 188
28. Ras Tanura Oil Terminal, Saudi Arabia — 191
29. Iraqi propaganda leaflet — 200

30. Status of forces, 15 February 1991   206
31. Map of Iraqi final deployments in Kuwait theater of operations   209
32. Iraqi "Tariq Project" in action   211
33. Opening assaults of Coalition ground operations   213
34. Coalition progress late on 24 February   222
35. Coalition attacks, 25–26 February   231
36. Iraqi troops surrender to Coalition forces   234
37. Collapse of the Iraqi defense   241
38. Republican Guard battles, 28 February 1991   242
39. Negotiations at Safwan, 3 March 1991   246
40. Video capture of Ali Hassan al-Majid kicking a rebel suspect   249
41. Republican Guard lessons-learned conference   263
42. Iraqi officers participating in a lessons-learned conference   265

Tables

1. General Purpose Iraqi Forces, July 1990   61
2. Kuwait's Navy and Coast Guard Fleets   76
3. Kuwait Air Force and Air Defense   79
4. Kuwaiti Ground Forces, July 1990   83
5. Iraqi Report of Aircraft Seeking Refuge in Iran from
   26 January to mid-February 1991   194
6. Iraqi Ground Order of Battle   204
7. Iraqi Air Force Status, June 1991   272

Foreword

The purpose of the Iraqi Perspectives Project is to provide the national security community with new insights concerning the long confrontation with Saddam Hussein's Iraq. It is the author's hope that this study and others in the Iraqi Perspectives Project will stimulate thoughtful analyses of currently accepted lessons of the 1991 Gulf War. Moreover, in support of U.S. Joint Forces Command's ongoing mission to develop operational lessons, this effort will help future warfighters and planners better understand the events of 1990 and 1991 as they wrestle with the challenges of today. It is in large part through *understanding* that lessons collected can, with significant effort, become lessons learned.

Karl Lowe, Director
Joint Advanced Warfighting Program

Preface

The Iraqi Perspectives Project (IPP) is sponsored by the Joint Center for Operational Analysis (JCOA), a directorate within the United States Joint Forces Command (JFCOM) responsible for operations research and lessons learned. JCOA's work informs JFCOM's transformation of the joint force by producing recommendations derived from direct observation and analysis of current operations, exercises, and experiments. In the past three years, JCOA has conducted collection and analysis missions in support of the Indian Ocean tsunami, the Central American mudslides, Hurricane Katrina, the Pakistani earthquake, U.S. Presidential Election events, the Global War on Terrorism, and Operations Iraqi Freedom and Enduring Freedom.

The Joint Advanced Warfighting Division (JAWD), responsible for the development and publication of this study, was established at the Institute for Defense Analyses (IDA) to serve as a catalyst for stimulating innovation and breakthrough change. It is co-sponsored by the Under Secretary of Defense for Acquisition, Technology, and Logistics; the Under Secretary of Defense for Policy; the Vice Chairman of the Joint Chiefs of Staff; and the Commander, JFCOM. JAWD includes military personnel on joint assignments from each Service and civilian specialists from IDA, a Federally Funded Research and Development Center.

Although only one author is credited on the front of this study, the work was accomplished through the efforts, dedicated support, and constructive reviews of a larger team of professionals. Elizabeth Nathan provided the day-to-day research, organization, and archival support required to keep this project moving toward completion. In addition to editing drafts daily, Elizabeth's efforts in managing thousands of pages of Arabic material in various stages of translation were Herculean. Dr. Williamson Murray's contributions to this work cannot be overstated. In addition to reviewing tens of thousands of pages of translated documents and helping to frame the larger issues, Dr. Murray made the entire process of sifting through the remains of a dictatorial regime an educational experience for all. Moreover, he helped draft Chapter 2 and provided numerous detailed reviews and rewrites of remaining chapters. Laila Sabara and Thomas Holaday provided invaluable research and translation support to this and related projects. The study author is in debt to JAWD's editorial staff, Katydean Price and Carolyn Leonard, for their attention to detail, style recommendations, and occasional English grammar lessons. Other members of the JAWD staff whose research and review support to this study was significant include: Mike Pease, Mark Stout, Jim Lacey, Alec Wahlman, and William Chou. The author would like to especially thank the study reviewers, Maj. Gen. Waldo Freeman, USA (Ret); Dr. Theodore Gold, and Dr. Richard White, for their thoughtful reviews and critical comments. A final thanks to Cdr. Al Musgrove, USN, for his contributions to and unwavering support for this project from its earliest inception. Notwithstanding all of the support listed above, any errors are the sole responsibility of the author.

A Note on Sources

This study represents a unique look at Operation Desert Storm and the events precipitating it from the perspective of Iraq's senior leadership. As a newly available perspective, it will fill in many of the gaps in previous histories of that campaign and should allow a new generation of histories to be written. From these, one hopes, will emerge a deeper understanding of the lessons from the first year of what would become a long conflict.

Events in this story of the "Mother of All Battles" (as Saddam designated the 1991 war) are drawn from primary Iraqi sources, including government documents, videotapes, audiotapes, maps, and photographs, captured by U.S. forces in 2003 during Operation Iraqi Freedom (OIF).[1] This study, and indeed the larger Iraqi Perspectives Project from which it is derived, is in the spirit of earlier works and studies of its kind that followed World War II.[2] Members of the former Iraqi regime considered most of this captured material as highly classified, never intended for outsiders' eyes. For clarity and context, this study supports the Iraqi archival material with information from other sources such as American military reports, Western histories, commentaries, and analyses.

There is much about the events of the 1991 Gulf War that historians will never know. Gaps in the record are one of the challenges that plague all historical research. Understanding the nature of the gaps can help place the available information in context and, in some cases, mitigate the impact of whatever is missing. In this study of the former Iraqi regime, the records have the following attributes:

- As extensive as the database collection of regime documents and recordings is, it is not complete. In many cases, the Iraqis simply failed to record key meetings. In other cases, information in the recordings themselves indicates that only a portion of a more complete record was captured.
- Saddam's regime collapsed in chaos, so there is no way to reasonably estimate what percentage of its records were destroyed by the war, or were lost or captured. This study relied heavily on the regime's national-level military, intelligence, and presidential office records.

Ba'ath party records and regional or local records of the various arms of the regime are much less complete and generally not central to the study.

- The Ba'athist bureaucracy was hardly an example of integrity in government. The incentive structures within the regime often resulted in carefully documented falsehoods embedded in extremely detailed correspondence. In addition, some of the material in this study comes from Iraqi lessons-learned discussions recorded after the war. It is clear that in some cases the Iraqi discussions suffered from distortions due to self-delusion or simple hindsight.

- Some aspects of the narrative may seem unbalanced (little detail on some major issues and much detail on seemingly minor ones), especially when weighed against general Coalition histories of the war. There are two primary causes. The first, as outlined above, is that the captured archive is in many ways incomplete and uneven. The second is that the Iraqi narrative is their own and often does not correspond with the one the Coalition developed. For example, an event deemed important to the Coalition may not have been recorded as such, if at all, in the Iraqi record, and vice versa. Moreover, even if the opposing sides similarly recorded the event, its implication may have differed. For example, most Coalition observers view the al-Khafji operation of 29–31 January 1991 as a disaster for the Iraqi army. The regime, however, hailed the battle as a victory from the start.

This work relies on English translations of Arabic documents and English transcriptions of Arabic audio and videotape. In some cases, the quality of the Arabic translations is uneven; however, care was taken to review all cited passages for clarity and accuracy. There is no doubt that in some cases the context, nuance, and meaning of specific discussions can be misconstrued or even lost in the process. Arab scholar Hisham Sharabi notes that translations from Arabic can convey meaning, but often fail to render the significance of allusions or psychological associations contained in the language and delivery. Sharabi describes how Arab orators do not appeal to their audiences by means of direct, purposeful, and precise explanations, but rather through repetition and an indirect approach.[3] A review of Saddam's public and private discussions, as collected for this study, supports Sharabi's contentions. Bernard Lewis reminds us that "few, if any civilizations in the past have attached as much importance to history as did Islam, in its education, in its awareness of self, in the common language of everyday talk."[4] Given the often stark differences in historical narratives between the

United States and Iraq, a significant degree of miscommunication was inevitable. As this study records, that miscommunication reverberates through the captured archives.

Through a broad examination of a combination of words and deeds, this study has endeavored to present the Iraqi regime's perspective, while at the same time accounting for the limitations and distortions in the translation. It should be remembered that these limitations are a given in the daily work of those charged with developing and implementing U.S. national security policy. The reality of the twenty-first-century's security environment means that most national security professionals will never have the time to master an adversary's language, not to mention its history or culture. Given that reality, an appreciation for the impact of such limitations is essential. Therefore, a study of how the "other side of the hill" saw the 1991 war represents a critical step, regardless of limitations, to learning lessons from that war.

Notes

1. The majority of Iraqi documents, videotapes, and audiotapes referred to in this study are held in electronic form in the Defense Intelligence Agency's Harmony database. The Harmony database holds the majority of documents captured during OIF, as well as a significant number of documents captured during Operation Desert Storm.
2. Published works such as B. H. Liddell Hart, *The Other Side of the Hill* (London: Cassell and Co., 1948), and Milton Shulman, *Defeat in the West* (London: Martin Secker & Warburg, 1947), as well as a large volume of U.S. government studies resulting from the German Military History Program conducted by U.S. Army in the 1940s and 1950s.
3. Cited in Ofra Bengio, *Saddam's Word: Political Discourse in Iraq* (New York: Oxford University Press, 1998), 7.
4. Bernard Lewis, *The Political Language of Islam* (Chicago: University of Chicago Press, 1988), 9.

Introduction

> If it is, indeed, one of the major functions of the historian to explain the present by deepening our understanding of the past, then a study simply of our own society will not get us very far. Our awareness of the world and our capacity to deal intelligently with its problems are shaped not only by the history we know but by what we do not know.[1]
>
> —SIR MICHAEL HOWARD

The events recounted in this study mark the beginning of a long military campaign by the United States and its allies to confront, contain, and ultimately depose the Iraqi regime of Saddam Hussein.[2] The campaign began in 1990 with the buildup of what would become a major air and ground campaign to eject Iraq from Kuwait in 1991. More than 390,000 air sorties enforcing "no-fly zones" in the north and south of Iraq followed during the next twelve years. Several air and cruise missile strikes punctuated the era in response to the regime's failure to comply with United Nations (U.N.) demands or for threatening those enforcing them. A new phase of this long military campaign began in the spring of 2003 with a large-scale, air and ground operation to oust the dictator.[3]

In the months following the Coalition's capture of Baghdad in April 2003, it became clear that ousting Saddam was a necessary but insufficient precondition to restoring any amount of stability in Iraq. So, one might ask, why explore the connection between events that occurred twelve years earlier? Can any lessons from the earlier conflicts of Saddam's regime help the United States navigate its way through current events? The answer depends on what one considers valuable about contemporary history.

Contemporary history has not always had obvious applications. As a reviewer of a 1947 official British history of the summer campaign of 1918 remarked, "It is difficult to see what purpose is served by the publication of this history at this time. . . . Nobody would read it for pleasure and nobody would study it to learn military art. It will go on the shelf of the military library and there remain, consulted occasionally . . . by one silver-haired veteran to refute another."[4] For many readers, the reviewer's opinion may be valid for this work as well. However, before rendering judgment, one should consider what makes the Iraqi case unique: the extensive, detailed, and most of all, contemporary access to the Iraqi perspective.[5] There is no shortage of narratives recounting the strategies and policies associated with recent Coalition military operations in Iraq. As useful as some of these histories may be, they suffer from the same malady they often (correctly) criticize in some Coalition planning—the lack of an Iraqi context. This lack of an Iraqi perspective should come as no surprise, given the nature of the regime. However, war is a two-sided contest and any analyses, beyond the most technical, that rely on only one side will inevitably fall short.

Do not worry. When you see that the world is dark, you should mock them and although we are not used to saying it, you should spit in their face. You must know that we are stronger than all of them. By God, I feel that we are stronger than all of them. Absolutely. The more they gather armies the more I feel the pride that fills us all as Iraqis and as a generation. . . . A man is for honorable deeds. He kills himself on the slaughter pad of honor, patriotism, pride, and [is] finished.[6]

Figure 1. Saddam Hussein, circa 1991 (Harmony Document Folder ISGZ-2005-601477)

Purposes of This Study

In addition to making the Iraqi perspective available, the narrative in this study lends itself to four general purposes: critical analysis, improving historical accuracy, red-team development, and a study of adaptation.

Critical Analysis

In Clausewitz's seminal work *On War,* he describes a process called "critical analysis." According to him, critical analysis is "the application of theoretical truths to actual events; [as such] it not only reduces the gap between the two but also accustoms the mind to those truths through their repeated application."[7] Theory, in this case, includes both the conceptual ideas (past and future) as well as a perception of what has occurred—in other words, historical knowledge. Clausewitz focused on developing a set of tools to answer questions such as: Will this concept or capability work on the battlefield? Did a particular concept or capability work? Can this or that warfighting theory explain what happened? Will an alternative theory work any better?

Critical analysis has three distinct, but closely linked "intellectual activities": 1) discovering and interpreting equivocal facts; 2) tracing effects back to their causes; and 3) what Clausewitz called the "evaluation of the means employed."[8] This third activity is where a lesson collected can actually become a lesson learned. Admittedly, this study does not venture into the third and most practical aspect of critical analysis. However, as this study should make clear, most lessons-learned analyses uninformed by an Iraqi perspective may require considerable rethinking. Such a project is clearly beyond the scope of this or any single study.

General Historical Accuracy

Through exploiting Saddam Hussein's records, the potential exists to develop a more complete history of the Middle East in the closing decades of the twentieth century. This should interest more than just historians. As Richard Neustadt and Ernest May contend in *Thinking in Time: The Uses of History for Decision Makers,* "Washington decision makers actually used history in their decisions . . . whether they knew any or not." Unfortunately, that history is the one that "falls within the remembered past."[9] If that remembered past is overly one-sided, then some decisions rest on a shaky foundation.

It is the nature of the processes of history that reputations—personal, technical, or institutional—often change over time. Since the nature of the states involved often determines how much of a conflict's context is open to scrutiny, open societies (especially the leaders of them) endure the most scrutiny.

This imbalance tends to skew contemporary history, possibly contributing to its reputation as an unreliable genre. Max Hastings, in his introduction to Milton Shulman's book on the Wehrmacht's perspective on defeat in WWII, noted, "Too many books have been written which focus upon the disagreements and difficulties of the Allied generals. It is essential not to consider the Allied command in isolation, but to compare it with that of the enemy. In that light, the dissensions between Eisenhower and Montgomery, Bradley and Patton, fade into insignificance."[10]

Such imbalance inevitably leads to an unhelpful, if understandable, tendency to overstate a particular side's successes and failures. The objective of the Iraqi Perspectives Project is to establish a more complete context from which one can learn useful lessons, not to minimize the actual strategic, operational, or tactical mistakes made by either side.

Improving Red Teaming

Taking advantage of the former Iraqi regime's archives must not result in templates of what a "generic" totalitarian regime will do in a given situation, but should expand the range of questions and open new avenues of investigation. The most practical use of such understanding is through an exercise called "red teaming."[11] A recent U.S. Department of Defense (DoD) study noted that red teaming "includes not only 'playing' adversaries or competitors, but also serving as devil's advocates, offering alternative interpretations (team B), and otherwise challenging established thinking within an enterprise."[12]

The study points out how critical this function is when America's adversaries look and act less and less like traditional foes. Using red teams "deepens our understanding of options available to adaptive adversaries and both complements and informs intelligence collection and analysis."[13] However, a red team, no matter how well informed, will never become omniscient. Even Saddam's closest neighbors failed to anticipate his actions during the tense months before he invaded Kuwait.

Ironically, a detailed study of a long-term adversary can suggest a lot about flaws in one's own forces. In this regard, as Sun Tzu notes, red teaming is a two-for-one investment: "So it is said that if you know others and know yourself, you will not be imperiled in a hundred battles; if you do not know others but know yourself, you will win one and lose one; if you do not know others and do not know yourself, you will be imperiled in every single battle."[14]

Finally, if, as the Defense Science Board noted in 2003, "the use of red teams can temper the complacency that often follows success," then using a realistic, three-dimensional red team can only improve the process.[15]

Study of Adaptation

A purpose related to improving red teaming is better understanding adaptation in war—defined in this context as a person's or group's change in behavior in response to new or modified surroundings. For the U.S. military, the 1991 war showcased the fruits of a twenty-year military reformation and hinted at a new generation of weapons systems and concepts. It also marked the beginning of a period of rapid change in the conduct and character of war with the increasing use of information technologies on the battlefield, and a rapid diffusion of military knowledge through globalization. As a result, adaptation—an endemic process of all wars—requires a fresh look. As combat operations since 2003 can attest, the speed and methods with which adversaries are adapting to U.S. capabilities have made dramatic strides since 1991. Understanding this obviously two-sided process requires more than a one-sided view of battlefield cause-and-effect.

An example of this process can be seen in the air campaign. Reflecting on a dozen years of conflict with the United States, a former senior Iraqi officer once told the author that "nobody knows more about absorbing precision munitions than Iraq."[16] Iraqi air defenses were not very effective during the 1991 war; however, in the dozen years that followed, they remained a viable and surprisingly adaptive threat to relentless, albeit small-scale Coalition operations. Some may ask why, after all that experience, Iraqi air defenses did not perform better. Moreover, why look to an air defense system with such a poor track record for insights that might help maintain the U.S. airpower advantage into the future? First, because the United States was seen as dominating the air domain during Desert Storm; critical analysis tended toward assessing performance against expectations rather than actual effects. This is understandable given available information sources, but may require reexamination. Second, it is only by examining what "almost was" that we can see what is changing on the battlefield over time and why. It is this process and its results that will provide insight into how the next adversary may fight.

The Iraqi archives afford researchers a rich set of two-sided data ranging from a baseline (1991), twelve years of air activity (Operation Southern Watch and Operation Northern Watch), and a capstone contest (OIF in 2003), with which to examine the interaction between modern air power and air defense. Furthermore, one can apply this methodology to doctrinal concepts, psychological operations, deception operations, and other conceptual components of warfighting.

Notes

1. Michael Howard, *The Lessons of History* (New Haven: Yale University Press, 1991), 16.

2. Dated from the Iraqi invasion of Kuwait on 2 August 1990 and ending with Saddam's statue being toppled in Baghdad on 9 April 2003, the military campaign against his regime lasted for twelve years, eight months, and seven days. The study period is limited to the formal government of Saddam Hussein and not his time in hiding or issues relating to the post-regime insurgency.

3. For a detailed summary of military operations associated with containing Saddam after 1991 (Operation Desert Storm) and before 2003 (Operation Iraqi Freedom) see: Alfred B. Prados, "Iraq: Post-War Challenges and U.S. Responses, 1991–1998," Congressional Research Service, Report for Congress 98-386-F (updated, 31 March 1999); and Alfred B. Prados, "Iraq: Former and Recent Military Confrontations with the United States," Congressional Research Service, Issue Brief for Congress, IB94049 (updated, 6 September 2002).

4. Cited in Hugh M. Cole, "Writing Contemporary Military History," *Military Affairs* 12, no. 3 (1948): 167.

5. The most significant examples of immediate access to enemy perspectives include the German and Japanese archives and senior prisoners following WWII. A smaller example is records captured following the 1983 invasion of Grenada. Significantly, adversary perspectives on the Cold War, Korean War, and Vietnam War, as well as a host of smaller operations, remain obscured.

6. Harmony media file ISGQ-2003-M0003629.

7. Carl von Clausewitz, *On War,* ed. and trans. Michael Howard and Peter Paret (New York: Alfred A. Knopf, 1993), 181.

8. Ibid.

9. Richard E. Neustadt and Ernest R. May, *Thinking in Time: The Uses of History for Decision Makers* (New York: The Free Press, 1986), xii.

10. Milton Shulman, *Defeat in the West* (London: Cassell Publishing, 2003), xiii.

11. So-called "red teams" of various kinds have been a staple of military planning staffs dating back to the mid-nineteenth century. Until recently, efforts at thinking about military problems from adversaries' perspectives have been ad hoc at best. Recent efforts, such as the U.S. Army's University of Foreign and Military Cultural Studies at Fort Leavenworth, Kansas, show promise of long-overdue improvement in this area.

12. Department of Defense, Defense Science Board, *Task Force on the Role and Status of DOD Red Teaming Activities,* September 2003 (Office of the Under Secretary of Defense for Acquisition, Technology, and Logistics, Washington, D.C.).

13. Ibid.

14. Sun Tzu, *The Art of War,* trans. Thomas Cleary (Boston: Shambhala Publications, 1988), 82.

15. Defense Science Board Task Force, "Role and Status," 1.

16. Interview of a former senior Iraqi air force officer with the author, Baghdad, Iraq, 26 November 2003.

Chapter 1

AN OVERVIEW OF THE GULF WAR FROM THE U.S. PERSPECTIVE

The truth is that Iraq began the war with an army of over a million men, approximately half of whom were committed to the Kuwait theater of operations, where they were mauled. Iraq took such a battering in the Gulf War that four years afterward, its army is half its original size. And within the Iraqi ranks, I am sure that horror stories are told about what it was like to endure the wrath from the skies and on the ground during Desert Storm.[1]

—GENERAL COLIN POWELL

To provide a clearer understanding of the Iraqi perspective during the events surrounding the Gulf War of 1990–91, this chapter presents a brief account of events leading up to the war and then the conflict itself from what can be generalized as a Coalition point of view. Pointing out milestones in the planning and execution of Desert Shield and Desert Storm will help the reader place Saddam's perceptions and assumptions about events in the context of what was actually happening on the Coalition side of the hill. We begin the discussion with the diplomatic background to the crisis and then move to descriptions of the air and ground campaigns.

The Diplomatic Background

The Iraqi invasion of Kuwait caught most in the West by surprise and there was considerable debate as to how the United States should react. The military side, with Chairman of the Joint Chiefs of Staff Colin Powell taking the lead, voiced doubts about trying to liberate Kuwait from the Iraqis, and there was little unanimity on the civilian side.

However, President George H. W. Bush was inclined to take a strong stand, an inclination that Prime Minister Margaret Thatcher of Britain echoed at a meeting in Aspen, Colorado in early August 1990, shortly after Iraq occupied Kuwait. The president set in motion the diplomatic and military responses that would lead to the Gulf War the following January.

The United States undertook a successful diplomatic campaign to rally world opinion against Iraq, as well as to build up allied military forces in the region. The United States garnered military and diplomatic support not only from America's traditional allies like Britain and France, but also from Arab nations like Egypt and Syria. Nevertheless, concerns raised both within and outside the U.S. defense establishment about the risks of a military campaign appeared to add to the dictator's conviction that he could get away with seizing Kuwait.[2]

Coalition-building proved easier than actually deploying military forces to the Gulf from the United States.[3] The early overestimate of Iraqi military capabilities by both the intelligence agencies and the U.S. military played a major role. Requirements for very large military forces[4] and their supplies drove planning processes, deployment schedules, and the eventual launch date for the war.[5]

Planning processes for the eventual campaign to liberate Kuwait were also complicated. As Coalition forces gathered in the deserts of northeastern Saudi

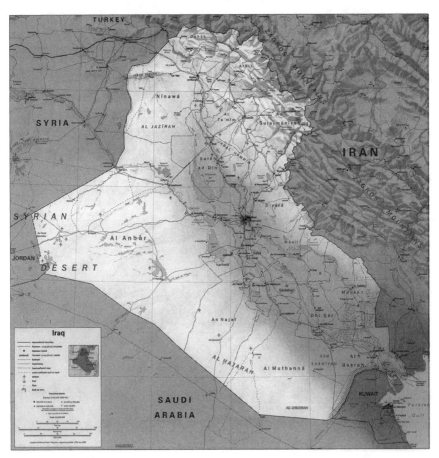

Figure 2. Iraq and its neighbors (Central Intelligence Agency)

Arabia, debate over the benefit and feasibility of immediate military operations continued inside and outside the American military. In Washington, Powell continued to press for sanctions over military action and war. The Commander of U.S. Central Command (CENTCOM), General H. Norman Schwarzkopf, echoed these sentiments in Riyadh. In a late-October 1990 interview with a reporter from the *Atlanta Journal-Constitution,* the CENTCOM commander went so far as to comment that "now we are starting to see evidence that the sanctions are pinching. So why should we say, 'Okay, gave 'em two months, didn't work. Let's get on with it and kill a whole bunch of people?' That's crazy."[6]

In Washington in mid-October, Schwarzkopf had briefed the initial ground plan to drive the Iraqis out of Kuwait. The president and his senior civilian advisers—influenced by estimates of Iraqi military capabilities, as were the military—saw the plan as unimaginative and carrying with it the prospect of considerable casualties.[7] Schwarzkopf's new plan called for adding a whole corps from Germany. The time to deploy such a large force and its support structure from Germany would mean that new and more ambitious plan of a deep envelopment into the deserts of Iraq could not begin until late February. However, this meant that there would be a considerable length of time between the air campaign's beginning and the Coalition ground forces' ability to begin operations with the newly arrived U.S. Army VII Corps.[8] The air campaign was to begin soon after the 15 January 1991 expiration date the U.N. had set for the Iraqis to leave Kuwait; the ground campaign was going to have to wait more than a month from that date to begin.

The Coalition's air plan, evolving from initial efforts that began in Washington in August, addressed the problems of taking down the sophisticated, integrated air defense system that the French and Soviets had built for the Iraqis— a system that pre-war Western analysts deemed effective and up-to-date.

The strategic difficulty that now confronted the Coalition was a major gap between the onset of the air campaign and the start for ground operations. Throughout that period of more than a month, Saddam would have the option of announcing the withdrawal of Iraqi forces from Kuwait. While many in the Coalition at the time would have seen an Iraqi withdrawal as a victory, it would have allowed Saddam to proclaim that his army had stood unbroken and undefeated in the field against the cowardly Westerners.[9]

The Air War

At 0300 hours local time on 17 January 1991, Coalition air operations began with a massive assault on Iraq's air defense system. The *Gulf War Air Power Survey* describes the aims of the attack as follows:

The . . . plan [aimed to attack] the heart of Iraqi [air] defenses; it aimed to break the connection between nodes in the Kari system and to swamp the defenses. . . . [The air attacks] would attack Iraqi air defenses from the inside out—in other words incapacitate the center where the Iraqis made their decisions. Above all, the initial waves would overload the Iraqi system with a massive attack on its heart. There would be no rollback or incremental approach; confronted with a massive attack at the war's onset, the Iraqis would have no time to adapt to Coalition tactics and attacks.[10]

The initial night's work played out better than Coalition air planners had hoped. Instead of the twenty to twenty-five aircraft losses some had expected, the early morning air attacks of 17 January suffered the loss of a single F-18, to a MiG-25.[11] Those attacks destroyed Iraq's integrated air defense system.[12] This did not mean the Iraqis were unable to fire unguided surface-to-air missiles at the attackers, or even to turn on their radars occasionally—there simply was no air defense *system* after the morning of 17 January.

Now began a sustained air offensive against an array of targets in Iraq and throughout the Kuwait theater of operations. Not surprisingly, Coalition air forces adapted in a number of ways during their operations as the campaign proceeded. The laming of Kari meant that attacking aircraft no longer had to avoid Iraqi missile defenses and radars by flying at low levels where Iraqi anti-aircraft guns were dangerous.[13] As massive Coalition air attacks destroyed targets throughout Iraq, Saddam scuttled from safe house to safe house. Coalition efforts during the first days of the air campaign focused on targets in Iraq itself, particularly command and control, transportation, the electrical grid, and weapons of mass destruction (WMD) sites. The attackers suffered few casualties, while inflicting extensive damage across the length and breadth of Iraq. Only on a single day, the third of the operation, did Coalition air attacks run into substantial difficulties, when the Iraqis managed to shoot down two attacking F-16s.

In early February, stealth aircraft stepped up attacks on the regime's political command and control centers. On 13 February, an attack occurred on the al-Firdos command post, which was also serving as an air-raid bunker for senior members of the Ba'ath elite and their families.[14] The result was heavy civilian casualties. In the initial portion of the air campaign, the regime had not emphasized civilian losses in its public statements. However, by early February, as the campaign continued in intensity, apparently beyond the point that the Iraqis had believed it would, the regime began trumpeting civilian losses to the Western media. This was effective at influencing U.S. policy. The result was that Coalition attacks on downtown Baghdad, the regime's controlling heart, became largely out-of-bounds for the remainder of the conflict.

By mid-February the air campaign's emphasis had shifted to Iraqi ground forces that lay in and around Kuwait. American F-111Fs, equipped with precision capabilities, switched from attacking strategic targets in the center of Iraq to striking Iraqi ground equipment in the Kuwait theater of operations. In retrospect, the precision attacks on Iraqi armor and artillery may not have been as successful as air force analysts thought at the time, but they did destroy substantial amounts of equipment and reduced the morale of Iraqi soldiers.[15]

The Ground War

On 29 January at Saddam's order, Iraqi forces attempted to initiate ground operations along the Kuwaiti-Saudi border by attacking the frontier town of al-Khafji. The Iraqis deployed forces from their III Corps, led by its best division, the 5th Mechanized, without Coalition intelligence recognizing what was happening. The Iraqis managed to surprise Coalition forces enough to brush aside the Coalition's screening units and advance to and capture al-Khafji. At Schwarzkopf's urging, the Saudis had evacuated the civilian population of al-Khafji earlier, because the town was within range of Iraqi artillery in Kuwait.[16] Thus, the town was empty except for a few liaison and special operations teams, which helps explain why the Coalition missed the Iraqi move.

From that initial point, things began falling apart for the Iraqis. On the morning of 30 January, the Coalition began air attacks. These raids wrecked the lead forces of the 5th Mechanized Division. One of its brigades was shattered in the middle of a minefield, when a precision strike disabled the lead tank. One survivor, a veteran of the Iran-Iraq War, later claimed to Coalition interrogators that all the brigade had endured in the ten years of the Iran War had not equaled what it suffered in a quarter of an hour in the desert north of al-Khafji.[17] Moreover, it appeared at the time that the 3rd Armored Division of Iraq's Regular Army never managed to deploy its maneuver units from their bivouac areas, so fierce were air attacks on its area of responsibility.

Nevertheless, Coalition commanders, believing the Iraqis were attempting to draw them into a ground battle, did not mount a ground effort to smash the attacking Iraqis north of the Kuwait-Saudi border. Instead, they continued to attack the Iraqi forces with air power and allow Arab forces in the area to drive the Iraqis out of al-Khafji itself. From the Coalition's perspective, that tactical achievement represented a victory.

By the end of February, the Americans had finished assembling the forces they believed necessary to break the Iraqis in the Kuwait theater of operations. At the last moment of 21 February, Soviet diplomats, with Iraqi concurrence, proposed an immediate cease-fire in return for an unconditional withdrawal from Kuwait by Iraq's military forces.[18] But Saddam's record for obfuscation and dishonesty—at least in Western eyes—was such that it was too late. Ground operations would begin in a couple of days.

Coalition ground operations would consist of three major drives. In the far west, XVIII Airborne Corps with the 82nd and 101st Airborne Divisions, the 24th Mechanized Infantry Division, and the French 6th Light Armored Division drove straight toward Tallil Air Base, just short of the Euphrates. Its drive represented an obvious and direct threat to Iraq's heartland and perhaps even Baghdad. In the east, I Marine Expeditionary Force (MEF) with two Marine divisions, supported by Arab Coalition forces and the U.S. Army's "Tiger" Brigade, which was equipped with M1A1 tanks, was to drive directly into Kuwait and focus Iraqi attention on the immediate threat to Kuwait City.

But the main blow would come in the center, well to the west of Kuwait itself. The U.S. VII Corps, consisting of four heavy divisions, an armored cavalry regiment, and one British armored division were to sweep north and then east to envelop Iraqi forces lying within the Kuwait theater of operations. Its operational success would rest on the flanking drives' ability to divert and hold the Iraqis, while the major blow gathered speed and enveloped Saddam's Republican Guard and Regular Army in a massive trap. In the end, not all the objectives were achieved, in particular entrapping the Republican Guard divisions.[19]

On 24 February at 0100 hours, the ground campaign officially began. In the west, the XVIII Airborne Corps was well on the way toward the Euphrates within hours. The French smashed much of the Iraqi 45th Infantry Division, capturing 2,500 prisoners on the first day. By 1030, the 101st had seized forward operating base "Cobra" 110 miles deep in Iraq, and its Apache helicopters were preparing to strike further north. By noon on 25 February, the 101st was within forty miles of the Euphrates and already putting down troops on Highway 8, one of the major highways running up the Euphrates Valley. XVIII Airborne Corps' heaviest unit, the 24th Infantry Division, was already seventy-five miles into Iraq by midnight on the first day.

In the east, I MEF's 1st and 2nd Marine Divisions were moving almost as fast, as units in front of them simply collapsed. In Schwarzkopf's words, the Marines "encountered no impassable mine fields, no walls of flame, no murderous gas barrage, and very little resistance."[20] In the first twenty-four hours, the 2nd Marine Division managed to capture the Iraqi 9th Tank Battalion virtually intact, with its thirty-five T-55s as well as five thousand Iraqi soldiers. In the same period, the 1st Marine Division destroyed twenty-one enemy tanks and captured three thousand Iraqi soldiers.[21]

The center drive was not supposed to begin until the next day, but early on the morning of 24 February, Schwarzkopf, recognizing that Iraqi defenses were unraveling, ordered the VII Corps to begin its advance as soon as possible. Mid-afternoon on the 24th it began its advance—a day early—but it did not match the speed of the drives on the flanks. By the next morning the corps' lead units were barely fifteen miles into Iraq, while some of its divisions had yet to cross the border.

On the second day of ground operations, the same pattern repeated itself. In the west, the 101st Airborne Division completed its mission of establishing a blocking position on the Euphrates to the west of An Nasiriyah, where the Marines would run into considerable trouble in March 2003. As a result, it had cut Highway 8. To the east of the 101st, the 24th Infantry Division, advancing at thirty miles per hour over rough terrain, closed in on the Euphrates.[22] Only growing bad weather hindered the division's advance.

To the east, the Marine drive was also moving faster than planners had calculated would be possible. For the most part, Iraqi forces were only sporadically resisting; most were either fleeing or surrendering in large numbers. Nevertheless, I MEF's advance was in effect pushing the Iraqis out of the trap that VII Corps was supposed to close in its advance. But as mentioned, the latter's advance did not begin until 24 February and then proceeded slowly compared with the pace on its flanks, while Iraq's Republican Guard and Regular Army units began a desperate rush to escape the Kuwait theater of operations.

On 26 February, the 24th Infantry Division had completed its advance to the Euphrates and swung east, while establishing a second firm blocking position on Highway 8. Furthermore, its units had captured the Iraqi airfields at Tallil and Jalibah. It was now in a position to advance down the Euphrates, adding to the powerful fist that would smash into fleeing Iraqis from the west. VII Corps formed the greater part of that fist and was now advancing to the east. Wretched weather, including rain showers, thunderstorms, and dust storms, accompanied the VII Corps' advance during the night of 25–26 February.

The Iraqis were already in considerable disarray as a result of the first two-day operations, on top of the intensifying Coalition air campaign. Saddam's withdrawal order also added to the confusion, while further air attacks exacerbated Iraqi difficulties. During the night of 26–27 February, Iraqi divisions were destroyed in their blocking positions, most of which were facing south. Also that night, VII Corps destroyed a substantial portion of the Tawakalna Republican Guards Armored Division, as well as the 12th and 52nd Armored Divisions and the 48th Division of the Regular Army. Much of the rest of the Iraqi Regular Army and the Republican Guard, which by then had fled the Kuwait theater

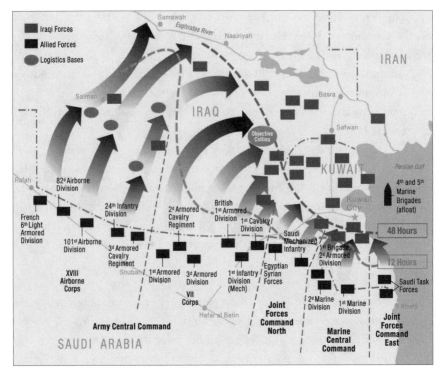

Figure 3. Operation Desert Storm Ground Offensive: Coalition Ground Operations 24–28 February 1991 ("The Persian Gulf—Ten Years After," *Joint Forces Quarterly* no. 27 [2000/2001], 10)

of operations, found shelter on the far bank of the Euphrates and were in no condition to resume the fight.

With considerable justification, the Battle of Seventy-Three Easting soon came to represent the war to many American analysts.[23] In that battle, Eagle Troop of the 2nd Armored Cavalry Regiment—under the command of Captain H. R. McMaster and equipped with nine M1A1s and thirteen Bradleys—crested the unmarked ridge at Seventy-Three Easting. They suddenly saw arrayed in front of them the forward elements of what was to prove an entire brigade of the Tawakalna Division. Within three minutes, Eagle Troop broke through the initial Iraqi defenses and was rolling through the enemy's rear areas. During the next quarter of an hour, Eagle troop fought its way through the entire Iraqi brigade without losing a single soldier or piece of equipment. Firing a combination of sabot rounds from M1A2s, TOW missiles, and 25-mm rounds from the Bradley chain guns, McMaster's Eagle Troop left a swath of wreckage: approximately thirty-nine burning tanks and forty to fifty armored personnel carriers and an equal number of trucks.

By the time President George H.W. Bush declared the war over at the end of one hundred hours of ground combat, Coalition ground and air forces had entirely liberated Kuwait, while to the west they had advanced to the Euphrates Valley nearly to An Nasiriyah. Coalition ground operations had managed to destroy virtually all of the Regular Army units Saddam had deployed to defend Kuwait.[24] However, the Coalition's ground offensive stopped on the right (southwest) bank of the Euphrates and did not deal with those Iraqi units that managed to cross the river. In effect, the Coalition granted Saddam's forces, especially the Republican Guard, a sanctuary where they were able to refit. Moreover, Saddam's forces, especially the Republican Guard, were ideally placed to deal with the political troubles that would erupt throughout the south. The regime's troubles were exacerbated when President Bush urged Iraqis to rise up and overthrow Saddam's regime, which had caused so much suffering, especially in the Shi'a areas.

But the locals, supported by expatriates in southwestern Iran, had already taken matters into their own hands. The same day that President Bush declared an armistice and the end of the one hundred–hour ground war, rebellion broke out in the southern Shi'a city of al-Basra. Positioning his tank in front of a great propaganda mural of the tyrant, the commander of a tank column fleeing Kuwait proclaimed in front of a crowd: "What has befallen us of defeat, shame, and humiliation, Saddam, is the result of your follies, your miscalculations, and your irresponsible actions."[25] Within hours, rebels had taken over al-Basra.[26] The rebellion soon spread throughout Iraq, reaching every province except al-Anbar. The extensive damage to Iraq's bridges and highways by the Coalition's air offensive exacerbated the extraordinary difficulties the Ba'ath regime confronted in attempting to put down the rebellion. For a moment, it appeared as if Saddam's tyranny trembled on the brink of collapse.

In the years following the war, the general Coalition view, as outlined above, has settled into a kind of commonly held "truth." To many in the West, the facts surrounding Operation Desert Storm are self-evident. Even as new historical facts are revealed through such things as memoirs, histories, and official documents, the general narrative remains constant with a distinctly Coalition perspective. But regardless of these presumed "facts," the current perspective of the war is only half right at best. Western assessments during the twelve-year confrontation between Iraq and the United States that followed the 1991 war used half-right perspectives as the baseline. Policymakers and analysts used this baseline to build new policies and to judge warfighting concepts. But the baseline is obviously skewed. Could it matter to the shape of subsequent events if

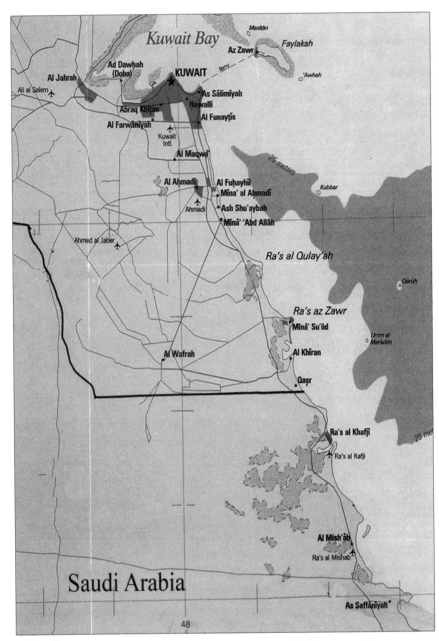

Figure 4. On 29 January 1991, the Iraqi Regular Army conducted a multi-division-size raid into northeastern Saudi Arabia (Central Intelligence Agency)

decision makers on both sides acted as if they won? Did these perspectives affect future decisions? Developing the requisite information necessary to even begin answering these questions is a major purpose of this project.

The remainder of this study will present the Iraqi perspective of events. In many cases, the Iraqi and Coalition narratives are two sides of a single coin. But in others, it is as if the competing narratives describe wholly disconnected events. An American historian said of the events in 1991 that "it is hard to envision a defeat more nearly total than that imposed south of the Euphrates."[27] Compare that statement to Saddam's 1992 pronouncement that "after their [the Americans'] previous experience with us, in which they did not achieve [their] ends regardless of [our] withdrawal from Kuwait, they might wonder how much force they need to deploy this time to achieve what they failed to do the last time."[28] It is this latter narrative that represents the history we do not know. As some events surrounding OIF attest, unknown histories have a significant impact on current and future events.

Notes

1. Colin Powell with Joseph E. Persico, *My American Journey* (New York: Random House, 1995), 525–26.
2. In July 1990, Saddam told the U.S. Ambassador, "Yours is a society which cannot accept 10,000 dead in one battle." Quoted in Jim Hoagland, "Outgoing Officers," *Washington Post*, 13 September 1990, sec. A33.
3. The first deployments to Saudi Arabia came nearly entirely from the U.S.: XVIII Airborne Corps, 24th Infantry Division, 82nd Airborne Division, and 1st Marine Division.
4. The initial deployment of U.S. forces was considered a defensive screen at best. Schwarzkopf told President Bush on 4 August that "if we ever wanted to kick the Iraqis out of Kuwait," it would require doubling the projected force and eight to ten months to prepare. General H. Norman Schwarzkopf with Peter Petre, *It Doesn't Take a Hero* (New York: Bantam, 1992), 301.
5. The overestimates largely resulted from the fact that Western experts believed that the Iraqis had displayed considerable military effectiveness in surviving the war with their much larger neighbor, Iran. Many others, especially in the media, also argued that the Iraqi military force represented a battle-hardened military that would display considerable powers of resistance.
6. Michael R. Gordon and Bernard E. Trainor, *The Generals' War* (New York: Little Brown and Company, 1995), 149.
7. In retrospect, given what we now know about the tactical superiority of U.S. forces, it might have been best to go with the plan and forces available and catch the Iraqis with their forces deployed well-forward.
8. In fact, VII Corps would not finish closing in theater with all its equipment until just days before the ground war began.
9. In other words, it would have created a situation analogous to what Germany was able

to get away with in 1919, when it claimed that its army had stood unbroken and undefeated in the field in November 1918 and that it had been tricked by Wilson's Fourteen Points into signing the Armistice—a complete untruth.

10. Williamson Murray, *Gulf War Air Power Survey, Volume 2: Operations/Effects and Effectiveness* (Washington, DC: U.S. GPO, 1993), 118.

11. Ibid., 136.

12. Ibid., 136–38.

13. The Kari system was a French-supplied integrated air defense command and control and battle management system built in 1987. Attack altitude was a major problem in the Vietnam War, when the North Vietnamese air defenses and missiles had forced down attacking U.S. aircraft to low levels, where anti-aircraft guns could inflict significant losses. The decision to attack at higher altitudes in Iraq in 1991 did come with some problems. While it minimized casualties, "the decision to bomb from medium altitudes did have a severe impact on the accuracy of munitions other than precision-guided in attacking fixed positions and equipment. In effect, the decision robbed platforms such as the F-16 and the F/A-18 of much of their ability to attrit enemy ground forces." Murray, *Gulf War Air Power Survey*, 155.

14. Coalition air planners had no idea that al-Firdos was also serving as an air-raid shelter. The irony of the attack was that if those in the bunker had remained in their houses, they would have been far safer, given that the Coalition was targeting no civilian areas. Murray, *Gulf War Air Power Survey*, 206–08. See also William M. Arkin's analysis of this issue in "Baghdad: The Urban Sanctuary in Desert Storm," *Airpower Journal*, no. 11 (1997): 4–20.

15. To read about the impact of air attacks on the morale of Iraqi soldiers, see the discussion based on POW reports in Murray, *Gulf War Air Power Survey*, 315–25.

16. For a detailed account of this story, see David J. Morris, *Storm on the Horizon: Khafji—The Battle That Changed the Course of the Gulf War* (New York: Free Press, 2004).

17. Murray, *Gulf War Air Power Survey*, 273–74.

18. U.S. News and World Report, *Triumph without Victory, The Unreported History of the Gulf War* (New York: Three Rivers Press, 1993), 279.

19. A contributing factor was the lack of overall control of the Coalition's ground forces.

20. Schwarzkopf, *It Doesn't Take a Hero*, 452–53.

21. Schwarzkopf, *It Doesn't Take a Hero*, 300. Standing on a captured Iraqi bunker complex laid out in the prescribed Soviet manner, which the Marines had captured without any losses, the commander of the 1st Marine Division, Major General Mike Myatt quietly commented "Thank God the North Vietnamese weren't here." Personal communication between Williamson Murray and Lt. Gen. Paul Van Riper, USMC (Ret.) (used with permission).

22. Schwarzkopf, *It Doesn't Take a Hero*, 381.

23. See Stephen Biddle, "Victory Misunderstood: What the Gulf War Tells Us about the Future of Conflict," *International Security* 21, no. 2 (1996): 139–79.

24. What the West and substantial portions of the Arab world saw were television images of Iraqi soldiers surrendering by the tens of thousands. None of those pictures were broadcast by Saddam's propaganda apparatus.

25. Kanan Makiya, *Cruelty and Silence: War, Tyranny, Uprising, and the Arab World* (New York: W.W. Norton & Company, 1993), 63.

26. The rebels "burned the palatial residence of the governor of al-Basra and attacked police stations wherever they could find them. They looted the security offices, destroying all files. The rebellion spread like wildfire, and within hours of those first shots in Sa'ad Square, the local residents from al-Basra and the returning soldiers from Kuwait had set up road blocks and were in control of the city. It was a classic revolutionary moment." Makiya, *Cruelty and Silence*, 60.

27. Richard M. Swain, *Lucky War: Third Army in Desert Storm* (Ft. Leavenworth: U.S. Army Command and General Staff College Press, 1994), 335.

28. Harmony media file ISGQ-2003-M0006753.

Chapter II

THE "VICTORY" AT AL-KHAFJI

> If we looked at things through purely military technical binoc-
> ulars, for example "we need more battalions," we would have
> been defeated a long time ago. We look at the battle through
> a creative strategic framework. Yes. These are all of the chapters
> from a battle and in each chapter that we achieve victory [we are]
> building up towards the strategic goal.[1]
>
> —SADDAM HUSSEIN

The small port town of al-Khafji, Saudi Arabia lies just over a dozen kilometers south of the Kuwaiti border. In August 1990, the town was well
within the range of Iraqi artillery and rocket batteries poised just inside
occupied Kuwait. Coalition military commanders decided the town's residents
should evacuate before any fighting began. By 17 January 1991, the entire population of fifteen thousand had evacuated. On the eve of war, the only people
left in al-Khafji were a couple of small detachments of U.S. Marines and Navy
SEALs inside the city as well as a few Saudi Marines and Coast Guard personnel
along the road north to the Kuwaiti border. For the Coalition, al-Khafji was
supposed to be an observation post, not a battlefield. As it turned out, the Iraqi
senior leadership had other ideas. On 29 January, Iraq launched a multi-division
operation into Saudi Arabia to seize al-Khafji and to disrupt the anticipated
Coalition operation.

The commander of Joint Forces, Saudi General Khaled bin Sultan described the Iraqi attack as a "bolt from the blue . . . threatening to disrupt the
Coalition's preparations."[2] The overall commander of Coalition forces, General
H. Norman Schwarzkopf, noted in his autobiography that he and his staff found
themselves "perplexed" by the Iraqi attack on al-Khafji. From the Coalition's
perspective, "it defied military logic."[3] In purely operational terms, Schwarzkopf
and his staff were probably correct in their assessment of the al-Khafji attack;
however, the attack was perfectly consistent with Saddam's strategic perspective.
For Saddam, al-Khafji was a demonstration of what Arab warriors can achieve
against a timid West when they unite under the right leader. . . . From its initial
hours, the regime saw the al-Khafji operation as a strategic, operational, and
moral victory. According to contemporary Iraqi accounts, after-action reviews,

Figure 5. Saudi port of al-Khafji as photographed by an Iraqi Air Force Reconnaissance MiG-25 in August 1990 (Harmony document folder ISGP-2003-00038521)

and official histories, the al-Khafji operation was well planned, well executed, and worthy of study. In this view, the battle at al-Khafji unhinged the Coalition's original plans and fundamentally changed the direction of the war. An official regime history confidently stated that the battle was a major victory that clearly underlined to the world that Saddam was "one of [the] most outstanding military strategists of our time."[4] Moreover, the Iraqi history noted that "the battle proved that the Iraqi forces were highly trained because they managed to launch a well-planned and successful attack during the night despite the enemy's spy satellites, drones, and surveillance aircraft and technical superiority. It also means that the Iraqi soldier was capable of taking part in a fierce war like that at al-Khafji—which will surely be recorded in the world's military history."[5]

According to Saddam's senior military officers at the time, the military utility of the operation was not in question.[6] Lt. Gen. Husayn Rashid Muhammed
explained that the logic of the mission was self-evident: "It is better that we
attack the enemy while we still have our capability . . . [it is] better than fighting
him while we are bending down. . . . [There were] several targets, and several
plans [but] the main purpose behind them was to drag the enemy into engagements with ground formations in the most expeditious manner or the fastest
way possible. . . . The aim was to destroy oil facilities, destroy them and then
return to the main launching area . . . the main aim was to wage a raid."[7]

Iraqi intelligence reports from 24 January 1991 noted that Coalition forces
between the Kuwait border and al-Khafji were lightly armed and assessed that
they would "withdraw when they sense the movement of our forces."[8] However, the authors of these same reports accurately warned that in addition to
the challenging cross-country navigation to the target city, "superiority of the
enemy's air force" would likely be the major obstacle to Iraqi forces attempting to reach the Saudi town. For Saddam, the tactical risks were never a major
concern. In pre-battle discussions, the only concern seemed to be how big
to make the operation. According to one of the Iraqi officers involved in the
planning, "The defense minister's report, and that of the joint chiefs of staff
. . . [recommended] that our forces [designated for] al-Khafji secure the city and
remain in it for a relatively long period of time in order to force the enemy to
engage in a land warfare that could lead to a war of attrition. There was also the
possibility that our forces could use the city as a safe base from which any [sic]
further attacks deeper in the Saudi territory, where the invaders forces were
concentrated, could be launched from."[9]

Several rough operational concepts for Iraqi attacks down the Saudi Arabia
coast date to as early as August 1990. For the most part these were contingency
plans written after the invasion of Kuwait. The Republican Guard staff developed three contingency plans—a close (the one actually executed), a medium,
and a deep. The medium plan called for an attack up to 150 kilometers into
Saudi Arabia, while the deep plan went beyond that. These two deeper plans, in
light of Coalition airpower, were formulated so that "in case we achieve success
in the close action, we have to [be prepared] to switch to the medium plan
within forty-eight to seventy two hours" and appear fanciful at best.[10] According to the former army chief of staff, Lt. Gen. Husayn Rashid Muhammad,
"[There] was really more than one plan, and more than one target. But only one
of the plans and targets was carried out. . . . There were several objectives and
each objective had its own plan and [Saddam] told us he will inform us which
plan we are to execute."[11]

Details of the final plans for the attack on al-Khafji were not complete until 0200 on 27 January 1991.[12] This was ten days after the Coalition air campaign began and less than two days before the al-Khafji operation started. Saddam was personally involved in both the planning and the final briefings to the commanders. In order to attend the final briefing with Saddam, some commanders in Kuwait made a dangerous 150-kilometer trip under blackout conditions and across bomb-damaged roads to a secret location in al-Basra.[13] After arriving, the commanders were secreted away from a headquarters building and "driven around for a short period of time" before arriving at a non descript house in a civilian suburb of al-Basra. After the war, Major General Mahmaud recalled the scene:

> We noticed there were some security and protection elements guarding the house. There was Col. Abid Hamid [Mahmud al-Tikriti], a close aide to Mr. President. We passed through a garden attached to the house where we entered a room located at the far end. Inside the room we found ourselves face to face with Mr. President Saddam Hussein, the commander in chief of the armed forces. [Saddam] stood up and welcomed us. Together with him, we also found the joint-chiefs of staff and a number of the members of the general command and a number of the commanders of the divisions and corps.[14]

Saddam asked the assembled commanders about the condition of their forces and their readiness for the coming battle. According to Major General Mahmaud, Saddam then dictated a series of directives for the upcoming attack. It is worth considering Saddam's al-Khafji directives in full, because they provide insight into Saddam's late-January view of the larger confrontation.

> After [telling] his Excellency about the condition of our forces and their preparedness, we [the assembled Iraqi commanders] started taking notes of his Excellency's directives: During the battle of al-Qadissiya [of the Iran-Iraq War] we took the initiative of challenging the enemy and attack[ed] it in the first two weeks of the war; then we stopped challenging it and the war dragged on for eight years until it ended at last with the liberation battles. When we got involved in a serious way, the image of the enemy, which had long been highly thought of, got tarnished and collapsed. Hunting the enemy down works and gives immediate results—should the hunting be done in a calculated way and with decisiveness. . . .

The enemy in front of us does not have the same level of determination as the Iranian enemy. . . . The enemy we are faced with would collapse, if we manage[d] to challenge and confront it in a determined way. The world capitals would then hear the news and many rulers' seats would be shaken as a result.

So are we to keep waiting? Your upcoming war, even if we think of it as a small [war], it won't be small in its political results and repercussions. Losses in this war will spare the blood of thousands of Iraqi people . . . hence we should take the battle very seriously due to its expected results.

You are all requested to convey the importance of this battle to the lowest-ranking fighter in the field; and since it will be the first confrontation for the forces, so should it fail, it would reflect negatively on our soldiers and result in a positive signal for the enemy. . . . Should we succeed, then the war duration will be short, and there will be less bloodshed and the enemy's wailing and mourning will be heard everywhere.[15]

The final plan for al-Khafji had two distinct parts, both sharing a common maneuver concept. In the first, designated as the main effort, elements of the Iraqi III Corps would attack to seize and hold al-Khafji. The overall main effort of the III Corps was led by the 5th Mechanized Infantry Division supported by the 3rd Armored Division. The second part of the operation, designated as the supporting effort, was given to the IV Corps. Its mission was to "conduct operations in depth"[16] in support of the III Corps' main effort. Both the main and supporting efforts required two divisions each and shared a similar concept. An armored division would draw the Coalition airpower's attention with a feint into lightly defended territory, while a mechanized division would conduct the cross-border raid.[17]

The IV Corps, located between the Wadi al-Batin (Kuwait's southwestern border) and the heel of Kuwait (midpoint of the Kuwait-Saudi border), would use the 1st Mechanized and 6th Armor Divisions for its portion of the operation. The plan called for the 1st Mechanized Division to attack twenty kilometers into Saudi Arabia and then circle east for twenty-five kilometers and re-enter Kuwait in the III Corps' sector (in front of the 7th and 14th Divisions). The division would be led by the 34th Armored Brigade followed closely by the 27th Mechanized Brigade. The division's third brigade would remain in Kuwait as a reserve force. The 6th Armored Division supported the 1st Division's cross-border operation. Its mission was to feint toward the border tri-zonal town of al-Ruq'I and draw Coalition attention away from the 1st Division's maneuver.

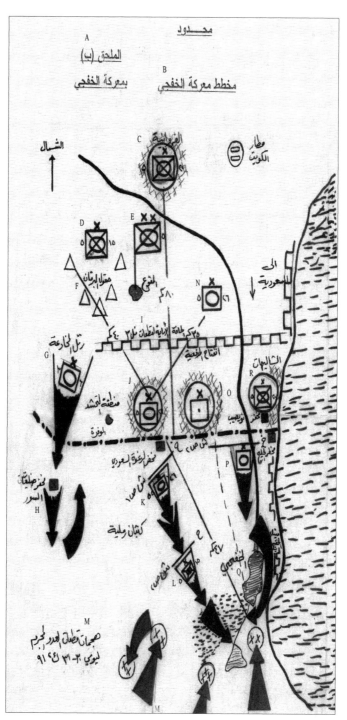

Figure 6. Iraqi concept sketch of attack into al-Khafji (Harmony folder ISGQ-2003-00055154).

A	Appendix B of al-Khafji Battle	L	15th Brigade, 5th Mechanized Division
B	al-Khafji battle Plan Sketch	M	The attacks of the criminal enemy for 30 and 31 January 1991
C	20th Brigade, 5th Mechanized Division	N	26th Brigade, 5th Mechanized Division
D	15th Brigade, 5th Mechanized Division	O	Artillery Brigade
E	5th Division HQ (al-Muquawa)	P	Border Station
F	al-Barqan Oil Fields	Q	Armor Brigade
G	Deception–6th Brigade, 3rd Armored Division	R	al-Khafji
H	al-Sur Dulai'at Border Station	S	20th Brigade, 5th Mechanized Division
I	III Corps Forward Troops	T	Artillery Opening (Rockets)
J	26th Brigade, 5th Mechanized Division (Defensive Posture)	U	To Saudi Arabia
K	26th Brigade, 5th Mechanized Division	V	Kuwait International Airport

Figure 7. Legend of al-Khafji map translated. The battle of al-Khafji became a centerpiece of Iraqi War College training after 1991.

In addition to supporting the III Corps, the IV Corps' tactical mission was to "inflict the maximum amount of casualties and to capture [Coalition] prisoners."[18] Corps warning orders for the close plan were issued on 27 January, immediately after the corps commander returned from his al-Basra meeting with Saddam. During the next two days, the division prepared shelters for its armor near the line of departure, pushed supporting artillery forward, and established paths through their own minefields. The engineering work was completed on time "despite the hostile air attacks."[19]

According to the 1st Division commander, Maj. Gen. Hussein Hassan Adai, "despite the intensity of hostile air power, it [the enemy] was unable to either identify or engage the divisions' deployment, its logistical transportation, or its shelters."[20] The lead vehicles of the 34th Brigade crossed the Saudi border at 2000 on 29 January followed closely by the 27th Mechanized Brigade. "We were able to achieve the complete element of surprise against the enemy," recalled the corps commander. According to the Iraqi version of events, the two brigades achieved their fifty-kilometer advance through Saudi Arabia almost without interference. General Adai described what he viewed as "random attacks" by Coalition aircraft and how the "defeated" Coalition forces retreated or "refrain[ed] from engaging our forces."[21] By first light on 30 January, both brigades re-entered Kuwait through the III Corps' lines without any significant casualties. After the war, the commander of the IV Corps praised the operation for its tangible effects on morale: "We witnessed an increase in the [corps] morale because our troops took off and returned with all their weaponry and with all [their] strength. . . . I witnessed myself during the conference in which we [issued] our directives to the commanders before and after the operation. They were all elated after carrying out this mission. They had high morale and [were] motivated to fight and preceded with the battle no matter the consequences."[22]

The commander of the Iraqi main effort, III Corps' Major General Mahmaud, spent most of the day on 28 January meeting with the commanders and staff of his 3rd Armored and 5th Mechanized Divisions in their respective field headquarters. Extensive planning went into repositioning the assault forces to avoid Coalition air strikes. The 5th Division took advantage of the and other built-up areas along the Kuwaiti coast to conceal its vehicles. Similarly, the 6th Brigade of the 3rd Armored Division used the al-Wafra Forest because it offered concealment "from the enemy's major air attacks."[23] The planning issues discussed in this final meeting included opening and closing minefields, using oil smoke from the al-Wafra oil fields to cover movement, firing FROG rockets against enemy positions in front of the 7th and 14th Infantry Divisions as a cover, and positioning counterattack forces near the breach in case of a large enemy reaction. The corps commander emphasized that the key to the operation was to get into al-Khafji quickly and then dig in. He emphasized sniper operations, anti-aircraft systems, camouflaging forward positions, and "bypassing small scale pockets of resistance during the advancing stage" because "[we] could later encircle and destroy them." Finally, in addition to telling them that they "should be underground before sunlight on the 30th," Major General Mahmaud announced that he had promised Saddam that the III Corps "would present al-Khafji as a present to him" on that day.[24]

The morning of 29 January, Major General Mahmaud inspected the 5th Mechanized Division as it moved to its final jumping-off points on the border. He was pleased that this first major part of the operation, moving the assault units to the line of departure, went off without any significant interference from the Coalition. A combination of thick smoke from some burning oil wells and good use of available cover and concealment meant that "the enemy didn't bomb [us] because [the targets] were considered unimportant."[25] According to the corps commander, his forces successfully repositioned from central Kuwait to the border at the cost of only two tanks.[26]

At 2000 hours on 29 January, the 6th Brigade of the 3rd Armored Division crossed the Saudi border near the al-Wafra plantation. The mission was to "rush in from the southwestern angle as a deception operation in order to cover up the actions of the 5th Mechanized Division." If conditions permitted, the deception was to proceed up to twenty kilometers into Saudi Arabia and "destroy some enemy elements and their wireless stations."[27] This maneuver, like the IV Corps operation just to the west of it, would provide Coalition aircraft a set of targets too good to pass up.

As it turned out, the Iraqi brigade had no trouble attracting Coalition attention. A sober assessment of the 6th Brigade's cross-border mission is found in an Iraqi classified official history: "At 2100 hours on January 29, 1991 the 6th Armored Brigade (the diversionary column) was met with fierce opposition at Dulay' at al Sur Station, [during which] the brigade *suffered major losses*, in spite of that, it was able to crush the opposition and advance to a depth of twenty kilometers. At 2330 hours, the brigade was told to return [to Kuwait] according to plan"[28] [Emphasis added].

The official history does not say what caused the 6th Brigade to "suffer major losses," but it was clearly an eye-opening encounter with Coalition tactical airpower. The losses to the 6th Brigade were almost total. According to one account, the brigade was "spiritually collapsed," their commander had to be relieved, and the "only thing that they had [left] was their name."[29]

Before the 6th Brigade's devastating experience, Coalition airpower had not significantly affected III Corps' armored vehicles. Nevertheless, Coalition air attacks did dramatically affect vehicle readiness even before the al-Khafji operation. A major issue for the Iraqi tactical commanders on the morning of the al-Khafji attack was basic vehicle maintenance. The primary cause of this sudden decline in readiness was attributed to a change in enemy aircraft tactics. A III Corps officer recalled that instead "of flying overhead for the purpose of dropping bombs and leaving," enemy aircraft started "flying continuously over our forces [just] beyond 75mm anti-aircraft artillery range."[30] This nearly continuous Coalition air presence meant the commanders in Kuwait were unable to move supply vehicles during the day. Routine maintenance was shifted to hours of darkness to avoid attracting attention. Numerous vehicles scheduled to participate in the attack had to be abandoned after arriving at the line of departure because of a lack of spare parts. Moreover, III Corps supporting artillery was "experiencing trouble with some of [its] artillery pieces due to [over] use or because [it] had been bombed" as many Iraqi POWs would later report.[31] It was not just vehicles that were suffering under conditions of enemy air dominance. The commander of the Iraqi 5th Mechanized Division recalled that, after making final preparations and establishing local security for the attacking force, his most pressing task was slaughtering 120 cattle from a local Kuwaiti farm to feed his troops.[32]

The tactical plan for the corps' main effort, in keeping with Iraqi raid doctrine and the experiences of the invasion of Kuwait, rested on speed. At 2015 on 26 January, 26th Armored Brigade of the 5th Mechanized Division crossed the Saudi Arabia border along the coast road. By 2115, the lead tank regiment completed its initial mission of clearing any resistance along the first fifteen kilometers of coast road. Just past the desalinization plant, the 26th Brigade established a hasty defense along the shoulders of the road, oriented west, and allowed the 15th Mechanized Brigade, augmented with an additional regiment from the 20th Brigade, to pass through on its high-speed run to al-Khafji. According to the Iraqi postwar retelling of events, the lead units of the 15th Brigade, after meeting only the lightest of resistance, reached the bridge at the southern end of al-Khafji at 2315. At 2130, the right arm of the 5th Division pincer left its forward staging area just to the west of the coast road, and raced toward al-Khafji. This arm consisted of the remaining two regiments of the 5th Division's 20th Brigade (2nd and 3rd Regiments). The initial attack moved to the southeast, paralleling the coast road, and then approximately fifteen kilometers into Saudi Arabia it executed a sharp turn to the east and into al-Khafji.[33] Slowed by the terrain and some "navigation challenges," the 20th Brigade finally secured the north and west sides of the town at 0100. The division commander was relieved that the only engagement until then was with a small Saudi Arabian border patrol. From the Iraqi perspective, these first five hours of offensive operations demonstrated to the world Iraq's military prowess.

After gaining control of the town, the priority for the remaining hours of darkness was to get all personnel and equipment "underground" before first light.[34] The 5th Mechanized Division quickly established communications with III Corps thanks to a thirty-kilometer phone line that was laid at the trail end of the initial assault.[35] At 0200 on 30 January, the General Command of the Armed Forces in Baghdad relayed to the III Corps commander that the decision to stay or withdraw from al-Khafji was his. According to a later official history, Major General Mahmaud "decided to keep the forces in al-Khafji considering it is a safe base for the operations that were agreed upon later and in preparation to advance to Mish'ab which was the target of the medium offensive."[36]

Meanwhile, the soldiers of the 20th Brigade were ordered to search the city and capture any Coalition forces that might have remained behind.[37] Sometime around 0300, the division commander reported that American helicopters arrived and made some tentative engagements, but after being fired upon "retreated back to their territory."[38] The commander also happily reported that

Coalition aircraft had attacked the division's line of departure along the Kuwait border, but by then "there were no [longer any] troops on it."[39]

At first light on 30 January, the 15th Brigade reported an American unmanned aerial vehicle (UAV) overhead. The curious novelty of being watched from a pilot-less drone quickly disappeared, when at approximately 0800 the division came under what would later be reported as "almost continuous air and artillery bombardment." At 0830, a group of some thirty Coalition tanks, supported by helicopters, approached the 20th Brigade positions on the city's northwest side. After an engagement with the brigade's tank company, the unidentified Coalition troops retreated.[40]

During his inspection of the defensive position, the 5th Division commander noted that "we did not have the [required] units in the al-Khafji port." While Iraqi documents on this part of the plan are lacking, he was probably referring to a force of Iraqi marines (probably from the Iraqi Navy's 440 Brigade) that had been intercepted and destroyed by Coalition helicopters and surface forces.[41] To make up for the force shortfall, the commander requested and received from III Corps the commando battalion from the 14th Division. The commander of the 5th Division recalled later that he was not impressed with these late arrivals. Compared to his troops, the men of the 14th Division were "ill-disciplined" and, as far as contributing to his mission, "this battalion was not good."[42] The commander's other major concerns on the first full day included a lack of a clear picture of the enemy, poor quality maps (some with coordinate errors of more than 500 meters), and the still-unknown duration of his mission.

The planned duration of the al-Khafji operation was a strongly debated issue within the Iraqi chain of command. In keeping with their doctrine, the 5th Division carried with it few supplies and only limited supporting arms. In the days leading up to the operation, the unanswered question of duration compelled the division commander to write a letter to the corps staff stating that "it was the division's responsibility to start their attack at the last light of the day, and to come back at the first light [of] the following day."[43] The corps commander acknowledged the letter but reportedly told him that the division would stay and defend al-Khafji once taken. The division commander later lamented that "the division was not designed to defend in the first place. . . . [We] did not have the ability to defend; especially under a heavy [enemy] air cover."[44] The division commander would prove to be the better judge of Coalition capabilities.

On 30 January at 1000 hours, the 3rd Armored Division, still stunned by the almost total loss of its 6th Brigade, received an order to move elements of the "Ben al-Walid" Armored Brigade to the border area of al-Wafra. The order stated that movement should begin after dusk and be complete by midnight. This deployment appears to be a case of the III Corps prematurely anticipating success. Less than twenty-four hours later, the division received the order to return to its previous location.[45]

The 5th Mechanized Division reported that Coalition air attacks continued throughout the day apparently "with the goal of demobilizing the roads and forward forces in al-Khafji."[46] At approximately 1830 on 30 January, the Iraqis recorded that they successfully repelled four to five attacks on the southern side of al-Khafji, near the boundary between the 15th and 20th Mechanized Brigades. At 2230, the Coalition probed the defense of the 26th Armored Brigade and again, according to the Iraqi telling, "the enemy was forced to retreat to the Saudi depth."[47] The 5th Mechanized Division commander recalled that his force held up well during 29 and 30 January; however, things went downhill quickly the next day: "On the 31st . . . at 0100 the enemy started to bombard [all of] our units. At the time I was going [around to] all the fighters. Each and every one of them . . . [told] me, sir; protect me from the air and I will fight and take care of the land units. I, as a division commander had no way to protect them from the air. . . . Our fighters were heroes, they were disciplined and the commanders were excellent. However, the enemy's technical ability is too great."[48]

At 0130, the Coalition launched a major attack on the left flank of the 15th Brigade along the al-Khafji–to–al-Mish'ab road. According to the division commander's recollection, "they [the Coalition] deployed airborne units from TOW helicopters behind the 20th Brigade . . . we fired artillery on them, and they retreated into the sea."[49] The intensity of the attacks by air increased and by 0415, the 2nd Regiment of the 15th Brigade "was destroyed by aircraft"[50] and through this gap the Coalition was able to gain a foothold in the southern edge of the city. Sometime on the morning of the 31st, the commander of the 5th Division requested permission from the III Corps to pull back into more defensible positions. According to a General Military Intelligence Directorate (GMID) history of the events, the Coalition attacks at 1130 and the seizure of the desalinization plant by "airborne forces" broke the defense of the 15th Brigade and forced the 26th Brigade to pull back to the far north side of the city.[51]

Sometime after noon on the 31st and "due to the criticality of the position of the 5th Mechanized Division,"[52] the commander of the III Corps requested, from the General Command, permission to withdraw. It is unclear from the record why, after being delegated the authority to determine the mission duration on the 29th, Major General Mahmaud would ask Baghdad for permission to withdraw at this point. Permission was granted shortly thereafter. However, the corps commander decided to delay the retreat until the hours of darkness. At 1800 hours, the 5th Division was ordered to pull out of al-Khafji and return to its original reserve position in east-central Kuwait.

In a postwar analysis of this decision, the 5th Division commander stated that it would have made more sense to withdraw during daylight hours, since waiting for darkness only prolonged the exposure to Coalition air attacks.[53] The official Iraqi version of events described the retreat under pressure as an early example of the kind of "victory" Iraq would later claim on a much larger scale: "On the 31st [of January], the 5th Division endured 360 air raids. By comparison; Egypt lost the 1967 war by [Israel's use of] 150 planes against it. Meaning, a country lost a war by [having] 150 planes used against it, while we had a division [endure] 360 attack against it."[54]

Most Coalition histories of the fight at al-Khafji describe the operation as a disaster for the Iraqis. Many count the 5th Division as being rendered combat-ineffective by the time it returned to Kuwait. While these descriptions might be true (physical evidence and the weight of Coalition documentation certainly suggest they are), these kinds of metrics were irrelevant to the strategic and operational leadership of Iraq. According to an Iraqi history, the 5th Division lost "only 20 percent" of its force during the al-Khafji operation.[55] The impact was even less, according to this version, when one accounted for the fact that immediately before the operation, two groups of 5th Division soldiers were on "vacation" and had, owing to movement problems in the theater, not yet returned to the unit before the operation began.

A later report was more specific about losses, but did not specify the units involved. For the Coalition, the Iraqi report recorded losses of four Chinook helicopters, eighty-eight armored vehicles, "large numbers of large and small vehicles," the capture of thirteen "officer and soldiers," as well as additional personnel losses. The exact number of Coalition casualties could not be determined, according to the Iraqi report, because "they remained inside Coalition territory." This is compared to Iraqi losses of 112 armored vehicles, 74 other vehicles, and 20 artillery pieces. Iraqi casualties are noted as 66 killed, 137 injured, and 566 missing.[56] Saddam once told his staff that Iraq would achieve a great victory if "a ratio of four Iraqi casualties to every one American" were achieved on the battlefield.[57] Reports like the ones out of al-Khafji certainly gave Saddam reason to believe his troops could achieve that "victory ratio" in future engagements.

Al-Khafji's other significant immediate impact was on Iraqi morale. Regardless of the morale of men who survived the al-Khafji mission, the morale of the overall force, as reported by the commanders, soared when the mission was completed. One officer, during a postwar review of the operation, related a degree of professional jealousy present in the Republican Guard just after the 5th Division retreated into Kuwait. The "daring men" of the Republican Guard were anxious to learn from the operation and do their part to "complete [similar] missions to the enemy's depth."[58] Saddam did not wait long to "learn lessons" from the al-Khafji operation. During the first week of February 1991, he reportedly offered several personal insights to his senior staff:

> The battle of al-Khafji had defamed the enemy, and it was considered a success. But the lessons learned and which we knew ourselves, and that we could address and correct must be remembered in the future.
>
> Going to al-Khafji [the next] time should be with different forces from what was the case the first time. We need to think of infantry soldiers, who could fight at the city's entrances without appearing outside the city.
>
> Our return to al-Khafji again is not necessarily for the same purpose the first time we went there. We need to discuss things in this spirit.[59]

The first ground combat action of what would become a twelve-year war ended, for all intents and purposes, in a draw. Regardless of how one assesses the military actions of 29–31 January 1991, both sides claimed victory and both sides acted accordingly.

For the Coalition, the battle confirmed Iraqi vulnerability to Coalition tactics and bolstered the confidence of the pan-Arab forces, but overall, according to Schwarzkopf, al-Khafji "was about as significant as a mosquito on an elephant."[60] The official U.S. Department of Defense history of the war was substantive with its assessment that "the battle of al-Khafji was important for the Coalition; the only ground offensive operation Saddam Hussein mounted had been defeated. . . . The strategic significance: Any Iraqi unit that moved probably would be struck from the air. Any unit that remained in place eventually would be struck whether from the air, or by impending ground assault."[61]

For Iraq's leadership, the battle was a success. An official regime history of the war recorded that in addition to Saddam's "courageous" leadership as "one of [the] outstanding military strategists of our time," the battle "proved that Iraqi forces were highly trained, [in part] because they managed to launch a well-planned and successful nighttime attack despite the enemy's spy satellites, drones, surveillance aircraft and technical superiority. It also meant that the Iraqi soldier was capable of taking part in a fierce [battle] like that at al-Khafji which will surely be recorded in world military history."[62]

Notes

1. Harmony media file ISGQ-2003-M0005309.
2. HRH General Khaled bin Sultan, *Desert Warrior: A Personal View of the Gulf War by the Joint Forces Commander* (New York: Harper Collins, 1995), 363. General Khaled bin Sultan

occupied a command position at the same level as that of General Schwarzkopf. The relationship between the U.S. Joint Forces Command (JFCOM) and CENTCOM was one of coordination. See Department of Defense, "Final Report to Congress," 556–58.

3. Schwarzkopf, *It Doesn't Take a Hero*, 424.

4. Harmony document folder ISGP-2003-00009833.

5. Ibid.

6. During the Iran-Iraq War, the Republican Guard developed a doctrine for "strategic preemptive attacks." The future commander of the II Corps, Ibrahim Abd al-Sattar Muhammad, delivered a lecture in 1985 where he described this type of attack having "political and international significance and consequences." The "indirect preemptive attack" [like al-Khafji], he argued, would have an "atmospheric effect" at the strategic level, which harms the enemy's plans and arrangements . . . rendering them incapable of meeting their objectives." In conclusion, Muhammad noted that Saddam was interested in this subject and offered his own instructions and comments to its author. Harmony document folder NGIC-96-0404.

7. Harmony media file ISGP-2003-10151507—Audiotape of Lt. Gen. Husayn Rashid Muhammad discussing 1991 Gulf War, dated 11 April 1995, 11 May 1995. Husayn was paraphrasing something Saddam told him and other senior officers at the time.

8. Harmony document folder ISGP-2003-00033524.

9. Harmony document folder ISGP-2003-00009833. Recollection attributed to Staff Lieutenant General al-Janabi.

10. Harmony media file ISGQ-2003-M0006183. Speaker is unidentified.

11. Harmony media file ISGP-2003-10151507.

12. It is difficult to pin down when the original planning took place. As early as August 1990, there clearly was intelligence being collected on al-Khafji as a place of interest, though it is unknown if it was for offensive or defensive purposes (see Harmony document folder ISGP-2003-00038521). The earliest detailed intelligence report supporting offensive operation on al-Khafji is dated 24 January 1991 (see Harmony document folder ISGP-2003-00033524). The Commander's concepts for the operation were discussed by the III Corps commander around 20 January 1991; see Harmony media file ISGQ-2003-M0003323.

13. In addition to Saddam and senior staff officers from Baghdad, those attending included Maj. Gen. Salah Aboud Mahmaud, commander of Iraq's III Regular Army Corps, the commanders of the 3rd Armored Division and 5th Mechanized Division, and the regional director of intelligence.

14. Harmony document folder ISGP-2003-00009833.

15. Ibid.

16. Ibid.

17. Most Western histories assume the purpose of both the Iraqi III Corps 3rd Armored and IV Corps 6th Armored Divisions was to link up with the attacks of the 5th Mechanized and 1st Armored Divisions respectively. A review of Iraqi plans and after-action reviews indicates that while there were options to reinforce success in Saudi Arabia, the primary mission of the armored divisions, to draw Coalition airpower away from the mechanized forces, was considered a success. The presumption that the armored divisions were "stopped" by Coalition airpower before they could reach their objective, while logical, does not appear to be accurate. See Gordon and Trainor, *The Generals' War*, 269; and

Kenneth M. Pollack, *Arabs at War: Military Effectiveness, 1948–1991* (Lincoln: University of Nebraska Press, 2002), 244.

18. Ibid.

19. Harmony document folder ISGQ-2003-M0006168.

20. Ibid.

21. Ibid. Destroyed Iraqi equipment on the Saudi side of the border indicates that, despite the Iraqi record of events, the operation was far from cost-free. For a thorough tactical retelling of the Coalition view of the 1st Division's attack see Morris, *Storm on the Horizon.* See also Gordon and Trainor, *The Generals' War,* 272–76.

22. Harmony document folder ISGQ-2003-M0006168.

23. Harmony media file ISGQ-2003-M0003323.

24. Harmony document folder ISGP-2003-00009833.

25. Ibid.

26. Ibid.

27. Harmony media file ISGQ-2003-M0006183. Speaker is unidentified.

28. Harmony media file ISGQ-2003-00054592. On this point, the Coalition and Iraqi narratives agree. In the Coalition version of this event, the lead brigade of the 3rd Armored Division was "devastated" in its attempt to cross the border at al-Wafra. See Gordon and Trainor, *The Generals' War,* 271. However, the presumption by some Western analysts that the al-Khafji assault force included three divisions, two of which were "stopped" by airpower, is incorrect based on information presented here. For example see Rebecca Grant, "The Epic Little Battle of Khafji," *Air Force Magazine* 81, no. 2 (1998).

29. Harmony media file ISGQ-2003-M0006183.

30. Harmony document folder ISGP-2003-00009833.

31. Ibid.

32. Harmony media file ISGQ-2003-M0003326. The only other provisions to cross the border with the assault were four tons of dates and a seven-day supply of bread.

33. Harmony document folder ISGP-2003-00033136.

34. Harmony document folder ISGP-2003-00009833. According to some Western reports, the 15th Division lost thirteen vehicles to AC-130 and USMC AH-1 helicopter fire before reaching the town. See James Titus, "The Battle of Khafji: An Overview and Preliminary Analysis" (Maxwell AFB, AL: Airpower Research Institute, Air University, September 1996), 13.

35. Harmony media file ISGQ-2003-M0006183.

36. Harmony media file ISGQ-2003-00054592. The reference to Mish'ab (a port town thirty kilometers south of al-Khafji) as a "medium offensive" was a concept to continue down the coast, if Coalition forces on the scene collapsed. There is almost no indication of serious logistical preparation for this concept.

37. There were in fact two reconnaissance teams of U.S. Marines remaining in al-Khafji after it was overrun.

38. Harmony media file ISGQ-2003-M0006181.

39. Harmony media file ISGQ-2003-M0006183.

40. Harmony document folder ISGP-2003-00033136. The Coalition troops were Saudi and Qatari tank companies. For some time after the war, the Iraqis convinced themselves they had faced down American forces in all but the final engagement.

41. On 29 January, Royal Air Force Jaguars detected fifteen Iraqi fast patrol boats attemp-

ting to move from Ras Al-Qul'ayah to Mina Al-Saud as part of an apparent combined operation to attack the port of Ras Al-Khafji. Lynx helicopters located and engaged the Iraqi boats with Sea Skua missiles, leaving two sunk or damaged and scattering the rest of the flotilla. Coalition aircraft then sank or severely damaged ten more of the fifteen small boats. Department of Defense, "Final Report to Congress," 195.

42. Harmony media file ISGQ-2003-M0006181.

43. Ibid.

44. Ibid. The commander's recollection notes that they were able to down two Coalition aircraft with SA-16 surface-to-air missiles. One was identified as an AC-130 and the other as a fighter.

45. Harmony media file ISGQ-2003-00054592. The fact that the Ben al-Walid Armored Brigade's movement was detected by a U.S. surveillance aircraft, resulting in a significant number of air strikes, likely affected the reconsideration of the order.

46. Ibid.

47. Harmony document folder ISGP-2003-00033136.

48. Harmony media file ISGQ-2003-M0006181.

49. Ibid.

50. Ibid.

51. Harmony document folder ISGP-2003-00033136.

52. Harmony document folder ISGQ-2003-00054592.

53. Harmony media files ISGQ-2003-M0003958—Military Seminar on the Um Al-Ma'arik, 10 May 1993. The speaker goes on to note the dilemma in choosing a day or night retreat under the enemy's air dominance. If the 5th Division retreated during the day, it was exposed to observation, but they could spread out and maneuver as individuals. Alternatively, if they retreated at night, they would have to remain in a formation (for navigation and passage of lines purposes), which made the Coalition's task of targeting them from the aircraft easier. The 5th Division commander's conclusion was that "retreating at night is no different than retreating during the day," as far as losses were concerned.

54. Harmony media file ISGQ-2003-M0006181. The speaker said he was quoting the director of the GMID at the time of al-Khafji.

55. The Coalition commander of the forces that retook al-Khafji counted Iraqi casualties as 32 dead, 35 wounded, and 463 taken prisoner. All told, he put Iraqi 5th Division losses at eleven T-55 tanks and fifty-one armored personnel carriers destroyed and another nineteen armored personnel carriers captured. HRH General Khaled bin Sultan, *Desert Warrior*, 387.

56. Harmony media file ISGQ-2003-00054592.

57. Harmony media file ISGQ-2003-M0001721.

58. Harmony media files ISGQ-2003-M0003958.

59. Harmony document folder IISP-2003-00026728.

60. Rick Atkinson, *Crusade: The Untold Story of the Persian Gulf War* (New York: Houghton Mifflin Co., 1993), 212.

61. Department of Defense, "Final Report to Congress," 133.

62. Harmony document folder ISGP-2003-00009833.

Chapter III

THE BEGINNING:
SADDAM'S NARRATIVE

The real chance is the one you use, not the one you think about.[1]

—SADDAM HUSSEIN

A Long View

For many in the international community, the Iraqi invasion of Kuwait on 2 August 1990 represented a "bolt out of the blue." Although tensions between Iraq and its small neighbor had made the news during the previous year, a regional war, and certainly one involving the United States, seemed like a ludicrous possibility.[2] To grasp the major elements of Saddam's strategic calculus on the eve of the 1990 invasion, one needs to go back to the late 1970s and the ruminations of an up-and-coming dictator. Saddam possessed a grandiose sense of not only his role in history, but also his responsibility to write the region's history through action. He would often remark that he was "writing the pages of history" when describing an event.

> You see that some of the foreigners say sometimes that Saddam Hussein is [being] imaginary in his thinking towards the Iraqis. He imagines them to be bigger than their actual size. Yes, correct, that's true. But not imaginary; I am interactive with Iraq's history to [such] an extent that the details interlock with every one of my cells. Regarding Iraq's history, I have a detailed comprehension and understanding of it. And I know the Arabic history and the spiritual meaning in the Arabic history, the significance of the missionary role in it. Hence, it is not imaginary.[3]

By observing events through his metaphysical historian's lens, one can see how Saddam maintained a remarkably consistent, if not predictable, narrative. An Iraqi historian once noted that "Saddam had an appointment with Iraqi history because a country with a great history always needs a great historical leader. The real history of modern Iraq began with [Saddam]; other leaders might end up in the 'trash bins of history,' but [Saddam] was inscribed in its annals by 'the pen of history itself.'"[4]

Saddam's public speeches and recordings of his private meetings reflect a striking consistency of strategic vision during the period 1978–90. In his view, unification of the Arab peoples, followed by the destruction of Israel and the expulsion of the "colonial" powers from Arab lands was the predestined course of development for any Arab superpower of the future.[5] Accordingly, the options, timing, and occasional compromises necessary to accomplish this vision remained at the center of all his calculations.

One such calculation came soon after the 1978 signing of the Camp David Peace Accords between Egypt's Anwar Sadat and Israel's Menacham Begin. Camp David was a seminal event framing Saddam's political and strategic outlook. In his view, Egypt's "surrender" was simultaneously a tragedy for the larger pan-Arab movement and an opportunity for a "true" Arab leader to step into the vacuum created by Sadat's betrayal. Saddam used the November 1978 Arab League Baghdad Summit to claim the leadership role he regarded as his duty. The declaration resulting from this historic meeting became Saddam's litmus test for Arab leadership.[6] It seems that as time went on it became increasingly clear to him that this was a test only a leader like Saddam could pass.

In March 1979 a visiting Palestinian representative asked then–Vice President Saddam Hussein, "Do you have an idea of the course of action that will take place against these Arab nations who do not abide by the decisions (of the Baghdad Conference)?"[7] Saddam replied, "We stated that they would be traitors and we would deal with them on that basis, by instigating the people to give all they can to topple the regime for treason. . . . I fear they [the "treasonous" regimes] think that those are just words for the public, but not for them. . . . We stand by what we have said."[8]

Saddam then went on to point out two specific examples of Arab nations that had pushed back from Baghdad's hard line: Saudi Arabia and Kuwait.

> We have told the [Iraqi] Minister of Foreign Affairs to tell them [Saudi Arabia and Kuwait] that they should not imagine that what was announced was incorrect but to tell them that was the position of the Iraqi nation and that we will apply it to the letter; it was not a slip of the tongue or a mistake. But rather it is a policy of the Iraqi nation stated with all its capabilities and political power which we will apply and consider any ruler who does not adhere to the resolutions of the Baghdad Summit to be as much a traitor as Sadat.[9]

During the coming decade, Saddam's call to action was not matched by action on the part of most Arab states. In 1990, on the eve of the Kuwait invasion, Tariq Aziz reminded Saddam that only one of the resolutions taken during the 1978 Baghdad Summit was complied with.[10] According to Aziz, the generally accepted excuse was that the Arab world was distracted because Iraq was "occupied with war . . . and when Iraq became occupied with [the Iran-Iraq War] people dragged their feeling away from facing the Arab-Israeli conflict."[11] Aziz went on to tell Saddam that he did not believe this excuse and that it reflected the Arab countries' "bad intentions." Saddam agreed and added that "this is the way of the Arabs," reflecting his oft-repeated frustration on this point.[12]

Notwithstanding his expressed pessimism on the potential for Arab cohesion and unity, Saddam repeatedly emphasized that these were the keys to his strategic vision. Arab unity, after all, lay at the heart of Ba'ath political philosophy. Over time, Arab leaders who did not subscribe to Saddam's view were going to be subject to the "instigation of the people in an organized manner to destroy [their] regime[s]."[13]

Saddam, who often conflated the concept of self and state, believed that Iraq was the only Arab state capable of carrying the Arab burden of history.[14] Countries like Syria (also nominally Ba'athist) would play a role, but only when "it becomes part of Iraq."[15] Saudi Arabia, whose rulers were often described as "temporary," could not rise to the leadership challenge because "there is a great deal of money. Yes billions, [earned] without sweat . . . the human is missing. There is no density of population and no quality. The one who is going to raise the Arab nation should be the one who is richer in scientific knowledge than the others. . . . There is no escape from the responsibility of leadership. It is not our choice to accept it or not. It is, rather, imposed on us."[16]

In these discussions, Saddam tended to mix his pan-Arab vision with a decidedly tribal outlook. He often described his burden as "the" leader or sheikh of all the Arabs. A time would come, Saddam predicted, when "our people will ask that we revolt against the illegitimate [leaders]." In this same conversation, Saddam used Sudan's President Muhammad Gaafur al-Nimeiry as an example of an illegitimate Arab leader.[17] Nimeiry's continued support for Sadat after the Baghdad Summit earned Saddam's anger.

Nimeiry is a traitor, a traitor like Sadat . . . and if one of you needs weapons and want to kill Nimeiry . . . these weapons are available from our embassy in France. And if the weapon is discovered that was sent through your embassy by diplomatic pouch, and is officially stated that it was sent from Iraq—we will admit it was sent from Iraq for the killing of the traitor Nimeiry, who is as much of a criminal as Sadat, just as we would do with Sadat. We do not vacillate when we take a stance, we state it as it is.[18]

One of the major reasons Saddam focused on Arab unity was his assessment of the nature and objectives of the enemy. He often noted, although rarely in public, that "the Zionist enemy is a smart and capable enemy, and we must not underestimate him."[19] It is sometimes easy to discount the "Zionist enemy's" central place in Saddam's long-term strategic calculations as simply rhetoric.[20] Based on a review of transcripts from hundreds of hours of recorded conversations, it is clear that for Saddam, the Zionist enemy was both a threat and a means to a much larger end. Much like Nasser before him, Saddam used his growing populist credentials to pressure other regional leaders from within their populations and as a tool to unify the Arab nations from without.[21]

Saddam once used the phrase "psychological quake," to describe the reaction of the Arab masses after the signing of the Camp David Peace Accords. According to him:

> If it hadn't been for the moves that led to the new relationship between Iraq and Syria and to the Baghdad resolutions at that time and the subsequent efforts up to now, I believe the Arab masses would have suffered from a psychological relapse that would have had dangerous strategic ramifications. . . . The Zionist presence definitely knows it too. The Americans, in spite of all their pride and all the mistakes they make in the situation will come to that conclusion. Thus, what's needed? Was the goal of Sadat's signing the accord to isolate Sadat from the Arab world? No, the goal was to make the whole Arab world bow down, not as governments but principally as people. As long as the masses have kept themselves on solid ground psychologically then they can wait for the unhealthy governments to be removed.[22]

Saddam apparently believed that his historic opportunity to unite the Arab peoples and deal with the conspiracies of his enemies would come only through war.[23] In the immediate aftermath of the Egyptian and Israeli peace accords, the objective for any future war would be Israel's destruction, not just reclaiming pre-1967 territory. But this time, Saddam was determined not to repeat the Arab mistakes of 1973. He had a different kind of war in mind:

> This is what we envision: we envision a war with the enemy, either with the unity nation [Iraq and Syria] or with the Iraqi, Syrian, Jordanian military effort . . . and for it to be a war that goes on for many months, not days and weeks. Whatever the enemy decides, we can get there. Does the enemy want a war where we quickly cross the miles to attack and then

fall back and withdraw? Or do we want the slow step-by-step war where every step we take becomes part of the land and we keep moving forward … and even more importantly what widespread cheering from the masses that will accompany each step we take forward from every corner of the Arab world. This is more important than the meter and kilometer we gain. … So we can guarantee the long war that is destructive to our enemy. And take our leisure each meter of land, that is bleeding with rivers of blood, we have no vision for a war that is any less than this.[24]

In effect, what Saddam was describing was not a military concept based on recent Iraqi or even Arab military experience, but a political concept designed to unite the Arab nation—the ever-elusive first step in the pan-Arab vision. In a preview of tragic things to come, Saddam described what a united Arab nation needed in order to defeat the "Zionist enemy":

What is required is a patient war, one where we fight for twelve continuous months and after twelve months we take stock and figure out how much we have lost and how much has been gained. And plan for losses amounting to thousands, thousands so that we plan to be prepared to lose in those twelve months, fifty thousand martyrs and injured.[25]

Saddam did not ignore the role of the United States in the coming conflagration. He apparently believed there could be no final defeat of the Israelis without forcing the United States out of the region, if not physically, then at least politically. He expressed his willingness to stand up to the challenge and see the confrontation through to the end.

But if we fight for twelve months in the Golan and God willing the day will come when we fight and the day we overlook the Sea of Galilee we will hear the Americans threatening that if we don't stop our advance they will throw an atomic bomb at us. Then we can tell them that, yes, we will stop … please let us know what you want. They in turn will tell us to stop and if we don't [we will be] hit by the atomic bomb. We will state that we have stopped, but not given up and that we will stay by the Sea of Galilee and watch for any changes in circumstances that will make us go further. We don't want to just go in and risk it. We either are victorious or are wiped out forever.[26]

All that remained for Saddam to fulfill his historic mission was to work patiently to unify the Arab peoples and prepare for the long war. He understood that timing was critical: "It has to be at the appropriate time," Saddam told his staff, "when I mentioned that it was a long process; I meant that it is a long way to victory."[27] Nevertheless, unification of the Arab nation would prove as elusive for Saddam as it had proven for Nasser. Becoming embroiled in a long war proved much easier. According to Saddam:

> Who can carry this role? It is no one else but Iraq. Iraq can make this [Arab] nation rise and can be its center post of its big abode. There are smaller posts, but it must always be that Iraq feels the responsibility and feels it is the central support post of the Arab nation. If Iraq falls, then the entire Arab Nation will fall. When the central post breaks, the whole tent will collapse.[28]

The Iran-Iraq War as Precursor

The Iranian revolution of February 1979 forced Saddam to rethink his calculations. In a self-imposed challenge like the one Hitler created in 1939, Saddam wrestled with an east and a west problem. His strategic vision was inhibited, as he saw it, by two natural enemies: the Zionists and the Persians. For Saddam the military problem to the west was clearly the most challenging, given the thirty-year history of disastrous Arab attempts to destroy the Jewish state. In his conception, the lack of an Arab victory over Israel was due to more than just the immature state of Arab leadership before Iraq's ascension, but was in large measure a result of a warfighting experience differential between Arabs and Jews. As Saddam once described it "considering that the current Arabic military and political commands did not get involved in the two World Wars" they could not possibly match "the gathered experience by the enemy."[29]

Saddam recognized that before a final battle with Israel was possible, the Arabs would need more experience with long-term, large-scale warfare. He acknowledged this when he told his ministers in March 1979 that a long war with the Zionists would

> not [be] this year—not this year and not in the next five years. . . . We are in the process of research and movement mobilization plans but the strategic visualization is what is important, so that you can't come and pump us up in the direction of planning a three-day war in which we neither win nor lose and end there. That is not what is needed with the Zionist Enemy.[30]

The rapid fall of the Shah of Iran in a Shiite-inspired popular revolution provided Saddam an unexpected window of opportunity to the east. Iraqi animosity toward Iran, and vice versa, was as ancient and complex as any in the

Middle East. The confluence of ancient grievances (never far below the surface) mixed fluidly with more recent conflicts over control of the Shat-al-Arab waterway, access to port facilities on the Gulf, long-standing demographic-political boundary mismatches in the north and south, and finally the ever simmering Sunni-Shiite seam running from Karbala and Najaf in Iraq to Qom and Mashhad in Iran.

In late 1979, Iraqi leadership closely monitored shifts in domestic and regional politics created by turmoil in Iran. Saddam was particularly alarmed by the revolutionary pan-Islamic messages emanating from Iran. Given Iraq's Shiite majority, the revolution next door had potentially dire consequences for Iraqi unity. A round of diplomacy by the new Iranian government directed toward the Persian Gulf States in the fall of 1979 created additional anxiety for Saddam and his inner circle. A senior member of this newly minted inner circle, Latif Nayyif Jasim, reported to him in November 1979 that with regard to Iran, the Gulf countries had passed through two stages. The first benefited Iraq because "at the beginning of the Iranian movement," the Gulf region "became a scary one."[31] The second stage was ongoing. It created a new and "dangerous" phenomenon, because Iran had reassured the Persian Gulf States that "there was no real or intrinsic threat from [Iran] toward the Gulf States and the region and that it is not necessary [for them] to side with Iraq."[32] Latif went on to point out:

> We must be very attentive to these phenomena. The Gulf people must be warned that the Iranian policy will remain that way whether their regime has changed quickly or it stays another year. . . . I believe they [the Iranian regime's leaders] are seeking to isolate Iraq; second, they desire that Iraq has limited political effects, adding to this that the new Iranian policies aim to make the Arabs believe that Iran does not have any problems with them and that Iran's problem is only with Iraq and the border issues . . . some Iranian media and some Western media started to talk about Iraq's attempt to acquire a leading role and that Iraq is restless and is pursuing a role outside its boundaries. . . . These actions [media and diplomatic initiatives] were not taken randomly, they were well studied and well coordinated . . . we must be proactive. We should not be complacent and let events lie down. We should acknowledge the real dangers in the region; we should be observant of all political activities whether it relates with the Palestinian problem, the Lebanon problem, the Gulf problems, and Iran's objectives in the region, all these events do not exist in isolation from each other.[33]

The threat appeared clear to Saddam and his inner circle. At a time when Iraq was ready to reinvigorate the drive toward Arab unity, events in the region were having a centrifugal effect on the Arab states. The political fragmentation along religious lines and external influences threatened to strangle Saddam's vision in its cradle. Earlier assessments that the Arab street and their more timid Arab leaders would naturally rally to him and the Iraqi Ba'ath party as the Iranian revolution continued were proving overly optimistic.

Nevertheless, Saddam wanted to proceed cautiously, especially since Iran seemed determined to challenge the United States directly before it had even consolidated its revolution. The fragility of revolutions was something the old hands at Ba'ath politics remembered well from 1963. Saddam lectured his ministers that they should not rush into any particular course of action, and certainly

[they] did not want to repeat the same mistakes that Nasser and Boumé-dienne have committed,[34] we are not going to fall into the same trap, even though the conflict with Israel continues. . . . Iran plans animosity for us from the beginning, as if the change that took place in Iran was designed with the intentions to be against the interests of Iraq. We have to be patient . . . we are not bargaining with Iran, we have treated them in a kind manner, [better] than they deserve.[35]

The problem, as Saddam saw it, was twofold. First, the Iranian appeal to Islamic unity was actively challenging Iraq's regional leadership role. This reality then led to the second problem. If non-Arab Iran successfully exercised political, economic, or religious influence with some portions of the Arab "nation," Saddam would find it impossible to unify the Arabs and lead them to the final battle with the Zionists. Saddam and his ministers voiced increasing frustration and disgust at the actions of the many Arab leaders for even talking to the Khomeini government. In this context, Saddam singled out the president of North Yemen as "not worth a *fils* [small coin]." Furthermore, he identified the actions of Libya, Syria, and even the Palestinian Liberation Organization (PLO) as not being helpful.[36] But he reserved his most venomous tirades for the Persian Gulf States.

The Arabs in the Gulf, Gulf Arabs, they do not change, God help us, they are the Arabs of decay, the Arabs of shame, Arabs whose values contradict all the values known in heaven and on earth, we were the first ones to realize their decay. Khomeini will not give them a chance to survive, slaughtering them is a blessing, a great deed, slaughtering them will prove to be beneficial because of their corruption and decay. All the decay of earth and all [that] you can imagine [are] found in the Gulf States.[37]

Saddam, in a prophetic moment, described Iraq's policy toward Kuwait in the context of his larger vision. This was long before the running dispute over Kuwait's manipulating the market price of oil or repaying a war debt began:

> We have to get rid of the rule of Kuwait, but if one overthrows the ruler of Kuwait he must be able at the same time to safeguard the interest of its people and to safeguard its Arab identity for its people. If we do not have these plans then we are against anyone who wants to carry out the change. . . . Only when an enemy attacks them [Kuwait] they cannot do without us.[38]

The solution to the twin problems of Arab unity and Iranian influence, like many strategic disasters in the making, appeared elegantly simple—at least to Saddam. It may be impossible to determine the moment when a plan to start a war with Iran came to life inside Saddam's inner circle. What is clear from the archival material is that the logic of war with Iran appeared to be the solution to Saddam's problems. He could leverage the historic fear felt by many Arab states with regard to Iran's rise to rally the Arab street and undercut those very same regimes.

Comrade Latif related to Saddam how at a recent Arab League conference the Kuwaiti foreign minister was "crying with fear" over news of Iran's activities and intentions. Latif went on to note that the opportunity for Iraq to open a "campaign against Iran at its fullest scale . . . [one] that could be achieved through instigation" might be at hand.[39] Such a campaign would influence the Arab masses to "imagine that Iraq wants to play a leading role, it wants to be the successor of Nasser's policies."[40] All that was lacking was an event to harness the opportunity.

The search for a coalescing event did not take long. After a series of increasingly aggressive border clashes during the fall of 1980, the Iraqi military surged into southern Iran in an attempt to destabilize the Iranian regime. In the eight-year war that followed, Iraq's initial successes were quickly forgotten as the war devolved into a World War I–style slugfest.[41] The details of the Iran-Iraq War are beyond the scope of this study and will be covered in future research. For Saddam, the war with Iran was never an end in itself but a means toward achieving both internal goals and progressing toward the long-term vision.

In a 1982 conversation with his senior advisers, Saddam provides another hint of the ultimate link between unfolding events.

> Now take a look at Israel. . . . It cannot tolerate Iraq walking out [of the Iran-Iraq War] victorious because there will not be any Israel . . . the Israeli strategic planners are the most knowledgeable on the implication that Iraq

is building and Iraq is winning military-wise. Technically they [Israel] are right in all of their attempts to harm Iraq. And I do not put it far from them that they might hit Iraq with an atomic bomb some day if they reach a certain stage. We are prepared, and if God allows it, we will be ready to face it.[42]

Saddam apparently believed the path to the ultimate confrontation with Israel would be, at least for the time being, an indirect one. The indirect approach was not just recognizing the military imbalance, but was, in fact, the strategy to overcome that imbalance.

The Coming War of the Elephant

Saddam's masterful use of language to establish his political truths and, all too often, Iraq's reality relied heavily on allusions to Islamic and even pre-Islamic history. One such story related the events on the Arab peninsula just before the birth of Islam in the year 570, a year that would later be called the "year of the elephant." The story tells of the power struggle between the Persian and Byzantine empires. The Byzantines allied with Christian Abyssinia to capture the city of Mecca. This operation was a part of the Byzantine drive to dominate the Arabian Peninsula and eventually invade Persia. After conquering Yemen, the Abyssinian soldiers, reportedly supported by war elephants, made their way to Mecca. A local Arab named Abu Righal acted as a guide during the Abyssinian's final approach march. As the battle was joined, so the story goes, Allah intervened by sending birds with stones to frighten the elephants and defeat the Abyssinian soldiers. In Saddam's updated version of the story, the Iranians logically played the part of the Persians; the United States was the Byzantine Empire, and the modern-day Abyssinia was Israel. Even the traitor Abu Righal found reincarnation in Saddam's myth as the modern Arab powers showing the infidels the way to Mecca.[43]

This story was a reservoir of material on which Saddam floated his worldview. The allusions in the story supported tactical as well as strategic purposes. The elephants represent the advanced weapons of the west; the stones are reminiscent of the weapons of the weak, and the divine birds—the people of Iraq.[44] But at a deeper level, Saddam seemed to be playing the role both of heroic Arab fighter against the odds and of the divine sender of the birds. In the period between the end of the war with Iran and the beginning of the Kuwait crisis, Saddam used the imagery from this story to not only explain the changes in the international balance of power, but also to justify his actions. The year of the elephant was also a seminal event in the advent of Islam as it was designated as the year of the Prophet Muhammad's birth. Such positive tidings fit nicely within Saddam's narrative of the glories to come.

At the end of their war with Iran in 1988, most Iraqis expected a rapid return to the kind of economic growth and prosperity Iraq enjoyed in the mid-1970s. It quickly became apparent that this was not possible. The war had severely damaged Iraq. In addition to the huge numbers of casualties, Iraq had a command economy built around war, exploding inflation, falling oil revenues, and a crushing war debt. To appreciate the magnitude of such an economic challenge, one must recall that in 1980, Iraq had more than $35 billion in foreign exchange reserves. By 1988, it was a nation saddled with more than $80 billion in debt and economic reconstruction needs of more than $230 billion.[45] In 1988, Iraq's gross domestic product was just over $38 billion. To make matters worse, Saddam could not afford to demobilize his huge army for fear of spurring dissent over a lack of jobs.[46] The solution, as leaders like this often resort to in times like these, was to focus on an external threat.[47]

One lesson Saddam learned during this long conflict with Iran was the degree of influence the international community had over events. The strategic calculus on how to establish leadership of the Arab Nation, consolidate Arab power, and complete his historic task was more complicated in 1988 than it had been in 1980. Some of these changes came about because of the internationalization of the Iran-Iraq War on issues such as the "Tanker War" and belated concerns over the use of chemical weapons.[48] But even more troubling developments resulted from changes inside the Soviet Union. A weak Soviet Union meant Iraq had a weak strategic ally. As a direct result of Moscow's troubles, the United States gained regional strength without expending any resources. The net effect in relation to Saddam's larger vision for himself and Iraq was a stronger regional adversary to the west—Israel.

On 4 September 1989, Iraq's ambassador to the United Nations in Geneva, Barzan Ibrahim al-Tikriti, wrote a long letter to his half-brother Saddam offering a strategic assessment of Iraq's new challenges. Barzan was motivated, he said, by a desire to "ensure that [our] victory is not kidnapped."[49] His analysis provides some insight into the dialogues of the inner circle during this short interlude of peace. Among Barzan's main points were:

> We have to identify the sources of danger. There is no danger from Western Europe now and for many reasons, namely because . . . we are able to "drag" a portion of its interests to our side like France. So we have to pay attention to our relation with France to ensure its continuity. . . .
>
> [While] there is no big danger from Europe, however, we can act in an

opportunistic manner economically wise and even politically [by] taking advantage of Iranian blackmailing, terrorism, and the kidnapping of hostages of these countries. . . .

The real danger is from the superpowers, the United States and the Soviet Union, but at the same time there are no major problems with the Soviets. . . . This is due to their positive view toward Arab causes in general and through the bilateral relations with Iraq in particular.

The real danger is the United States and its follower Israel. The Americans want to control the region and we are the only obstacle in front of them.[50]

Barzan's letter went on to describe the five main elements of the "American campaign" against Iraq. The first, and largest, "weapon" was a public and private campaign of "psychological warfare," which he described as "non-stop." The major themes of this campaign were "Human Rights issues, Kurdish rights, sectarian divide, and other allegations that are designed solely for one aim which is to defame Iraq and dilute the efficacy of our victory."[51] The second major element was an economic war imposed on Iraq by the United States' manipulation of oil prices, which was exacerbating Iraq's debt. The third was the American attempt to "invade us from the inside out." However, on this point, Barzan was confident that "they do not stand an opportunity of success." The fourth element was particularly troublesome to Saddam's long-term view. According to Barzan, "the United States has tried for a long time to isolate us [Iraq] from the rest of the Arab World." While Iraqi initiatives like the Arab Cooperation Council (ACC) had "positive results" in hindering the American plans, Barzan did not believe it destroyed them.[52] In fact, he suspected that two of the ACC member countries were being "opportunistic" because they had known ties to the United States. In a statement reflecting the sometimes-convoluted conspiracy logic at work in this regime, Barzan wondered if the ACC actually might be an American plan "aimed at Iraq."

Barzan ended his analysis of the American threats by reminding Saddam that an American assassination (of Saddam) was also a serious threat. He wrote, "Your Excellency knows that if an assassin is determined on killing someone, even if he sacrifices his life, there isn't any security procedure that could be taken to prevent him from achieving his objective."[53]

In Barzan's estimation, the Americans would not conduct the operation themselves, but would hire someone from the many different groups with a potential anti-regime bent. Of particular concern was a group of thousands of Iraqi soldiers still held as prisoners of war in Iran. He noted that "the situation [potential assassination] will become more complex when prisoners of war return home, moreover, part of the religious craze is still active—we can safely say that it has diminished, but we cannot say that it has ended . . . there are still people out there who have been brain-washed and influenced by such craze to the extent that they are willing to sacrifice themselves. It is beneficial to mention those individuals who have detonated their bodies in vehicle borne explosives at some official sites."[54] Clearly, Barzan accepted as fact the idea that the Americans and Iranians were working closely to achieve their nefarious aims.

Actual changes in the general or specific situation outside Iraq never seemed to shake certain conspiratorial explanations for events. For many in the inner circle, the changes only revealed new dimensions of the already accepted truth. In many future conversations relating to Iraq's foreign policy, the major issues articulated in this 1989 letter would be repeated time and again.

Notes

1. Harmony document folder IISP-2003-00045177.

2. For a summary of Iraq's complaints and Kuwait's rebuttals see Lawrence Freeman and Efraim Karsh, *The Gulf Conflict (1990–1991): Diplomacy and War in the New World Order* (Princeton, NJ: Princeton University Press, 1993), 42–63. For a detailed description of Iraq's justification (after the collapse of Iraq's "it was a republican revolt" cover story) and Kuwait's response see "Press Release by the Press Office of the Embassy of the Republic of Iraq, London, 12 September 1990," and "The Association for Free Kuwait: Kuwait—An Independent State, 28 November 1990," in E. Lauterpacht, et al., eds., *The Kuwait Crisis: Basic Documents* (Cambridge: Grotius Publications Ltd., 1991), 73–77, 78–82.

3. Harmony media file ISGQ-2003-M0007540. Saddam goes on to remind his audience that God is the one who put the Iraqis in this position of historical superiority, "so why should we give it up? . . . An Arab disdains only [those] who try to look down upon him. Otherwise . . . he is modest, but a modesty [born] out of capacity not weakness. Plus, God . . . doesn't like the weak."

4. Sabah Salman cited in Ofra Bengio, *Saddam's Word: Political Discourse in Iraq* (New York: Oxford University Press, 1998), 167–68.

5. This "vision" was not entirely original. Political unification of one type or another among the Arabs had been a rallying call since the rise of the Ottoman Empire in the fourteenth century. The focal point, acute issues, political philosophies, and iconic leaders have changed along with the larger issues of the region. During the past century, the rallying cries for Arab unification have ranged from the European-encouraged nationalism during World War I, the Zionist movement of the 1930s, the post-colonial era, more recently the existence of a Jewish state, and finally the rise of radical Islam.

6. The final statement of the Baghdad Conference included five basic principles for confronting "the dangers and challenges threatening the Arab Nation, particularly after the results of the Camp David agreements." 1) "The military, political, economic, and cultural danger the Zionist enemy constitutes against the entire Arab Nation" requires that all of the Arab Nation share in the conflict. 2) Arab countries must offer "all forms

of support to the struggle of the Palestinian resistance." 3) Reaffirmed commitment to the Arab summits of Algiers and Rabat. 4) It is "impermissible for any side to act unilaterally to solve the Palestinian question." 5) No solution to the Palestinian question shall be accepted "unless it is associated with a resolution by an Arab summit conference." Middle East Research and Information Project, "Baghdad Summit: 'The Palestinian Question Is the Essence of the Conflict," *MERIP Report*, no. 73 (1978): 22–23.

7. Harmony media file ISGP-2003-10151758. Saddam Hussein became Iraq's vice president (deputy chairman of the Ba'ath party and vice chairman of the RCC), after participating in a Ba'athist coup on 16 July 1968. On 17 July 1979, Saddam became the president after he forced President al-Bakr to resign and purged the ranks of the Ba'ath party of dissenters, potential rivals, and past enemies.

8. Harmony media file ISGP-2003-10151758.

9. Ibid.

10. Tariq Aziz's comments reveal his assessment that only resolution #2 (that all Arab countries must offer "all forms of support to the struggle of the Palestinian resistance") was complied with. Harmony media file ISGQ-2003-M0003677.

11. Ibid.

12. Ibid.

13. Harmony media file ISGP-2003-10151758.

14. Saddam, like Nasser before him, struggled with the Gordian knot of Arab unity. As a national leader, Saddam appealed to state nationalism (as opposed to regional nationalism) in order to build the kind of physical strength and political clout necessary to press for a political philosophy (Pan-Arabism) that eschewed state nationalism.

15. Harmony media file ISGQ-2003-M0003811.

16. Ibid.

17. Muhammad Gaafur al-Nimeiry was president of Sudan from 1971 to 1985. A one-time vocal Arab revolutionary, he was influenced by the ideas of Gamal Abdel Nasser's Free Officers Movement. In 1969 he helped lead a military coup of the civilian government, eventually becoming Sudan's president. Nimeiry was the only Arab leader to back Egyptian President Anwar al-Sadat in his peace negotiations with Israel.

18. Harmony media file ISGP-2003-10151758.

19. Ibid.

20. See, for example, Otto Friedrish, "He Gives Us Hope," *Time* 136, no. 9 (27 August 1990). For an examination of the issue, see Barry Rubin, "The United States and Iraq: From Appeasement to War," in *Iraq's Road to War*, Amatzia Baram and Barry Rubin, eds.

21. One Middle Eastern specialist noted that "the importance of Arab public opinion to the foreign policies of Arab states derives from the very absence of electoral legitimacy and the prevalence instead of transnational symbols of legitimacy . . . any Arab government must present credentials on those issues." Shibley Telhami, "Arab Public Opinion and the Gulf War," *Political Science Quarterly* 108, no. 3 (1993): 439.

22. Harmony media file ISGP-2003-10151758. Saddam is referring to the short-lived attempt to restart the failed United Arab Republic (UAR) concept with a political "union" between Iraq and Syria in 1978.

23. The role of conspiracies in policy-making for this regime cannot be overstated. Saad al-Bazzaz, the former head of the Iraqi News Agency, said in an interview (after his

defection) that Saddam would "turn to disasters for silly reasons; they [the regime] base their policy on conspiracy theories." See "Saad al-Bazzaz: An Insider's View of Iraq," *Middle East Quarterly* 2, no. 4 (1995).

24. Harmony media file ISGP-2003-10151758.

25. Ibid.

26. Ibid.

27. Harmony media file ISGP-2003-10151704.

28. Harmony media file ISGQ-2003-M0003811.

29. Harmony document folder ISGP-2003-00010140. Saddam credits the Israeli exprience in both World Wars to the immigrant nature of its population. This was such a concern that he suggested Iraq use all of its political influence to prevent individuals with more recent war experiences (like Vietnam) from immigrating to Israel.

30. Harmony media file ISGP-2003-10151758.

31. Latif Nayyif Jasim was Saddam's minister of culture and information and one of the most senior Shi'a in the regime. Harmony media file ISGQ-2003-M0004353.

32. Ibid.

33. Some of the "suspicious" diplomatic activity Latif mentions included Syria's Hafiz al-Assad's and Libya's Muamar Kaddafi's trip to Iran, the Palestinian Liberation Organization's (PLO) Yasser Arafat's trying to intercede with Iran for the release of American hostages, and the rising American strategic military influence in the Gulf region resulting from its tensions with Iran. Harmony media file ISGQ-2003-M0004353.

34. The comment about Egyptian President Gamal Abdel Nasser is likely a reference to his failure to defeat Israel in the 1967 war after establishing and promoting the power of a pan-Arab ideology. The reference to Houari Boumédienne (president of Algeria from 1965 to 1978) is likely to the disastrous economic policies and social policies instituted under his rule. Boumédienne pursued a non-aligned policy and stoked independence movements in North Africa.

35. Harmony media file ISGQ-2003-M0004353.

36. Ibid.

37. Ibid.

38. Ibid.

39. Ibid.

40. Ibid. Latif was apparently referring to Nasser's pan-Arabist philosophy and early successes before the disastrous war with Israel in 1967.

41. Casualty figures from the eight-year Iran-Iraq war are a subject of continuing debate. According to sources cited in Dilip Hiro's work, *The Longest War: The Iran-Iraq Military Conflict* (New York: Routledge, 1991), 250–51, "conservative Western estimates put the total number of war dead at 367,000—Iran accounting for 262,000 and Iraq 105,000. With more than 700,000 injured, the total casualties were over one million." According to Hiro, in 1991 dollars "Iran spent between $74 and $91 billion to conduct the war, and Iraq between $94 and $112 billion. . . . If the direct damage caused by the warfare and the indirect loss of income from oil and agricultural produce were added to the cost of conducting the war then . . . the aggregate direct and indirect cost of war to Tehran [was] $627 billion, and to Baghdad [was] $561 billion."

42. Harmony media file ISGQ-2003-M0005346.

43. Bengio, *Saddam's Word*, 194–202. The "treachery of Abu Righal" is a common theme in the

creeds of many Salafi jihadist groups aimed at delegitimizing secular governments across the Middle East.

44. Several of the Scud missiles that Iraq fired at Israel in the 1991 war reportedly had concrete warheads. Iraq dubbed these missiles "*hijarat ababeel*" (flying stones).

45. Freeman and Karsh, *The Gulf Conflict (1990–1991)*, 39.

46. In addition to the direct costs, Saddam cited the failure to demobilize after the war with Iran as a major factor in the poor discipline and readiness of some of the army units deployed to Kuwait. The Iraqi army was simply too large to maintain proper training and discipline standards. Harmony media file ISGQ-2003-M0006905.

47. For a good description of the combination of internal and external factors implicated in Saddam's decision-making after 1988, see Amatzia Baram, "The Invasion of Kuwait: Decision-making in Baghdad," in *Iraq's Road to War*, Amatzia Baram and Barry Rubin, eds.

48. The so-called "Tanker War" (1984–88) refers to the attacks on civilian tankers and supporting oil facilities in the Persian Gulf by both Iraq and Iran during the Iran-Iraq War.

49. The "victory" Barzan is referring to here is of the Iran-Iraq War. Harmony document folder ISGZ-2004-001472.

50. Ibid.

51. Ibid.

52. The ACC was founded in 1989 with Egypt, Iraq, Jordan, and Yemen as the charter member countries. Its purpose was to promote economic cooperation among the member states, including issues of free movement of workers and joint projects in transportation, communications, and agriculture. The stated long-range goal was the eventual integration of trade and monetary policies. The ACC disbanded with the withdrawal of Egypt in 1994.

53. Harmony document folder ISGZ-2004-001472.

54. Ibid. According to Iraqi documents, soldiers repatriated after the Iran-Iraq War were subject to suspicion, investigation, harassment, and sometimes incarceration based on rumors of Iranian "brainwashing." This is not unlike some Soviet POWs returning from Nazi captivity after WWII.

Chapter IV

SADDAM'S STRATEGIC CALCULATIONS

If you decide to fight your enemy, then you have to make him look like the aggressor.[1]

—SADDAM HUSSEIN

Kuwait

In the late 1980s, Saddam was consumed by the pressing concerns of recovering from the lingering effects of the Iran-Iraq War. But no sooner had the dust from his Pyrrhic victory settled, than Saddam was again facing the same strategic situation he articulated in 1979. To the east was a weak but still troublesome Iran, to the west was a strong Israel, and the Arab population was as fractious as ever. Saddam needed a way to focus Iraq's internal aspirations and simultaneously demonstrate leadership in the Arab world. Saddam's calculations followed the same logic as on the eve of war with Iran: a confluence of historical, economic, geographic, and political factors brought Saddam to the conclusion that this time Kuwait might be the answer to Iraq's challenges.

In 1989, a series of seemingly positive and stabilizing interactions between Iraq and Saudi Arabia actually exacerbated long-simmering tensions with Kuwait. In March of that year, Saudi Arabia's King Fahd signed a non-aggression and military assistance pact with Saddam. Saudi Arabia followed this agreement by converting a significant portion of Iraq's wartime debt into gifts. Iraq's offer and quick ratification of the non-aggression pact with Saudi Arabia was in part a pressure tactic by Saddam aimed at Kuwait. The emir of Kuwait found himself under pressure to follow King Fahd's lead on the war debt issues, as well as to open talks on long-standing border disputes with Iraq.[2] In a November 1989 visit to Baghdad, the emir and his negotiators failed to resolve either issue. In an effort to move the Iraqis forward in the negotiations, Kuwait's emir began to push for repayment on Iraq's wartime debt. Saddam, ever wary of conspiracies in the unfolding of significant events, came to believe that the United States and its regional ally Israel were somehow involved in encouraging Kuwait to press its larger neighbor in such a "disrespectful" fashion.[3] Of course, for Saddam, the issue was bigger than Kuwait.

In a 1996 interview, Tariq Aziz recalled that "by the end of June [1990] we started to realize that there is a conspiracy against Iraq, a deliberate conspiracy against Iraq, by Kuwait, organized, devised by the United States. So when we came to that conclusion, then we started thinking of how to react against the future aggressors on Iraq."[4]

To many Iraqi leaders it seemed that, in this case, time was not on their side. Saddam once described Iraq's situation as "like an army standing before a landmine, when they stop, the artillery will finish them. [T]o overcome the landmines, they must pass it as quickly as possible and not stand before it. It is the same thing with the International [community], if we were to stop, we could be exposed to the death of our regime."[5]

Figure 8. Map of Kuwait. "Kuwait" in Arabic can be translated as a "fortress built near water." (Central Intelligence Agency)

Immediately after the invasion, there was much debate surrounding the content and interpretation of this meeting. Some accused the U.S. ambassador of "giving Iraq a green light" to invade Kuwait. Others contended that such an interpretation of the meeting owed a lot to hindsight. A full version of the Iraqi transcript of this meeting can be found in Micah Sifry and Christopher Cerf, eds., The Gulf War Reader (New York: Times Books, 1991), 122–33. For insights into how the discussion was interpreted by the ambassador at the time, see declassified cable from the U.S. Embassy Baghdad to the Secretary of State dated 25 July 1990, titled "Saddam's message of Friendship to President Bush," www.margaretthatcher. org/ (accessed 15 November 2006). When asked by a reporter "Why had the Washington government's policy before August 2, 1990, failed to deter Saddam from ordering an invasion of Kuwait?" Ambassador Glaspie replied "because we foolishly did not realize he was stupid, that he did not believe our clear and repeated warnings that we would support our vital interests." Washington Post, 21 March, 1991, sec. A23.

Figure 9. U.S. Ambassador April Glaspie and Saddam Hussein, 25 July 1990 (Harmony document folder ISGQ-2003-00049397)

In 1991, the U.S. ambassador to Iraq, April Glaspie, stated that the Iraqi senior leadership at that time believed that a growing set of conspiracies were threatening its state's security. According to the ambassador, the Iraqis were "quite convinced the United States . . . was targeting Iraq. They complained about it all the time. . . . Day after day, the Iraqi media since February [1990]— literally every day—was full of these accusations. And I think it was genuinely believed by Saddam Hussein."[6]

Figure 10. Saddam and Yasser Arafat, summer 1990 (Harmony document folder ISGZ-2004-026434)

Conspiracy theories big and small were not just fodder for Saddam's public speeches; they were seemingly at the heart of Iraq's strategic decision-making process. Saddam spoke about a willingness to confront this "conspiracy" in an April 1990 discussion with Yasser Arafat: "Just like when you prayed in Beirut and said, 'death tastes good'" [to which Arafat responded, "Yeah."]

> According to us, it is a done decision. Since all the small players have been isolated, there has been no possibility other than for America to play the game directly. I swear to God we are ready. We are ready to fight America. And if God wills, we will fight them. With the help of God we will fight them and kick them out of the entire region . . . it is true that America has a lot of planes and [our] planes are humble and few . . . it is true that America has a lot of rockets and our rockets are humble and few, but I believe that the Arabic public, when they see a real stance, not just words, I believe that they will fight America everywhere. . . . We are prepared to fight America whenever they fight us. If America wants to strike us, we will strike back. Wherever they have a naval base in the Gulf, we will send our planes to fly over it and bomb it. We will announce, for example, that "today our aircrafts have conducted continuous attacks on the American bases wherever they are."[7]

The fact that this meeting was videotaped with a small number of Iraqi and Palestinian dignitaries in the room implies that the words were selected to demonstrate confidence and leadership as much as any other purpose. However, it is instructive to see the degree to which Saddam saw the United States as the primary threat, months before the Kuwait invasion. Buoyed by Arafat's praise, Saddam continued with a somewhat rambling motivational monologue:

> If America were to hit us we will hit America back. We have stated these words before. As you know, we are not the kind of people who will mumble on the microphone and tell stories. . . . We mean all the things we say. Perhaps we cannot reach Washington, but we can send a strapped person [a suicide bomber] to Washington. Our rockets cannot reach Washington, but I swear to God that if it could reach Washington, we would hit Washington. . . . We can send a lot of people. Move them. Move a strapped [person] on to Washington and retaliate just [like] the old days. This is the thing. [A man] strapped with a bomb and throws himself on Bush's car. . . . Let us prepare ourselves on this level. We cannot be intrigued by words. Words are nothing. It is all about taking a decision and having a commitment. . . . The necessity states that right now we have to stand up tough. . . . When we decide, we decide.
>
> Arafat: Just like you always decide.
>
> Saddam: I am very confident; I am filled with faith . . . if [someone] comes in and shuts the door for the Arabic nation's development and the door of hope for Palestine [then] we have no hope but to fight.[8] I swear to God that we will fight! We will fight! . . . We will not get engaged in a few days [of] battle. We are not familiar with a few days battle or a few months battle. That is how it is. Once we agreed we are going to keep on doing it because that is what the people ask for. How many years is it going to last? Let it last! We might become quiet for twenty days, but after twenty days, you will be surprised to see boom, boom, boom, boom, and the rockets along with the planes will be striking. . . . We have no middle solution. We do not negotiate, we do not use a middle man, and we do not want any of that. Isn't that true Abu Ammar?
>
> Arafat: A hundred percent!
>
> Saddam: Sabawi, what kind of old school stuff do you have?[9] Pull out your old books. . . . Coordinate with the intelligence director and your Palestinian brothers. When it comes to the region of the Middle East, we want to know where each American individual is, even those who come to do business. . . . This is the battle, so let us resist, and when we resist, let us be beasts.
>
> Arafat: Beasts indeed!.[10]

Saddam closed his meeting with Arafat on two thoughts. Both represent a different aspect of his calculations. First, he says that

> [this] battle will develop. It is true someone might do calculations in regards to the nation. I do not calculate the abilities of the nation. I do not calculate them in a classical way. How many artilleries, how many planes. . . . This is important but what is more important—is that the son of the nation be able to touch the future with his fingers, if he stretches his arm [out] while dying? This is what is important to me."[11]

Saddam's second thought was darkly prophetic. It may have been a logical extension of Saddam's bravado about conventional war with the United States, or it may have been the only result imaginable to a man absorbed by his historic mission. He warned that they "did not ask for [this] evil but America might be in need for some discipline. Hopefully America will bring its army and come in here and occupy Iraq. Let them do it so that we can kill them all! Finish the Americans. Finish them period!"[12]

In most cases, Saddam's confidence with regard to confronting the United States was an eclectic mix of naiveté and bravado. However, it also increasingly appeared to reflect his judgment that America was unwilling to decisively use military force. During a speech in February 1990, he articulated this growing belief, derived from reading recent history. Saddam commented, "we saw that the United States, as a superpower, departed Lebanon immediately when some Marines were killed" and since that time the United States had "displayed some signs of fatigue."[13] No doubt, the rapidly dissolving power and stability of the world's only other superpower, the Soviet Union, reinforced Saddam's belief that the prefix "super" was transitory.[14]

Notwithstanding the complex mix of grand strategies, conspiracy theories, and regional animosities, the dispute between Iraq and Kuwait finally came to a head in 1990 over money. The economic impacts of the war with Iran and the depression in oil prices through OPEC inaction were ostensibly costing Iraq $1 billion per year for each $1 decrease in the price of a barrel of oil.[15] In mid-July, Iraqi pressure directed against Kuwait over the economic question came to a climactic point. Saddam dispatched his final "demands" to the emir. Iraq reportedly demanded $2.4 billion in compensation for the disputed Ramalia oil field; $12 billion for Kuwait's role in depressing oil prices in general; forgiveness of Iraq's $10 billion war debt; and a long-term lease on Bubiyan Island.[16]

A 31 July meeting, hastily arranged by Egypt's President Hosni Mubarak, between the vice-chairman of Iraq's Revolutionary Command Council (RCC),

Izzat Ibrahim al-Duri, and Kuwait's Crown Prince (and Prime Minister) Sheikh Saad al Abdullah as Salim, failed to provide a workable solution.[17] In fact, it may have had the opposite effect. Iraq's al-Duri, playing the role of regime enforcer, reportedly replied to the Kuwaiti Crown Prince's rejection of Iraq's "offer" with "how do you confront me without a solution? [This] means you are driving me to kill you."[18] Apparently, in al-Duri's conception of diplomacy, not accepting Iraq's "reasonable" list of demands constituted confrontation. At the conclusion of the meeting, the Kuwaitis were concerned, but generally unfazed. The emir of Kuwait reportedly dismissed the brewing crisis as a "summer cloud," which fairer winds would blow away.[19]

The View of Senior Ba'athists

It is not clear when in the summer of 1990 Saddam decided to invade Kuwait. Given what is now known about Saddam's compartmented style of decision-making, it is not surprising that this kind of decision is not in the record.[20] Saddam's penchant for making important decisions in small, closed groups guaranteed that many of his key decisions were never documented. Nevertheless, there are some unique records, recorded immediately after the invasion of Kuwait, that provide glimpses into the issues, preconceived notions, and strategies at play during the run-up to war in the summer of 1990.[21]

A transcript of a meeting that took place on 4 August 1990 between Saddam Hussein and the visiting president of Yemen suggests much about Iraqi thinking before the invasion.[22] After brotherly welcomes to various delegation members, Saddam immediately turned to the issue at hand, stating that "Kuwait is Iraqi land. . . . I don't make ambiguous statements, we may become silent and we don't want to talk but if we talk . . . we are sincere in our talks. [A month ago] we didn't have any plans against Kuwait, but when we perceived the conspiracy against us . . . which causes division in our region . . . we started planning and searching for an exit from this deadlock."[23]

In an indication of how acute Iraq's economic circumstances were, Saddam explained that he could not accept the economic privations brought on after the Iran-Iraq War "because it means our failure."[24] He continued to recite the oil conspiracy, wherein the Persian Gulf States accumulated billions of dollars, leading to poverty in other Arab nations, disunion among the people, and the empowerment of the colonialists. Saddam declared to his guest, "the Arab Nation is decaying now and the reason is the Arab oil."[25]

Journalist John Cooley once described Saddam Hussein's action in the crisis of 1990–91 as the "perfect illustration of what might be called the 'Al Capone' theory of international relations. According to this theory what happened in the Gulf region was a kind of 'protection racket.'"[26] While Saddam might have disagreed with the comparison to an infamous American criminal, he certainly would have recognized the modus operandi. As he told his Yemeni guest, "Iraq ... who defends them [the Arabs] for ten years [and] they consider his defense as a liability against [Iraq]? ...The time has come for every person to say ... I'm Arabian.... I'm Saddam Hussein.... [If] Iraq will pay this amount of money to develop the Arab nation and to defend it [then] the other Arab countries must pay this amount of money ... if they don't we will fight them."[27]

A long, rambling discussion between Saddam and his senior ministers recorded on 7 August 1990—five days after the invasion—also captured some of Iraq's pre-invasion sentiments. Saddam began the meeting with a loaded question to assembled Ba'ath leadership. He stated that the "authority [the RCC] decided on full merger without delay explaining that this would be the correct method, which is to return the branch [Kuwait] to its original [tree]. Now I am presenting the same question to the Minister Council Members, how [do] the Minister Council Members see this?"[28]

The fact that Iraq had already invaded and that everyone in the room knew the decision rested solely with Saddam undoubtedly limited "dissenting" opinions. However, a careful reading of the responses provides a glimpse of not only the regime's internal logic in the days preceding the attack, but the peculiar dynamics at the top as well.

The first unidentified minister couched his answer in grand pan-Arabist terms, while repeating the preemptive justification:

> The Arabs will wake up from their rest, and they will gain their culture back. The culture they had abandoned for a long time. This culture that your people and your soldiers managed to retain with this specific victory ... all the Iraqis have been praying for [it]. This situation [could] not be postponed. Our enemies are looking for reasons to attack us, but with God's will we are stronger than them because we are doing the right thing. In reference to your question, I believe merging is the only solution.... This is an opportunity that we can not pass because our alternative is to lose everything.[29]

Another minister discussed the invasion of Kuwait in geopolitical terms. He said, "Mr. President. I believe that the present circumstances in the world today have given us the opportunity of a lifetime, and this opportunity would not happen again in fifty years. Therefore the situation is ready ... and we are behind the command decision in merging [Kuwait]."[30]

The minister of justice addressed the inevitability of Arab unity and the political cost of failing to achieve it, saying he remembered "after a month or two of the first August revolution [referring to the 1963 Ba'ath coup] and the separation of our national parties. . . . We are looking for unity Mr. President. I believe the biggest mistake that Gamal Abdel Nasser made in his life was when the separation happened when his army withdrew and the movement stopped. [H]e was for unity alone, if he was determined we would not have to deal with Hafiz al-Assad and the smiley guy [a reference to Egyptian president Mubarak]."[31]

The minister of agriculture and irrigation believed "that we had accomplished a miracle and more than a miracle; this would never be accomplished under any leader in history. Without your brave leadership [of the] revolution, this huge miracle and our dream would never happen." Blissfully unaware of the military realities, like many of his fellow Ba'ath loyalists, he continued, "*We should keep going without boundaries and we are here waiting for direction*"[32] [Emphasis added].

The minister for higher education and educational research, after offering the obligatory praise, noted that "a few days ago we started to live a historical event. . . . I consider the second of August a historical change in the Arab nation."[33] He then proposed that, since Kuwait had "returned to the mother," it was time to do some retroactive research on the "legal issues of this matter." For international examples of "merging unity" he offered to look into the examples of Switzerland and America. Recognizing the potential complexity of absorbing a state with its own laws "in regards to people's ethnicity and physiological environment," the minister recommended studying a historical example for the implementation "of some kind of local administrative system. . . . [W]e should focus on the historical event, such as the war between France and Germany in 1870 and during the First World War when France retrieved the Alsace Lorraine region and kept it united under regional policy laws, municipal laws, and autonomy after the First World War. France gradually extended its authority to this region until it became internationally and constitutionally part of France."[34]

The minister of education, perhaps voicing a populist pan-Arab line of reasoning, offered, "What was only a dream yesterday became a reality under your command today. [It] is not possible for a small state like Kuwait to be self governed; the Kuwaiti people are against self government. They [the European powers] made this country [Kuwait] feel that it has history, tradition, culture, and they gave them a different lifestyle that they acclimated themselves with. They [Kuwaitis] got accustomed to luxury, travel, and constant contact with foreign companies. . . . I say they were ungrateful; therefore Mr. President the combined unity will bring them back to normal life."[35]

The minister of endowment and religious affairs lived up to his title. He avowed his support for Saddam's "courageous decision in finishing this irregularity, which is a cancer that used to live in Kuwait." Using sweeping historical and religious terms, he said that "Saladin did not liberate Jerusalem till he crippled all the leadership in the cities of Homs, Aleppo and Mosel . . . and then liberated Jerusalem. . . . Kuwait [had seceded] from the motherland of Iraq and it needs to be united again; this serious step is the only path to bring the nation together, then people will shift to liberate Jerusalem. Saddam Hussein is [carrying the] Saladin mission from Iraq in order to liberate Jerusalem and Arab occupied lands."[36]

A close military adviser and future Minister of Defense Sa'di Tuma Abbas al-Jabburi provided a military geography rationale. In addition to the "obvious geographical and ethnic composition," Kuwait is a natural part of Iraq because

> this piece of land (Kuwait) has what Iraq needs. From the military aspect, its importance for Iraq lies in the fact that it's bordering the sea. This is a problem we have suffered a lot from . . . it is difficult to secure our needs with regards to our access to the high seas . . . [t]herefore the main ports [of Kuwait] will serve Iraq and secure direct access to [the] high seas and the outer worlds. I will leave it [to] you to make the decision on how the relation should be between Kuwait and Iraq. The most important thing is that this generation managed under your command accomplished many victories for Iraq and the Arab nation . . . [for example] when Iraq secured the eastern door [referring here to the Iran-Iraq war] for eight years . . . this was not only to secure Iraq only but it was for all the Arab nations.[37]

During a Ba'ath party reception recorded sometime later in August 1990, Saddam summarized his public position on the decision to invade Kuwait, its continuity with past events, and future goals:

> Allah who honored this generation with witnessing of this victory that was attained not only for Iraq, where it was a great victory, but not only that, it was a great victory for the entire Arab nation, beginning with the victory that was attained in the Second Qadissyyah and its legitimate child, the Day of the Call, August 2nd of this month. There is no doubt that these victories will have a large impact, not in themselves, but in the coming days, in the lives of Arabs as a whole and in particular that which is related to Arab unity, that a large number of believers have fought for and only

a few of them were able to experience its successes, sporadically and for short periods of time. But I am absolutely certain, exactly as I believe in Allah, the Almighty, that the coming days will open a door that will never be shut again in the face of the national fighters to achieve the great Arab unity, which is rising from its unwavering base, the new Iraq.[38]

Notes

1. Harmony document folder IISP-2003-00045177.
2. The border disputes included formal borders near the oil-rich Rumalia oil fields as well as Iraq's long-standing demands for long-term leases to Bubiyan Island.
3. U.S.-Kuwait defense and political relations warmed considerably during the final years of the Iran-Iraq War. Iran's attacks on tankers in the Gulf drove Kuwait to request U.S. military assistance. The United States responded with a naval escort and tanker re-flagging program (Operation Earnest Will) designed to protect not only Kuwaiti but also international shipping from Iranian naval attacks. U.S. policy goals toward Iraq in late 1989 included normalizing relations, moderating Iraq's behavior on issues such as WMD, human rights, and regional stability. See National Security Directive 26, Subject: U.S. Policy Toward the Persian Gulf, 2 October 1989 (Secret-declassified 26 May 1999), http://bushlibrary.tamu.edu/research/directives.html (accessed 1 December 2006).
4. PBS Frontline, "The Gulf War," original broadcast 9 January 1996, www.pbs.org/wgbh/pages/frontline/gulf/oral/aziz/1.html (accessed 1 September 2006).
5. Harmony media file ISGQ-2003-M0003473.
6. Ambassador Glaspie's testimony to the Senate Foreign Relations Committee, 20 March 1991; cited in Donald Neff, "The U.S., Israel, and Iran: Backdrop to War," *Journal of Palestinian Studies* 20, no. 4 (1991): 35.
7. Harmony media file ISGQ-2003-M0006048 – Saddam Hussein Meeting with Yasser Arafat, 19 April 1990. Date established by Harmony media file ISGQ-2003-M0006248 – Video of meeting between Saddam Hussein and Yasser Arafat, 19 April 1990, which appears to be a partial recording of the same meeting. On 2 April, Saddam gave a speech to the Iraqi armed forces, made public, in which he threatened to "burn half of Israel," if Israel preemptively struck at Iraq's industries (harkening back to the Israeli preemptive strike at Iraq's nuclear facility in 1981).
8. In this discussion, Saddam offered Arafat proof of the "conspiracy goal of the Americans and Israelis." According to Saddam, the conspiracy "known to everyone" was called Iran Gate and "was conducted [by the United States] so that the Iranians could reach al-Faw and then [defeat] the regime." Harmony media file ISGQ-2003-M0006048. Saddam was referring to the U.S. political scandal known as Iran-Contra. During the mid-1980s, members of the Reagan administration sold arms to Iran, a nation America did not have diplomatic relations with, and used the money from the sales to fund the anti-communist guerrilla organization in Nicaragua, known as the Contras.
9. Sabawi Ibrahim al-Tikriti, half-brother of Saddam Hussein, was leader of the Iraqi secret service, the Mukhabarat, at the time of the 1991 Gulf War.
10. Harmony media file ISGQ-2003-M0006048.
11. Ibid.

12. Ibid.

13. Foreign Broadcast Information Service, translation of a Saddam Hussein speech given in Amman, Jordan, 27 February 1990; cited in Neff, "The U.S., Israel, and Iran," 35.

14. In other conversations, some of Saddam's inner circle tempered this long-term view with concerns about America's growing freedom of action in a world without counterweight.

15. Saddam reportedly announced in a closed session of the Arab Summit on 30 May 1990 that Iraq's losses were a billion dollars per year each time the price of oil dropped by one dollar. "This is a kind of war against Iraq," he said. John K. Cooley, "Pre-war Gulf Diplomacy," *Survival* 33, no. 2 (1991): 127.

16. Janice Gross Stein, "Deterrence and Compellence in the Gulf, 1990-1991: A Failed or Impossible Task?" *International Security* 17, no. 2 (1992): 150.

17. In addition to pressing its original demands, Iraq actually added a demand for an additional $10 billion loan guarantee. See Cooley, "Pre-war Gulf Diplomacy," 125–39.

18. Anecdote as told by Saddam Hussein to the president of Yemen on 4 August 1990. Harmony document folder ISGQ-2003-00044897. According to the former head of the Iraqi News Agency, Saad al-Bazzaz, the same thing happened in the June meeting with the Kuwaitis when Deputy Prime Minister Sa'dun Hammadi reported to Saddam that the emir of Kuwait had not been "deferential enough." Sa'dun complained to Saddam that "the emir didn't respect me and by that he didn't respect you for I was representing you." See "Saad al-Bazzaz: An Insider's View of Iraq," *Middle East Quarterly* 2, no. 4 (1995).

19. Steve A. Yetiv, *Persian Gulf Crisis* (Westport, CT: Greenwood Publishing Group, 1997), 9.

20. Kevin Woods et al., *Iraqi Perspectives Project: A View of Operation Iraqi Freedom from Saddam's Senior Leadership* (Washington, DC: U.S. GPO, 2006).

21. The audiotaped and videotaped portions of the captured Iraqi archive provide a unique window into Saddam Hussein's regime. Many of the captured media files are incomplete records. Some tapes lack a complete context, some have unidentified speakers, and others are clearly part of a larger set of tapes. However, most of these conversations were never intended for public release and therefore capture a moment in history in a most intimate way.

22. Harmony document folder ISGQ-2003-00044897. This document appears to be a transcript that was in the process of being reviewed and edited in February 1993 by the principals involved. It includes Saddam's handwritten corrections in the margins.

23. Ibid.

24. Ibid. For a succinct external description of Saddam's rational calculus for invading Kuwait see Michael T. Corgan, "Clausewitz On War and the Gulf War," in *The Eagle in the Desert— Looking Back on U.S. Involvement in the Persian Gulf War*, William Head and Earl H. Tilford Jr., eds. (Westport, CT: Praeger, 1996), 267–89.

25. Harmony document folder ISGQ-2003-00044897.

26. Cooley, "Pre-war Gulf Diplomacy," 125.

27. Harmony document folder ISGQ-2003-00044897.

28. Harmony media file ISGQ-2003-M0003852. Saddam's historic argument over Kuwait carried emotional weight in many parts of the Arab world, but had little support beyond. In terms of international law and existing agreements, there were varying interpretations, but little real debate. The boundaries of the modern state of Iraq were generally

established in its 1932 application to the League of Nations. Those boundaries were reaffirmed by Iraq in 1963 when it formally recognized Kuwait and accepted it as a member state in the Arab League.

29. Ibid.

30. Ibid.

31. Ibid. The reference to "separation of our national parties" probably refers to the collapse of the UAR. The UAR was an early attempt at a pan-Arab state (Egypt, Syria, and Yemen). It was led by Egypt's Nasser during its existence (1958–61) but collapsed after Syria withdrew following a military coup. Egypt continued to use the name UAR until 1971.

32. Ibid.

33. Ibid.

34. Ibid.

35. Ibid.

36. Ibid. Saladin captured Jerusalem shortly after defeating a combined crusader army at the Battle of Hattin on 4 July 1187 CE.

37. Ibid.

38. Keeping track of the names of wars in the Middle East requires some effort. The Iranians called the Iran-Iraq War the "Imposed War." Most of the world referred to the 1980–88 war as the Gulf War until the conflict in 1991 was given the same name in the West. This in turn led to many confusing references in Iraqi documents to the first or second Gulf Wars. Most official Iraqi documents use the term "Qadisiyyah Saddam" or the "First Gulf War" (after 1991) to describe the war with Iran. Harmony media file ISGQ-2003-M0003853.

Chapter V

RESTORING THE BRANCH TO THE TREE

At the time when the second of August arrived to be the legitimate newborn son of the second Qadisiyya and its people . . . it and its consequences shall be the beginning of a new, lofty, and rising stage in which virtue will spread throughout the Arab homeland.[1]

—SADDAM HUSSEIN

Planning an Invasion

For the Iraqi military, the period between the end of the war with Iran in August 1988 and the invasion of Kuwait in the summer of 1990 would prove a short respite. The physical and human costs of the war with Iran had been devastating. Notwithstanding the butcher's bill of the previous eight years, Iraq's military emerged from the war with a cohort of experienced combat officers and a large but generally exhausted force.[2]

In the summer of 1989, the Iraqi military began conducting combined-arms training for the first time since the end of the Iran-Iraq War. Delegations from other militaries had begun to make pilgrimages to Iraq to garner insights from its eight years of combat experience and in some cases to explore the market for new and replacement weapons. Recovery would be slow owing to economic constraints, but Iraq's professional officer corps, their confidence at an all-time high, threw itself into the task.

Lt. Gen. Aayad Futayyih Khalifa al-Rawi was the chief of staff of the Republican Guard in the summer of 1990. Saddam came to him early that summer and asked him to "take a look at the Iraq/Kuwait border."[3] The motivations behind this task were well known to General al-Rawi. Since early in the year, the growing tensions with Kuwait and indicators that "foreign interference was possible" dominated the regime's public and private rhetoric. However, during this period the military's general focus was on the threat posed by Israel, not Kuwait. The next day, General al-Rawi reported the results of his reconnaissance to Saddam and received an order to "write up a detailed plan to accomplish the task of retrieving Kuwait and massing the troops in the area."[4] The broad outlines of a plan were quickly pulled together by a small, highly secretive planning staff that was closely supervised through a series of meetings with Saddam.

TABLE 1. General Purpose Iraqi Forces, July 1990

Manpower		Total Combat Aircraft**	513
Total Active	1,000,000	Bombers	20
Regular	425,000	Fighter/Attack	284+
Reserve	850,000	Recce/Interceptor	223+
Paramilitary	40,000	Recce/FGA Recce	10
Army and Guard		AEW C4I/BM	1
Manpower	955,000	Other Combat trainers	157
Regular Army Manpower		Transport Aircraft	63
Reserve (Recalled)	480,000	Tanker Aircraft	4
Total Main Battle Tanks (MBT)	5,500–6,700	Total Helicopters	584
Active MBT	5,100	Armed Helicopters	160
Active AFIV, Recce, Lt. Tanks	2,300	Other Helicopters	424
Total APC	7,100	SAM Launchers	600+
Active APC	6,800	Total Naval Manpower	5,000
ATGM Launchers	1,500	Naval Vessels	44
Self-Propelled Artillery	500+	Major Surface Combatants	4
Towed Artillery	3,000+	Patrol Craft Missile	8
Multiple Launch Rocket Systems	300+	Patrol Craft	6
Mortars	5,000	Mine Vessels	8
Surface-to-Surface Missiles*	230	Amphibious Ships	6
Light SAM Launchers	1,700	Landing Craft	9
AA Guns	unknown	Support Ships	3
Air Force Manpower	40,000		
Air Defense Manpower	10,000		

* Based on Iraqi documents
** Differs slightly from Iraqi documents

Source: Order of Battle data derived from Anthony H. Cordesman, The Gulf Military Forces in an Era of Asymmetric War—Iraq *(Washington, DC: Center for Strategic and International Studies, 28 June 2006), 9–10; and International Institute for Strategic Studies,* The Military Balance: 1989–1990 *(London: Brassey's, 1989), 104–05.*

In support of the planning efforts during July 1990, the GMID produced a series of studies. According to a postwar summary, the Directorate produced five influential reports before the invasion:

> As per Saddam Hussein's "verbal orders [and] in our top-secret and perso-nal correspondence" dated 12 July, the Directorate provided the commander of the Republican Guard with an analysis of the theater of operations, details of Kuwaiti order of battle, and video of the Iraq-Kuwait borders.
>
> On 24 July, the Directorate provided the commander with information on all embassies and communications centers in Kuwait. Moreover, it completed a report on the Kuwait Air Force and Air Defense.
>
> On 25 July, the Directorate provided an "evaluation on probable foreign military intervention" in case of any armed conflict with Kuwait. The report hinted that Kuwait would try to "internationalize" any crisis and noted that the United States had declared that it would intervene to help Kuwait.
>
> On 31 July, it completed a summary report of all actions the Kuwait military had taken between 19 and 29 July, as well as a list of all of Kuwait's "vital" targets.
>
> On 31 July, it provided to the Republican Guard a detailed listing of members of the Kuwait government, the national council, and senior military figures.[5]

Even as the number of supporting tasks grew, military planning for the invasion remained limited to a small team around Saddam. He successfully kept major portions of his government entirely ignorant of the planning for war. The army chief of staff at the time and hero of the Iran-Iraq War, Gen. Nizar al-Khazraji, recalled "the invasion was staged by the Republican Guard forces without my knowledge. It came as a surprise to me . . . [when] I was informed of the situation."[6] Like the chief of staff, for many of the military formations that would participate in the invasion, notification and planning came only hours before the invasion began.

Preparing the Republican Guard

Brig. Gen. Ra'ad Hamdani, a future Republican Guard Corps commander during OIF, commanded the 17th Armored Brigade of the Republican Guard's Hammurabi Division during the summer of 1990. He recalled the period as one of dramatically rising tensions. Between August 1989 and July 1990, rumors of

Zionist military conspiracies, including the possibility of an Israeli preemptive strike against Iraq, kept the Republican Guard busy. Saddam's public rhetoric concerning the "economic and media conspiracy" leveled against Iraq found its counterpart in a series of secret warning orders to the Republican Guard. On 2 July, Saddam told a group of senior Republican Guard officers that a conspiracy of "external" forces was controlling the events afflicting Iraq. Moreover, Kuwait played a major role in the conspiracy. Like many of his fellow Republican Guard officers, Hamdani accepted the regime's logic that Iraq deserved nothing but gratitude and respect from its fellow Arab nations. After all, it was Iraqi soldiers who had just spent eight years defending them at a horrendous cost. Saddam ended his meeting by leading a detailed discussion of the capabilities and readiness of his Republican Guard.[7] In hindsight, it seemed to Hamdani as a less-than-subtle indication of how Saddam was planning to engender Kuwaiti gratitude.

On 15 July, Hamdani received a short-notice movement order to deploy his brigade from its garrison location near al-Kut to an area southwest of al-Basra.[8] When asked by his subordinates for an explanation, Hamdani told them the movement was probably just "a show of force and the threat of using it was a political maneuver to pressure Kuwait and permit the resolution of our political crisis."[9] It would be almost a week before even he knew the real purpose for the hasty maneuvers.

On the morning of 20 July, Hamdani completed the deployment south. His brigade was arrayed in a tactical assembly area just north of Kuwait's border. Later that same day, Hamdani was ordered to report to the Hammurabi Division headquarters. In a scene likely played out in numerous headquarters across the Republican Guard, he received a heretofore highly classified briefing on the general concept for a new war.

> When I entered my commander's caravan, I saw a Koran on his table in a very prominent position, which was very unusual. We had a short conversation about how the [final] massing of the forces was going and then he asked me to stand up and take an oath to keep Project 17 (the plan for Liberating Kuwait) secret. I was stunned by the size of the mission. For I thought that at the most we would only reclaim the part of the border which Kuwait had taken from us and which contained quite large oil reserves belonging to the southern Iraqi oil fields. In astonishment I asked, "We are going to occupy Kuwait ... our neighboring country?"[10]

Not only was Hamdani's division going to participate in the invasion of Kuwait, but his brigade, the 17th Armored Brigade, was to be the spearhead unit. As briefed, the plan was still more concept than order. It lacked many of the details necessary for execution. Between 20 and 31 July, Hamdani and his staff feverishly developed courses of action and war-gamed scenarios on a large sand table replica of Kuwait. The other brigades were doing the same under the close guidance and supervision of the division commander. In his memoirs, Hamdani described his division commander, Maj. Gen. Qais Abd al-Razaq, as "a very practical man who concentrated on getting our directions right while giving us ample opportunity for initiative"—not a description usually given of Iraqi generals.[11]

During the next ten days, working from a bare mission outline, Hamdani's officers considered how to conduct an armored dash from southern Iraq to the beaches immediately south of Kuwait City—a distance of 160 kilometers. This mission presented unique challenges to a force still more heavily influenced by defensive slugfests with the Iranians than WWII German-style armored thrusts.

Hamdani later recounted some of the considerations, limitations, and challenges in planning the initial assault. First and foremost, he recalled "speed was the most important factor to achieving surprise and surprise was the most important factor in achieving mission success." Another challenge resulted from the fact that neither Hamdani nor his troops held any enmity for the Kuwaitis and therefore planned to minimize casualties, military and civilian. According to his plan, there would be no preliminary shelling or "protective [artillery] fires."[12] Hamdani went so far as to require his tanks to fire only high-explosive shells, not sabot, which are armor-piercing, in an attempt to "frighten the occupants, but not destroy the vehicle."[13]

Many of the planning limitations were directly related to a lack of tactical intelligence. Republican Guard planners reported an urgent need for detailed information on the enemy and terrain. Enemy order of battle briefings consisted of limited descriptions of the six Kuwaiti brigades and their peacetime garrison locations.[14] To make matters worse, planners had to work with a limited number of out-of-date, 1:100,000 scale maps.

One of the most significant operational challenges in the plan was the need to make the assault forces self-sufficient. Logistics and administrative support for the attack forces would follow the operation by upwards of twenty-four hours. The planners decided the armored units would use civilian fuel stations, water sources, and hospitals as necessary to maintain the speed of the attack.

To support their staff's mission analysis, Hamdani and his fellow commanders conducted numerous personal reconnaissance missions along the Iraqi side of the border. By the end of July, Hamdani received permission to conduct an even more detailed reconnaissance of his proposed attack route on the Kuwait side of the border. He planned to enter Kuwait disguised as an Iraqi army sergeant on a routine logistics mission to pick up supplies in the Kuwaiti port of Ahmadi.[15] During the pre-dawn hours of 31 July, just as Hamdani was preparing to depart on his "covert" reconnaissance mission, his division commander cancelled the mission and ordered him to return to his unit.[16]

During the commander's update briefing on 31 July, Hamdani learned that his superiors had cancelled his mission for two reasons. First, the commander of the Republican Guard had already dispatched one of his deputies, disguised as a merchant, to scout the invasion routes and the details of his report were now available to the division staffs. Second, and more important, the date for the invasion was now set for 2 August at 0400 and final unit preparations took precedence over reconnaissance.

The Hammurabi division commander personally briefed his brigade commanders on the Republican Guard plan. The guard's mission consisted of two distinct tasks. First "commence attack at the 0400 hour on Monday 2 August against enemy locations between Umm Qasr, al-Salmi, and al-Shagayir, and . . . occupy the city of Kuwait and other Kuwait cities that are identified on the spot." The second task, which included the plan for the Republican Guard Forces Command, was "to defend locations that it has occupied."[17]

As the commander explained it, the Republican Guard scheme of maneuver consisted of a main effort, a supporting effort, and a special operations raid. The main effort followed the major highways from southern Iraq into northern Kuwait supported by a commando air assault into the highway choke point just north of Kuwait City. The supporting effort was a ground attack across a secondary road through western Kuwait. An additional commando air assault was planned into Kuwait City to capture the ruling family as well as senior government officials. A small reserve force, positioned in southern Iraq, would support the overall operation.

The main effort had three distinct trident-like prongs of attack. The central prong was led by the Hammurabi Armored Division, which was to attack along the main road from Safwan (Iraq) through Abdali, Mutla, Jahra, and then to the capital Kuwait City. The Hammurabi was to be followed by the Nebuchadnezzar Infantry Division, whose primary mission was to occupy the center of Kuwait City.

The al-Fao Infantry Division supported the Hammurabi with an attack along the coastal road running between Umm Qasr and the capital Kuwait City. It served as the easternmost prong of the attack and controlled the restricted terrain along the northern Kuwaiti coast.

The third prong of the main effort was led by the Tawakalna Division. The Tawakalna Division deployed to the west of the Hammurabi Division. Its immediate task was to "take the Kuwait's Ali as-Salim Air Base and wait for the passage of the Medina Division from the western axis." The Tawakalna's secondary mission was to move to and seize the area around al-Wafra and Sa'ud Port south of Kuwait City.

The supporting attack was led by the Medina Armored Division, which would attack from the west, on the axis of Rumaila al-Mabar, al-Abraq, Ali as-Salim Base, and the port at al-Ahmadi. The Medina was to be followed by the Adnan Division, and then the Baghdad Division to "take the coastal area between al-Ahmadi and the Saudi Border."

Supporting the primary ground operations were a series of commando assaults designed to seize key terrain and political objectives. Elements of the 16th Republican Guard Special Forces Brigade infiltrated Kuwait before dawn, taking the Abdali-Jahra-Kuwait City Road with the aim of attacking the "vital points" in the capital. Its primary task was seizing the Sabah ruling family. The 3rd Republican Guard Special Forces Brigade was to be dropped by helicopters on the Mutla Barricade. According to Hamdani, its mission was to "ensure the safe passage of our armored vehicles through this mountain pass." Finally, the 6th Armored Division (Iraqi Regular Army) was assembled near Sanam Mountain in southern Iraq to act as the reserve force for the overall Republican Guard effort.[18]

Final preparations for the invasion included applying some lessons from the Iran-Iraq War. One example was the addition of a reserve infantry brigade to each armored division. The Republican Guard commander explained that, because mission success depended on speed, they would need the reserve infantry to attack and clear "security checkpoints" between the border and the objective area. Another lesson focused on water. The Hammurabi Division commander, recalling the lack of water during summer battles in the Iran-Iraq War, ordered insulated tanks manufactured and attached one to each armored vehicle alongside the traditional extra fuel tank. This same commander also borrowed a lesson from the Iranians for conducting night operations. In order to maximize the speed of the assault, he directed 130-mm artillery detachments to follow just to the rear of the assault formations. As the force moved forward, the artillery would fire illumination shells forward of the advance at increasing five-kilometer ranges. After the war, one commander recalled how his attack speed in the initial phases of the operation increased from twenty kilometers per hour (his planning rate) to forty kilometers per hour during the actual attack.[19]

Operationally, the Republican Guard plan was relatively simple. However, a lack of detailed information on the primary objective, Kuwait City, limited detailed tactical planning. For example, late on the evening of 31 July, Hamdani received "two very important documents," which he recalled as "critical" to

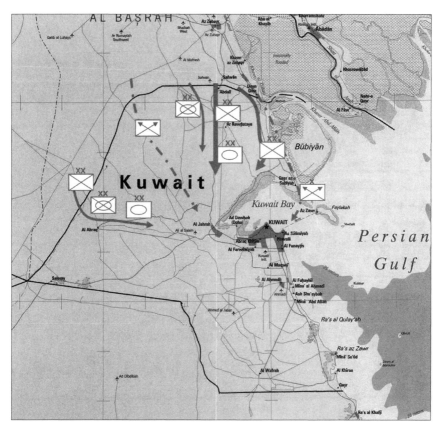

Figure 11. Invasion of Kuwait: Phase I—Republican Guard Kuwait Invasion Plan (Central Intelligence Agency)

his success. The first was a set of recent aerial photographs of Kuwait City. The second, more importantly, were detailed tourist maps of the city that he could distribute to his subordinate commanders. Hamdani noted in his memoirs that without the photographs and tourist maps, that his troops could not have operated inside Kuwait City.[20]

Early on 1 August, Hamdani completed a final personal reconnaissance along the line of departure with the commander of his brigade's commando company. Satisfied with the preparations, Hamdani assembled his commanders and briefed them on the details of the brigade plan.

> The commando company would seize the Kuwaiti Border Control Company located at Sideriya Fort. The intent was "to take prisoners but not spill blood."
>
> "Speed during execution would ensure that the two major Kuwaiti maneuver threats would not be a factor. Speed would prevent the Kuwaiti

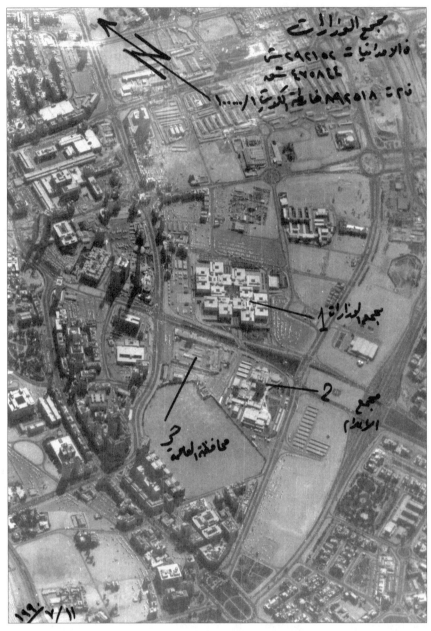

Figure 12. Annotated pre-invasion aerial photograph of military objectives in Kuwait City taken by Iraqi Air Force on 11 July 1990 (Harmony document folder ISGP-2003-00038233)

6th Mechanized Brigade (defending forward of the Mutla Pass) from withdrawing into it. Speed would also prevent the Kuwaiti 35th Brigade from reaching and blocking the pass from its base forty kilometers to the south."

"The main body of the brigade would initially assault in two columns driving through the desert for fifty kilometers before turning to the east at dawn. (A point between Abdali and Jahra)."

"At dawn the brigade would turn south and split into two flying columns." The left column would attack toward the position of the Kuwait 6th Brigade; the right would "advance quickly" across the Mutla Pass before the Kuwait 35th Brigade could arrive. Once both columns crossed the Mutla Pass (having successfully dealt with or bypassed the Kuwait resistance) they would split into three "combat legions."[21] Each legion had a distinct objective in Kuwait City:

The first legion was a tank battalion. "Its objective was to take the Circular Fifth Road and occupy the Royal Palace, the international hotels, and the Kuwaiti Ministry of the Interior."

"The second legion was to follow the main effort to take the Seventh Circular Road and take Kuwait International Airport and the colocated air force base."

"The third legion, and the brigade's main effort, was an armor battalion augmented by infantry, engineers, artillery, and anti-aircraft troops." Hamdani personally led this force. It was to advance to the Sixth Circular Road "through the capital city, dealing with all resistance, if any, as well as with the police force and the Kuwaiti Royal Guard." The limit of advance was the Arabian Gulf where they would circle back and link up with the first legion.[22]

No matter what, Hamdani repeatedly emphasized to his men, speed of action would take priority over all other aspects of the plan.

The night before the invasion, Hamdani reviewed the final intelligence reports and finalized last-minute logistical issues, such as provisioning extra fuel and water for each vehicle. He met with the commander of his sister unit—the 8th Brigade, Hammurabi Division—to coordinate actions for the next day. Over dinner, the two commanders watched the latest regional news on a Kuwaiti television channel. Hamdani recalled that

"the Kuwaiti TV news showed the Kuwaiti Crown Prince arriv[ing] at the airport back from Saudi Arabia. He hinted that the poltical negotiations with Iraq had failed, because the Iraqi leadership wanted them to fail. We exchanged comments about this statement and he [the 8th Brigade Commander] said, "I had hoped that this crisis would end while we still had our finger on the trigger."[23]

Iraqi Airpower—Confidence Abounds

The Iraqi Air Force (IAF) spent the last half of the 1980s rebuilding its capacity, its confidence, and in some cases, its reputation with the Ba'ath regime. The decade did not start well. The losses to the qualitatively better Iranian Air Force in the first half of the Iran-Iraq War nearly devastated Iraq's air force.[24] Saddam preserved what remained only by the partial evacuation of his best aircraft to sympathetic Arab countries.[25] The inability to stop the Israeli air raid on Iraq's nuclear facility in 1981 only made matters worse for the "Falcons" of Iraq. Notwithstanding this inauspicious start, things had markedly improved by 1986. The IAF conducted successful economic interdiction missions in the Gulf, flew deep strategic strikes on Iranian cities, and used a revised air-ground doctrine to good effect along the Iranian front.

By 1988, the IAF generally completed its transformation and became a growing source of pride for Saddam. This was in part due to successful operations against Iran, as well as its growing reputation in the region. Airpower in the Middle East had a deterrent effect and Saddam learned early to carefully husband its potential.[26] As Iraq's most technologically advanced force, Saddam saw the air force and related air defense forces as a critical capability in fulfilling Iraq's historic mission with regard to confronting "Zionist aggression."[27]

In the months just before invading Kuwait, the regime was confident in its airpower abilities. According to a 1991 top secret study prepared by the Iraqi Air Force and Air Defense Command:

> Prior to 2 August 1990, it was clear that [given] the magnitude of the air force and air defense, considering the planes [we] possessed as well as the weapons and available systems, [we] had the power to face the adversary threat of the neighboring countries, each one separately, especially Iran. . . . As to the Zionist enemy [Israel], our military [situation] required that Iraq participate with the Arab countries in any potential confrontation. For this reason, our air force and air defense were assigned to confront the potential Zionist aggression by responding in the form of air attacks with limited number of planes targeting the strategic and vital targets in the Israeli depth and later on by expanding the mission.[28]

From the captured documents, it is not clear when the IAF was brought into the invasion planning. Its first hint of what the regime was thinking may have been in early July when it was assigned a series of high-priority reconnaissance missions. In the first two weeks of July, Iraqi reconnaissance variants of its Soviet MiG-25s successfully executed four aerial reconnaissance missions over Kuwait. These flights resulted in more than eight hundred images of key facilities and would prove critical to the success of upcoming ground operations.[29]

Beyond the reconnaissance task, the air force's primary mission during the invasion was eliminating the Kuwait Air Force and its air defense assets. Air force planning for the invasion was complicated by the same tight security imposed on the other services. One commander recalled being ordered to "swear on a Koran not to tell anyone [about the plan] until one day before the battle."[30] Maintaining this kind of secrecy was made more difficult by the pressing need for detailed pre-invasion imagery of Kuwait City and other critical targets.

Planning near simultaneous joint military operations under conditions of near total secrecy proved more difficult for the air force than it did for Iraq's other military branches. For Iraqi ground commanders, overwhelming the relatively small Kuwait ground forces were never an issue. However, ground commanders were concerned that if the Kuwait Air Force did enter the battle, it might reduce the speed of attack enough to jeopardize the entire operation.

For example, one of the IAF's specified planning tasks was to make the airspace over Kuwait safe for the helicopter insertion of the Iraqi commando forces. Early drafts of the Republican Guard's plan called for swift commando raids on the Kuwait Air Force bases at al-Salim and al-Jaber, as well as the international airport, to ensure their neutralization. However, during a meeting just before the invasion, the commander of the IAF and air defenses, Gen. Muzahim Sa'b Hasan al-Tikriti, assured Saddam that "we can bomb the runways and stop the enemy air force; therefore assuring [that helicopter] flying will be safe."[31] Moreover, the air force commander assured Saddam that they could simultaneously take care of the Kuwaiti air defense, especially the American-made HAWK missile batteries at minimal cost.[32] The commando raid option was eventually dropped in favor of the air force–only concept.

In the summer of 1990, Iraqi air defense forces were oriented on the ever-present "Zionist air threat which targeted mainly [our] advanced scientific [facilities]."[33] In light of the Israeli threat, Iraqi leadership ordered the air defense forces to focus on the defense of more than 200 national "headquarters and projects" of which 125 were military. Preventing a potential repetition of the 1981 Israeli strike on the Iraqi nuclear facility at Osiraq (Tuwaitha Nuclear Research Center) was seen as critical, given Iraq's recent "scientific and technological

advancement" and advanced military manufacturing.[34] Given the focus on operational security for the upcoming invasion, as well as the concern that the
ongoing verbal battle over WMD between Saddam and Israel might precipitate
Israeli preemptive action, the air defense forces were generally excluded from
pre-invasion planning. Orders to develop a plan for the air defense of Kuwait
were issued after the invasion was complete.

The Iraqi Navy's Mission—A Daunting Task

The Iraqi Navy had very little planning time and almost no preparation
time in the run-up to the invasion of Kuwait. Compared to their counterparts
in the navy, Hamdani and his fellow Republican Guard commanders were well-
off in terms of preparation.

According to the commander of the Iraqi Navy, RAM Gha'ib Hasan, on
the morning of 31 July, Saddam called him to Baghdad for an unscheduled
meeting. During the meeting, Hasan received a briefing on Project 17 (the plan
to invade Kuwait). Saddam personally and repeatedly emphasized the importance of secrecy and concealment in the Navy's preparations.[35] Immediately
following his audience with Saddam, the chief of operations provided Hasan
with a specific list of twenty military tasks his service was to accomplish. Given
that the invasion was less than thirty-six hours away, it is not clear if the last-minute mission notification was an expression of confidence (unlikely), or a lack
of trust. The tasks included:

- Liberate Faylakah Island and defend it.
- Be ready to assume command of the [Kuwaiti] naval bases from the
  Republican Guard and defend [them].
- Prevent any ship from entering or exiting [Kuwaiti] waters.
- Consider the Arabian Gulf region as the new field to stop the enemy's
  advance.
- [Do] not interfere with . . . Iranian navigation.
- Benefit from the Kuwaiti ships after [gaining] control over them.
- Relocate the surface-to-surface radar station to higher ground to iden-
  tify enemy targets.[36]

In complete secrecy, Iraq's most senior naval officer returned to his Baghdad
quarters to personally prepare the plan to execute the assigned missions. He
found his planning effort hampered, as had the Republican Guard, by a "lack
of maps, or [a] clear picture of the situation [in Kuwait] and other matters."[37]

Nevertheless, Hasan completed a plan in a few short hours and obtained approval from the general staff in Baghdad to brief and prepare his units. It was already 1 August when Hasan flew to al-Basra to brief his subordinate commanders. He noted that as part of his plan to "practice secrecy and confidentiality," he needed a "diversion" to justify the frenzy of planning activity. Hasan's solution came in the form of a cable from the Directorate of Military Intelligence to the navy warning of an impending Israeli operation in the "next few days."[38]

Yum al-Nida (Day of the Great Call)—The Invasion

The Iraqi Navy

At 0700 on 1 August, naval Col. Muzahim Mustafa, commander of Iraq's missile boats and its coastal artillery units, was standing in the ad hoc naval command center near the port of Umm Qasr. To enhance operational security, the commander of the Iraqi Navy selected an old hangar away from the main facility for his headquarters. Joining Mustafa was Col. Hasan Sawadi, commander of the 440th Naval Infantry Brigade, as well as most of the Iraqi Navy's senior staff.[39] The evening prior, they had all received a warning order (Gha'ib Hasan's cover story) about a possible Israeli operation against Iraq. Now, however, their commander was explaining that the real purpose for all the activity was the invasion of Kuwait, scheduled to begin in less than twenty-four hours. The invasion would begin at 0400 (designated H-Hour) on the morning of 2 August.

Colonel Mustafa's primary mission was to seize the large Kuwaiti naval installation located fifty kilometers south of Kuwait City, followed by the "liberation" of the Kuwaiti islands (Faylakah and several small, mostly uninhabited islands within Kuwait's territorial waters). When it came to essential information necessary to plan, it seemed the tactical commanders were no better off than their commanding officer had been the day before. According to Colonel Mustafa, "we did not have information or prior knowledge regarding its (the Kuwaiti naval base) approaches, the marine routes leading to it, or its defenses."[40] Notwithstanding this challenge, the officers quickly built a plan around two naval task forces, one assigned to neutralize Kuwait's navy and the other to secure Faylakah Island.[41]

The first task force centered on one of the Iraqi Navy's Soviet-made missile boats with 160 men from Colonel Sawadi's brigade. This ship would rendezvous with a second missile boat at the tanker port of al-Bakr to form the assault force for the main effort.[42] This task force was to seize the Kuwaiti Navy's headquarters at al-Qulayah Navy base almost one hundred kilometers south of where they were staging.

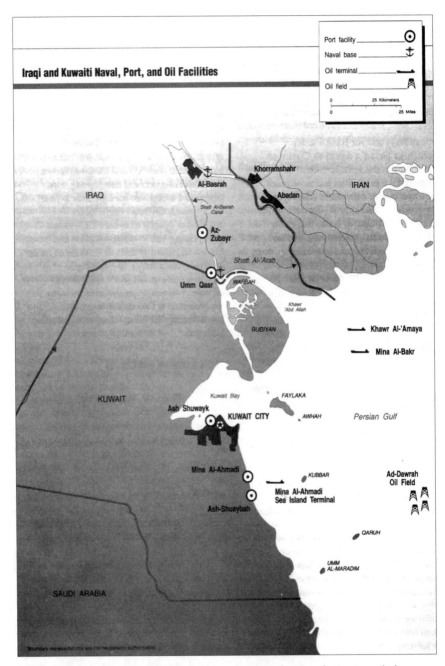

Figure 13. Naval Battlespace: Major facilities and areas of interest for Iraqi naval planners, August 1991 (U.S. Department of Defense, "Final Report to Congress, Conduct of the Persian Gulf War," 189)

The second task force consisted of a battalion-sized infantry force, also from the 440th Naval Infantry Brigade. Commanded by Lt. Col. Saed Jalio, it would eventually receive assets made available after the first task force completed its mission. One assumption of the initial plan was that after capturing the Kuwaiti Navy, the second task force's mission of securing Faylakah Island would be completed with ease.

At 2330 on 1 August, Colonel Mustafa deployed his missile boat with its embarked naval infantry from Umm Qasr to al-Bakr. The journey took three hours. Apparently, the rapid planning and the extensive secrecy did not account for the realities of time-distance navigation through coastal waters at night. Colonel Mustafa coordinated a change to the timeline with the naval head-quarters. His task force would not arrive at its objective until three hours after H-Hour. The difference was potentially disastrous since it would result in not only a daylight assault but one well after the Iraq ground invasion had provided warning of what was to come. The new assault time for the Kuwaiti Naval Base was now 0730 and was timed to coincide with the arrival of Republican Guard forces attacking from the land side.

At 0430, the ships departed al-Bakr heading toward southern Kuwait with orders to "cruise at suitable velocities and take certain routes so as to make them [the boats] appear as a commercial convoy heading south."[43] The mission did not go well from the start. One of the two missile boats "suffered a number of technical malfunctions [and] could not navigate."[44] It eventually had to stop to make repairs. According to the task force commander, the ship eventually got underway again only because "[t]here were Russian experts on board for the purpose of training the [the missile boat] crews."[45] The second boat also had problems with its radar and navigation systems, but Mustafa managed to continue the mission despite the challenges of directing the second boat by radio, in low visibility, and while navigating through water "abounding with marine obstacles."[46] Despite the maintenance delays, the task force continued south. By 0600, two hours after the ground invasion had begun, the small force was nearing its objective area.

As the main Iraqi task force neared the Kuwait coast, it came under fire from two Kuwaiti patrol boats operating near Saudi territorial waters. According to Mustafa:

> It was not possible to engage these boats because the [missiles] on one boat were broken down and the second boat was without radar. The first boat, which was the command boat, suffered two busted cannons. To evade the bombardment [from the Kuwaiti ships] we resorted to evasive maneuvers in course and speed—meaning zigzagging. We were successful, but the

TABLE 2. **Kuwait's Navy and Coast Guard Fleet**

Manpower	2,100
Fast Patrol Craft Missile	
Istiqal (FPB-57)	2
al-Boom(TNC-45)	6
Amphibious Craft	4
Logistics and Support	3
Miscellaneous Boats and Craft	15

Note: Kuwait's small navy and coast guard were equipped with eight modern German patrol craft equipped with Exocet missiles. Order of Battle data derived from Cordesman, Gulf Military Forces, *11–22; and International Institute for Strategic Studies,* Military Balance, *104–05.*

second boat sustained a direct hit to its command cabin causing injuries to a number of personnel. Additionally, moving in a zigzag manner caused the boat to deviate [from its path] which caused it to [run into] the jutting rocks . . . its propellers were smashed.[47]

The remaining Iraqi ship, containing Mustafa and the seventy-five naval infantry continued its mission to seize the Kuwaiti base. According to his account, the Kuwaitis continued to fire at the lone attacking ship as it approached the harbor. Mustafa noted, however, that their "bold assault" caused considerable confusion among the defenders, who "couldn't believe they were being attacked by one [missile] boat . . . they may have believed that this boat [was] a lead up to a larger force to arrive later."[48]

Once inside the harbor defenses, the Iraqi infantry quickly "dispersed throughout the base using their weapons in the face of various light resistance."[49] At 0745, Colonel Mustafa captured the base commander, an officer he personally knew from friendly military-to-military contacts during the Iran-Iraq War. The Kuwaiti was apparently so disoriented by the events that he asked his Iraqi captor if these attacks were a real event or some kind of training exercise. Whatever the purpose, the base commander complained angrily that it was occurring without his knowledge. Accordingly, he demanded to know when the Iraqis planned to withdraw. To calm the officer and secure his cooperation, Mustafa assured him this assault was indeed an exercise and it would all be over in a couple of hours. The Kuwaiti officer no doubt realized the truth later that morning when he found himself on a barge en route to a POW camp near Umm Qasr in Iraq.

By 0830 on 2 August, Iraq's newest naval base on the Persian Gulf was secure. At 0930, the commander of the Iraqi Navy passed the word to Saddam, who congratulated him on the victory. The Iraqis had accomplished the entire operation from planning through final execution in little more than a day. The success resulted from a combination of three things: luck, an inept Kuwaiti defense, and an uncharacteristically aggressive Iraqi tactical commander. At the cost of one dead and several wounded, the Iraqi Navy captured 271 members of the Kuwaiti Navy (including the base commander and 43 of his officers) as well as 213 contractors and third-country nationals. Moreover, at the cost of one missile boat, the Iraqis had acquired three large missile boats, three light missile boats, three supply and provision ships, and eight smaller vessels.[50]

The initial success, however, was almost short-lived. Although the small Iraqi task force received twenty-five additional troops later that morning, the two kilometer-square Kuwaiti naval base was still held by less than one hundred lightly armed Iraqis.[51] At 0700 on 3 August, this small force came under a vigorous attack by unknown troops approaching from the mainland side of the base. Colonel Mustafa described "firing and loudspeaker sounds demanding that we lay down our weapons and surrender. Some of our fighters, who earlier were dispatched to reconnoiter the [area around the base], were able to make out the red triangle insignia identifying those fighters as members of the Republican Guard. We then raised the Iraqi flag to assure them we were like them . . . they were unaware that the [base] was liberated. The Republican Guard arrived twenty-four hours after the appointed time."[52]

The second Iraqi naval task force, under the command of Lt. Col. Saed Jalio, left Umm Qasr in mid-morning of 2 August to seize Faylakah Island. This secondary mission suffered from the same paucity of intelligence that afflicted the primary one. According to Colonel Mustafa, "[we] had no information about the island and the weapons scattered thereon; we inferred the information from the available naval charts."[53]

Jalio reported to the navy command at 1755 that the small Iraqi flotilla was in place and was "bombarding the shoreline with missiles." The bombardment continued throughout the next six hours. By midnight on 2 August, the task force commander reported the landing force as going ashore using rubber boats.[54] According to the commander of the Iraqi Navy, the landings were complete by 0245. Iraqi reconnaissance patrols were fanning out across the island to locate reported Kuwaiti anti-aircraft batteries. Resistance on the island was generally nonexistent. The big triumph of the operation was capturing a seven-man Kuwaiti radio broadcasting station in the late afternoon of 3 August. At 1900, the task force commander reported mission complete.[55]

During the next several days smaller operations cleared three smaller Kuwaiti islands and captured a few remaining members of the Kuwait Navy or

Coast Guard.[56] The defense of Faylakah Island became the priority mission for the Iraqi Navy after 4 August. Eventually, a commando company and a squadron of light tanks reinforced the small assault force on the island. According to Colonel Mustafa, the island "gained an unprecedented importance after field visits by some members of the general command who gave a great deal of attention to the strengthening of its defenses. The forces assigned there were charged with a suicidal defense of the island."[57]

A senior Iraqi naval officer summed up the accomplishments of their small force as: increasing Iraqi's shoreline from 30 nautical miles to 160 nautical miles; increasing the number of passages for direct deployment in the Arabian Gulf; possession of the Kuwaiti naval base at al-Qulayah, which now allowed Iraq to influence events in the Straits of Hormuz; the addition of Kuwait, which dramatically increased Iraq's access to ports, docks, and vessels; and finally, and probably most importantly for Iraq's navy, it now had "a greater capability in maneuvering its naval vessels in the open sea."[58]

Iraqi Airpower—Weaknesses Exposed

IRAQI AIR FORCE

According to the invasion plan, joint operations between Iraqi ground and air forces were critical. The coordinated attack time (H-Hour) was 0400 on 2 August. Despite the pronouncements of confidence, the missions to destroy Kuwaiti air defense batteries and to catch its air force on the ground, as well as neutralize four airfields simultaneously proved much more complex in reality. As a result of the onerous security restrictions imposed on Iraqi air planners and because of the mission's complexity, critical failures became apparent as soon as the first Iraqi sorties attempted to depart for Kuwait.

On 2 August, the weather in Kuwait was perfect for air operations, but weather at some western Iraqi airfields delayed take-offs for more than an hour. The delay allowed the small Kuwait Air Force to get airborne, just as the Republican Guard officers had feared it would. Moreover, coordinating take-off times and in-flight link-up procedures for aircraft departing from multiple Iraqi airfields resulted in significant confusion and a number of accidents.

Between 0500 and 0600, Kuwaiti A-4s attacked the two Republican Guard divisions still moving toward Kuwait City from the west. During one rather heated postwar analysis, an unidentified Republican Guard officer lambasted the commander of the IAF because he "gave a promise in front of the president," but had failed to accomplish his mission. The Republican Guard officer continued, "You said you could stop the air force because we have the airplanes. The [Kuwaiti] air forces were bombing us until 0500. You were in Kuwait and you saw the effects!"[59]

The commander of the IAF defended his efforts and claimed that, when compared to the worst-case scenario, his mission was successful. He noted that, despite all of the challenges they faced with weather and "other conditions," his pilots managed to strike the Kuwaiti airfields at 0625, 1220, and 1600.[60] In addition, he noted that, "the [Kuwaiti] air force should have flown ten times the number of sorties it flew. The Kuwait Air Force accomplished only 10 percent of their attacks. I stopped 90 percent of their attacks. . . . I believe the [Iraqi] air force accomplished its mission completely. If the Kuwait Air Force flew four-teen missions and they had six air defense missions, this does not mean that the [Iraqi] air force did not accomplish [its] mission."[61]

As one might expect, the air force commander's Republican Guard peers were not impressed with his performance. One critic sarcastically complained that the only reason sorties stopped flying from Kuwait's Ahmed al Jaber airbase had nothing to do with the IAF but was because "the [Iraqi] troops were right next to it!" However, the air force commander noted that even if Iraq had used surface-to-surface missiles against the Kuwaiti bases, it would not have mattered. After the initial Iraqi air raids, the Kuwaitis were taking off from roads, not runways.

The air force commander's sometimes-spirited defense of Iraqi airpower was not convincing. Clearly, the ground officers were convinced that the air

TABLE 3. **Kuwait Air Force and Air Defense**

Manpower	2,200	Transport Planes	
Fighter Interceptor		L-100-30	4
F-ICK Mirage	20	DHC-4	2
F-1BK	4	DC-9	2
Lightning	12	**Helicopters**	
Hunter	4	SA-342 Gazelle with HOT	17
Fighter Ground Attack		AS-332 Super Puma	6
A-4KU	24	SA-330 Puma	10
TA-4KU	3	**Air Defense Systems***	
Combat Capable Trainer		Improved HAWK Battalion	1
Hawk MK64	12	Aerostat AN/TPS-63 Radar	1

*Does not include man-portable SA7/14s with the Kuwait Army

Order of Battle data derived from Cordesman, Gulf Military Forces, *11–22; and International Institute for Strategic Studies,* Military Balance, *104–05.*

force was more interested in its own force protection than mission accomplishment. One Republican Guard officer noted sarcastically, "We believe that there is not a force that can harm the Iraqi Air Force! . . . When they [the Iraqi Air Force] take off, they can reach and bomb Tehran and other places." The air force commander could only rebut with, "we should not look down on any force, even if it was a force the size of the Kuwaitis."[62]

In the same postwar discussion, Ali Hassan al-Majid (aka "Chemical Ali") recalled that in addition to using roads near their own airfields, the Kuwaitis also flew sorties from Saudi fields. He added that there were also Kuwaiti aircraft in Saudi Arabia as a part of a Gulf defense exercise. One officer added that, during an interrogation, a Kuwait Air Force commander revealed that just as the invasion began he "smuggled eighty planes to Saudi Arabia."[63]

According to Majid, the failures of the IAF during the invasion came down to simple poor planning. Directing his comments to the air force commander, Majid complained that he failed to account for weather: "You did not think that maybe there will be a change in the weather that affects the airports in Iraq . . . meanwhile there is good weather in Kuwait?" Moreover, Majid noted there should have been contingency plans so that "if the first command [the air force] did not finish their duty, then this becomes the second command's [the Republican Guard] duty to finish."[64]

Despite the overall success, Majid pinned the major tactical failures during the invasion squarely on the IAF. He noted, "We all know that one of our missions was to arrest the corrupted Sabah family, the previous rulers of Kuwait. All the time we were thinking the air force would bomb the airports and that the Kuwaiti royal family [would] have no place to go. It seems to me that we relied, wrongly, on [the air force]."[65]

Overall, the lack of serious coordination between the IAF and the Republican Guard, combined with excessive secrecy, was a recipe for failure. As Majid conceded, "the whole country was in complete secrecy . . . the people who put things into effect were informed forty-eight hours before the zero hour."[66]

ARMY AVIATION

One result of the overwhelming secrecy imposed on planning was that the pilots of Iraq's assault helicopters were "informed at . . . midnight," that they would begin the largest air assault in Iraq's history at 0350 that morning.[67] One senior officer remarked after the war that the operations were "not planned very well and in enough time . . . meaning [planning] was spur of the moment."[68] The plan, as far as one could call the hasty mission preparation, required some ninety-six helicopters to lift elements of the Third Special Forces Brigade from southern Iraq to three-to-five landing zones in Kuwait and the 16th Special Forces Brigade to downtown Kuwait City.

At 0425, after some delays, the helicopters departed for their designated landing zones in Kuwait. For most of the Iraqi pilots, night flights were rare, formation night flights were unheard of, and as they discovered, unrehearsed night air assaults, without night vision equipment, were a nightmare.

According to one participant, the Iraqi losses exceeded "more than forty helicopters hit and destroyed."[69] In some cases the "hits" were attributed to the Kuwait Air Force and HAWK surface-to-air missiles. In other cases, the Iraqi helicopters hit power lines, each other, and the ground "during landing operations."[70] An officer, identified as Lieutenant General Sabir, recalled that "this matter was investigated after the operation by direct instructions from the president. It was proven that the Kuwait Air Force hit three or four aircraft . . . the army aviation aircraft that were destroyed were destroyed for two reasons. The first reason was poor visibility. Many aircraft collided with each other in mid-air. The second reason is the areas [selected] for landing. The landing areas were sandy . . . therefore the aircraft collided with each other."[71]

He went on to note that a large number of the helicopter losses occurred because they hit power lines while trying to avoid the HAWK missiles that the Iraqi Air Force promised, but failed, to destroy. Majid also noted that he personally saw that "the helicopters crashed into the [power] lines and [even] destroyed some of the towers"[72] during the power line strikes at Mutla Ridge. He added that "we must ask why there is this big number of downed aircraft. If the reason is the sand as what was said by the commander of the air force, then we should have [selected] several [landing] areas. We have to keep in mind the direction of the wind. . . . We have to think about how to land all of these air-craft so we don't have a pile of them. We had [helicopters] taking off and others landing, and they both crashed at the same time."[73]

The commander of Iraqi special forces recalled that his forces suffered more than sixty casualties as a result of helicopter crashes. One Republican Guard officer matter-of-factly remarked that "this is collateral damage for such a large number of aircraft. . . . This is acceptable." When one of the helicopter pilots complained that the landing areas were too sandy, this same officer replied that was a poor excuse since "all of Kuwait is sandy."[74]

The Republican Guard's Blitzkrieg

For the Republican Guard, the invasion of Kuwait began with a series of commando assaults on Kuwait's lightly manned border posts. One such attack was on the post known as Sideriya Fort located near the main highway crossing into Iraq from northern Kuwait.[75] At 0100 on 2 August, a company of Iraqi commandos from the 17th Brigade of the Hammurabi Division slipped over the border to surround the lightly armed fort. Less than two hours later their brigade commander, Brigadier General Hamdani, saw three green flares rise over the fort indicating a successful and bloodless mission. At 0300, Hamdani gave the order to his two maneuver columns, the Faris Regiment and the 17th Regiment, to advance across the border. By 0300, the lead Iraqi armored forces were in Kuwait and moving at thirty kilometers per hour toward their objectives in Kuwait City and beyond. As Hamdani recalled, "the night maneuver of the two columns had begun. . . . Despite the screeching of our armor and the long thick belt of dust that obscured the sky above us, there was a horrific silence. Our [radio] communication equipment was not picking up any signals from our command or from any of the remaining formations. My staff officers began to believe that the whole mission was cancelled and that our brigade was the only one on the way to Kuwait City."[76]

At dawn, the Iraqi helicopters ferrying special forces to Kuwait City on their way to attempt to capture the emir over-flew Hamdani and his assault columns.[77] The tanks of Hamdani's brigade arrived just north of the Mutla Ridge at 0600, when they came under direct fire from what he assumed to be elements of Kuwait's 6th Mechanized Brigade. The small Kuwaiti force, consisting of British-made Vickers tanks and newly arrived Soviet-made BMP-2 armored fighting vehicles, destroyed one of the lead Iraqi tanks at less than three hundred meters. But this initial action did not slow the overall advance. As planned, Hamdani had his left column turn off of the highway to engage the Kuwaiti force. After a one-sided exchange of fire the small Kuwaiti force withdrew after losing several of its armored vehicles. Meanwhile, Hamdani's right column continued at full speed toward their interim objective—the Mutla Pass.

The Hammurabi Division commander later interviewed the commander of the Kuwaiti 6th Brigade in a prisoner of war camp. The Kuwaiti commander was asked why he had not put up more of a fight in that first firefight of the invasion. He replied that he thought the tanks of the 17th Brigade were only a small scout element for the Iraqi main body. The Kuwaiti colonel explained that when his tanks engaged the lead Iraqi tank, the Iraqi column did not stop and deploy as expected. Furthermore, the mission of the 6th Mechanized Brigade was to delay any Iraqi invasion force for forty-eight hours. He did not want to become decisively engaged with the first Iraq reconnaissance unit he saw. Moreover, the key to Kuwait's defense plan was to delay long enough for the Kuwait Air Force and allied air forces to intervene and stop Iraqi armor in the Mutla Pass.[78] The Hammurabi commander was no doubt pleased that the decision to use raw speed instead of mass and firepower had successfully neutralized Kuwait's only defensible terrain.

TABLE 4. **Kuwaiti Ground Forces, July 1990**

Manpower	**23,000**	**Armored Personnel Carriers**	**512**
Army	16,000	M113A2	200
Paramilitary	7,000	TH 390 Fahd	100
Combat units	**6**	Saracen	130
Army Reserve Brigade	1	V-150	20
Armored Brigade	3	V-300 Commando	62
Mechanized Infantry	1	**Artillery**	**112**
Artillery Brigade	1	SP Mk F3	20
Tanks	**281**	Sp M-109A2	36
M-84	6	Mortar 120-mm RT-F1	40
Chieftain	165	TOWED 105-mm M101	16
Vickers MK	70	**Anti-Tank Weapons**	**396**
Centurion	40	TOW M-901	56
Reconnaissance	**190**	Vigilant	200
Saladin	100	AT-4 Spigot	120
Ferrett	90	HOT	20
Infantry Fighting Vehicles	**245**	**Surface-to-Surface Missiles**	**12**
BMP-2	245	FROG-7	12

Source: Order of Battle data derived from Cordesman, Gulf Military Forces, *11–22; and International Institute for Strategic Studies,* Military Balance, *104–05.*

The sight of Iraqi T-72 tanks cresting the highway at Mutla Pass no doubt came as a surprise to the civilian truck drivers on the four-lane highway that ran through it. The truckers were not the only ones surprised. As the lead Iraqi tanks exited the pass to the south, they ran into Kuwaiti Chieftain Tanks, still in column formation, moving north. According to Hamdani, after a few rounds from the lead Iraqi tanks, the Kuwaitis abandoned their vehicles and "turned around and started to flee, while leaving most of their tanks with their engines running behind them."[79] This lead element of the Kuwaiti 35th Brigade was, as the Iraqi planners expected, moving to block the pass. Once again, the speed of the Iraqi attack surprised them and made short work of the second Kuwaiti defense attempt in as many hours.

Soon after crossing the pass, Hamdani's two formations rejoined to envelop Kuwait City. The commander of the Faris Regiment took the Fifth Circular Road toward Shiyukh Port and Ra's al-Rad—the easternmost portion of

Kuwait City. Hamdani remained with the 17th Regiment to continue on to the Sixth Circular Road, en route to Kuwait International Airport. Hamdani was relieved to note that urban navigation was going to be easier than he had anticipated thanks to the "green and blue road signs pointing out places and directions" depicted on their tourist maps.[80]

As Hamdani and the 17th Regiment approached the airport near an area described as the "pilgrim rest house," elements of the Kuwaiti 35th Armored Brigade again tried to delay the attack. Ineffective Kuwaiti fire failed to delay the force long, however, and the attackers withdrew west into the desert after destroying a single Iraqi tank. Elements of the Kuwaiti 35th Brigade would continue to conduct hit-and-run attacks to the west of Kuwait City until late on the second day of the invasion.

Hamdani's forces soon entered a major urban area and confronted one of the inevitable side effects of having achieved surprise—panicked civilians. He noted, "[We] were really shocked by the terror of the Kuwaiti and other Gulf citizens. The roads were full of civilian cars. There was a general atmosphere of surprise, worry, and panic. We tried our best to quiet them down and stop the traffic, but the panic was so great that I was afraid that one of our armored vehicles might run into one of the civilian cars."[81]

By 0830, the roads around Kuwait City had reached an "indescribable stage of gridlock."[82] Hamdani and his force slowly inched their way through the crowds. Along the way, they passed groups of civilians making panicked runs on local banks. Kuwaiti police and security personnel were passively watching both the civilian panic and the invasion in stunned silence. Hamdani realized that at this point the challenges were changing rapidly from those of military operations to those of logistics and civil affairs.

Before the 17th Brigade could reach its final objective—the Masila Hotel beach resort—Hamdani and his force ran out of fuel. Although he had hoped to avoid this problem, the original logistics plan called for drawing fuel from Kuwaiti stocks once Iraqi forces had exhausted their limited assault supply. The plan, however, did not account for panicked crowds rendering access to civilian fuel stations difficult, if not impossible. Hamdani's creative solution was to simply ask the Kuwaitis for help:

> My vehicle had run out of petrol and the communication vehicle behind me was on its last drops. I called the nearest Kuwaiti police officer . . . and asked him for two things. I said, "Firstly, there are 1,000 more tanks behind me,"(I exaggerated), "So could you and your comrades help open the roads so that we can proceed without running over some innocent

Figure 14. Iraqi reconnaissance photograph of Kuwait International Airport. Brigadier General Hamdani's brigade's attack route followed the large road just to the left of the airport terminating at the Persian Gulf (Harmony document folder ISGP–2003–00038256)

civilian and secondly, could you please help us refuel?" He was very scared, but I quieted him down and he obeyed me . . . the roads opened and one of the [Kuwaitis] who was refueling my vehicle (we pumped the gas out of the police cars), also showed us how to get to the Masila Hotel.[83]

At 0930, the main element of the 17th Brigade reached the hotel and waters of the Gulf. Hamdani later linked up with the Faris Regiment, which had completed its tasks after a sharp engagement with a small Kuwaiti force guarding the palace. He immediately began establishing security throughout the city by placing tanks at every intersection and establishing roadblocks with orders to arrest "government officials, army officers and anyone else they thought important."[84]

Because of poor communications, the Republican Guard assault forces were only vaguely aware of their sister units' locations and status. By late afternoon, brigades of the Nebuchadnezzar Division had secured their portions of Kuwait City. A series of engagements with the Kuwait Air Force and Army delayed, for almost a day, the Medina Division. The Medina's mission was to secure the coastal areas to the south of Kuwait City. The delay facilitated the escape of large numbers of Kuwait residents and military units to Saudi Arabia.

According to a Republican Guard after-action report, the Medina Division formations became disoriented and separated during the long assault across Kuwait from the west. At 1410, the 14th Brigade of the Medina ran into Kuwait forces to the west of al-Jahra, the same forces Hamdani believes he ran into coming out of the Mutla Pass early that morning. Fighting with the Kuwaiti 35th Brigade continued on and off for several hours. The 14th Brigade, after being joined by its sister unit the 10th Armored, finally cleared the remnants of the Kuwaiti force. Medina Division did not arrive at its final objective, the port city Ahmadi, until 3 August at 0130.[85] A few hours later, it linked up with the naval brigade after narrowly avoiding a major fratricide incident at al-Qulayah Naval Base.

Small engagements with isolated elements of the Kuwait Army continued for the next two days. However, rumors of large counterattacks were rampant. Hamdani recalled how he was summoned to meet with the incoming province chief of intelligence, Sabawi Ibrahim Hasan al-Tikriti, at 2300 on the day of the invasion. Sabawi told Hamdani that he had "intelligence indicating that the [Kuwaiti] Crown Prince had gathered two brigades on the border with Saudi Arabia and intends to attack tomorrow."[86] Hamdani was more than a little skeptical:

I told him that in my opinion, this man [the Kuwaiti Crown Prince] had six brigades and was not able to sustain fighting for even one hour in the morning of that day. How was he to gather the remains of his forces and execute an attack that required three times the number of soldiers he had while there were eight Iraqi divisions in Kuwait? Saba'awi responded, "this is the information, you do what you decide to do." So I thought it was appropriate to give them one of my high-frequency communications stations so that he could contact the commander of the Republican Guard.[87]

Hamdani never did receive orders from the Republican Guard to move south to meet the mysterious Kuwait counterattack. Since the 17th Brigade had been out of communication with the Republican Guard headquarters since 1000 that morning, Hamdani thought it a safe bet that Sabawi would fail to get the required orders to make him move any time soon.

By the end of the day on 3 August, the military invasion and conquest of Kuwait was complete. Compared to the kind of warfare experienced by the men of the Republican Guard during all but the first and last months of the eight-year Iran-Iraq War, the invasion was an overwhelming triumph. To the surprise of many commanders, the cost had been light. Captured records are incomplete, but it appears most of the Iraqi divisions completed their assigned missions with fewer than one hundred killed-in-action. Equipment losses were, when compared to what would occur six months later, trivial. The worst single incidents were suffered by the Baghdad Division after coming under Kuwaiti A-4 Skyhawk attacks at midday or the commandos lost in helicopter accidents in the initial hours. Hamdani's division, which carried the critical main effort tasks, counted its losses as minor compared to military operations of just a few years before. A Hammurabi Division command after-action report recorded that the division suffered 99 killed, 249 wounded, and 15 missing during the invasion of Kuwait.[88]

Despite the satisfaction arising from their military accomplishments, many Iraqi officers would later question the long-term value of their mission. Brigadier General Hamdani recorded an observation in his memoirs that would become increasingly common within the Iraqi military:

To tell the truth, the erroneous Iraqi policy of occupying Kuwait is something history will never forgive. Most of the disgraceful phenomena that we [saw] occurring there after the occupation began by the top political and security officials and a few military officials as well. And in spite of there being many honorable and good men in the Republican Guard

Forces, the foremost of them being the commander Staff Lt. Gen. Aayad Futayyih Khalifa al-Rawi, the reputation of the Republican Guard and the Iraqi army was forever smeared by this criminal minority which feared neither Allah nor law, and had no military honor. This will forever remain a black page in our history.[89]

Notes

1. Saddam Hussein's "Victory Day" message as read by an announcer on Baghdad Radio, 7 August 1990. FBIS-NES-90-153, 8 August 1990. In typical Saddam prose, he explicitly connects the success of the Iran-Iraq War (the second Qadisiyya) with the invasion of Kuwait.
2. By some estimates, the Iraqi army in 1989 was the fourth-largest ground force in the world.
3. The exact date is unknown. Documents from the GMID indicate an increase in intelligence and terrain studies of Kuwait beginning in May 1990. The memoirs of the commander of the Iraqi missile forces indicate that operational planning occurred as early as the middle of June 1990. Actions that appear to be enablers include: on 19 June, he was ordered to move a "Luna" missile battalion (FROG-7) to the vicinity of al-Basra; and on 22 June, he was ordered to release the Republican Guard troops under his control (in the western desert) back to their parent commands. See Hazim Abd al-Razzaq al-Ayyubi, "Forty-Three Missiles on the Zionist Entity," Al-Arab al-Yawm (Arabic), Amman, Jordan, 27 October 1998, 12.
4. Harmony media file ISGQ-2003-M0005371.
5. Harmony document folder ISGP-2003-00033136.
6. Open Source Center, FTS19960416000591, Salamah Ni'mat, Interview with Staff General Nizar al-Khazraji, al-Hayah (Arabic), London, 16 April 1996.
7. Ra'ad Hamdani, "From the Golan to the Collapse of Baghdad: Six Wars in Thirty Years" (title trans. from original Arabic), unpublished memoirs, 130. An expanded version of General Hamdani's memoirs has subsequently been published in Arabic under the title Before History Left Us (title trans. from original Arabic) (Beirut: Arab Scientific Publishers, 2006).
8. According to the former U.S. national intelligence officer for warning, Charles Allen, the first military indicators of a move toward Kuwait were identified twelve days (approximately 21 July) before the attack. Charles E. Allen, "Warning and Iraq's Invasion of Kuwait: A Retrospective Look," Defense Intelligence Journal 7, no. 2 (1998): 33–44.
9. Hamdani, "From the Golan to the Collapse of Baghdad," 130.
10. Ibid., 132. Hamdani's 17th Brigade was the lead Republican Guard armed force into Kuwait on 2 August.
11. Ibid., 133. In postwar after-action reviews, Major General al-Razaq's description of the Hammurabi Division's planning process and his command concepts are notable for how much they resemble western military planning and leadership techniques. See Harmony media file ISGQ-2003-M0006038.
12. According to a member of the small U.S. military assistance team in Kuwait at the time of the invasion, in late July "CENTCOM dispatched a courier with satellite photos to

provide to the ambassador and the Kuwaiti government further proof that the Iraqi forces posed along their border were ready to strike." The intelligence noted, however, that "*the only missing piece of the puzzle* was that Iraqi artillery had not been brought forward" (Emphasis added). LTC Fred L. Hart Jr., "The Iraqi Invasion of Kuwait: An Eyewitness Account" (Carlisle Barracks, PA: U.S. Army War College, 1 May 1998), 9–10.

13. Hamdani, "From the Golan to the Collapse of Baghdad," 137.

14. Ibid., 133. The Kuwaiti forces described to Hamdani on 21 July by the Republican Guard Military Intelligence were the Kuwaiti 6th Mechanized Infantry Brigade (stationed north of Mutla Ridge), the Kuwaiti Commando Brigade (south of the Mutla), the 35th Armored Brigade (forty kilometers south of Mutla), the Royal Brigade (in Kuwait City), the 15th Armored Brigade (south of Kuwait City), and the border control brigade (dispersed along Kuwait's borders).

15. Apparently, a routine agreement established during the Iran-Iraq War that allowed Iraqi military logistics convoys to access Kuwaiti ports was still in effect. The port of Ahmadi lies just south of Kuwait City.

16. Hamdani, "From the Golan to the Collapse of Baghdad," 134.

17. Harmony document folder ISGQ-2003-M0006038.

18. Ibid. and Hamdani, "From the Golan to the Collapse of Baghdad," 134.

19. Harmony document folder ISGQ-2003-M0006038.

20. Ironically, Hamdani would complain to the author about the same issue after OIF. A lack of accurate maps of Baghdad made his attempt to defend the approaches to the capital during the American invasion of Iraq in April 2003 much more difficult. Brig. Gen. Ra'ad Hamdani, interview with author, 10 November 2003.

21. A combat legion was the term applied to battalion-size combat task forces.

22. Hamdani, "From the Golan to the Collapse of Baghdad," 135–37.

23. The Kuwaiti Crown Prince was returning from the 31 July negotiations in Jeddah, mediated by King Fahd and Egyptian President Mubarak. Ibid., 137.

24. See David Segal, "The Iran-Iraq War: A Military Analysis," *Foreign Affairs* 88, no. 5 (1988): 946–63. Iran actually solved a major portion of Iraq's qualitative deficit by purging many of its most experienced air force officers during the early years of the war.

25. Dilip Hiro, *The Longest War, The Iran-Iraq Military Conflict* (New York: Routledge, 1991), 40. Saddam dispersed parts of his air force to Jordan, Kuwait, Saudi Arabia, and Oman for safekeeping. This gambit was one Saddam would use again in January 1991, but with a decidedly less successful result.

26. In 1981, Saddam reportedly said, "We will not use our air force. We will keep it. Two years hence our air force will still be in a position to pound [Iran and its] collaborators." Ronald E. Bergquist, The *Role of Airpower in the Iran-Iraq War* (Washington, DC: U.S. Government Printing Office, 1988), 46.

27. On 1 August 1990, the Iraqi Air Force consisted of 18,000 personnel operating a mix of Soviet and Western aircraft. Of significance were the more than 700 fighter/fighter-bombers including MiG-29s, MiG-23s, and Mirage F-1s.

28. Harmony document folder ISGP-2003-00031468.

29. Harmony document folder ISGP-2003-00033136. This detailed Iraqi top secret history notes the 124 specific targets covered in the Kuwaiti reconnaissance. Captured Iraqi target folders indicate that the same Iraqi aircraft conducted reconnaissance flights over or

near northern Saudi Arabia and the Persian Gulf States around the same period. Among the captured archives are dozens of target folders prepared by the Iraqi Air Force in July 1990 for targets in Kuwait, Saudi Arabia, and several Persian Gulf States. For an example, see Harmony document folders: ISGP-2003-00038232—Aerial Photograph of Kuwait City; ISGP-2003-00037981—Aerial Photograph of Saudi Arabian Naval Base; ISGP-2003-00038524—Aerial Photograph of Kuwaiti Desalinization Plant.

30. Harmony media file ISGQ-2003-M0005879.

31. Harmony media file ISGQ-2003-M0005872.

32. Kuwait had several batteries of the U.S.-made I-HAWK (Improved Homing All the Way Killer) (MIM-23B) missiles. Iraq saw these systems as the most significant threat to Iraqi aircraft during the operation.

33. Harmony document folder ISGP-2003-00031468.

34. Ibid. The name "Osiraq" is a combination of the French name for the reactor (Osiris – Egyptian god of the dead) and Iraq.

35. Harmony media file ISGQ-2003-M0006198.

36. Ibid.

37. Ibid.

38. Ibid.

39. In 1990, Iraq's navy was by far the smallest of its conventional military forces. It consisted of approximately five thousand personnel supporting a mixed fleet of eight Soviet-built OSA-class patrol boats (equipped with Soviet-made SSN-2A/B Styx surface-to-surface missiles), a collection of small coastal and river craft capable of surface mining, coastal missile batteries (Chinese-made CSSC-3 Silkworms), and seven Super Frelon helicopters capable of firing modern anti-ship missiles (French-made AM-39 Exocet).

40. Later in this same recording, Colonel Mustafa states that he was provided with a facilities sketch of the interior layout of the base during the final planning stage. Harmony media file ISGQ-2003-M0006198.

41. In July 1990, the Kuwait Navy's primary purpose was coastal defense and police functions. The approximately 1,800-person force operated eight German-built fast-attack patrol boats and a variety of smaller coastal craft. Faylakah is a small island (twelve kilometers long by six kilometers wide) situated approximately twenty kilometers northeast of Kuwait City. The island had one settlement of approximately six thousand inhabitants.

42. Known as Mina al-Bakr (renamed al-Basra Oil Terminal in October 2003), this is an offshore oil transfer terminal located off the mouth of the Shatt al-Arab waterway. It is less a naval base than a sprawling collection of pilings, pumps, pipes, and metal buildings built over the water.

43. Harmony media file ISGQ-2003-M0006198.

44. Ibid.

45. Ibid. Estimates vary, but there were approximately 5,000 to 7,000 Soviet specialists and more than 190 Soviet military advisers in Iraq when Kuwait was invaded. See Robert O. Freeman, "Moscow and the Iraqi Invasion of Kuwait," in *The Middle East after Iraq's Invasion of Kuwait* (Gainesville: University Press of Florida, 1993), 88–90.

46. Harmony media file ISGQ-2003-M0006198.

47. Ibid.

48. Ibid.

49. Ibid.

50. According to the commander of the Iraqi Navy, sometime on the morning of 2 August one of their Super Frelon helicopters was sent to support the assault force, but never arrived. He noted they later discovered that it and its coveted Exocet missile were downed by a Kuwaiti HAWK missile battery operating in the vicinity of the base. Harmony media file ISGQ-2003-M0006198.

51. The additional troops arrived in the same Iraqi coastal vessel that then transported the Kuwaiti officers to their POW camp in Iraq.

52. Apparently, Coalition forces were not the only ones challenged by friend-or-foe identification and inter-service rivalries. Harmony media file ISGQ-2003-M0006198.

53. Ibid.

54. The lack of information on safe approaches to the island required the assault force to use the standard ferry channels. The assault focused on the settled portion of the island at its southwestern tip.

55. Harmony media file ISGQ-2003-M0006198.

56. According to the Iraqi record of events, on 5 August the Iraqis seized Um al-Maradem and Kobbar Islands. On 6 August, they seized Qarooh Island as well as a small Kuwaiti missile boat and its crew. Ibid.

57. Ibid.

58. The speaker is identified on the tape as Iraqi Staff Commodore Huessin Sabri. Ibid.

59. Harmony media file ISGQ-2003-M0005879.

60. If not for the quick thinking of some Kuwaiti airmen, most of the early Kuwaiti sorties would not have happened. The initial Iraqi attack on al-Jaber Airbase closed the runways with air-scattered mines. The returning Kuwaiti Mirage F-1 and A-4 Skyhawk jets landed and were serviced on the perimeter fence road. John Levins, *Days of Fear: The Inside Story of the Iraqi Invasion of Kuwait* (Dubai: Motivate Publishing, 1997), 25–26.

61. Harmony media file ISGQ-2003-M0005879.

62. Ibid.

63. Ibid. It is not clear if the Kuwaiti officer was misquoted here or if it was a deliberate exaggeration on his part to confuse his interrogators. The Kuwait Air Force did not have eighty aircraft.

64. Ibid.

65. Ibid.

66. Ibid.

67. Ibid.

68. Harmony media file ISGQ-2003-M0005872.

69. Ibid.

70. Independent analysis of the losses is difficult to obtain. Various Western sources credit sixteen Iraqi helicopters to the Kuwait Air Force, and four to HAWK missiles, leaving twenty destroyed due to mishaps.

71. Harmony media file ISGQ-2003-M0005872.

72. Harmony media file ISGQ-2003-M0005879.

73. Ibid.

74. Harmony media file ISGQ-2003-M0005872.

75. In addition to the Sideriya Fort, Hammurabi Division units simultaneously seized the Abdali Customs House (disrupting communications from all border stations to Kuwait

City), the Kuwaiti Farms Police Station, al-Izam Police Stations, and the al-Sulaibikhat Police Station. Most were taken, as planned, without a shot being fired.

76. Hamdani, "From the Golan to the Collapse of Baghdad," 138.

77. According to some accounts, the emir and most of the royal family began their escape soon after the American contractor-operated radar balloon located on the Mutla Ridge reported significant movement of Iraqi forces before 0200.

78. Harmony media file ISGQ-2003-M0006027. For a good description of this and many other incidents during the Republican Guard's initial assault on Kuwait from a Kuwaiti point of view, see Levins, *Days of Fear*, 22–50.

79. Hamdani, "From the Golan to the Collapse of Baghdad," 139.

80. Ibid., 140.

81. Ibid.

82. Ibid., 141.

83. Ibid.

84. Ibid., 142.

85. "Fourteenth Mechanized Infantry Brigade, Republican Guard, General Staff, Analysis of Yom al-Nida Battle in the Kuwait Sector of Operations (2-18 August)" in Hussain 'Isa Mal Allah, comp., *The Iraqi War Criminals and Their Crimes During the Iraqi Occupation of Kuwait* (Kuwait: Center for Research and Studies on Kuwait, 1998), 134–50. This official Kuwaiti government history contains English translations of documents captured during the Coalition liberation of Kuwait in 1991. The Iraqi documents published in this Kuwaiti government report appear valid after comparing them to Iraqi documents captured by U.S. forces during OIF as well as statements by Iraqi veterans about the Kuwait invasion.

86. Hamdani, "From the Golan to the Collapse of Baghdad," 144.

87. Ibid. The "counterattack rumors" are also recorded in the documents contained in Hussain 'Isa Mal Allah, comp., *Iraqi War Criminals*, 168.

88. "Letter by Hammurabi Forces Command (Republican Guard) on analysis of Kuwait Liberation combat, dated 5 September 1990," in Hussain 'Isa Mal Allah, comp., *Iraqi War Criminals*, 170.

89. Hamdani, "From the Golan to the Collapse of Baghdad," 149.

Chapter VI

OCCUPATION AND CONSOLIDATION

In this world, the more time passes, the more it becomes our advantage. Their planning is based on the economic embargo and they think that the more time passes the more it becomes their advantage.[1]

—SADDAM HUSSEIN

A New Historical Juncture

The day of the invasion, Iraq's deputy ambassador to the United Nations, Sabah Talat Kadrat, told the U.N. Security Council (UNSC) that "the events taking place in Kuwait are internal matters which have no relation to Iraq." He went on to explain that "the Free Provisional Government of Kuwait requested my government to assist to establish security."[2] Within a few days the thinly constructed story that Iraq was supporting an internal "republican rebellion" against the Kuwaiti ruling family would collapse.

In the days immediately following the invasion, the Iraqi regime considered the implications of regional and international reactions. However, given its stunning success, it is not clear that Saddam anticipated anything more than a muted reaction. On 4 August he told his ministers, "Do not worry about the small things; only pay attention to what is going on in Kuwait. At this time Comrade Ali Hassan al-Majid and the Minister of Industry, Comrade Husayn Kamil were [both] stationed there [in Kuwait] according to their specialty, and from the military side we have al-Sabawi, who is handling the security [and] other issues. Any of these men calls . . . for any assistance to help our people in Kuwait City, you should give them prompt assistance."[3]

On 7 August 1990, Saddam Hussein addressed his national assembly about events in Kuwait. He reminded them that the historic implications of Iraq's military success in Kuwait were apparent, since "you are today, like all the great Iraqi people, before a new historical juncture. . . . The word today means a new will and the new future. It means determination, resolve, and will, whereby we should put things right so that Iraq will go forward and the banners of victory will flutter everywhere, and so that Iraq will be the new launching base for all the Arab free men."[4]

Figure 15. Saddam and the Kuwaiti Quisling. Hussein congratulates Alaa Hussein Ali, the new prime minister of the Kuwaiti puppet government. (Harmony media file ISGQ-2003-M0003354. Alaa Hussein Ali went into exile after the 1991 liberation of Kuwait. In 2000, he returned, was convicted of treason, and sentenced to death by hanging by a Kuwaiti court. In 2001 his sentence was commuted to life in prison.)

Saddam's reasoning for following through with the invasion was, as always, a complex mix of predicable "strongman" tactics, regional power politics, and it can be argued, naive grand strategy. But as with most major events in Saddam's political career, he drew strength from a kind of ruthless confidence that both terrified and motivated his followers. In a moment of feigned reflection immediately after the invasion, Saddam wondered aloud, "Are we going in the right direction? If we are, then we depend on Allah and Allah's will, and we continue in the same spirit. If we receive a negative criticism of our policies, *we will correct the critic* and keep going . . . we must move forward and keep moving"[5] [Emphasis added].

Saddam underlined his confidence in an early August 1990 conversation he had with then-president of Yemen, Field Marshal Ali Abdullah Saleh. After a rambling recitation of Iraq's historical claim to the "nineteenth province," Kuwaiti interference in Iraq's economy, and the need to distribute the oil wealth "fairly" across the Arab Nation, Saddam addressed himself to the potential for an international military response:

We considered that America and Israel may attack us . . . without ground forces . . . they may attack us with airplanes and missiles, [but] we will destroy them. And we will attack their fleets in the Gulf as the Kamikaze . . . they may attack us by the atomic bombs . . . we are ready for that. [W] e considered the economic blockade . . . if Saudi Arabia closed our oil lines we will attack them [with] 100 divisions and we'll increase the cost of oil up to 1,000 U.S. dollars. We will destroy the palace of the Emeriti people in occupied Kuwait. . . . The dignity of the Arab nation can be restored.[6]

A few days after his conversation with Saleh, Saddam sat down for a two-hour discussion with the U.S. chargé d'affaires Joseph Wilson, and passed the following message to President Bush:

You should refrain from being pushed into taking an action on wrong advice after which you will be embarrassed. If what President Bush wants in fact, is the preservation of U.S. interests as he has described them, then escalation of the tension and the military alternative is against these interests. I will tell you how you will be defeated. You are a superpower, and I know you can hurt us. But you will lose the whole area. You will never bring us [Iraq] to our knees. You can destroy some of our economic and

Figure 16. U.S. chargé d'affaires Joseph Wilson meets with Saddam Hussein, 8 August 1990 (Harmony document folder ISGQ-2003-00049397)

industrial base but the greater damage you cause, the greater the burden to you. In such a situation [military], we will not remain idle against your interests in the region.[7]

Extending Ba'ath Control

Saddam saw the invasion of Kuwait as a complete triumph of not only Iraqi arms but also of his will. Occupation proved to be a much more difficult task. For a regime used to police-state controls, the early acts of resistance, scattered protests, and even non-violent actions, like a general worker strike, were shocking and demanded an immediate response. In the weeks following the invasion, Saddam and his ministers worked to establish Ba'ath control over these new Iraqi citizens. The bureaucratic issues associated with occupation quickly overwhelmed Iraq's ministries. A section of the Iraqi Ministry of Defense with the very non-secular sounding title of "Directorate of Moral Guidance" issued a book in late October titled "Iraqization of Kuwait Handbook" to help clarify a myriad of issues faced by occupation troops.[8]

In a meeting, which included many of Saddam's senior advisers, the newly appointed governor of Iraq's nineteenth province, Ali Hasan al-Majid, made the following observations and recommendations:

> The Kuwaiti "governorate" must become less developed than the other eighteen Iraqi governorates—because the other Iraqi governorates deserve more. "The former rulers of Kuwait and the people of Kuwait and most of those present in the land of Kuwait have conspired against Iraq, some of them directly and knowingly were aware that they were hurting Iraq."
>
> His position had allowed him to "study the corrupt behavior of the Kuwaiti social, family, and sexual life." He noted that the Kuwaitis "only care about money and not moral values."
>
> Iraq needs to "create ways to limit the freedom of Kuwaitis." For example, deporting the "rich" as well as limiting food and gas supplies.
>
> He noted that Iraq could live on resources in Kuwait for two years. "As for cows, now we have approximately thirteen thousand that we could slaughter and live off . . . for years . . . [y]es, yes, everything is there, the good is there and the bad is there, I mean, they have everything."
>
> "Kuwaitis must not be treated like other Iraqis." The Kuwait opposition had already attacked Iraqi troops several times and "many were killed." Killing Kuwaitis in response was "not done for pleasure, but was necessary to make them obey Iraqi law."[9]

It is difficult to know with certainty what specific incidents Majid is refer-ring to, or if in fact the reports filtering into the headquarters accurately re-flected conditions. A sampling of security reports from Kuwait between August and October 1990 provides some indication of what the regime thou-ght it was facing.

> Kuwaiti security services "operating out of al-Khafji [are] building car bombs to send into Kuwait." The car bombs are "intended for places where Iraqi troops gather." There are indications that "specialized" Lebanese experts were paid to help the Kuwaitis.
>
> "Citizens of the former Kuwait were booby-trapping appliances that . . . interest Iraqi soldiers like video players and air conditioners." More-over, "Kuwaiti girls were putting poison in tea and others were putting arsenic in food stuffs to kill Iraqi soldiers."
>
> Rumors have been heard that the Kuwaitis have paid a "Japanese suicide network" to enter Kuwait City and execute suicide operations against Iraqi forces.
>
> American forces were training "assassination teams" to infiltrate Kuwait. The report also noted that "foreign doctors (such as Pakistani and Egyptian) working in Kuwait hospitals" had received instructions "to inject wounded Iraqi soldiers with poison."
>
> Finally, Kuwaiti saboteurs were using "feminine elements" as a cover because Iraqi soldiers at checkpoints were not checking women.[10]

In this same meeting, Saddam's half-brother, Sabawi Ibrahim Hasan al-Tikriti, newly appointed as chief of security in Kuwait, added his own obser-vations about security conditions and possible solutions. Sabawi told Saddam that, in the three weeks he had been on the job, his forces learned to treat the Kuwaitis in an appropriately "harsh way." The security tactics were simple and effective because they made the Kuwaitis feel "miserable and depressed."[11] Sabawi explained that after his forces captured resistance suspects, they were immediately interrogated about their plans and sources of information. "After we complete the interrogations," Sabawi noted, "we treat them harshly, really harshly, then kill and bury them." For example, Sabawi told Saddam that Iraqi security forces had recently killed all twenty-eight members of an opposition group known as Al-Fuhud. This group of Kuwaiti policemen, led by the former Kuwaiti drector of homeland security, was responsible for "numerous acts of sabotage."[12]

In order to comply with Saddam's order to eliminate the Kuwaiti oppo-sition, Sabawi reported that he had instituted a new set of counterinsurgency techniques. Again, simplicity was the key. The security chief explained that it was now occupation policy that "when a single bullet was fired from a neighborhood, the entire neighborhood was attacked." A related method was to "take captured resistance members to their neighborhoods, call out the neighbors, and kill the resistance member in front of them." For added effect, the resistance member's house was then burned to the ground.[13]

Iraq's security chief also noted that newly instituted population control techniques for Kuwait were having some positive effects. Under new regulations, all Kuwait identification documents were required to be immediately replaced with Iraqi documents. Thanks to the recently issued presidential decree, if Kuwaitis failed to obtain the proper Iraqi documents, they would lose all of their "civil rights," which would include such "privileges" as buying food and cooking gas.[14]

Despite all of the harsh measures instituted by Sabawi during the first few weeks of the occupation, the Kuwaiti resistance was having an effect. He described how Kuwaiti citizens had lured Iraqi soldiers into their homes, got them drunk, and then "slaughter[ed] them like sheep, using knives." What made these kinds of incidents worse, complained Sabawi, was that they all stemmed from "the army's leniency" with the population. Perhaps more worrisome for the regime than the loss of a few dozen ill-disciplined soldiers was the attempt by the Kuwaiti resistance to execute a "scorched earth" policy.

Sabawi explained to Saddam that the Kuwaiti resistance had started an arson campaign in warehouses all over Kuwait in early September. The apparent purpose was to deny the Iraqis material benefit from their invasion. Sabawi went on to report that "daily we stop no less than twenty to thirty arsons."[15] Sabawi's description of the threats to the material wealth in Kuwait got Saddam's attention. Earlier in the day, an unidentified minister explained to Saddam that since "this city is apparently full of warehouses . . . and everywhere you turn your eyes you see commodities," therefore the effect of the international embargo on Iraq will be minimal.[16] Despite the bounty, the minister explained Iraq's near-term challenge, noting that he had "requested about one hundred and fifty [extra] trucks from Jordan," and continued, "I now have about four hundred trucks. Four ships are now working between ports in Kuwait and the port of al-Basra. One warehouse has about 15,000 tons of barley. Another one has likewise steel and another lumber. It is really a commercial state. There is a great deal of plumbing supplies and construction materials. There is so much that I don't know what [Iraq] will do with it!"[17]

Saddam directed his ministers to work together efficiently to manage the transportation assets of Iraq's ministry of trade and transportation and those of

Figure 17. Saddam closely supervised the details of the Kuwait occupation through Sabawi Ibrahim Hasan al-Tikriti, Ali Hassan al-Majid, and Taha Ramadan. (Harmony media file ISGQ-2003-M0003354)

the army to move Kuwait's riches into Iraq quickly. Always looking to couch his actions in Iraq's larger historic purpose, Saddam reminded his ministers: "Our situation, thank Allah, is full of bounty, and we are not going to waste it. We will share it with the Arabs and a great deal more. As for Iraq's national interest [this] is great too. It is not only a great thing but a great honor."[18]

Saddam closed the meeting by designating Taha Ramadan as the minister responsible for the organized looting of Kuwait, to include such things as camel herds. To emphasize the point, Saddam directed that his ministers personally ensure that Kuwait's remaining warehouses were systematically "emptied."[19]

For the citizens of Kuwait and the hundreds of thousands of third-country nationals residing there, the post-invasion days were chaotic. As Brigadier General Hamdani recalled in his memoirs, the exodus through the Saudi Arabian border that was spurred on by "foreign media hype" continued at a frenzied pace throughout August and September.[20] As Hamdani later recalled, the problems with the exodus were twofold. First, in the open deserts of southern Kuwait, many of those trying to "escape" were without benefit of air-conditioned cars and succumbed to the heat. Second, as noted later in a memorandum from the III Corps commander, the Kuwaitis leaving the country constituted "important sources of information about all of the defensive arrangements of our troops." He recommended that, if those living in Kuwait were going to be allowed to leave, they should only depart by way of al-Basra, so they could not observe the construction of defenses.[21]

The soldiers of the Republican Guard spent the better part of August consolidating their temporary garrison positions and conducting a variety of "occupation missions." Those missions included carrying out local security in support of Iraqi intelligence services and securing convoys moving the material wealth of Kuwait to Iraq. Cadres of Ba'ath officials, units of the Regular Army, and what some Republican Guard officers described as "undisciplined" units of the Iraqi Popular Army soon joined the Republican Guard.[22] It was the Iraqi Popular Army that was blamed for much of the lawlessness in Kuwait during the early days of the occupation.

The Iraqi Popular Army was formed in 1970 to "maintain the achievements of the revolution, support and protect the party from local conspiracies, and sacrifice and struggle."[23] During the dark days of the Iran-Iraq War, Saddam and his advisers saw the Popular Army as a way to get fresh troops to an increasingly outnumbered front without being delayed by such time-consuming things as training. The Popular Army was often described by Iraqis as neither very popular nor much of an army. During the Iran-Iraq War, many Iraqis actually dubbed it the "unpopular army," and it was generally held in contempt by the armed forces.[24] One Western analyst described them as "a pool of Ba'athist officials designated for tasks similar to those performed by the officers in the regular army. . . . The main tasks for the popular army were related to filling the areas behind the regular forces and, in some instances, participating in actual combat—often with catastrophic results."[25]

A few days after the invasion, Saddam, in response to reports of Iraqi-initiated chaos in the streets, ordered that all Iraqis serving in Kuwait be in military uniform. He was shocked when told that most of the Popular Army, already deployed, did not have any uniforms.[26] A military intelligence report at the time noted that the lack of discipline was deadly, since "many among our troops left their weapons and went for a walk in a disorganized way which caused some of them to be murdered."[27]

For some of Iraq's professional soldiers, the Popular Army's actions during the occupation tainted what they viewed as an otherwise brilliant military operation. Although he avoided details, Hamdani recalled later, "I could no longer bear [the rampant violence and criminal activity] I was seeing, for the human misery would have softened a mountain. What made things worse was that a few of the military personnel, the security apparatus, and the Iraqi citizens were undisciplined and started misbehaving. You could add to that what the non-nationals who lived in Kuwait were doing to the country."[28]

Official reporting during the first few weeks of occupation reflected some of the chaos but remains unclear on who was to blame. One detailed memorandum dated 4 August described the confusion of the early days and the impact of poor post-invasion planning:

- There is a great concentration among our soldiers in specific areas while many areas don't have any soldiers. [This] helps some Kuwaitis open fire on the military vehicles of our troops which happen to be passing by those areas without backup.
- The enlisted men were seen destroying shops, restaurants, breaking their doors and looting them especially the shops.
- There are rumors that a number of Palestinians asked the Kuwaitis to furnish them with weapons in order to fight Iraqi troops.
- There is an inability to control the curfew in Kuwait City and the other provinces.
- Some troops complain about food shortages which forced some of the enlisted personnel to go to private homes to ask for food. This case has a negative repercussion in so far as food is not available and also there is a strong possibility that our soldiers could be kidnapped or killed.
- Some enlisted [soldiers] confronted [Kuwaiti] families without authorization.
- There are rumors [that] some Iranians and Kuwaitis robbed some gold shops and this theft was attributed to the Iraqi soldiers.[29]

A memorandum from the GMID dated 7 August reported that the Kuwaitis "committed acts of sabotage such as bombing oil wells so that it would be attributed to the Iraqi troops and tarnish our image." Additionally, these Kuwaiti groups were "breaking into the homes of the wealthy people."[30] To some of the Iraqi officers on the ground like Hamdani, the growing chaos resulted from compartmented pre-invasion planning, limited planning for an occupation, and a lack of administrative experience. Later he wrote, "I asked myself—When are we going to create a military government for civilian affairs before it is too late and we lose control over the security? There were more migrants in this country than nationals, and evil was bound to happen. We might be good at dealing with the external threat, but we were useless as policemen and internal security forces, 'and some of us are righteous and others are not; we follow different ways'"[Qu'ran 72:11].[31]

By early October, despite almost eight weeks of chaos, the internal security situation in Kuwait had largely stabilized. Iraqi forces were still manning checkpoints, conducting security patrols and executing large-scale sweeps, but the level of public violence had generally subsided. Iraq's infamous security services required some time to adapt to the new "human terrain" of the nineteenth province, but soon established the same kind of brutal equilibrium that existed in other restless areas of Iraq.

Interestingly, official documents from the late fall of 1990 explicitly recognize the role that Iraqi forces played in the chaos as well as their attempts to control it. One example is a 24 November 1990 order from the Kadhima Forces Command to units of the special forces and Popular Army to conduct a search of a neighborhood in Kuwait City. The mission was to "arrest suspicious individuals and confiscate any banned weapons, ammunition, and equipment they find."[32] Most of this standard field order would be recognizable to any American military unit conducting a cordon and search operation with the exception of the warning to the troops:"Violation of the property or possessions of citizens for any reason is forbidden (absolute integrity). Anyone stealing will be executed."[33]

One factor that greatly helped to tame Kuwait was the gradual depopulation of the small country. By some estimates, the pre-invasion population of 2.4 million had fallen 60 percent by February 1991.[34] Large areas of Kuwait City were virtual ghost towns, greatly simplifying the security challenges.

In several postwar reviews of the invasion, Saddam took note of the lawlessness reported in Kuwait during the occupation and expressed regret, not for the lawlessness, but for the effect it had inside Iraq:

> The parties [anti-Ba'athist] played an important role in corrupting the morals of our army, including corrupting our soldiers' integrity. . . . Such corruption did not involve everyone, yet it became contagious. . . . At least the police officer if he tries to steal, he will steal half and leave the other half behind, because he is aware of the law and well-trained on theft issues. On the other hand, if the army soldier attempted to utilize the same method by using his weapon, it will be a crisis, since he is inexperienced in such a matter. Unfortunately this corruption [has] extended to our nation, which is very hurtful! The people used to trust our army, and leave their doors wide open, not any more, now if they observe our army, they lock up their homes.[35]

This mistrust came back to haunt the regime during the early stages of the March 1991 uprisings in al-Basra. Recalling the looting in Kuwait, Saddam explained that "people learned to extend their hands to the public property. We did not tell people that Kuwait was not Iraq and they could go and loot it . . . although Kuwait was Iraqi, the looting continued in it. So it created [a] kind of mixed understanding towards the public property.[36]

Reaction and Iraqi Counteraction

The Arab World

Immediately following the invasion of Kuwait, the Arab League issued a statement that sharply condemned Iraqi "aggression" against Kuwait and called for the "immediate and unconditional withdrawal" of Iraqi troops. The statement also opposed any intervention by foreign forces.[37] The Iraqis, no doubt hoping to take advantage of the wording of the Arab League statement, offered to withdraw their troops "as long as there emerges no threat to the security of Kuwait or of Iraq."[38] Unfortunately for Iraqi leaders, "threats" quickly emerged in the form of UNSC Resolution 660 as well as statements by numerous world leaders condemning the invasion.

The Security Council,

Alarmed by the invasion of Kuwait on 2 August 1990 by the military forces of Iraq,

Determining that there exists a breach of international peace and security as regards the Iraqi invasion of Kuwait,

Acting under Articles 39 and 40 of the Charter of the United Nations,

1. *Condemns* the Iraqi invasion of Kuwait;
2. *Demands* that Iraq withdraw immediately and unconditionally all of its forces to the positions in which they were located on 1 August 1990;
3. *Calls upon* Iraq and Kuwait to begin immediately intensive negotiations for the resolution of their differences and supports all efforts in this regard, and especially those of the League of Arab States;
4. *Decides* to meet again as necessary to consider further steps to ensure compliance with the present resolution.

Figure 18. United Nations Security Council Resolution 660 of 2 August 1990 (http://www.un.org/Docs/scres/1990/scres90.htm)

The governments in the Arab world were openly split on the question of the invasion. For those opposing Iraq—like the now-exiled Kuwaitis, Saudi Arabia, and most of the Persian Gulf States—the primary issue was an existential security threat. For others opposing Iraq, for example Egypt and Syria, the issues were both of security and a matter of long-standing competition for regional leadership. Arab League members who refused to endorse the resolution condemning Iraq, such as Yemen, Jordan, the PLO, Sudan, and Mauritania, did so, in most cases, to stand with their champion.

Iraq, in addition to supporting the revolutionary movements within many of the more supportive Arab states, had more recently been a strong advocate for pooling regional oil revenues to redistribute to the "have-nots." Most of the Arab have-nots did not lose sleep over Kuwait's predicament. Still others— Tunisia, Algeria, and Libya—tried to remain on the fence throughout the conflict. Saddam was not happy that, once again, the Arab Nation did not rally to his vision for remaking the Middle East. Most of the blame was placed on what Saddam saw as "weak leaders" such as Libya's Muammar al-Qaddafi. After being told that Qaddafi, while not supporting Iraq, had urged Arabs to unite against any foreign interference in Arab affairs, Saddam opined, "Do you know why that is? It is not because he is worried about Iraq, but because he knows that the Iraqis will shatter the skull of the foreigners and he [Qaddafi] will end up being a forgotten cigarette butt. Everyone acts depending on their own motives, even if they lie."[39]

On 12 August, Iraq made a public offer to "make a formulation of arrangements for the situation in Kuwait" in exchange for an immediate and unconditional Israeli withdrawal from Palestinian territory [the Gaza Strip and the West Bank], the Golan Heights, and Syria's withdrawal from Lebanon.[40] The international community saw this as yet another excuse for invading Kuwait and a cynical ploy to play on Arab opinion. Given Iraq's pre-invasion rhetoric about economic warfare, few took this offer of "linkage" as a serious way forward.[41]

Rallying the Arab Nation was one of the underlying, though not exclusive, drivers of the invasion of Kuwait, just as it was for embarking on the Iran-Iraq War. Unifying the Arab Nation under Saddam's leadership was, after all, at the core of his Ba'ath vision. Saddam spent a significant amount of time in the weeks after the invasion trying to build support in the Arab world for his actions. His attempts at coalition-building were designed to do more than build a bulwark against international reaction. He saw it as yet another opportunity to claim pan-Arab leadership. Saddam did not find many sympathetic ears. Saddam's tacit claim was that because borders in the Middle East, such as Kuwait's, were "imposed" by former colonial agreements, their validity was questionable.

Even if Saddam's historical facts were true, his rhetoric on the subject threatened the territorial legitimacy of more than just Kuwait.

Saddam's other tack was to appeal to the idea that Arabs should be left to solve their own problems without international interference. He insisted that "it is easier to be flexible in the Arab arena than it is in the international arena with its evil powers."[42] Once again, Saddam chose a tactic that seemed to threaten the very leaders he was trying to win over. After all, the emir of Kuwait said the same thing just before Saddam invaded. At this point in the crisis, Saddam's lack of Arab support did not seem to weaken his confidence or resolve. In a statement recorded after the invasion, Saddam showed that, on the issue of an Arab compromise, even he had his limits, declaring that "any state that takes us further and brings our enemies closer to their evil goals, we must refuse, even if our blood reaches our chest. That is my resolve."[43]

The Iranians

One of Saddam's more surprising attempts at building regional support for the invasion was his outreach to President Rafsanjani of Iran. Following the end of the Iran-Iraq War and with the encouragement of the United Nations, Iran and Iraq made tentative steps toward normalizing relations and settling several postwar issues. An exchange of letters between these bitter enemies began in early 1990 and continued during the rising tensions over Kuwait. In a 30 July letter to Rafsanjani, Saddam all but abrogated most of Iraq's public justifications for the eight-year war.[44] Saddam's purpose, he said, was "to ensure they are spared from the schemes of enemies of peoples, who endeavor—God-forbid—to turn back the clock in our two countries to the situation as it was before August 1988 . . . and in that event, losers will be losers, without any evident gain."[45] In a letter of 3 August, Saddam spoke not only of his "intent for peace," but a "quick peace" in view of the "winds of change" swirling around Kuwait.[46] Apparently, the issues at the heart of the bloody war with Iran were not as valuable to Iraq as possessing Kuwait.

In another letter to Rafsanjani dated 14 August, Saddam asks that a new relationship be established between Iraq and Iran based on "fraternal relations with all Muslims" in order to "extricate Iraq and Iran from the blackmail and intrigues of malicious international forces and their adjuncts in the region."[47] In this same note, Saddam reiterated his willingness to comply with the 1987 UNSC Resolution 598 on exchanging the thousands of prisoners still held after the war. Additionally, and as a measure of "good faith," Saddam promised to pull Iraqi soldiers out of occupied Iranian territory and back from the borders on 17 August regardless of Iran's response to his letter.[48]

Not all of Saddam's advisers were comfortable with this initiative, but most saw both the potential short- and long-term benefits. In a conversation recorded on 17 August, Comrade Tahir stated that although he supported the initiative, he had serious concerns.[49] He was perhaps influenced by a GMID report dated 14 August noting that recent statements from Iran implied "that it does not accept the changes" in regional balance of power resulting from the invasion.[50] Tahir commented that the Iranians were "black-hearted," and all they were interested in was the fall of Saddam's regime. Saddam responded that regardless of the initiatives, "Iraq's army is ready, if Iran acts aggressively."[51]

Comrade Sa'di recommended that Iraq immediately publicize the Iranian letters. He reasoned that the "psychological effect will be in favor of the Iraqis," because the Americans would be forced to reevaluate the regional situation. Finally, Comrade Izzat al-Duri noted that the offer was worth the effort even if Iran did not reply because it would free up troops for the Kuwait theater. More importantly, given the paucity of allies lining up with Iraq, it might "mobilize the Arab and Islamic people and governments." This, in turn, might cause nations such as France to consider the long-term dangers of American action on their regional interests.[52] The response from Tehran was non-committal and early hopes of shifting the regional status quo on a "fraternal basis" soon faded.

The International Community

One of the most serious issues in the international community, after the invasion itself, was the fate of more than eight hundred Western hostages held by Saddam as human shields at potential strategic targets throughout Iraq.[53] In addition to holding these unfortunate individuals, Saddam refused to grant thousands of other non-Iraqis exit visas. These "guests," as he called them, were consolidated in several hotels in Baghdad under constant threat of being used as human shields. This group included more than 350 passengers and the crew of an unlucky British Airways 747, which had landed at Kuwait International Airport on a routine refueling stop at the height of the invasion.[54] Despite an international outcry and four UNSC resolutions condemning the Iraqi behavior during August and September, many in the regime viewed the hostage policy as an effective tool of statecraft.

On 1 November, Saddam met with his diplomatic staff to discuss the details of Iraq's hostage policy. One of his advisers pointed out the psychological effect the hostage issue was having on American leaders: "Bush knows we are not going to start this war. Then when there is nothing happening he [Bush] began talking about the hostages and had some other excuses. We all know this is an excuse. . . . Bush stated 'I lost my patience regarding the hostage situation and this is really hurting me.'"[55]

This same adviser cautiously told Saddam that he thought the decision, on 23 October, to release more than three hundred French hostages and "guests," was a mistake. He noted that since time was obviously in the Iraqis' favor on this issue, they should have taken advantage of French sensitivity by holding the hostages longer. Saddam agreed that gaining time was a critical task and noted that "the purpose of prohibiting some foreigners from leaving the country [Iraq] is to increase the obstacles for the wicked enemy's intentions, especially the American officials . . . [and] to gain some time."[56]

According to Saddam, negotiating limited releases was designed to allow an international peace movement to build momentum and frustrate "the one who was in a hurry for war."[57] Creating frustration, explained Saddam, was why he insisted that the Iraqi National Assembly discuss the hostage matter country by country.[58] As Saddam explained it at the time:

> Why do I insist that the National Assembly discuss this matter? There are three reasons: first of all, I want the world to know that we have a national assembly that is elected and discusses issues, etc., and even though I made the decision on it [the hostage issue] they still get to discuss it . . . the other issue is to show respect to our assembly, this assembly we elected and we want it, shouldn't we give it consideration? . . . The third reason is that we don't want to allow any country to do what they like and make it too easy for them. Any country that wants its citizens must make a political effort and take a political stand and convince not one or two or four, rather he must convince 250 people.[59]

Managing the hostage issue was an important and personal part of Saddam's strategy. Between late August and November, Iraq entertained more than thirty delegations (private and governmental) from more than twenty countries. Each went to Baghdad to petition for release of their fellow citizens or a particular category of hostage. A select group of these delegations met with Saddam in a highly publicized ritual of "mutual" respect usually resulting in a token gesture of humanity on Saddam's part. Lesser delegations were limited to making their pleas through the secondary officials and the quasi-governmental entity known as the "Friendship, Peace, and Solidarity Organization."[60]

Saddam confidently told his ministers that a number of countries were soon going to join Iraq to "demonstrate peace" by declaring their opposition to war. Ironically, this new, Iraqi-led "peace" movement would renounce the use of military force or threat of military force in the entire region, especially in the Palestinian situation. According to Saddam, all Iraq needed was two members of the UNSC to side with peace in the region and "we will release the foreigners ... we will release [all] the foreigners except the Americans."[61]

In a conversation recorded in late September 1990, Saddam dismissed the growing chorus of threats from countries both in and out of the Middle East. In an apparent reference to the American president's remarks to Congress that "[o]ur quarrel is with Iraq's dictator and with his aggression. Iraq will not be permitted to annex Kuwait. That's not a threat, that's not a boast, that's just the way it's going to be," Saddam remarked to Tariq Aziz that "[i]t looks like the old man Bush is beginning to warn us. He must be crazy."[62] He then previewed what would become a constant refrain during the coming decade about America's influence over the United Nations: "The more they [the U.N.] increase [its] resolutions, the more unbending we become. I hope [they] will not end up being too adamant, because this kind of world in fact does not deserve respect. This low level of being subservient to America does not meet with any kind of respect from us at all ... it is disgusting the way America is leading them [the U.N.] under its whip and brings them to any decision it wants from them."[63]

According to Saddam, the United Nations and the members of the Security Council had been bought and paid for by the United States. He said that "the United States has publicly and on TV bought the support of Russia. The United States and Saudi Arabia have done that. How can we respect something called the resolution of the Security Council, which comes out of this dirty mess? How could I respect such a resolution? ... This is not an international organization ... this is an organization that belongs to Bush."[64]

Saddam's disdain for the United States and its supposed puppet the U.N. was very public. In private, Saddam's opinion of more sympathetic states like France could be just as bitter. When some of his ministers expressed concern about French reaction not only to the invasion, but more recently the decidedly undiplomatic treatment of their delegation in Kuwait, Saddam was dismissive. He reminded his less confident ministers that Iraq would go its own way, "even if he [French President Mitterrand] wanted to take action, let him go to hell. We do not beg for a positive relationship with anybody. What matters to us is what we say."[65]

Perhaps the most surprising aspect of this long conversation was Saddam's comments about his erstwhile ally the Soviet Union. After Tariq Aziz reported he would meet Soviet Minister of Foreign Affairs Eduard Shevardnadze on 28 September, Saddam ordered, "When you meet with Shevardnadze, I want you to tell him that we noticed that their [the Soviet Union] position is getting worse. We will never ask the Soviet Union for a favor any more. ... We shall take matters into our [own] hands and not depend on [them]. ... You should explain to

Shevardnadze that, if you think that Iraq can be flexible under the guns of America, then you are wrong. That America will come in, and hit, and destroy us, this ploy we know. . . . We have decided that we shall go through the battle till the end."[66]

In early October, in one of what would become many attempts by the Soviet Union to moderate Iraqi behavior, President Gorbachev dispatched a member of his presidential council, Yevgeny Primakov, to Baghdad. During a 6 October meeting, Primakov provided Saddam with details of the recently concluded superpower summit at Helsinki. Primakov then expressed confidence that Gorbachev had made progress with the Americans. According to Primakov, President Gorbachev was confident he could put Bush on "the path of political work."[67] Primakov noted the Soviet Union had two major interests in trying to work with the Iraqis to achieve a political solution. First, they wanted to link the solution in the Gulf to the other issues in the Middle East, especially the Arab-Israeli conflict. The second reason was the long-standing Soviet belief that "the existence of a strong Iraq is a necessity to keep a balance in the area."[68] The idea of a link between a Kuwait solution and the Israeli–Palestinian conflict of course resonated with Saddam. Keeping the Palestinian cause alive, but not necessarily resolved, had always been a central component of Saddam's long-range strategy.

Overall, Saddam struck a pessimistic tone with his Russian guest during their 6 October meeting. "[L]et me be frank with you," Saddam admonished Primakov, "you cannot bring an end to the American siege of Iraq."[69] The Iraqi president went on to explain that, even if he gave Primakov a promise to pull out of Kuwait, Saddam was convinced the siege would continue. Saddam insisted that any sign of flexibility on his part would be a sign to King Fahd, President Bush, and Israel to continue "bargaining and blackmailing."[70] He lamented that "America is the strongest [country], but they are not giving us the chance to solve the problem with dignity!"[71]

Saddam reminded Primakov that in the past, conflicts in the Middle East were only solved when the parties involved received adequate time to negotiate. "Why were the Americans insistent in their approach to Iraq?" Saddam asked. "Why are they so patient when it comes to Israel?" he wondered.[72] After reiterating his position that the solution to Kuwait must include a solution to the Israeli-Palestinian conflict, Saddam made his negotiating position crystal clear. According to Saddam, President Bush's demand that Iraq withdraw from Kuwait or face war was "utterly unacceptable."[73]

From 1979 through the fall of the regime in 2003, Tariq Aziz was Saddam's personal window into the world. During this crisis he was also the most visible member of the Iraqi government, appearing almost nightly on international

television screens from different capitals around the world. During private discussions within the regime's inner circle, Aziz was often the only voice with any
experience outside the Middle East. The two countries with which Aziz was
most familiar and where he cultivated extensive personal relations were France
and Russia. Based on this history and in the run-up to the U.N. vote on the
use of force, Aziz's opinions carried significant weight with Saddam. During a
2 November meeting with his advisers, Saddam was frustrated at the series of
seemingly contradictory statements made by Soviet leadership on the outlook
for peace or war in the Middle East. Aziz assured his boss that he had "no indication that the Soviet Union has any [independent] interest, when we discuss
war or peace, they are always seeking our interest."[74] He went on to place the
Soviet position in context:

> As I have shared my opinion with you, deducing that the Soviet Union
> has no interest in a war of this manner happening and at this large scale.
> Maybe at the beginning and at different intervals the idea of a surgical
> [military] operation came up. [T]o hit Iraq and force it to withdraw from
> Kuwait, as maybe a disciplinary move for Iraq; it possibly entered their
> mind, but when they saw the reality and the fact that the Iraqi power was
> not something they could control in days or weeks and that this war will
> lead to major destruction in the region and to political and economic
> imbalance; and because the Soviet Union is worried about Europe and
> has internal problems, sir, they couldn't imagine that the situation would
> explode in the Middle East, seeing that it is their southern border. If a war
> of this manner happens the situation will explode, the Islamic factor, the
> nationalistic factor, the oil, and security all these would explode . . . and as
> Primakov said to you when you met, after you told him that we would hit
> Israel, that that was a nightmare they didn't want to see. . . . [A] nightmare
> to the Soviet Union, not out of love or care for us, but a nightmare.[75]

Notwithstanding his assessment of the Soviet Union's interests, Aziz was
apparently not completely convinced Iraq could rely on this "ally." While he
estimated that the Soviets had "no interests in a war," he questioned whether
they would "do all in [their] power to stop it." The question remained "[could]
the Soviet Union stop the war?"[76] Aziz explained to Saddam how recent
changes inside the Soviet Union had created two leadership camps in Moscow.
On one side were "the pragmatists," led by Shevardnadze and "closest to and
influenced by the American position."[77] The second group, inclined to support
Iraq and "full of nostalgia for the Cold War" was, unfortunately for Iraq, much

weaker. Aziz described a meeting with one of Gorbachev's advisers from this latter camp: "When he saw me speak with conviction and intensity, his eyes would shine and I could see memories of the old communist, who sees a man coming from the Middle East, an Arab speaking against imperialism, and he feels an affinity for me. . . . There are still some Russians, who for seventy years, sir, were raised to hate the Americans and to face them head on, those you can't easily make follow the United States, the Russian nationalistic fervor is still strong in them."[78]

Aziz did offer some hope for the Russian position when he noted that "Gorbachev's policies are somewhat flexible," and despite the tensions inside the Kremlin, Gorbachev "could handle these [policy] differences."[79] For his part, fellow Saddam confidant Taha Ramadan was not as hopeful as Tariq Aziz. His assessment at the beginning of November was that "the Soviet Union does not wish to sacrifice its newly formed relationships with the U.S. and the West for our sake."[80]

For Aziz, the French position was somewhat more complex than the Russian one. He explained to Saddam that "[I]t is clear, sir, that France, particularly in all of Western Europe, does not want war and considers war to be a very dark cloud, which will hurt its relationships with the Arab and Muslim World."[81]

As leader of the Francophone world, Aziz explained, France carried a significant amount of influence with many countries, and many of those are Arab and Islamic.[82] Aziz continued:

> France knows that a war of this nature, if it starts, will not only be a military conflict, but as Claude Cheysson said "a conflict of culture and civilizations." [So] what is the deal with France? France has over four million Arab Muslims in the country . . . the question is: can France stop the war? That is a question we must follow up on. They will exert an effort but at the same time they are against Iraq taking all of Kuwait, which is obvious.
>
> [French President] Mitterrand said, "Let Iraq express a desire to withdraw and everything is possible"—yes you know that the French language has some ambiguity—basically he is saying, you [Iraq] state that you want to withdraw and after that everything is possible. Which means what? His statement is ambiguous towards Kuwait or the whole Middle East, and he intends for it to be ambiguous at this stage because he doesn't want to answer questions and doesn't want to seem like he is offering any concessions.[83]

Aziz continued articulating the positions of the countries on the UNSC. Iraq's diplomatic emphasis was to find countries that might yet offer it the international maneuvering space it needed to avoid a direct confrontation on American terms. Aziz shared many of these same issues with Saddam, albeit with a more cynical outlook, in the run-up to the 2003 war.[84] Aziz told Saddam:

> What Primakov came up with is in the same vein—"that we cannot gua-rantee for Iraq"—he didn't say we, he said the group that he wants to get together guarantees for Iraq what it wants in Kuwait. So they are against Iraq taking all of Kuwait, but they are not against Iraq reaching some kind of settlement with Kuwait. The Soviet Union and France are not in danger of the current Iraqi power; they are probably uncomfortable with the idea of chemical weapons . . . they have their private irritations—which we understand—since they are a European nation in the process of chemical weapons disarmament . . . but it is not in their interest for the Iraqi power to weaken, because what could they benefit from making Iraq weaker?— and what threat does Iraq present to them? France is a friend of Israel, but a "mild" friendship meaning that it wouldn't sacrifice its interests for Israel . . . it will help maintain the security of Israel, but not more than that. It is not a friend of Israel's expansionist dreams. Therefore it is not in their [French] interest to destroy Iraqi power, but also it is not in their interest that Iraq become the leader in the region and control the region, therefore it is not out of love or hate towards Iraq.[85]

Another longtime Saddam confidant, Izzat al-Duri, was inclined to agree with Aziz's assessment of international interests. "[W]hen a nation becomes strong," al-Duri noted, "an air of independence takes over." This independence is "not what the big players want," he added. However, in al-Duri's assessment, none of the big players had immediate interests in either war or serious eco-nomic sanctions. His recommendation at this stage was to focus diplomatic efforts on France, in hopes that it would in turn influence "official European positions." Al-Duri also noted that "European countries hide behind the French position if they want to compromise and take a more conciliatory stance toward us, or to distance themselves from the American sanctions."[86] It was important for Iraq to focus its diplomatic and political campaign at this point, al-Duri emphasized, because it had already brought "many good results" and besides, "this way we [can] prevent the matter from growing into a war they will lose, they probably estimate that they won't lose, when Bush convinces the American people and their leaders, that the American civilization will be destroyed if . . . Saddam Hussein controls the region, and its oil, then they will enter into a full fledged war."[87]

Finally, Taha Ramadan offered Saddam his assessment of the international situation. By his estimate, the chances for peace were better than fifty-fifty and growing.

> The Soviet Union, which I don't disagree that it is important, but the Soviet Union, because of their president and current policies and distance from us will not be a security buffer for us—I still think that if we get closer to France, they will be a better security buffer for us. Of any country in the Security Council outside of the United States or Britain which would be able to prevent the war it would be France, not Soviet Union and not China . . . in the last 15 years, even during the Iran-Iraq War, if one or two members lean towards peace [China] joins them, but it never initiates it, or vetoes or causes problems. Which leaves France—France is important and France is able through its contacts to influence two or three other countries [like] Italy, Germany, [or] Spain. That also makes France want to go ahead and help us, to [appear] as someone who initiated the process. . . . But this is war, it's not just a regular problem and the results aren't your everyday results.[88]

During the last half of November, U.S. diplomats and others completed the wording in UNSC Resolution 678. From a Coalition point of view, time seemed to now be working against Iraq. Every month without a settlement only increased the number and severity of UN sanctions. In a discussion recorded at approximately the same time as the U.N. deliberations on Resolution 678, Saddam indicated just how differently he assessed the situation: "We are gaining time on our side; at the moment time is working on our side they [the Americans] will fall into our hands. This is excellent. . . . Because now the time is great! Because when the world [gets] in a frenzied state, everything will become possible."[89]

As late as the end of November, senior members of Saddam's inner circle parroted Saddam's reasoning. Taha Ramadan, referring to the new UNSC Resolution, told Saddam,

> "Mr. President, I hope that this resolution [UNSC 678] will be the last one. Many countries will realize the injustice and abuse in it. Nowadays, issuing such a resolution is not like the resolution 660 or 61 or 62 in the first week. Now we have supporters. There is a peace movement in Europe and America. People are running back and forth. There is a crack in the economic sanctions and the people are starting to send stuff [to us]. . . . I do not believe that the results [of any war] are going to be negative on the Iraqis and the Arabs. It is going to be negative on the other side."[90]

The Americans

Both Saddam and Tariq Aziz seemed to understand that depending on assistance from Russia or France, while worth pursuing, was not likely to dissuade the United States. As Aziz explained to Saddam:

> Concerning the American position . . . the American position these days is dangerous, meaning that, starting tomorrow, Saturday [3 November 1990], and until the day of the elections, or the day after, if they don't carry out a military operation, I expect they will push it [an unknown voice says "After Christmas"]. Not only after Christmas . . . the Secretary of Defense said that they needed a hundred thousand soldiers, [the request] is either to con us—or it is a bluff, then so be it—it means the hit is near—but if the timeframe of the expected political hit passes—then he cannot continue bluffing—he has to come out and say that he is not going to send a hundred thousand soldiers.[91]

Saddam agreed. He noted somewhat optimistically that in recent statements to the press, the American administration was "pulling back from discussing details, they are making general statements." Aziz cautioned Saddam that American public statements are probably not as well thought out as Saddam's because "these Americans are under daily [press] questioning, God help them, even the Americans, sometimes I see them being chased by the journalists . . . cornering a person . . . even [Secretary of Defense] Cheney has to give a response."[92]

For Saddam, if American statements, actions, and deployments were not a bluff, then anticipating the timing of any attack was critical. Aziz reported in early November that "the commander of the British 'Desert Rats'" said publicly that he "would be ready for a strike on November 15." Again, reflecting on the nature of public statements in the West, Aziz added that the British commander

> has to be committed to his word because he is going to be held accountable—if the journalists and newspapers hold them accountable then they will investigate them—but if November 15 passes, then I expect that they will avoid Christmas time because of emotional reasons. . . . Christmas and New Years are not something they are willing to compromise on. . . . And the president who brings corpses [home] to his country at Christmas time will be skinned alive in the U.S. Because if war happens, they know it will not end between November 15 and December 15—it will not end in one month and they know it.[93]

The other factor, as Aziz tried to educate his boss, was the effect electoral politics had on the American decision to go to war. According to Aziz, the 1990 congressional campaign season was a major factor in America's decision on a war. Moreover, "Bush has a problem in his running of the country . . . he is a Republican and both houses are Democratic."[94] Aziz explained that "Congress is Democratic, as usual, and the Senate is also Democratic, and they are giving him [Bush] a very hard time . . . thus, for this reason he may consider war to gain a Republican majority, which would strengthen his chances of ruling the U.S. and in staying for another term. This is the only reason, as I explained to you sir, I have no other reason."[95]

Saddam, apparently still unclear about how an American decision for war might be made, asked Aziz, "if he can't reach an agreement with the opposing party, would the president be able to make a monumental decision, if both parts of the house were from the opposing party?" Before Aziz could answer, Saddam asked, "[if] they [Congress] are not going to take responsibility and that he [Bush] would have to do it and bear full responsibility on his own—would he be able to do that?"[96]

"Well, he [Bush] met with the leaders of the Congress the day before yesterday," Aziz answered, "and then they came out and said that they support the president in his current policies—but they also advised him to be a little more patient." The good news, in Aziz's estimation, was that congressional caution was actually lessening the likelihood of a military strike and "for a while more [this caution] allows a chance for negotiations." The bad news was that the American administration was still aggressively pushing the use-of-force resolution in the Security Council.[97]

Returning to the issue of timing for a possible attack, Taha Ramadan offered Saddam his assessment of the situation: "Time is not on the side of the Americans or those calling for a war, because the later they are—the more the coalition disbands—and international opinion is now leaning towards peace. Therefore I think that if they can, they will [attack] within a short period. . . . I think the decisive time [will] be between the 5th and 15th [November]."[98]

Moreover, Ramadan noted, President Bush had announced he would visit the troops in Saudi Arabia on 20 November. So while there was an increased danger around the American elections, "if there isn't a strike between now and the 15th, then it means that during the rest of the year there won't be a strike . . . [and] time will be on our side."[99]

Saddam, in a display of his finely tuned survival instinct, cautioned his advisers to always look for the deception in their adversary's actions. He explained that since this is a sensitive time and we can't know the exact dates, we shouldn't ignore Christmas and the holidays. [I]f they wanted to strike, these dates are not going to stop them, and it might actually help in the element of surprise.[100]

Taha Ramadan agreed with his boss and noted that if the United States felt that the Coalition was weakening, "then it will strike before the break becomes permanent so it will not appear like it is fighting Iraq on its own."[101] He noted that regardless of all the machinations in the United Nations, "what is obvious though is that the American administration and Bush have the final say in the decision. It does not matter what Mubarak wants, what Fahd wants, France's role and support, the role of Britain and Israel. It is clear that the U.S. can decide to strike and can decide not to strike."[102]

Ramadan went on to present Saddam with a prophetic prediction of what would likely occur in any American attempt to sustain an international economic embargo against Iraq:

Who says they will strike and leave . . . how will they strike and leave? We have stated that the first strike we get we will in turn fire on Saudi [Arabia] and Israel—they can't just come and hit and run—we are not a little secondary country [that they can] just come and strike us and say . . . they hurt us and then have the Security Council issue a resolution, declare a cease fire, and withdrawal of [our] troops and then the United States begins to withdraw and so on and so forth. I don't believe the whole war structure will be like this.

First of all we will not just sit there quietly, if we are attacked, and hope that they won't do it again. What is the size of the strike that will happen and how do we know that, if we don't respond, they will not repeat it?

It will not be in this scenario. Well, how will they withdraw? I expect that after three months if the situation continues in this manner, the economic sanctions will start to fracture. . . . this one [country] will say we are not against the Security Council, the other [country] will [send a] plane that is carrying medicines, and so on. Any beginning, however small, will highlight the nations that will complain of shortages and of the economic pressure on it and therefore find it as an opportunity to cooperate with Iraq.[103]

In conclusion, Ramadan recommended that they consider a way to "establish or encourage a channel with the two sides, the United States and Saudi Arabia, a secret communications channel," because it would benefit both. He then asked rhetorically, "How do you calm a big commotion and also save face?"[104]

This was not a question, at least in early November, that Saddam appeared ready to answer.

Like his fellow members of the RCC, Izzat al-Duri was somewhat optimistic that if the United States did not strike before the New Year, then the chances of an attack would decrease over time. He cautioned, however, that any planning that depended on that scenario would risk catching Iraq "unawares or dreaming and end up losing."[105] His version of a worst-case scenario was much darker than the one presented by Taha Ramadan. Al-Duri told Saddam that Iraq should consider their adversary's interests:

> America, if it strikes, will not [conduct] a six-day strike, once it is convinced . . . nor [a] six-month strike. . . . It is possible that the United States will plan to be here three or four years. If it sees and remains convinced that the issue of Iraq will harm American interests in the region, then it becomes in America's fundamental interests in the region. Then it becomes in America's fundamental interest to enter in a world war, an international war, not a small war as if disciplining a little child, to go smack him with some airplanes and [go] back. This is a different opinion than that stating that they will come and do a quick strike and leave. . . . we will not allow them to do that to us.
>
> How does the United States see Iraq now? Since World War II no nation in the world has stood in the face of the United States and threatened it, except the Soviet Union, when the U.S. threatened it, then the Soviet Union threatened the United States back. The Soviet Union did not threaten the United States on its own, [it] responded to the United States threats. Now the United States has destroyed the Soviet Union. It is destroyed; you [can] see it disbanding, falling apart, the people and the military. That is the international situation. Now what is the outlook [in] the region?
>
> Since 1948 there has been a conflict between the Arabs and Israel, with the United States supporting [Israel]. . . . How does Fahd deal with the United States now? How does he see the U.S.? How does Hosni [Mubarak] deal with the United States? . . . Zayed . . . al-Khalifa . . . al-Hassan . . . Hussein? They see the U.S. as bigger than Allah! And they make the United States feel that it is bigger than Allah to them.[106]

It is difficult to judge how much influence al-Duri's version of history either reflected or influenced Saddam's view of the world or Iraqi policy in November 1990. However, after conflating the American threat to Iraq as a threat to all nations, al-Duri explained Iraq's unique advantage:

Bush is losing his mind, he is going crazy, and he can't figure out where this little country has come from and made such a bold move, [who would] want to do such a thing? He is wondering: Are they mentally stable? Are they crazy? Are they bluffing? Will they really fight or not? The United States is stunned . . . stunned! The whole world is stunned at the situation, but especially the Americans. They are not used to this, and have not seen this since the establishment of the American nation. . . . Since both World Wars I and II they have been masters, not one village was bombed, they were [only] hit in the far regions. The Japanese hit their port suddenly. So this is how the United States sees and understands the situation.

In my opinion, if the United States has decided through its analysis and the analysis of its friends and agents in the region, that Iraq will chase the oil and that if Iraq entered Kuwait then it will enter Saudi [Arabia], and other oil-rich areas, and that is the strategic policy. Then the United States will enter the war, it will enter a comprehensive war with us . . . and if it decides on that basis, then its chance is this month [November 1990]. Outside of this month it will not have a chance, or at least its chance will lessen significantly.[107]

Minister of Communications Latif Nayyif Jasim offered that, if the United States had initiated a war in the first few months, then "in the eyes of history" the Iraqis would not be considered martyrs. Immediately after the invasion of Kuwait, Jasim explained "the whole world wanted war, war, war, to save Kuwait." However, during the first month American power was insufficient for anything other than attacking "factories, command centers, and political centers. But now," he continued, "after three months of managing the worst crisis that has ever faced humanity on the face of the earth," Iraq would be considered martyrs of any United States action.[108]

Notes

1. Harmony media file ISGQ-2003-M0003629.
2. Extracts from the debates of the U.N. Security Council (provisional verbatim record, S/PV.2932, 2 August 1990). Lauterpacht, et al., *Kuwait Crisis,* 100. The so-called "Provisional Free Government of Kuwait" consisted primarily of nine junior Kuwaiti military officers hastily installed by Iraqi intelligence on 2 August 1990. The charade dissolved six days later after Iraq announced it had decided to annex Kuwait, and Saddam installed his cousin, Ali Hassan al-Majid (aka "Chemical Ali") as the governor. Chemical Ali was then replaced by Saddam's half brother, Barzan al-Tikriti, on 2 November 1990.
3. Harmony media file ISGQ-2003-M0003852.
4. "Saddam Hussein Address to National Assembly 7 August 1990," recorded speech broa-

dcast on Baghdad Domestic Radio Service [in Arabic] 1653 GMT, 8 August 1990, FBIS-NES-90-154, 9 August 1990, cited in Ofra Bengio, *Saddam Speaks on the Gulf Crisis: A Collection of Documents* (Tel Aviv: Tel Aviv University, 1992), 116–18.

5. Harmony media file ISGQ-2003-M0004608.

6. From a transcript of a 1990 meeting. The recording was transcribed in 1993 and with Saddam's hand written notes correcting and deleting some wording. Saddam did not expect ground action by the United States as a serious possibility in this early stage of the confrontation. Harmony document folder ISGQ-2003-00044897.

7. Cable from the American Embassy Baghdad to Secretary of State, 6 August 1990, Subject: "Main Points of Chargé's Meeting with President Saddam Hussein." (Declassified on 11 August 1999.) www.margaretthatcher.org/archive/displaydocument.asp? docid=110715 (accessed 22 August 2006).

8. Harmony document folder ISGP-2003-00026600.

9. Harmony media file ISGQ-2003-M0005325.

10. Harmony document folder IISP-2003-00036124.

11. It is difficult to determine from the Iraqi record what "a harsh way" means. One U.S. postwar investigation noted that the Iraqis "established more than two dozen torture centers" in Kuwait City during the occupation. The activities in these centers included the most gruesome forms of torture and abuse imaginable. See Summary of the Report on Iraqi War Crimes (Desert Shield/Desert Storm), U.S. Department of Defense (19 November 1992). For a compelling narrative of conditions in Kuwait during the occupation see Levins, *Days of Fear.*

12. Harmony media file ISGQ-2003-M0005325.

13. Ibid.

14. Ibid.

15. Ibid.

16. Harmony media file ISGQ-2003-M0003629.

17. Ibid.

18. Ibid.

19. Harmony media file ISGQ-2003-M0005325.

20. Hamdani, "From the Golan to the Collapse of Baghdad," 148.

21. Harmony document folder ISGP-2003-00026610.

22. Not surprisingly, almost all of the captured documents and testimonies associated with the Republican Guard downplay any incidents of looting, rape, or wanton destruction on the part of Guard soldiers that occurred during the first few weeks of the occupation. Western eyewitness accounts of this period give a very different account of events. See Martin Stanton, *Road to Baghdad – Behind Enemy Lines: The Adventures of an American Soldier in the Gulf War* (New York: Ballantine Books, 2003), 47–97; and Levins, *Days of Fear,* 114–71.

23. Harmony document folder IISP-2003-00043745. Many Ba'athists saw the Popular Army as an insurance policy designed to protect the ruling Ba'ath party from a military coup.

24. Ahmed Hashim, "Saddam Husayn and Civil-Military Relations in Iraq: The Quest for Legitimacy and Power," *Middle East Journal* 57, no. 1 (2003): 24.

25. Abbas Kadhim, "Civil-Military Relations in Iraq (1921–2006): An Introductory Survey," *Strategic Insights* 5, no. 5 (2006): 11.

26. Harmony media file ISGQ-2003-M0006909.

27. Harmony document folder ISGP-2003-00029600.
28. Hamdani, memoirs, 148.
29. Harmony document folder ISGP-2003-00029600.
30. Harmony document folder ISGP-2003-00029600.
31. Hamdani, "From the Golan to the Collapse of Baghdad," 146.
32. Harmony document folder NGIC-96-0528. This document was captured in 1991 during Operation Desert Storm. When Iraq officially annexed Kuwait on 8 August 1990, it renamed Kuwait City "Al-Kadhima."
33. Ibid.
34. Sharon Stanton Russell and Muhammad Ali al-Ramadham, "Kuwait's Migration Policy since the Gulf War," *International Journal of Middle Eastern Studies* 26, no. 4 (1994): 574. Interestingly, of the 2.4 million people in Kuwait in 1990, only 572,000 were Kuwaiti citizens. The majority of the population consisted of non-citizen labor including more than 400,000 of Palestinian descent.
35. Harmony media file ISGQ-2003-M0005373.
36. Harmony media file ISGQ-2003-M0006905.
37. United Nations, "Resolution 3036 as adopted at the 'Extraordinary Session of the Council of the League of Arab States,'" Cairo, 2 August 1990, in Lauterpacht et al., *Kuwait Crisis*, 293.
38. Letter from the permanent representative of Iraq to the United Nations addressed to the Secretary-General, 3 August 1990, in Lauterpacht et al., *Kuwait Crisis*, 293.
39. Harmony media file ISGQ-2003-M0006909.
40. Saddam summarized the proposal in a public radio address with "because the spark of war, if it begins, will burn many people and inflict many catastrophes. . . . I propose that all issues of occupation . . . in the entire region be resolved in accordance with the same principles, and premises to be set by the U.N. Security Council." To make this possible, U.S. and "other forces that responded to its conspiracy" will withdraw from Saudi Arabia, and "all boycott and siege decisions against Iraq shall be frozen." If Iraq did not receive a satisfactory reply to its initiative, Saddam promised that "the evildoers will regret their actions after they leave the region defeated, cursed, and humiliated." FBIS-NES-90-156 (FOUO)—Saddam Hussein, Speech on "Linkage," read by an announcer on Baghdad Domestic Radio Service [in Arabic], 1530 GMT, 12 August 1990, 13 August 1990, in Bengio, *Saddam Speaks*, 124–26.
41. Brigadier General Hamdani noted in his memoirs that it was well understood that the offer was "totally impractical, as well as not being genuine and it was mostly aimed at embarrassing the other Arab countries." Hamdani, "From the Golan to the Collapse of Baghdad," 151.
42. Harmony media file ISGP-2003-10151576.
43. Ibid.
44. Phebe Marr, *The Modern History of Iraq* (Cambridge, UK: Westview Press, 2004), 232. The letter is dated 30 July 1990.
45. Lauterpacht, et al., *Kuwait Crisis*, 64.
46. Ali Asghar Kazemi, "Peace through Deception: The Iran Iraq Correspondence," in Farhang Rajaee, ed., *Iranian Perspectives on the Iran-Iraq War* (Gainesville: University Press of Florida, 1997), 115.
47. Letter dated 14 August 1990 from the president of Iraq to the president of the Islamic

Republic of Iran. Lauterpacht, et al., *Kuwait Crisis*, 67. According to various discussions with his ministers in August 1990, Saddam sent letters to President Rafsanjani on at least five occasions (30 July and 3, 8, 14, and 17 August). See Harmony media files ISGQ-2003-M0004189) and ISGQ-2003-M0007111.

48. Harmony media file ISGQ-2003-M0007111.

49. This is probably Tahir Jalil Habbush al-Tikriti, then the director of the Iraqi Intelligence Service.

50. Harmony document folder ISGP-2003-00033136.

51. Harmony media file ISGQ-2003-M0007111.

52. Ibid.

53. The hostages were held at up to seventy strategic sites including dams, refineries, factories, and suspected weapons facilities. Central Intelligence Agency, "Putting Noncombatants at Risk: Saddam's Use of 'Human Shields,'" (Washington, DC: CIA, January 2003), 2.

54. Rumors and even civil lawsuits concerning British Airways Flight 149 continue to this day. The most persistent rumor, strongly denied by the British government, is that the aircraft was allowed to land, despite the invasion, in order to insert a special operations team into the Kuwaiti capital. There is no evidence in the Iraqi documents of this or any other suspicious activity. According to the commander of the 17th Brigade of the Hammurabi Division, the aircraft was actually trying to depart when his troops stopped it. Hamdani, "From the Golan to the Collapse of Baghdad," 146.

55. Harmony media file ISGQ-2003-M0004608. The speaker is unidentified, but is in a relaxed and direct conversation with Saddam.

56. Ibid. Iraqi officials hoped to split the Western members of the Coalition by favoring its long-standing relationship with France. Instead, this may have had the opposite effect, actually causing some French officials to take a harder line in keeping with its "role and rank" among the great powers. See David S. Yost, "France and the Gulf War of 1990–1991: Political-Military Lessons Learned," *Journal of Strategic Studies* 16, no. 3 (1993): 339–74.

57. Harmony media file ISGQ-2003-M0004608.

58. Although a part of the 1970 constitution, the 250-member Iraqi National Assembly was not seated until 1980. The electoral process for this body all but guaranteed that it was 100 percent Ba'athist. Its nominal constitutional function was to ratify or reject legislation forwarded to it by the RCC.

59. Harmony media file ISGQ-2003-M0004608.

60. See Levins, *Days of Fear*, 455–73. From 1990 through the fall of the regime, chapters of the Iraqi Friendship, Peace, and Solidarity Organization located around the world served in part as fronts for the regime's intelligence operations as well as outlets for information campaigns directed against sanctions imposed by the U.N. For an example, see Harmony folder ISGZ-2004-00028216.

61. Harmony media file ISGQ-2003-M0004608. On 4 November, Saddam publicly announced that he would free all the hostages if Japan or Germany, plus one permanent member of the Security Council, would say that they opposed military action against Iraq.

62. Harmony media file ISGQ-2003-M0003629. The remark attributed to President George H.W. Bush appears to be from "Remarks by the President to the Joint Session of Congress," 11 September 1990.

63. At the time of this conversation (20 September 1990), the U.N. Security Council had already passed seven resolutions against Iraq, ranging from condemnation to comprehensive sanctions and a blockade (UNSC Resolutions 660, 661, 662, 664, 665, 666, and 667). Harmony media file ISGQ-2003-M0003629.

64. Harmony media file ISGP-2003-10151576. It appears Saddam is referring to President Bush's announcement in late September 1990 of the Gulf Crisis Financial Coordination Group and various G-7 initiatives. However, Saddam was not above offering economic incentives to gain supporters. On 10 September, he announced on Baghdad TV that Iraq would, in the future, supply free oil to the Third World.

65. Harmony media file ISGQ-2003-M0003629.

66. Saddam was referring to the dramatic shift in Soviet Middle East policy, especially in relation to the United States, following the invasion. For example, on 3 August the Soviet foreign minister and the U.S. secretary of state issued a joint condemnation of the invasion; the USSR consistently supported the early UNSC Resolutions aimed at Iraq; and finally, the "new world order" statements emerging from the Bush-Gorbachev summit in Helsinki on 9 September seemed to link the approaches of the two superpowers against Iraq. Harmony media file ISGQ-2003-M0003629.

67. Harmony document folder ISGQ-2003-00045740.

68. Ibid.

69. Ibid.

70. Ibid.

71. Ibid.

72. Ibid.

73. Ibid.

74. Harmony media file ISGQ-2003-M0004609.

75. Ibid.

76. Ibid.

77. Ibid.

78. Ibid. Tariq Aziz identified the Gorbachev adviser as Alexander Yakovlev. Ironically, Yakovlev resigned within a year, after warning that hard-liners were plotting "a party and state coup."

79. Ibid.

80. Ibid.

81. Ibid.

82. Ibid. Tariq Aziz listed the Francophone nations as Senegal, Niger, Ghana, Mali, Morocco, Mauritania, Algeria, and Tunisia.

83. Ibid.

84. Iraqi frustrations with French and Russian duplicity continued for the next twelve years. After the collapse of Saddam's regime in April 2003, Tariq Aziz told a debriefer that despite significant under-the-table oil contracts, "France and Russia did not help Iraq, they helped themselves." See Woods et al., *Iraqi Perspectives Project*, 90.

85. Harmony media file ISGQ-2003-M0004609.

86. Ibid.

87. Ibid.

88. Ibid.

89. Harmony media file ISGQ-2003-M0004608.

90. Harmony media file ISGQ-2003-M0001716—State Command and Revolutionary

Command Council meeting, November 1990. By the beginning of November, there had been peace rallies in Amman, Tokyo, Paris, New York, Boston, San Francisco, and Los Angeles. Various delegations from Western countries (official and non-governmental) had made trips to Baghdad to negotiate for the release of their citizens, and many had made statements supporting negotiations over the Kuwait issue.

91. Harmony media file ISGQ-2003-M0004609.
92. Ibid.
93. Ibid.
94. Ibid.
95. Ibid.
96. Ibid.
97. Ibid. In addition to the Security Council resolution, Aziz noted that the United States was pushing to freeze Iraqi assets around the world. Naively, Latif Nayyif Jasim offered that, in response, Iraq could retaliate by passing its own "freezing law" that would "allow us to control their assets."
98. Ibid.
99. Ibid.
100. Ibid.
101. Ibid.
102. Ibid.
103. Ibid.
104. Ibid.
105. Ibid.
106. Ibid.
107. Harmony media file ISGQ-2003-M0004608.
108. Ibid.

Chapter VII

THE IRAQI PLAN FOR THE DEFENSE OF KUWAIT

Indications point to America winning the war; I say Iraq will win
the war. Yes, factories may be destroyed, let it be, the factories are
idle because of the sanctions anyway. We say to the Iraqis; this is
the way it is. Iraqi public opinion is to die rather than withdraw.
. . . Any retreat will mean a crushing; a despicable defeat on the
Iraqi and Arab level. Thus we have to deal with the issues in a
way Iraq will not come out defeated. If Iraq was a superpower
this would be easy.[1]

—SADDAM HUSSEIN

On 29 August 1990, the Director of the General Military Intelligence
Directorate (GMID) sent a "top secret and confidential" report to the presidential secretary entitled "The Essence of the Intelligence Service's
Opinion."[2] The document provided an "abridged [version] of the Directorate's
opinion about the probability of Western aggression." The major points were:

"The U.S. administration gave us clear instructions to withdraw our forces."
"The European countries showed great solidarity with the American administration."
"The goal of the colossal American military buildup is to try to bring
back the agents among the Gulf citizens . . . and re-alienate Iraq from
Kuwait. Logical analysis compels us to believe in the probability that
the West will impose an embargo by force, while continuing their
threat[s] to achieve their goal. If they fail (and this should take a [few]
weeks at least), or find it useless, they will resort to an expanded military aggression."
"The most dangerous probability is that the Americans might move forward
with their hostile agenda without waiting for the results of the embargo.
They might come up with many pretexts such as the fact that they are
not satisfied with the expected upcoming discussions with [U.N. Secretary General] de Cuellar as far as their requests for an unconditional
withdrawal."[3]

Based on this analysis, the GMID's rather weak recommendation was that Iraq "use our forces accordingly."[4] It is not clear from the report what the Directorate meant by "accordingly," but a few days later in a radio message to "the Iraqi people, faithful Arabs, and Muslims everywhere" Saddam made clear his determination:

> As for America's sea and air fleets, its armies and those who slipped with it into the abyss, they will only strengthen in us, the leadership, and the great people of Iraq. . . . The rattling of their weapons and the use of these weapons will only increase our determination to respond. . . . The motto of the faithful is: There is no going back; the believer will advance. . . . Under the banner of faith and jihad, many heads will roll—heads that have never filled with pride and whose owners never knew the path of faith. Let those who have been promised martyrdom have it.[5]

Preparing for the "martyrdom," as Saddam said, required significant action on the part of the Iraqi military. After a short period of consolidation, Iraqi ground forces in Kuwait repositioned and reorganized to shift their posture from offensive to defensive. Based on a review of Iraqi documents from the time of the initial Kuwait invasion, there are no indications of a serious military plan for invading Saudi Arabia as a part of the initial invasion.[6] Republican Guard forces deployed two divisions to the south of Kuwait City during the invasion, but these units were without significant logistics or even organic supporting units. As noted earlier, plans were developed as early as the third week of August 1990 for Republican Guard–led "raids" into Saudi Arabia (al-Khafji and Ras al-Mishab), but these appear to be contingency plans for spoiling attacks and little more. In early September, the Republican Guard completed a relief in place with divisions of the Iraqi Regular Army and units of the Popular Army. The Republican Guard divisions involved in the invasion pulled out of Kuwait into southern Iraq to act as the theater reserve and a hedge against Iranian adventurism. Moreover, the Guard's position astride the lines of communications likely served to help stiffen the resolve of the largely conscript army.

Part of Saddam's response to the Coalition force buildup was to increase the size of Iraqi ground forces. In what might be called a "pufferfish" defense, Saddam reached back to one of his lessons from the war with Iran—you don't have to be bigger than your adversary, just big enough to give your enemy pause.[7] In a May 1991 conference, Saddam recalled when, after failing to dissuade Iran from firing missiles at Baghdad, Iraq hit Tehran hard with Scud missiles. According to Saddam, "the Iranians said 'Wow! This is a Soviet rocket, I guess they are serious' . . . [the Iranians] said 'we never expected this from Iraq.'"[8] Saddam then explained, with more than a touch of hindsight, how, after the invasion of Kuwait, "we expected the entire world to react; we could not believe how long it took them to enter [the area]."[9] Saddam announced that in anticipation of a clash with the Americans, he ordered the creation of thirty-five new divisions; the purpose of which, according to Saddam, was to communicate with his new adversary, "as if we were saying to the enemy, 'We are warning you! Do not involve yourself.'"[10] In addition to expanding the Regular Army and Republican Guard, Saddam designated two new headquarters, the Jihad and Gulf Operations commands, to provide command and control for Kuwait and a second echelon defensive belt.[11]

Assessing the Coalition Threat

Anticipating potential military reactions to the invasion was the job of the GMID. In the days just after the invasion, its reports were full of rumors of immediate retaliatory strikes by the United States and its Israeli allies. Throughout late 1990, the Directorate issued reports, often without significant analysis, containing information collected by its attachés, agents, and "supporters" throughout the world. In one early August report, the director of military intelligence informed the presidential secretary that, according to information "supplied to us by the Palestinian Liberation Organization," the Israeli and American governments had completed retaliatory preparations. This operation would "depend mainly on air raids" and focus on missile facilities within one hundred kilometers of the capital. The report further warned that the operation might begin as early as 9 August "if a diplomatic solution is not reached."[12] But even with a flood of material from traditional intelligence sources, a significant stream of information came in the form of open source press reports.

According to a senior member of the regime interviewed in 2003, soon after the 1991 war Iraqi officials came to believe that in hindsight, their most accurate source of strategic and operational military intelligence was the Western press.[13] The officer recalled that a study of the issue conducted sometime in the mid-1990s determined that, if military plans appeared in Western newspapers such as the *Washington Post* before they were executed, the Iraqis could generally depend on the accuracy of the report.[14]

Regardless of the accuracy of the Western press on such matters, the problem for Iraqi officials was sorting through the sheer number of "credible" Western news sources. Speculation about possible Coalition military plans received a lot of coverage during the run-up to war.[15] In some cases, this wealth of "intelligence" often created a situation in the Iraqi intelligence services of mutually exclusive enemy courses-of-action. Having limited means to independently verify many of the reports, Iraqi intelligence officials often reported all of them equally. In other cases, significant intelligence—such as the western shift of Coalition forces after 17 January 1991—came too late in the war for the Iraqi military to make significant adjustments.

Judging from the complaints of Republican Guard commanders and the commander of Iraqi missile forces, even the flood of Western media reports could not make up for the paucity of tactical military intelligence provided by the GMID. One of the best examples of the intelligence problem was Iraq's inability to secure basic military maps. As Brigadier General Hamdani noted, the invasion of Kuwait was conducted primarily on tourist maps and unmensurated overhead imagery.[16] With the invasion over and the mission shifting to defense, the requirement for maps grew exponentially.

On 2 September, the Directorate of Military Surveying reported that it had only sixteen out-of-date planning maps (1:250,000 scale) of Saudi Arabia, and they were all distributed. The Directorate reported that it intended to develop smaller scale maps (1:100,000 and 1:50,000 scale), but it was hampered by a lack of a scale sample or adequate overhead imagery of Saudi Arabia. GMID correspondence from October 1990 indicates that deliveries of contracted French and Russian satellite imagery for the region were still incomplete.[17] Iraq's military intelligence officials sent an urgent call to its deployed attachés to secure maps of Saudi Arabia; however, because of the crisis, the attachés reported that military maps were no longer available—at least not to them. The Directorate was left to modify large-scale tourist maps for most of Saudi Arabia to satisfy Saddam's instructions to "prepare information regarding the vital targets [and] to prepare topographic information regarding Saudi [Arabia] to a depth of no less than 120–150 kilometers."[18]

Unlike many of the optimistic political assessments, most early intelligence assessments the GMID prepared did not minimize the challenges ahead. As early as 8 August, Directorate reports warned of the "qualitative and quantitative air superiority" of the developing international Coalition. The reports recommended developing defensive measures designed to survive the growing threat, such as digging trenches, using extensive camouflage, developing deception measures, and establishing alternative headquarters. Another report even proposed "transferring some of our aircraft outside Iraq to avoid sudden air strikes."[19] A sample of the early threat reporting and assessments from the Directorate include:

12 August: "We can conclude from the information and the hostile activities that the aggressive intentions against Iraq are . . . serious, especially when it comes to air operations at this time; it is more likely to carry out air operations prior to the other operations (land and naval)."

14 August: "The attack against Iraq will begin once the required preparations are ready and [the Americans] have exhausted all diplomatic means. If we consider that these troop concentrations are only a part of a large psychological warfare plan, which aims to force us to withdraw our troops, we might be taken by surprise; because accelerating events do not support the psychological warfare theory. Moreover, the volume of propaganda statements and the [scale] of American activities suggests the seriousness of the American administration to wage this war against Iraq."

23 August: Based on recent developments the GMID recommended that Iraqi forces "complete their protective procedures as soon as possible." Moreover, this report cautioned that "while the basic American forces consist of airborne troops, it is necessary that our defensive plan entail protecting important junctions and critical points located south of al-Basra." This was essential because "our troops will not execute large maneuvers during [combat] operations" to avoid "being exposed to air strikes." Finally the report recommended that Iraq focus its defenses along the main roads because "the enemy will make use of the main roads to penetrate in depth due to the harshness of the desert and moving sand."

24 August: In a report titled "The Possibilities of Hostile Operations," the GMID noted that "the number of conventional hostile land forces is insufficient to carry out operations against our troops." However, "while waiting for more troops to arrive, the Americans will mainly depend on [their] air superiority."

27 August: In a report titled "Analysis of the Probable Hostile Operations," the author reiterated the assessment that Coalition forces in Saudi Arabia exceeded the number required for such a threat.[20] Moreover, such a concentration of troops exceeded what is "required to stop or hinder a probable Iraqi advance towards Najd and al-Hijaz [Saudi Arabia]." The number of troops indicated an intent to attack Iraq's "vital targets [in order to] dismantle [its] political, economic, and military" capabilities.

29 August: "The continuous concentration of American troops in the region affirms the intention of the coalition forces to launch the attack. [T]hey believe that the embargo policy is insufficient as a political measure, also they will not wait for long before they attack."[21]

The Iraqi armed forces chief of staff, Lt. Gen. Husayn Rashid Muhammad, noted that Saddam involved himself in all aspects of planning for the defense of Kuwait—especially enemy scenarios.[22] His guidance was described as "continuous" and the meetings were recorded so that military staffs could "follow . . . [Saddam's directives] to the tiniest detail."[23] The general went on to note that "these directives were accumulated and consequently the picture became much clearer about the invasion and about [enemy] directions and possible routes."[24] According to Husayn, Saddam thoroughly considered all the possible Coalition scenarios: a sea landing, an assault through Wadi al-Batin, possible routes through Turkey, and even large airborne operations. However, in addition to potential Coalition actions, Husayn was personally concerned about a possible Iranian threat. In conspiratorial fashion consistent with the rest of the regime, Husayn said that he "was expecting a ferocious and direct attack [by] the Iranians. . . . I mean . . . what was the guarantee that the Iranians were not instigating the [war?]"[25]

Despite its limitations, the Iraqi military put its reconnaissance capability to good use during late 1990. It collected oblique photographic imagery, signals intelligence, and electronic air intelligence, as well as Side-Looking Airborne Radar (SLAR) images of Iraq's southern and western borders.[26] Most of the collection was only effective to a depth of forty kilometers into Saudi Arabia. Nevertheless, it was useful during early operations, such as al-Khafji. Iraqi signals intelligence, ground and air, was also actively trying to confirm the Coalition's order of battle and specific deployment scheme. Iraqi signals collection reports between late September and early November noted increasing levels of reconnaissance and tactical communications on the Coalition's part. The scale of the American reconnaissance efforts by 4 November convinced one Iraqi intelligence officer that "the mobilization of the [enemy] forces is almost complete . . . the enemy is now waiting for the time of the attack."[27] In another report a few weeks later, the GMID reiterated that "the American administration is serious about attacking Iraq, but we have not received any intelligence evidence that enables us to identify the right timing for the attack."[28]

Even if the timing was still a mystery, most Iraqi analysts had settled on the character of any potential Coalition attack. Regardless of attack direction, nearly every assessment of Coalition courses-of-action started and ended with airpower. Saddam would say after the war that, while he expected "the prewar aerial bombardment" to be intense, he did not expect it to continue "for a month and a half."[29] Regardless of its unexpected length, Lt. Gen. Husayn Rashid Muhammad reminded Saddam that because of his constant warnings about air attacks,

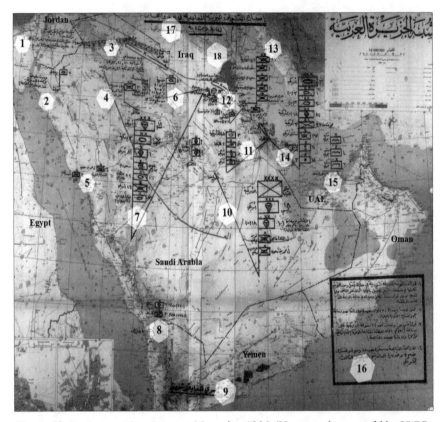

Figure 19. Iraqi enemy situation map, November 1990 (Harmony document folder ISGP-2003-00032772. With some exceptions, this map is generally accurate for Coalition order of battle as well as the "forward defense" deception being portrayed by the Coalition at the time. See Gary P. Melton, "XVIII Airborne Corps Desert Deception," Military Intelligence Professional Bulletin 17, no. 4 (1991): 43–45.)

we informed the soldiers and told them that the good fighter is the one who curls up and hugs his weapon, when the strike comes, and after the strike to look and see if there is movement . . . [they] protect themselves and their weapons [for] when the land attack occurs.[30]

First Priority: Prepare for a Long Air Campaign

According to the Republican Guard chief of staff, Saddam's priority mission for fall 1990 was to maintain a "wide dispersion and [keep] large distances between different sets of troops" in anticipation of large-scale air attacks.[31] Thus, Saddam "stressed the dispersion principle . . . the stacking up of supplies and taking care of air defense weapons."[32] In the decade after the 1991 war, the "dispersion principle" became the dominant characteristic of Iraqi military

1	Barrier System (Under Construction)
2	British 7th. *Additional comment: We have received information saying it moved to the east of Hafir al-Batin.*
3	10th Brigade [Saudi] National Guard. 41st, 42nd, 43rd, and 44th Mechanized Infantry
4	Egyptian 3rd Brigade. *Additional comment: A part of it moved to the northeast of Hafir al-Batin.*
5	Mohammed Bin S'aud Brigade and Medina Brigade
6	6th French Brigade. 1st Armored, 2nd Armored, 21st marine and 1st Para Battalions. *Additional comment: We have received information on the possibility of its move to the east of Hafir al-Batin (under follow-up).*
7	U.S. 18th Airborne Corps. 2nd Armored Division, 82nd Airborne Div (1st Brigade), Saudi Fayal Bin Zaki Brigade, 2nd Tank Battalion, 2nd Motorized Regiment, 24th Mechanized Brigade, and a "Fugitives" formation.
8	Bengali and Pakistani Brigades
9	Top Secret and Personal [Iraqi Classification]
10	U.S. Command Headquarters. 18th Airborne Corps, 101st Airborne Division, Saudi National Guard King Khalid Brigade and Mohammed Bin S'aud Brigade (Riyadh)
11	Unidentified American units including Ranger and Special Forces (Dhahran)
12	The Corps of the King S'aud National Guard. A mix of the Saudi 10th, 11th, 13th, 14th, and 15th battalions. A mixture of forces from Morocco, Syria, Egypt, and Abu-Bakr ?. Units of American artillery, Egyptian Mechanized, and other Saudi forces.
13	U.S. 24th Mechanized Infantry Division. The 1st and 20th Saudi National Guard brigades, and unidentified Brigade and forces from the Peninsula Shield Force
14	U.S. III Corps. 1st Armored Division, 2nd Armored Division, 82nd Airborne Division, 7th Infantry Division, 197th Mechanized Brigade, 11th Aviation Brigade, and the 18th Artillery Brigade
15	1st, 2nd, and 7th marine Brigades (units aboard ships)
16	(1) The Syrian armored division is still on the move; it is expected to be integrated mid next month toward the north of Hafir al-Batin. Taking into consideration they already have a brigade that arrived in full at the beginning of the crisis to the same area. (2) We have (11) Saudi Brigades that opened and we are still following-up on the size and opening of the other brigades. (3) A part of the 101st American airborne units have moved to (20) kilometers toward the area across from al-Wafra (in front of the 3rd Corps sector) and we are still following up. (4) The follow-up continues regarding the opening and arrival of the 3rd armored corps and the 7th (UI) corps related to the 3rd American Corps.
17	The Opening of the Hostile Land Forces in Nejd and Hejaz until 11/25/1990

Figure 20. Legend to Iraqi enemy situation map in Figure 19.

doctrine—regardless of service. As Saddam later recalled, "it was good of us that we were able to imagine this scenario even though it is unprecedented, and there is nothing like it . . . in military history. These events are not part of military history anywhere in the world—it is not part of it."[33]

Camouflaging the dispersed force was another critical activity for Iraqi forces during this phase. One general proudly noted that his fortifications were so concealed that "you could come to a site and you would not see anything . . . only if you whistle, then you would see [the soldiers] coming out."[34] Decoy armored vehicles were added to the mix to enhance the effectiveness of both the dispersion and camouflage. In October, the army chief of staff ordered more than 500 "deactivated or destroyed" tanks sent into Kuwait in order to "confuse the enemy" and oblige him to strike all possible targets.[35] The Iraqis tried to stimulate innovation in its camouflage program by sponsoring a suggestion campaign within various government departments, such as the Military Industrial Commission (MIC). A special scientific competition was even held to develop the most effective smoke for obscuration.

At Saddam's direction, the Iraqis conducted experiments on the utility of burning oil to obscure targets with smoke and of setting fires to "drag heat rockets" away from their targets. According to Saddam, the experiments with the smoke were a great success and created clouds rising to "500 meters where they could not see the plane."[36] He directed his subordinates to apply this technique to "the entire state," but especially around troop concentrations and "sensitive facilities."

In November, Saddam directed a scientific conference to explore ways to defeat American cruise missile technology. Some of the scientists present were skeptical about the potential to defeat a substantial number of stand-off weapons. Nevertheless, the conference produced various suggestions for smoke, camouflage, and creating "mirages" to fool the cruise missile guidance system. An unidentified representative of the Ministry of Defense, reflecting Saddam's optimism in such matters, reminded some of the skeptics working on these projects that "the West publishes great propaganda about these weapons, especially in the present. Therefore, many people would think that such weapons are undefeatable and they become depressed and frustrated. Actually, any weapon has its own points of weakness, to vanquish any weapon, it requires scientific, intelligence, and academic study [focused on] that weapon."[37]

Some in the Iraqi military were even confident that Iraq's forces could avoid satellite detection. According to the commander of the Republican Guard, his forces carried out large-scale satellite avoidance drills "day and night." They were confident that they were not observed by the United States because "we knew exactly the number of satellites charged with monitoring our movements." Moreover, he continued, "[we] knew the time during which each of the satellites would pass over our units [and] . . . therefore we were cautious."[38]

Additional passive air-defense measures included restricting the use of electronic communications. Lieutenant General Rashid recalled that Saddam went so far as to order the commands "not to use the phones . . . there were microwave phones and landlines, he prohibited us from using [them all], all messages were to be hand delivered through liaison officers."[39]

In the late fall, Saddam directed a series of live-fire test-ranges be built in order to test all of these solutions in a realistic combat environment.[40] According to Rashid, "[Saddam] said 'prepare a defensive site . . . exactly the same site as the one you [built] in Kuwait, the same soil, the same region' and [then] he told us to bomb it ferociously, as if simulating an enemy's attack and even more . . . and place items that are affected by the damages and then inspect and determine the percentage of damage."[41]

According to Rashid, they even placed animals inside the structures to test physiological effects. After subjecting the Iraqi defensive position to heavy attacks by air and artillery, they determined the percentage of damage as "very low."[42]

The III Corps commander later recalled that a follow-on demonstration called the "Resistance and Liberty Exercise" took place on 19 December and was attended by all the "corps, division, brigade, and unit commanders." They claimed that, "based on what we observed, we reached a conclusion that the digging in, underground preparations and mobilizations secured by proper deployment and along the front and middle minimizes the losses despite the heavy bombardment. . . . The outcome proved our defenses were adequate."[43]

Not surprisingly, commanders touted the results throughout their formations. According to the generals involved in the "experiments"—men whose personal survival was far less dependant on these structures than that of their troops—the results "raised the level of confidence" of soldiers in the Kuwaiti occupation force that they could survive any air campaign. One key task of these experiments was to perfect shelters that could survive a precision air attack. The shelter design, dubbed the al-Faw project, was to withstand a direct hit from a 250-pound bomb. In a postwar conference, Staff Lieutenant General al-Rawi recalled that these efforts provided "big results. When the enemy bomb[ed] one of the [command] shelters belonging to the Tawakalna 'Ala Allah forces, with a direct hit, while the commander and his advisors were there, nothing happened, because it was well fortified."[44]

Even after the war, Saddam was satisfied with the emphasis placed on preparing for the air campaign. In fact, as he would repeat during the next decade, the inability of American airpower to accomplish its objectives (as assumed by

Saddam or otherwise) demonstrated Iraqi spiritual, if not physical, superiority. In fact, Saddam often referred to the air campaign as a "prewar aerial bombardment." His emphasis on "prewar" was apparently meant to emphasize that only face-to-face forms of combat were worthy of the term "war."

Preparing a Naval Defense

On 17 September 1990, Saddam directed the commander of the Iraqi Navy to establish a "comprehensive plan" for defending Iraq's newly expanded maritime region.[45] Saddam approved the plan, with some minor modifications, on 3 October 1990.[46]

The naval defense plan emphasized mining, air defense, surveillance and reconnaissance, and a counter-landing component. Throughout planning, the disparity in naval capabilities between Iraq and the Coalition limited the options. Iraqi naval planners determined that their best weapon would be sea mines. In a postwar lecture, Iraq's senior naval officer noted that "it is well known that a mine is a preemptive weapon and the decision to use it [is] a political one. Indeed, when the leader president, may Allah preserve him, ordered the use of water mines in our just war of defense, it was considered a wise and just decision."[47]

The Iraqi Navy's problem in fall 1990 lay in the limited number of mines available to protect a greatly expanded coastline. By early November, more than 60 percent of Iraq's naval mines were already deployed, but the requirement kept expanding. Saddam ordered his MIC to rapidly develop and deploy an indigenous Iraqi mine. It is unclear how many mines they produced, but after the war the commander noted that "these [Iraqi] mines proved [their] lethality and effectiveness . . . they caused havoc within the enemy force." Altogether, the plans called for the Iraqi Navy to deploy "more than 1,300 mines of different types," across seven minefields.[48]

In a postwar conference, the commander of the Iraqi Navy pointed with pride to comments made about the effectiveness of Iraq's minefields in the memoirs of Coalition commanders, saying that, "during the epic Mother of All battles, this weapon [mines] was utilized effectively and successfully to disrupt the allies' plans in launching any operation from the sea. General [Peter de la Billière] mentioned in his biography . . . that the allied fleets faced a major peril, which was the mines embedded by the Iraqis."[49]

In addition to mines, the navy developed a series of defensive plans for a range of amphibious contingencies. One example was titled naval "Defense Plan Number One." This plan generally consisted of force protection measures and limited active defense activities. As with the other branches of the Iraqi military, the navy's planning priority was preserving the force. Its key tasks included:

Figure 21. Saddam inspecting naval mines. Iraq deployed more than 1,300 naval mines in the Gulf between September 1990 and January 1991. (Harmony document folder ISGZ–2004–026434)

- Spread naval force elements in order to absorb enemy air strikes.
- Constantly move air defense elements around so they do not become targets.
- Conduct surveillance and early warning from the sea.
- Prepare and operate underground command centers.
- If required, "plan to evacuate from the occupied islands of Qarwa, Maradim, and Faylakah. . . . Additionally, be prepared to pull out of al–Bakr and Al–Amiq port facilities."[50]

The counter-landing component of the plan was long on concept, but short on practical "how-to." The major components were:

- Challenge any troop landing using all available naval forces.
- Establish seven defensive minefields "in the shape of a bow" stretching from al-Khafji (Saudi Arabia) to al-Amiq (near the Shaat al-Arab).
- Plan to disrupt airborne attacks near coastal facilities.

- Plan to destroy Kuwaiti port facilities. Specifically, destroy the concrete platforms and destroy all support equipment associated with the port.
- Plan to use oil as a weapon. "By leaking petroleum as a weapon to confuse the enemy and pollute [his] ports [in order] to complicate the movement of enemy naval forces." The inventories of this weapon were Iraqi oil tankers, floating oil platforms, and Kuwaiti industrial facilities, where oil "could be directly pumped out" into the Gulf.[51]

Using oil as a weapon was a key component of the plan. A meeting of the General Command of the Armed Forces in Baghdad first discussed this concept on 17 or 18 September. Staff Rear General Admiral Hasan recalled during a postwar conference that,

> his Excellency [Saddam] had a proposal to consider the idea of using oil in the battle, on the ground and on the sea. . . . [Saddam] ordered the formation of a committee under the leadership of LTG A'mir Moham-mad Rasheed, director of military manufacturing and the oil ministry. The motive behind using the oil [was] to protect the troops from the influence of the enemy guided weapons.[52]

During a series of meetings in early October with petroleum and military engineers, the navy fleshed out Saddam's ideas for "oil in the battle." The overall operation, which would eventually go by the code name of "Project Tariq," had three distinct tasks. The first task was to use oil "in front of the troops" to protect them from air attack. The second task of the project was to use oil along the Kuwait coast and around Bubiyan Island. The third task was to create a large "oil stain" (spill) that would extend outward from the Kuwait coastline. This third project area was assigned to the naval command.

Saddam personally approved the details of Project Tariq. Those involved were directed to plan "without using any [documentation], in order to ensure complete secrecy."[53] The commander of Iraq's navy assembled a panel of experts including employees of Iraq's civilian oil industry. The naval task consisted of two parts. Part A was to pump oil from the shore-based pumping stations and the "industrial island" directly into the sea. The second part, known as Part B, was to pump oil from the tankers currently in Iraqi and Kuwaiti waters. For part A, Hasan recalled, "we assigned some generals and naval ranks by name to carry out the operation . . . they were trained by some oil experts without knowing the reasons behind [the training]."[54] Part B, involving the oil tankers, was more complex and required the building of "special systems" (modified pumps). Once the pumps were manufactured, they were installed on five tankers holding more than 535,000 tons of crude oil. The tanker captains were briefed "in complete secrecy" and told to "carry out the order whenever it is given . . . without any discussion or arguments."[55]

The Ground Defense Concept

Saddam clearly believed that airpower would dominate any confrontation involving the Coalition. Moreover, if there was going to be a ground fight it would be a conventional one, not unlike the recent war with Iran. The linear deployment of slow-moving forces, the construction of defensive fortifications, and the placement of reserves all hint at Saddam's expectations. Although the Iraqi records do indicate the kind of plans and level of effort they put into preparing for the ground defense of Kuwait, they do not indicate how much of this was in support of a strategic psychological campaign aimed at dissuading Western populations from supporting their governments' moves to attack. It appears that raising the specter of bloody battles in Kuwait was a part of Iraq's deterrence scheme.

During a 1 November meeting with his senior staff, Saddam emphasized an additional concept—urban operations. Referring to a potential battle for Kuwait City, and presaging discussions on the eve of the 2003 war, Saddam said his intent was "to affect their [the Coalition's] fighter, when their fighter comes knowing that we know [his] limitations he comes to fight us with a different morale."[56] In support of this concept, Saddam said he was "stressing the necessity of fighting within cities." He went on to say he "expected the fighting in the cities to take place with unfamiliar methods."[57] Saddam told his staff he was assigning Hussein Kamel as a corps commander under the supervision of Ali Hasan al-Majid. This new position was required because "when the fighting takes place with civilians who are militarily able, the fighting takes on a new form. It becomes important to encourage and cheer [them] on, because they are contained, so we must organize them in this way to allow for command and control."[58] Despite the apparent emphasis at the top, it appears that with the exception of coastal defenses near the city, there were few serious preparations for an urban defense of Kuwait City.[59]

The Regular Army corps staffs conducted most of the planning for defending Kuwait, which reflected a very conservative approach. A review of orders from this period suggests that the initial plan was a simple forward defense.[60] In triangular form, every division would put two brigades forward and keep one in reserve. This same structure was reflected in the brigade plans below them. For the most part, the frontline defense was static, reminiscent of the French Maginot mentality of 1939. The little maneuver planning that was done related to the division arrayed on the "second line" of defense in the center of Kuwait.

The best example is the position of the 5th Mechanized Division near the Kuwait International Airport.

Soon after deploying to Kuwait, the commander of the 5th Mechanized Division issued "Maneuver Plan No. 1" to his brigades and attached units. The 5th Division had deployed into Kuwait as a part of the Iraqi IV Corps' second line of defense.[61] The 5th Division's mission statement was simple: "Conduct an aggressive defense at all costs within the sector of responsibility and prevent the American enemy and forces allied with them from penetrating the borders."[62] The basic scheme of maneuver, was to create an "impenetrable set of strong points" to dissuade or ultimately to defeat any attack that penetrated the first line. Major elements of the "maneuver concept," as described in the 5th Division plan, included:

Detect and destroy the enemy at "maximum ranges using all weapons."

Fully understand enemy scenarios and prepare to counter them "without the need to await higher headquarters."

Units must be self-sufficient in all aspects "for at least one week, holding out under various threat condition, not leaving the position regardless of cost."

Retain the "maximum reserves, especially mechanized infantry and armor."

Hold key terrain in strength and "do not surrender it regardless of cost."

All reserves must be able to "defend from their hide sites while simultaneously prepared to leap into counterattack to destroy enemy troops that have succeeded in penetrating positions."

Hold road intersections and "nodes" in strength, "holding out and not surrendering regardless of cost."

Finally, "always remember that the enemy has new scenarios that we have no knowledge of."[63]

This order included an early military assessment of the "likely enemy scenarios." The scenario judged "most likely" was an American ground attack toward Kuwait City in two columns, one along the coast and the other bisecting Kuwait from its far southwestern border. Both American columns would conduct a link-up operation with a large airborne landing on Mutla Ridge just northwest of Kuwait City. The scenario judged "most significant" would be a large "air landing" on the Mutla Ridge, supported by a sweeping attack along the Wadi al-Batin following the Kuwait-Iraq border to the north and then east. A Marine landing north of Kuwait City near Bubiyan Island would support these two operations. Both scenarios, as well as many elements of the lesser three, were close to the so-called "one corps plan" developed by the U.S. Central Command Staff in October. This plan was ultimately rejected by the senior leadership in Washington because "success could not be guaranteed without an additional corps."[64]

During September and October, the Iraqi Army created the kind of trenches, bunkers, and minefields it believed necessary to hold its positions "regardless of cost." Notwithstanding their confidence in the defensive battle, Iraqi commanders were always troubled by the Coalition's operational agility. What if the enemy did not choose to face the Iraqi defense head-on? The III Corps commander described the challenge during a postwar conference: "We

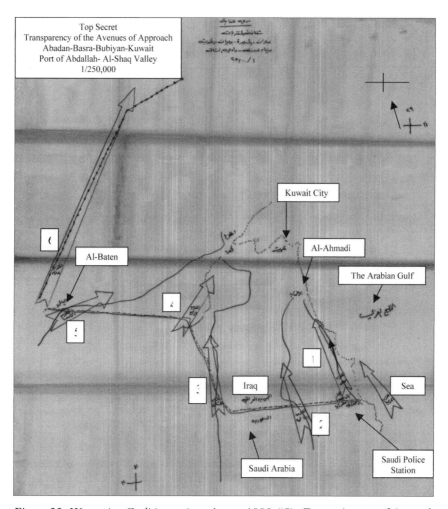

Figure 22. Wargaming Coalition options, August 1990. "Six Enemy Avenues of Approach Sketch," General Military Intelligence Directorate (Harmony folder ISGP-2003-00033503).

had to consider the possibility that the enemy could be air-dropping Marines. So we had to dedicate part of our resources to carry out that mission or we could face an airdrop deep against our bases. Thus, some of our formations would not deploy unless there was a grave necessity to do so."[65]

By late November, as the Coalition's capabilities and, more importantly, intentions became clear, Saddam directed a major shift in operational strategy.[66] On 18 November, Saddam issued a set of directives through the armed forces general command that shifted the form of the defense. The III Corps commander recalled the logic was to "derail the enemy's efforts" by positioning forces to the rear so that the new position would "come as a surprise to the enemy."[67] Iraqi forces in Kuwait shifted from a forward defense to a modified defense in depth with an eye toward more operational flexibility or possibly, though unstated, withdrawal. According to correspondence from the III Corps, Saddam directed the following:[68]

> "We must benefit from past experience gained during al-Qadisiyya [The Iran-Iraq War] with respect to all matters standing in our way at the present time."
>
> "We must make vicious circles of their calculations. Every time they calculate what is needed for the next action, we will surprise them with something else. This will force them into continual recalculation in light of our surprises and unconventional methods."
>
> "Our enemy's ambition grows as they see us engaged in classical calculations as if we were at war with Iran because classical calculations ensure unilateral superiority. We must reduce the front for the depth and reserve, establish a rear position, and retain cover troops with combat capability, but [the cover troops] is not the main position."
>
> "Give the position the chance for anonymity by making it unobservable from the borders and give the [artillery] the opportunity to deal with [enemy] targets."
>
> "We will go to positions that allow us to economize [our] force."
>
> "[We will use] lofty determination and swift effort to establish the new position as quickly as possible to gain time."

Based on this guidance from Saddam and updates from the GMID, the staffs in Kuwait drafted a list of "presumptions" about the Coalition's approach to the coming war:[69]

> "The enemy will rely greatly on his air assets, which he considers the main effort in any operation. He will target reserves, missile and artillery

positions, and headquarters. Enemy actions will include operations to land airborne forces at road junctures, headquarters, and areas which are suited to . . . the isolation of our troops."

"The enemy will use the indirect approach to achieve a rapid decision and avoid a large number of losses. This approach [rests] on exploitation of intense aerial strikes and a rapid advancement on primary axes to threaten as many of our troops as possible by attacking from unexpected directions and carrying out deep penetrations that target headquarters and road intersections."

"The enemy will conduct naval landing operations simultaneously with land and air operations to isolate as many troops as possible and support land operations from the sea with heavy artillery fire."

"The enemy will conduct attacks on secondary axis using Kuwait and Saudi troops and some multinational troops to fragment our effort and fix our reserves along this axis."

Iraq's III Corps took a number of actions in response to the commander in chief's new directives and the resulting "presumptions" about the enemy. Among the major changes directed were: forward defensive positions were reduced by almost half, infantry divisions were redeployed from a forward to a defense-in-depth posture, and infantry battalion task forces augmented by tank and anti-tank companies took up the front line as covering forces for the deployed brigades. Elaborate deception operations were instituted to both cover the new positions and hide the activity that might signal the change. As a corps commander later recalled, "Decoy tanks and camouflaged nets were deployed as a cover-up. Destroyed vehicles were used so that no tank would be withdrawn unless a decoy tank was placed in the same position. And no cannons were pulled away unless a decoy one was placed in that same position."[70]

Given the linear nature of the Iraqi deployment, it is reasonable to assume that similar changes occurred with the Iraqi IV, VII, and possibly, but to a lesser degree, I and II Corps. On 22 November, seven additional Regular Army divisions moved into the Kuwait theater from the north and east of Iraq to augment the new second echelon. This move, as one officer recalled, was more than just a military one, it "necessitated the re-evaluation of the [strategic] situation by the enemy, for it required a noticeable increase of their army elements in an environment of popular rejection of military solutions, and it also gave us some time to improve our defenses and fortifications."[71]

In addition to finalizing its defensive schemes, the Regular Army prepared for operations that would seem to indicate a degree of pessimism for the idea of holding onto Kuwait in the long term. On 8 December, Iraqi headquarters in Kuwait conducted a command post exercise for "conveying the sabotage orders." This was followed by additional training and an exercise on 13 December, when one of the Tariq Project trenches was set ablaze. The II Corps commander recalled the exercise with satisfaction noting that "the flames [above the oil trench] reached fifty meters high . . . and the smoke reached 400 to 500 meters . . . and it was black and thick."[72] The training and exercises were considered both a practical and a psychological success.

While the conscripts of Iraqi Regular Army prepared for operations in Kuwait and along the Saudi border, Iraqi's elite force was busy in southern Iraq making its final preparations. The Republican Guard's planning scenarios were simpler than their Regular Army peers. The Republican Guard signed over its last sector of Kuwait to the Regular Army on 7 September. It then repositioned to much the same location from where it launched the 2 August attack and settled into a series of loose defensive lines with general orders to act as the theater reserve and, if conditions permitted, a "striking force." Like the Regular Army, the Republican Guard also went through a rapid expansion in response to the Coalition buildup. During fall 1990, four brand new divisions, the Al-Nida, al-Quds, al-Abed, and al-Mustafa forces became part of the Guard's order of battle.[73]

According to the commander of the Republican Guard at the time, LTG Ayyad Fateeh al-Rawi, the mission of his command with regard to Kuwait's defense was threefold:

"Carry out operations to abort the enemy's attacks in the depth of the region."

"Carry out counterattack operations in the locations where the enemy was able to achieve a foothold."

Serve as "a reserve force and establish a confrontation line for the defense of al-Basra, if the situation required it."[74]

To support this mission, the staff developed three counterattack plans and one offensive plan during the fall of 1990. The counterattack plans were coordinated with the III and IV Regular Army Corps staffs in Kuwait and focused on "dealing with the enemy's possible attack routes." In a postwar discussion of the plans, the commander described with apparent satisfaction how "the possible areas that the enemy was likely to attack were obvious [so] we put the forces in these areas in order to enable them to mobilize and head to their targets in a speedy manner."[75] Postwar descriptions by Republican Guard tactical com-

Figure 23. Saddam meeting with Republican Guard officers, 31 December 1990 (Harmony document folder ISGQ-2003-00049397)

manders about the dispersion and the functional burying of armored vehicles to protect them from an enemy air attack, makes it difficult to see how the word "speedy" would describe any possible execution.

The only offensive plan for the Republican Guard at this point was mentioned briefly in a postwar discussion as an attack "into the heart of the enemy" by occupying al-Khafji and al-Mish'ab in Saudi Arabia.[76] Little written evidence of this concept has been uncovered; it was probably a variation of the contingency plans prepared in August. Perhaps the Iraqi III Corps eventually executed the al-Khafji portion of this concept on 29 January 1991.

On 23 November 1990, the entire Republican Guard leadership assembled around a large sand-table near al-Basra to review the preparations for war. A series of staff officers spoke in great detail to the assembled tactical commanders about the "enemy's capabilities, intentions, and expected plans." The officers then launched into a "comprehensive presentation of the whole defensive plan."[77] The presentation, according to one of the officers in attendance, was "not convincing and the presented numbers [of Coalition forces] were much lower than the real ones. The general plan presented for our defense was based on the environment of our war with Iran . . . as if we were going to fight the Iranian Army."[78]

The participants were asked, "If you were the American commander of the allied forces, what would be your plan of operations against the Iraqi forces

defending Kuwait?"[79] Most of the answers followed a predictable "how the Iranians would act" framework. Brigadier General Hamdani, as he would be again
in the 2003 war, was out of step with many of his peers. As a student of Western military "ideology and strategy," Hamdani suggested the Americans would
leverage airpower to an unprecedented extent and then attack "based on the
notion of [the] indirect approach."[80] In what could be a case of biased memory,
Hamdani recalled that the enemy commander, General Schwarzkopf, defined
the "crucial tactical target" as the destruction of Iraqi capabilities, which would
precipitate the liberation of Kuwait. Accordingly, Hamdani calculated that the
Americans would pound critical targets for not more than one month, sweep
up the Wadi al-Batin to isolate Iraqi forces from reinforcements, and then link
up with airborne and amphibious assaults in northern Kuwait to try to destroy
the remaining Iraqi forces. Hamdani did not receive a positive response during
the conference, but by January 1991, Iraqi intelligence assessments and Coalition deception operations were telling the same tale.

Air Force and Air Defense

The airmen's tone of optimism that characterized the days immediately
before invading Kuwait changed precipitously just after it, which was not a
surprise, based on the critical assessments of their performance. The air force's
clear-eyed understanding of the qualitative and quantitative differences between
Iraqi and American air forces stood in stark contrast to the overconfidence of
many senior army officers. For the most part, planning documents relating to
the Iraqi Air Force before 17 January 1991 focused on preserving the force, not
necessarily participating in the coming confrontation. During a postwar conference, a senior IAF officer captured a more mature version of what, in 1990, was
fast becoming Iraq's air doctrine, saying that "the main goal for our air force in
overcoming the allied countries . . . is [by] preventing him from destroying our
air force through the directional defense method, such as mobilization, cooperation with the air defense and through exploiting any opportunity to protect
our planes from being destroyed."[81]

The mission of the Iraqi Air Force on the eve of battle, while retaining the
language of the fight, reflected a degree of realism not present in many ground
force plans or intelligence assessments:

> The mission of the air force comprises two aspects. The first one is the mis-
> sion against the coalition countries by undertaking *limited* air interceptions,
> infiltration in *selected* targets and supply of air support to the ground and
> naval forces. The second aspect is the mission against the Zionist enemy
> by undertaking an air interception for a *total* reprisal with all available air

power capability including the ground attack planes to handle the maximum targets possible and to achieve a vindictive retaliation provided that the retaliation is immediate and as soon as possible within thirty-six hours once the order is issued in this respect [82] [Emphasis added].

The Iraqis carefully circumscribed missions against the actual threats (like the growing Coalition) with terms like "limited air interception" and "selected targets." In contrast, the second half of the IAF mission focused on a mission less likely to occur, but one that carried with it the potential for glory. Given the IAF's assessment of the deployed Coalition air forces, it is not surprising its focus would be on surviving to fight another day. In the section of their prewar assessment titled "Enemy's Potential," Iraqi Air Force planners described their enemy in almost admiring terms:

> The enemy could use his full air power in Saudi Arabia, the Gulf countries, the aircraft carriers, in Turkey, with participation from Israel, from multiple axes, in different directions, in large numbers of planes, with different consecutive and continuous waves, for long periods of time and around the clock, in all weathers, on several targets simultaneously, and he could use remote guided weapons [as well as] traditional weapons. . . . The enemy's quantitative potential and qualitative superiority compared to our potential accounts for a proportion of one to four in favor of the enemy when quantitatively comparing the force of the interceptors, and a proportion of one to eight in favor of the enemy, when qualitatively comparing the force of interceptors. The coefficient of general superiority amounts to more than one to twelve in favor of the enemy, when making a general comparison. [83]

Enemy superiority ratios notwithstanding, the air staff in Baghdad did develop a series of seemingly daring concepts between September and November 1990. According to Iraqi after-action reviews, only a few of these concepts ever matured into a plan and only one was attempted during the war. That operation, a high-risk mission to strike Saudi coastal oil facilities (Ras Tanura and al-Baqiq) will be discussed in a later chapter. The contingency concepts included: [84]

> Air strikes on Gulf desalinization plants: Although this target set was eventually judged to be inappropriate for air strikes, planners developed strike plans for the Saudi Arabian plants at Jubayil, Khobar, and

al-Khafji. The Iraqi planners calculated that they would lose 50 percent of their aircraft and subsequently judged the mission "economically worthless compared to the expected damages which will be incurred by our sophisticated ground attack planes."

Air support to Iraqi naval operations: This mission was planned, approved, and prepared (i.e., crews briefed and weapons distributed). Final planning was completed in late 1990 and the mission was placed in an "on-call" status as of 10 January 1991. The plan called for the Iraqi Air Force to "handle the naval landing ships" of any amphibious task force landing in Kuwait. The concept required daylight "waves" (eight to ten aircraft) of Mirage F-1, Sukhoi-22M4, -24, and -25 aircraft carrying a mix of radar-, laser-, and TV-guided air-ground missiles. The captured document does not include an estimate of Iraqi losses.

Air support to operations in defense of Kuwait: Given the dangerous nature of low-altitude operations in the vicinity of Coalition ground forces, air planners limited this mission to ten Sukhoi-25 airplanes. Air-to-ground ordnance for this level of support was judged sufficient for ten to fifteen days of operations. The planners did not want to use the "rest of the advanced ground attack planes since they are dedicated to other [strike] duties." The concept's bottom line recommendation was that Iraq should "avoid the use of ground attack planes for the [ground] support duty except in emergency cases and only after the first phase of the adversary aggression . . . and [not] until the direction of the adversary ground attack is determined."

Air support to Iraqi offensive operations into Saudi Arabia: This concept was discussed with the minister of defense and the chief of staff of the Army as early as 1 September 1990. The basic idea had two phases. First, air support to Iraqi ground units "up to twelve kilometers south of the international borders with Kuwait." The second phase would "be up to the logistics target (Dhahran City)."[85] The plan assumed that attacking Iraqi troops would be exposed to enemy airpower from their western flank and from enemy naval power on its eastern flank. The planners concluded that under such circumstances, the Iraqi Air Force could only maintain its strength while supporting such an operation for a short time. Accordingly, they recommended that "there should be planning for making the joint ground-air battle quick and sudden and to have our force work by night to minimize the effect of the adversary air force."

"Plan for handling the aircraft carriers": This was less a plan than a study to confirm what the Iraqi air planners already knew about the American carriers: "we cannot handle them because they are outside the radius of operation of our planes." The odds of the Iraqi Air Force defeating an aircraft carrier's "very intense" 350-kilometer protective screen were judged to be limited. This was due in large part to the air force's "inability to achieve surprise," the ships' "sophisticated weapons jamming," and the fact that "the naval operation [area] does not offer us any chance for maneuver." Nevertheless, the planners determined that if they were ordered to try, "the best way to disrupt the operation of the aircraft carrier" was to use eighteen Sukhoi-22 M4 planes carrying twelve C28L [Kh-28] missiles, four Mirage F-1 planes carrying AIM-39 missiles, and twelve Mirage planes carrying AS-30 missiles. Of the thirty aircraft required for the mission, "only twelve of them will reach the target and [these] won't come back after their duty is over." Moreover, the study continued, "the loss of thirty-four advanced ground attack planes to disrupt one aircraft carrier out of [the] nine carriers mobilized by the enemy in the region was ineffective."

Plan for "Duty 66": "Duty 66" was the code word assigned on 25 November to an IAF mission to "target some cities in which some important commanders and officials were present." The summary of the "Duty 66" mission does not specify the cities or the names of the "important commanders," except to say that with the exception of Riyadh, all the cities were outside the combat radius of Iraqi aircraft. The operation was considered "high risk" because of the need to conduct air-to-air refueling, the inability to achieve surprise, and the lack of detailed information on the locations of the individuals to be attacked.

Other operations considered but not planned in detail were strikes on the seven largest Saudi airports, operations to interdict "adversary helicopter drops," and battlefield illumination operations over Kuwait during any ground fighting.

The operation that the Iraqi Air Force is most remembered for in the West, evacuating its aircraft to Iran, appears to have had little, if any, preplanning. The only mention before late January 1991 of the evacuation was in a GMID intelligence report dated 6 August. This report assessed the strong probability of "enemy troops and the probable foreign intervention" as a result of the Iraqi "liberation" of Kuwait. Based on this likelihood, the report's authors asked the command to "consider the idea of transferring some of our aircraft outside Iraq to avoid sudden air strikes."[86] It seems unlikely that Saddam would have authorized such a plan during a time when he needed all of his military potential to execute his "pufferfish" defense.[87]

In sharp contrast to his air force, Saddam apparently had high expectations for his air defense forces. The standing mission of the Iraqi air defense forces to "provide the air defense of the Iraqi airspace and the defense of the civil and military vital targets, strategic projects, and ground units," did not appreciably change after the invasion of Kuwait. At the time of the invasion, the Iraqi air defense protected strategic headquarters (8 military), very important headquarters and projects (21 military), and 135 important headquarters and projects (96 military).[88] In the months before the war, Iraq's air defense staff dedicated its efforts to expanding the air defense to cover new headquarters in the new nineteenth province.

The prewar distribution of air defense assets reflects not only the Iraqi planning priorities, but also something about the expectation of the enemy. Iraq's air defense forces had seven priorities:[89]

"Deploy six brigades of Iraq's most capable defense systems (SA-2, SA-3) to protect Baghdad, Project 777 [nuclear research facility], Project 922 [production facilities for sarin, mustard gas, and VX chemical weapons] military manufacturing facilities, fuel and electric facilities, and, the phosphate complex in al-Qaim [used for the production of yellow cake from 1984 to 1990]."

"Six SA-6 missile battalions augmented the manufacturing facility defense, defense of Project 777, and the al-Waleed Air Base (near Jordanian border)." Three battalions were assigned to "the Republican Guard headquarters in al-Basra."

"The four Roland missile battalions were divided between vital military and civilian headquarters. Four batteries of Roland missiles were assigned to protect airfields and the Mutla Ridge in Kuwait."

Approximately twenty (SA-7) missile batteries were divided between "vital projects (priorities one and two) and ground units in Kuwait and al-Basra."

Kuwait's HAWK missile units were split: "One battery to the Project 777 site and one battery to defend the Mutla Ridge in Kuwait."[90]

The thirty-nine radar-guided anti-aircraft artillery (37-mm) battalions were "divided among the vital sites as well as air fields in Iraq and Kuwait."

The thirty-six non-radar-guided anti-aircraft artillery (all calibers) battalions were "deployed to ground units."

In addition to the asset reallocation, the Iraqis added a fifth air defense sector—Kuwait. The new sector would control various warning control battalions, thirty-eight visual observatories along the southern border, and fourteen radar systems of various types. In the days before the air campaign began, the air defense sector commands completed work on all of the alternative command centers and backup wire communications means.

For all of its challenges, the Iraqi air defense force had a unique legacy in Iraq's military confrontations with the United States. In the nearly thirteen-year confrontation, the air defenders were the alpha and omega of the regime's conventional defense. At 0230 on 17 January 1991, the air defense command sent the first message to Baghdad that "enemy planes violated our airspace." More than twelve years later, at 1600 on 8 April 2003, the command sent what was probably one of the last reports with "the enemy continues to violate the sanctity of our airspace."[91]

Surface-to-Surface Missile Forces

In 1998, LTG Hazim Abd al-Razzaq al-Ayyubi, former commander of the Iraqi surface-to-surface missile (SSM) corps, published a memoir entitled *Forty-Three Missiles on the Zionist Entity*, which described in considerable detail the preparation, planning, and execution of Scud missile operations during Um Al-Ma'arik. His account is surprisingly candid and generally consistent with captured Iraqi documents on the subject.[92] According to al-Ayyubi, the planning for the eventual use of Iraq's Russian-made Scud and modified-Scud missiles (designated by Iraq as al-Husayn missiles) in the 1991 war actually began in October 1988.[93] Over a two-year period, al-Ayyubi and his staff developed a fixed and mobile missile capability to strike "industrial targets in the Zionist entity, if it [Israel] attacked our military and industrial installations."[94] Anticipating a preemptive attack, Iraq's SSM force expended an extraordinary amount of its limited resources to support tasks such as enhancing air defense of missile sites; securing redundant communications; and most importantly, camouflaging, concealing, and stockpiling missiles and associated equipment.

As tensions rose in early 1990, the best of the Iraqi SSM force deployed to the western desert and oriented on targets in Israel.[95] Frequent rumors of Israeli preparations for a surprise attack kept them busy throughout the summer. Honing skills they would soon use, Iraqi missile brigades rehearsed mobile launch procedures during late July, but were not part of the invasion of Kuwait. Instead, in the eyes of Iraq's leadership, they performed the critical role of guarding Iraq's back. In his memoirs, al-Ayyubi noted that he was not informed of the invasion plans, but was on alert in response to what turned out to be part of the invasion's deception plan.

In the days just after the invasion of Kuwait, the 223rd and 224th Missile Brigades, already deployed in Iraq's western desert, readied their equipment, strengthened their air defenses, and integrated the plans "for missiles with chemical warheads" in anticipation of a "Zionist" response.[96] Within a few weeks, the mission expanded and, like his colleagues in the Republican Guard, Regular Army, and air defense forces, al-Ayyubi had to reorganize his force. The new mission required supporting not only the traditional missile operations in the west, but also missile and rocket operations in the south oriented toward Saudi Arabia. On 16 August, Iraq established what it called the "Missile Control Center" out of the headquarters of the 225th Missile Brigade and deployed it to Kuwait.[97] This center would be responsible for all missile operations in support of the southern sector as well as locally deployed corps headquarters. The challenge for this headquarters, as it had been for the Republican Guard during the invasion, was a severe lack of detailed maps or of any useful information on enemy troop locations. As was the case for many in Iraq's military, the missile force staff had never envisioned targeting anything outside of Israel or Iran. Once again, much of the early mission planning was conducted on tourist maps.

Iraq's missileers spent most of the autumn perfecting their camouflage techniques as well as reducing the time required to reposition, prepare, and fire a missile. These "dry-run" operations ended with test firing an al-Husayn missile (modified Scud) on 2 December. On 7 January, al-Ayyubi met with his brigade commanders and finalized their respective missions. On the 8th, he received specific instructions "about the special weapons." In Iraqi military jargon, the phrase "special weapons" was commonly used to refer to chemical or biological munitions. Saddam ordered the special weapons to be deployed in such a way that they "would be ready to use the moment a pertinent order is given, or in the event of a massive strike against Iraq."[98]

A prioritized set of targets, based on long-standing intelligence estimates as well as Saddam's new directives, was completed in early January. Target area priorities in Israel were the cities of Tel Aviv and Haifa. In Saudi Arabia, the priority was American troop concentrations in Dhahran, Dammam, al-Jubayl, and Hafir al-Batin. A major secondary Saudi target included the capital, Riyadh. On the eve of the war, Saddam personally made clear to al-Ayyubi that conventional weapons would be the first response option in case of a Coalition attack.[99] In case this last piece of guidance changed, Saddam dedicated a trusted bodyguard to manage a special code word communication system with its own dedicated radio and phone network to ensure communication with the missile commander.

Iraq's missile program would remain a source of great pride for the regime after the war. The fact that the regime, not known for publicly discussing its military capabilities, allowed publication of the commander's memoirs in 1998 is strong evidence of this fact. The missile commander recalled in his memoirs that "for the first time in history, the Zionist entity was now within the range of an effective weapon held by the Arab hands of the valiant soldiers of Iraq. . . . I wished that at least some Arabs, both on the popular and official levels, were with us as we stood ready to execute our mission. . . . Had this been the case, the Zionist entity would have backed down and submitted to Arab will."[100]

Unconventional Preparations

The Iraqi regime developed, deployed, and appeared prepared to use two major unconventional capabilities in the looming conflict with the Coalition. The first was WMD, specifically, but not limited to, chemical weapons. The fact that Iraq had recently demonstrated a willingness to use chemical weapons (against Iran, 1984–87) and threaten their use (against Israel in 1990) was significant in the minds of operational and strategic decision-makers in the Coalition. A U.S. intelligence estimate from 15 January 1991 put the threat bluntly: "we have strong indications that Iraq is prepared to use chemical weapons in any conflict with U.S. forces over Iraq's invasion of Kuwait."[101]

The second unconventional defense was the use of so-called fedayeen to conduct commando and terrorist operations in the region, and if necessary, around the globe. In some cases, fedayeen operations were associated with or were part of existing groups affiliated with Iraqi Intelligence. In other cases they were newly formed teams of volunteers designed for autonomous action. An Arabic word, *fedayeen* means "one that is ready to sacrifice his life." As translated, it is most commonly used in association with the Iraqi organization founded in 1994 known as "Fedayeen Saddam." At the time of the 1991 war, however, fedayeen referred to passionate volunteers willing to conduct paramilitary operations best described as "very high risk." Some Iraqi documents indicate that at least some of these operations included plans for suicide missions.

As it turned out, neither the threat nor use of chemicals or fedayeen had any effect on the outcome of the 1991 campaign. It is still difficult to determine the degree to which deterrence, interference, or ineptitude played a role in this failure. However, more than any other capabilities, these two would come to dominate the operational and strategic friction between Iraq and the United States until the fall of Saddam's regime in 2003.

"SPECIAL WEAPONS"

One of the most significant issues for U.S. policy makers and military planners during the buildup to war was the implications of Iraq's WMD arsenal.

Therefore, it should be no surprise that the potential for similar retaliatory use by the United States also concerned Iraqi military planners.

Iraqi leaders were no strangers to the use and deterrent effect of WMDs. In the two years between the end of the war with Iran and the invasion of Kuwait, the priority for Iraq's WMD programs was simple: Speed up the program. In a 1989 letter to his half brother Saddam, Barzan Ibrahim al-Tikriti argued against those in the regime who advocated abandoning Iraq's nuclear and missile programs,[102] writing, "With regard to military industrial and nuclear power . . . we have to hurry in order to reach the point through which we can completely achieve the deterrence objective. Moreover, we have to concentrate on producing weapons according to their importance as identified in the [Iran-Iraq] war. [Because] we are in a constant race with Iran and Israel . . . to achieve the objective we want, which will in turn enable us to defend our sovereignty and independence . . . before being attacked or becom[ing] subjected to a conspiracy."[103]

Early the next year, Saddam publicly threatened that if Israel dared to "strike at any [Iraqi] metal industries . . . I swear to God that we will burn half of Israel."[104] The proximate cause of Saddam's threats against Israel was the subject of some debate. Most Western analysts now believe it represented an attempt by Saddam to deter Israel from reprising the successful 1981 air strike on Iraqi's nuclear reactor, but this time against its military industries.[105] Whether Saddam's concerns were borne out by the facts on the ground in 1990 or not, they were a consistent part of his long-term calculations. To understand the central drive to protect his nuclear investment, one need only consider what then-vice president Saddam told a group of military officers in 1978:

> when the Arabs start the deployment [atomic weapons], Israel is going to say, "We will hit you with the atomic bomb." So should the Arabs stop or not? If they did not have the atom, they will stop. For that reason [the Arabs] should have the atom. If we were to have the atom, we would make the classical [conventional] armies fight without using the atom. . . . [If] they said, "We will hit you with the atom." We will say, "We will hit you with the atom too. The Arabic atom will finish you off, but the Israeli atom will not end the Arabs."[106]

Even after a significant amount of study, the question of how close Saddam was to a nuclear device on the eve of the 1991 war remains unclear. According to postwar International Atomic Energy Agency (IAEA) analyses, Iraq was possibly on track to develop a nuclear weapon by the end of 1992. While the regime did go on a "crash" development program after the Kuwait invasion, it did so with considerable caution. Sometime in late September 1990, the infamous nuclear weapons proliferation network run by Pakistani scientist A.Q. Kahn offered to provide Iraq with "project designs for a nuclear bomb." An IIS staff officer reviewing the Kahn proposal thought the offer was too good to be true. He prepared a memorandum stating that, because of the "known policy of entrapment adopted by the opposing parties," Iraqi Intelligence should require that Khan provide a "sample of the detailed [nuclear bomb] diagram and its calculations" before proceeding. Apparently the start of the war three months later disrupted any follow-up and ended a potential shortcut to Iraq's development of an atomic bomb.[107]

The logic of which side in the Arab-Israeli standoff could withstand significant losses extended to the standoff with the United States following the invasion of Kuwait. In a November 1990 discussion with his senior advisers, Saddam restated privately what he had recently hinted at in the open media:

> We will hit them [the Coalition] with everything. The Americans asked me themselves on American TV. They said; "Are you going to use chemicals, atomic, and whatever else?" I said to them, "First of all we do not have atomic weapons and if we did we would not be ashamed to say it, but in all scenarios, we will not give up Iraq." . . . But if we wanted to use chemicals, we will beat them down. . . . We have discovered a method where the destructive ability is 200 times more than the destruction ability for the same chemical type that we used against Iran . . . we have superiority in the chemical and in the biological weapons. In the world there are only two countries on our level or maybe one or maybe none in regards to the quantity and quality. We have biological weapons that can kill, even if you step on it forty years later.[108]

Bombast aside, Saddam's challenge with regard to his WMD capability was that he needed a way to deter his enemies, regional and international, without exposing Iraq to preemption. Preemption by Israel was, to many Iraqi leaders, a matter of when and not if. As the prewar threats and rhetoric heated up, Israel was not the only perceived source of a WMD threat to Iraq.

According to the commander of the Republican Guard in 1990, the potential for the United States to use WMD either preemptively or in retaliation was a serious planning consideration.[109] The Iraqis developed and partially exercised an elaborate civil defense plan for the evacuation of Baghdad in case "of a nuclear or weapons of mass destruction [attack] by America or its allies."[110] It is unclear if this contingency plan was in reaction to the belief that the United States would retaliate with WMD for any Iraqi use of WMD or if the Iraqis actually believed a preemptive WMD strike was part of an offensive Coalition war plan. At a purely military level, given Iraq's recent experience with Iran, some of this planning was simply normal defensive activity when faced with an adversary possessing "special weapons."[111] In a discussion recalling the planning considerations for the defense of Kuwait, Commander of the Republican Guard at the time Lieutenant General al-Rawi stated, "We also called in the Chemical and Biological Weapons Commander and requested that he give us a plan to defend against a nuclear and biological attack. [A]s it turned out, the American forces had within their arsenal [in Saudi Arabia] Pershing missiles which have nuclear warheads. We studied these missiles and their effects carefully and decided on a wide deployment."[112]

While the Iraqi military was considering the detailed implications of WMD use, the senior regime's inner circle seemed almost oblivious to the same. In a surprisingly casual dinner conversation recorded sometime in early January 1991, Saddam and his senior advisers discussed the potential use of WMD in the coming battle:

Saddam: I want to make sure that—close the door please [door slams]—the germ and chemical warheads, as well as the chemical and germ bombs, are available to the "concerned people," so that in case we ordered an attack, they can do it without missing any of their targets.

Husayn Kamil: Sir, if you'll allow me. Some of the chemicals now are distributed; this is according to the last report from the Minister of Defense, which was submitted to you sir. Chemical warheads are stored and are ready at air bases, and they know how and when to deal with, as well as arm these heads. Also, some other artillery machines and rockets missiles are available from the army. While some of the empty "stuff" is available for us, our position is very good, and we don't have any operational problems. Moreover, in the past, many substantial items and materials were imported; now, we were able to establish a local project, which was established to comply with daily production. Also, another bigger project will be finalized within a month, as well as a third project in the coming two to three months that will keep us on the safe side, in terms of supply. We, Sir, only deal in common materials like phosphorus, ethyl alcohol and methyl—[interrupted].

Saddam: Etc. . . this is not important to me.

Husayn Kamil: So, Sir, regarding the germs and [he pauses]

Saddam: And the chemicals.

Husayn Kamil: No, we have some of the chemicals available—[interrupted]

Saddam: So, we qualify that the missiles, by tomorrow, will be ready on the 15th.

Husayn Kamil: Sir, we don't have the germs.

Saddam: Then, where are they?

Husayn Kamil: It's with us.

Saddam: What is it doing with you, I need these germs to be fixed on the missiles, and tell him to hit, because starting the 15th, everyone should be ready for the action to happen at anytime, and I consider Riyadh as a target.[113]

This conversation continued with a review of the details of storage, delivery method, and the various "doomsday" command and control options available.[114] Saddam and his advisers discussed additional targets such as Jeddah, and "all the Israeli cities, all of them" as well as growing American force concentrations. Saddam offered a hint as to what criteria he might apply for WMD use when he commented, "Only in case we are obliged and there is a great necessity to put them into action."[115] Captured Iraqi documents support the notion that physical preparations were indeed made to use chemical weapons even as release procedures were being developed. In early January 1991, operational distribution of chemical weapons, preparing "special warheads," and the precautionary movement of chemical munitions were significant priorities.

One document gives some indication of the scale of Iraq's prewar WMD preparations. Several documents indicate a significant effort was made to disperse Iraq's WMD stockpile before Coalition air strikes could destroy it. For example, the al-Muthanna storage complex was a particular concern because, according to a defense ministry memorandum, it was "one of the strategic targets which might be attacked; [and] this will affect the movement of the munitions during the battle. We suggest that you receive the munitions and store it in areas near expected fields of operations to secure its movements whenever we need to use it and to avoid massive contamination near Baghdad, if it were hit or destroyed during the battle."[116]

The scale of the chemical weapons dispersal task was not trivial. According to this same memorandum, the Muthanna required more than 120 trucks to move the 1,232 aircraft bombs and 13,000 artillery shells filled with mustard agent. Moreover, 8,320 Grad rockets (122-mm) filled with nerve agent had to be moved, in addition to the examinination and securing of 25 "special warheads."

Despite the regime's capability, plans, and preparations to employ WMD, it never did. The reasons were not documented. The most plausible explanation remains that Saddam was deterred by implied and explicit Coalition threats of "significant" retribution if chemical or biological weapons made an appearance. Despite his public pronouncements to the contrary, there is no indication that Saddam was willing to martyr himself or his regime in defense of his Kuwait policy.[117]

COMMANDOS, FEDAYEEN, AND OTHER "ARAB FIGHTERS"

At the other end of the capabilities spectrum from Iraqi WMD were the special forces paramilitary forces, fedayeen (commandos), and volunteer Arab "fighters." The use of special operations forces or paramilitary intelligence commandos as a part of a conventional military campaign is a commonly recognized, though not always acknowledged, facet of most modern military campaigns. Saddam's military campaigns were no exception.

Iraqi intelligence agents, operating out of embassies and commercial interests throughout the world, clearly had the capability to conduct paramilitary operations. One such example occurred during the 1978 fratricidal warfare between Palestinian factions. A hit team from one Palestinian faction tried and failed to assassinate the Iraqi ambassador to France. The bungled operation resulted in a hostage crisis at the Iraqi embassy in Paris. As Saddam recalled a short time later, saying, "We have issued only one order so far and that we asked the comrades in Paris not to let the perpetrators escape alive and [to] kill them even if that means killing them while they [are] in the custody of the French police. One of the comrades was shot dead by the French police as he tried to approach one of the perpetrators [who] were in the custody of the French police."[118]

A more conventional example came during the invasion of Kuwait. Iraq tried, with limited success, to integrate its military special forces and intelligence operations into its Republican Guard blitzkrieg. During late July, it was reported that Iraq had infiltrated a significant number of intelligence operatives into Kuwait City. In addition to giving some life to the "republican revolution" cover story, these agents were to conduct link-up operations with heliborne special forces on the morning of the invasion and to seize the royal family and key facilities.[119]

During the buildup to the 1991 war, the regime engaged in a range of activities in keeping with the expected norm. Iraqi commando teams were designated to kill the deposed Kuwaiti royal family, who had taken refuge in

Saudi Arabia. Moreover, the Iraqis prepared plans for a range of Iraqi Intelligence Service (IIS) operations in overseas locations directly and indirectly related to the Coalition assembling against Iraq.

In addition to the "professional" forces described above, Iraq developed a capability that could be characterized as "highly motivated amateurs." Through its sponsorship of various regional factions, revolutionary movements, and terrorist groups, Iraq had a pool of operatives trained and equipped to conduct paramilitary and terrorist attacks around the world. Some of these groups shared the Ba'ath pan-Arab dream, while others were only interested in Saddam's largesse. Nevertheless, a diverse array of groups received some level of political, financial, and logistical support from the regime. In many ways, Iraq acted as a sort of venture capital resource for numerous violent political factions. The dangerous web of terrorists born of these venture capital programs continues to affect the region even after the fall of the regime.

The groups that benefited the most from Iraqi support, and in turn were the most reliable when it came to quid pro quo, were the many Palestinian factions. In the run-up to the war, there were offers of support from some of the beneficiaries of Saddam's pan-Arab support efforts. One of many examples was "the group of Abu Nidal," which a September 1990 intelligence service memorandum noted "has mobilized its components, who are mostly college students in the European countries, in order to strike the American and Saudi interests with the cooperation of other organizations. One of the groups [is] headed to Brussels in order to strike American targets to include the American embassy. The operations [are] expected to take place in the near future."[120]

Saddam's strategy of supporting a wide array of non-Iraqi groups makes tracing terror connections an inexact process. For example, Saddam's relationships to groups ostensibly opposed to the Ba'ath regime's very existence indicates an ability to ignore mutual animosity and work together against a common enemy.[121] A specific case comes from a member and chronicler of today's Salafi Jihadist movement, Abu Mus'ab al-Suri.[122] Recalling the events in Syria during the early 1980s before the Syrian regime brutally decimated a growing Salafist movement, Al-Suri wrote:

> Open military camps were established in some countries with groups opposed to and waging war against the government. Among them was our camp in Syria, where Jihadists from the Fighting Vanguard and the Syrian Muslim Brotherhood [helped] establish *frontline military camps in Iraq, which the Iraqi regime supplied with abundant military and material assistance.* As a result from 1980 to 1983 Jihadists, who had undergone

general and specialized training in artillery and antiaircraft weapons, launched a number of attacks. . . . *I saw with my own eyes these experiences in Iraq. . . . They were tremendously beneficial and we gained from them a high level of expertise.*[123] [Emphasis added]

The "Arab fighter" program also seems to have introduced, or at least influenced, a new doctrine in Iraq—that of the suicide volunteer. Recruiting for suicide volunteers was not limited to the radicalized fringe but included efforts to get volunteers from within the ranks of Iraq's military, the Ba'ath party, as well as the "independents." Documents indicate that this effort was the brainchild of Izzat Ibrahim al-Duri. In a November 1990 memorandum to al-Duri with the title "Training Courses for Suicide Volunteers," the director of military intelligence reported that, as ordered, his directorate "had begun and continues to open a number of special courses, including fedayeen and suicide volunteers from their positions as 'officers, commissioned officers, and the ranks,' as well as a number of suicide volunteers from the two parties and the independents who have declared their readiness . . . to participate in any task that may be assigned."[124]

The fedayeen training program began just after the invasion of Kuwait, and by the time of the November memorandum more than 270 students had graduated from one of four "suicide volunteer courses." For unknown reasons, the courses were disguised behind the code name of "Concentrated Fire Courses."[125] The Iraqis opened the courses to non-Iraqi volunteers shortly after the first class. The documents fail to make clear how many were ultimately trained, what missions (if any) they may have conducted, or what the nationality composition of the volunteers was. Nevertheless, as other documents make clear, the non-Iraqi participation in the overall volunteer program was not trivial. In order to participate in a military parade on 15 October 1990, the ministry of defense required fifty-five busses and forty additional vehicles to move Sudanese volunteers from the Ta'mim camp, and a similar number to move Egyptian volunteers from the Diyala camp, Syrian volunteers from the Karbala camp, and Palestinian volunteers from the Babel camp.[126]

In the end, Iraq's attempt to use external terrorist organizations, intelligence service paramilitaries, and fedayeen to support its fight against the Coalition did not add up to much. The U.S. State Department's 1991 annual report on terrorism noted that "although many of the Palestinian groups threatened to conduct terrorist operations against the international Coalition opposing Baghdad's invasion of Kuwait, few such attacks actually occurred. Most incidents recorded during the Persian Gulf War were bombing attacks outside the Middle East region, and most of these were against commercial property belonging to coalition countries' firms. Few of these attacks were carried out against civilians."[127]

Notwithstanding the limited success of such efforts, the regime continued to deliberately, if not cautiously, cultivate non-Iraqi "Arab fighters" and their organizations in support of Saddam's causes over the next twelve years.

Iraq's Net Assessment of the Coming War

On 29 November, the U.N. Security Council approved Resolution 678.[128] The resolution set 15 January 1991 as the deadline for compliance with the Security Council or "all necessary means" would be used to force Iraqi compliance. Saddam and his inner circle debated the appropriate response. The defiant tone of Iraq's response to the United Nations' authorization of force was classic Saddam, three parts bravado and one part rational policy.[129] Saddam's perspective reflected his regime's unique "net assessment" of the coming war. A net assessment is both a comparative analysis and a process for studying "the issues that are important but overlooked."[130] The distinction between what Saddam and his advisers found important and those that were important in the West is often striking.

A few weeks before the vote in the Security Council, Izzat al-Duri provided Saddam and the other members of the RCC with a darkly optimistic assessment of the coming war:[131]

We must be aware of [the United States] and expect that they are willing to enter into a full fledged war, until we make the rulers [and] the American nation tear apart like what happened in Vietnam. Once we expect the war to be on [this] basis when they come in, we can fight the United States with our heavy artillery [and] with the weapons we now make.[132]

We can fight the [American] agents in the region. We can fight for every inch of this country, from the south of Kuwait to Zakho. And when we need to, we can go to the mountains and fight either officially or in guerilla wars. I imagine this war to be thus and based on these expectations, to allow us to face the United States.

I don't think it will do some [for the Americans to use] air strikes and let the Arabs come and take Kuwait, that doesn't make sense, is not logical and or practical. They won't just come and fight like this. We must also expect that the United States could hit us with a nuclear bomb, because the United States, as I said, [and] I am very convinced, cannot imagine our situation, cannot fathom how a little country stands in defiance in front of the United States and dares to challenge it and to win.

It is possible that if the United States hits us and after six or seven months did not get the result and saw that the war is going to start tearing the [American] people apart, it is possible that it will use nuclear bombs to strike two or three cities.[133]

Taha Ramadan was also optimistic. Moreover, he predicted long-term benefits arising from the coming war, saying

I believe the war with America [will be] easier than the war with Iran. Mr. President, America has no borders with us. The American fighter is not like us or the Iranians, nor is the Iranian sitting in his land. Where is the American? According to us, no Saudi is going to fight us, nor Egyptian, or Syrian. It is going to be an ideal war.[134]

Taha continued with his analysis of the situation, which considered the possible longevity of any confrontation. Perhaps imagining a static war similar to the war just completed with Iran, Taha estimated that the American forces could "only fight for three years." In addition to highlighting Iraq's long war experience as one of its strengths, Taha added that Saddam could use American military deployments as the rally cry for Iraqi leadership of the Arab Nation:

We should not worry ourselves with it [long-term American deploy-ments]. In fact, it is a good thing that the American forces will stay in Saudi Arabia. You may ask "why good?" The revolutionary struggler needs an excuse to [discredit] the fakers. The Saudi supporter, the Emirates sup-porter, people carrying flags, and the Syrian supporter, they are all fake. . . . As long as American forces stay in Saudi Arabia, it will be a load and it will shorten the life of those rulers . . . the Arabic people hate the existence of the foreigner on their land. In the 20s, the Arabic people were all barefoot and illiterates. Was there any Arabic person that did not sacrifice to kick out the foreigner?[135]

One Iraqi strategy used during this period was the threat to expand any war. Since the late 1970s, Saddam had included direct and indirect threats against Israel as an almost axiomatic response to any Western threats to the region. Threats to attack Israel (regardless of how serious) played to Saddam's leadership of the Arab Nation strategy, while at the same time giving pause to a cautious international community. As a result of the growing international and Arab resolve to reverse the Kuwait invasion, many of Saddam's advisers were split on whether to expand the threats against regional enemies (like Israel) or to concentrate on the far enemy (the United States) exclusively.

Deputy Prime Minister Sa'dun Hammadi advocated a policy that concentrated on the far enemy. His logic, as he explained to Saddam, was simple. By focusing on the United States, Iraq could leverage the tension on the Security Council between the United States, China, Soviet Union, and France. Besides, "the Americans are insisting on picturing the battle as if it were between Iraq and the international community and not between Iraq and the United States."[136]

Comrade Mohammad generally agreed with Sa'dun, but expanded the argument to a dual-track approach. He agreed with the focus on limiting the international battle to the American threat, but recommended that Iraq's declared regional policy move beyond threats against Israel and "be clear that our strike is going to be hard on the Saudi rulers."[137] He explained that "once anything happens with us we should hit the Saudi rulers with powerful strikes . . . we can cause them very big losses. What I mean is that as long as the battle stays in Saudi Arabia it will have enormous benefits. Let the entire Gulf States understand along with the Gulf rulers, that we are going to hit."[138]

Taha Ramadan, among others, advocated a first strike against the American forces assembling in Saudi Arabia. Mohammad picked up on this theme, but again focusing on the regional targets, he said, "Let us be clear . . . the Saudi Rulers are going to be the first targeted, just like we are going to hit the American forces that are going to hit us. We are targeting Fahd and the rule of Fahd in a complete way."[139]

In purely military terms, this strategy appeared impractical at the very least. After the initial deployments of Coalition airpower, Iraq was capable only of limited ground thrusts to the south and firing SSMs. However, Mohammad was not speaking on military terms; he focused on the "important, but overlooked," psychology of the Arab states, especially the Persian Gulf States.

He said that "it is very necessary that [the Gulf rulers] understand . . . [that] they know themselves that they are going to be struck. . . . I believe regardless of how much the Americans will tell them that they are not going to be struck, I believe that they will stay scared and hesitant, which is going to cause the cases of frustration."[140]

Weighing into the assessments, Tariq Aziz shifted the conversation away from military strategy to the issue of the strategic battle of wills and public perceptions, saying,

Sir [referring to Saddam Hussein], I do not have anything to add, but I do have quick points in regards to . . . this resolution [678]. From my follow-up on the American stance, statements, and TV, the very thing that annoys the Americans is our solidness. They see us calm and steady, speaking logically and [with] convincing words, and they go angry. The interviews of you sir on the American TV and the answers [you gave] were strong and solid.[141]

Accordingly, Aziz recommended that Iraq's response to the resolution be a calm one and that they avoid "looking angry like we want to throw a fit."[142] Besides, he pointed out, the resolution gave a definitive time frame for a possible war (15 January) and this "gives us plenty of time" for further preparations.[143]

Picking up on the preparations for a possible war, Saddam articulated his version of the classic insurgent "win-by-not-losing" strategy.[144] In this version, to win, Saddam needed to challenge the legitimacy, not necessarily the militaries, of his near and far enemies. His first target was the Arab states, most of which were either cooperating with the Americans or refusing to support their "brothers" in Iraq beyond a few speeches and official rallies. The Arab populations in these states "want [their governments] to act like Iraq does" and would, in accordance with Ba'ath political lore, prefer to stand together behind a strong Arab leader.[145] The second target was the legitimacy of American leadership in a changing international environment. Target populations of this far enemy were in countries interested in checking America's growing power in the international arena. In some cases, they were even potential constituencies within the Coalition. Iraq would communicate with these constituencies through its "principled" actions. As Saddam described it, "As long as our blood is less, as long as our breath lasts longer, and at the end we can make our enemy feel incompetent. I mean the lower the devastation in our economy, the longer we can last . . . the more we can make our enemy hopeless."[146]

Tariq Aziz agreed that "we should show the enemy how much harm he is going to cause himself, even if it is outside of Iraq."[147] Aziz then offered Saddam his insights into the thinking of their far enemy:

Why did they [the Americans] make such a military mistake? In the beginning they wanted to bring forces in order to hold the ground and get basing in the region. They needed time to exist here and I am not talking about [just] rockets and planes, I am talking about a physical existence. But when they had seen our preparation and the growth and the improvement of our preparations which made them bring more, and more, and more.

At that critical moment and before they do anything, they are going to take into consideration our preparations and capabilities. . . . If they were to find out that the battle is going to be long, they would not attack. That is the important thing; that is the important thing.[148]

Saddam concurred with this assessment. He declared, "We will show them in reality it is going to be [a] long [war]."[149] Saddam went on to describe how Iraq could frustrate Coalition bombing strategies by distributing electric generators, building alternative means of communication, and stockpiling food. Thus, Iraq could show that it was being strategically firm, "just like being firm on the front."[150] Saddam asked his inner circle if they believed Iraq could remain "firm" for a period of three to six months. Most agreed, with their well-practiced parroting of Saddam's ideas. One, Comrade Sa'dun, cautioned that "they [the food distribution managers] believe, if we give the citizens a supply for six months, [they] would eat it in one month and come back to us and throw a fit for the next five months."[151] Seemingly on the strength of this analysis alone, Saddam settled on a compromise—he directed his staff to prepare Iraq's civil defense for a two-month siege.

In a final—and from a Coalition perspective out-of-touch--assessment of Iraq's options, Saddam proposed that, in response to the U.N. Security Council Resolution authorizing force, Iraq should sponsor a resolution of its own. He told Aziz to request "permission [to] crush the American forces, if they refuse to withdraw. . . . Actually, request permission [from] the Security Council to permit us to kick out the American forces, if they do not agree to pull out their last soldier in the same period of time that it took them to deploy . . . ask them to give us the authority to use force to kick them out."[152]

Several of Saddam's ministers were optimistic that the Iraqi counter-resolution would at least have a chance for a hearing, since the rotating president of the Security Council would be Yemen in December. As one participant in the meeting optimistically said, "Yemen is an Arabic state and a brother state that is on our side."[153]

Notes

1. Harmony document folder ISGQ-2003-00045740.
2. In the language of the Iraqi security bureaucracy, the term "confidential" normally signified a limited distribution to only the top-level officials in the regime.
3. Harmony document folder ISGP-2003-00033219 (FOUO). U.N. Secretary General Javier de Cuellar met with Tariq Aziz on 31 August and 1 September in Oman. Iraq offered to release all foreign nationals, if the multinational forces promised not to initiate military action.

4.   Harmony document folder ISGP-2003-00033219.

5.   "Saddam Hussein repeats call for Jihad," read by announcer on Baghdad Domestic Radio Service in Arabic, 1500 GMT, 5 September 1990; FBIS-NES-90-173, 6 September, cited in Bengio, *Saddam Speaks*, 139. In this same speech, Saddam evoked the war of the elephant story to place King Fahd and President Mubarak in the role of the traitorous Abu-Righal.

6.   There is a lingering controversy about the acuteness of the Iraqi threat to Saudi Arabia in early August 1990. During the first two weeks after the invasion, there were approximately eleven Iraqi divisions either in or moving toward Kuwait (Republican Guard and Regular Army). Given the inability of most intelligence services (including those in the Middle East) to divine the intent behind many of Iraq's military movements, analysts were left with few options. The United States understandably opted for a worst-case scenario explanation of Iraq's military formations south of Kuwait City.

7.   The pufferfish inflates itself to several times its normal size when threatened in hopes of dissuading its attacker. Additionally, through a powerful neurotoxin within its flesh, the fish can exact a fatal revenge on any predator not fooled by the inflated show before the fight. This seems to be an apt analogy for Saddam's regime.

8.   Harmony media file ISGQ-2003-M0005373.

9.   Ibid.

10. Ibid.

11. Harmony media file ISGQ-2003-M0005371.

12. Harmony document folder ISGP-2003-00033248. This document number includes a large collection (481 pages) of similar material. Reports from the PLO were particularly inflammatory during early August; in one case the PLO contact described a pending Israeli nuclear strike and in another the deployment of the Israeli fighters and tanks to Saudi Arabia with "the Israeli sign camouflaged." For the most part, the General Military Intelligence Directorate did not appear to place much stock in these reports, but nonetheless passed them to the presidential secretary.

13. LTG Zuhayr Talib Abd al-Satter al-Naqi, interview with author, 14 November 2003, Baghdad, Iraq.

14. BG Ra'ad Hamdani, interview with author, 10 November 2003, Baghdad, Iraq. No copy of the referenced study has been recovered.

15. One postwar study noted 145 major U.S. news articles alone referring to or speculating on U.S. Central Command war plans before and during combat operations. See Sarah Pitman and George J. Walker, *Desert Shield / Desert Storm: Evaluation of Public Domain Battle Plans* Volume II. SAIC study prepared for U.S. Central Command, 31 May 1991.

16. Hamdani, "From the Golan to the Collapse of Baghdad," 135.

17. Harmony document folder ISGP-2003-00026600.

18. Harmony document folder ISGP-2003-00033248. This is another example of pre-invasion secrecy complicating post-invasion operations. The GMID noted that the original requests for new military maps of Kuwait, Saudi Arabia, Jordan, and Syria went out on 8 July 1990, but were rejected because there were none in stock.

19. Harmony document folder ISGP-2003-00033136.

20. By the end of August, total U.S. military personnel in the presumed theater of operations exceeded 82,000. In addition to major elements of three army divisions, there were four

carrier battle groups, two amphibious ready groups, and more than 250 ground-based strike aircraft.

21. Harmony document folder ISGP-2003-00033136. Iraqi GMID documents cited are numbers 11599, 11770, 12484, 12513, 12749, and 14419 respectively. Many of the original reports are included in Harmony document folder ISGP-2003-00033248.

22. Iraq's previous chief of staff, LTG Nazir Khazraji (July 1987–October 1990), reportedly fell out of favor with Saddam after questioning Iraq's ability to withstand the military power lining up against it. Khazraji was replaced by Husayn Rashid Muhammad. See Hashim, "Saddam Husayn and Civil-Military Relations in Iraq," 30. Khazraji was no shrinking violet. He was suspected of carrying out chemical attacks on Kurdish civilians in 1987 and defected to the West in 1995. He was reportedly assassinated in southern Iraq in April 2003 while working with Iraqi expatriate groups during OIF.

23. Harmony media file ISGP-2003-10151507.

24. Ibid.

25. Ibid.

26. Harmony document folder ISGP-2003-00033136.

27. Harmony document folder ISGP-2003-00031515. The increased Iraqi dependence on signal intercepts for intelligence on Coalition movements enhanced Coalition deception efforts aimed at masking movements.

28. Harmony document folder ISGP-2003-00033136. Iraqi document cited is number 16616.

29. Harmony media file ISGQ-2003-M0005371.

30. Ibid.

31. Ibid.

32. Ibid.

33. Ibid.

34. Harmony media file ISGP-2003-10151507.

35. Harmony document folder IST-A5053-002. According to other documents in this collection, the Iraqis eventually deployed 689 "destroyed" tanks and "war-booty" armored vehicles plus 211 obsolete cannons of various types to serve as decoys in the Kuwait theater.

36. Harmony media file ISGQ-2003-M0001716.

37. Harmony media file IZSP-2003-10103729.

38. Harmony document folder ISGQ-2003-00046040. Some of this "official history" reflects a significant degree of revisionism verging on the fanciful. There is no indication that the Iraqis knew at a technical level the satellite capabilities of the United States or that they actually carried out large training operations during this period.

39. Harmony media file ISGP-2003-10151507.

40. Harmony document folder IST-A5053-002—General Command of the Armed Forces, "Orders and Instructions" log, reference letter no. 6033, 10 November 1990. According to this document and its follow-on correspondence (no. 1077, 10014, 6397 in the same log), the order to establish a test range was issued on 10 November. The actual test firing occurred at 0930 on 2 December 1990 in the presence of the minister of defense, army chief of staff, the director of general military intelligence, the commander of the air force and air defense, and associated deputies.

41. Harmony media file ISGP-2003-10151507.

42. Ibid. The III Corps Commander recalled that the position was extensive, measuring 2,200 meters by 1,200 meters. The test position was designed to accommodate four infantry companies, a tank platoon, and an artillery battery. See Harmony media file ISGQ-2003-M0003323.

43. Ibid.

44. Harmony media file ISGQ-2003-M0005889. Of the more than 148,000 general-purpose bombs the USAF dropped during Operation Desert Storm, most were 500- and 750-pound variety. None were as small as 250 pounds.

45. Harmony media file ISGQ-2003-M0006195. Speaker is identified as Staff Rear Admiral Hasan.

46. Ibid.

47. Ibid.

48. Ibid.

49. Ibid. General de la Billière noted in his account of the war that the Iraqi free-floating mines were a "severe constraint on ship movements." Peter de la Billière, *Storm Command: A Personal Account of the Gulf War*, paperback ed. (London: Harper Collins, 1993), 255.

50. Harmony media file ISGQ-2003-M0006195.

51. Ibid.

52. Harmony media file ISGQ-2003-M0006201. The potential impact on naval operations from Saddam's threat to create "rivers of fire" and set the Gulf on fire is unclear. The obvious dangers included fire, toxic fumes, and clogged cooling systems on ships. U.S. Navy analysis determined that under near-optimal conditions the best Saddam could do was create a short-term fire of fewer than seventy square nautical miles, which could be easily avoided. Marvin Pokrant, *Desert Shield at Sea—What the Navy Really Did* (Westport, CT: Greenwood Press, 1999), 207.

53. Ibid.

54. Ibid.

55. Ibid.

56. Harmony media file ISGQ-2003-M0004609.

57. Ibid.

58. Ibid.

59. This same phenomenon repeated itself during OIF in 2003. Despite a significant effort on the part of regime propagandists to play up the regime's intent to create a "Stalingrad on the Euphrates," most of the actual preparations were limited at best.

60. Related documents captured during Operation Desert Storm include tactical plans from the Iraqi 3rd Armored Division, 5th Mechanized Division, 8th Mechanized Division, 15th Mechanized Division, 20th Infantry Division, and III Corps Artillery. See respective Harmony document folder numbers FM8625, FM9108, FM8617, FM8556, FM8621, and FM8607.

61. The 5th Mechanized Division was reassigned to the Iraqi III Corps sometime between the publication of this order and the attack on al-Khafji on 29 January 1991.

62. Harmony document folder FM9108.

63. Ibid.

64. Robert Scales, *Certain Victory* (Washington, DC: Brassey's, 1994), 128. General Schwarz-kopf was concerned about the human cost of executing this operation, but judged it the

best option given the forces available. U.S. defense leaders ultimately rejected the "one corps" option on 10 October.

65. Harmony media file ISGQ-2003-M0003323.

66. Coalition activities possibly precipitating the Iraqi change include: On 25 October, the United States announced that 100,000 additional troops and additional heavy armor were being deployed to the Gulf; on 8 November, President Bush announced that additional troops were required "in case offensive action becomes necessary"; on 15 November, Coalition forces conducted a large-scale military exercise ominously named "Imminent Thunder." Iraqi documents suggest the order to re-evaluate the defensive strategy resulted from a high-level review that began on 10 November 1990 with the formation of a series of committees to "evaluate the current defense and decide on new procedures" and to report not later than 12 November. See Harmony document folder IST-A5053-002.

67. Harmony media file ISGQ-2003-M0003323.

68. Harmony document folder FM9108. This document related the contents of a III Corps (Iraqi top secret and personal) letter 8224, dated 24 November, that reported the results of discussions between the army chief of staff and the corps commanders in Kuwait on 20–21 November.

69. Harmony document folder FM8625.

70. Harmony media file ISGQ-2003-M0003323. The commander noted that they were able to take advantage of the local junkyards to use "a great number of pipes, tanks, and everything else that we could" to make their decoy targets.

71. Hamdani, "From the Golan to the Collapse of Baghdad," 157.

72. Harmony media file ISGQ-2003-M0003323.

73. Harmony media file ISGQ-2003-M0005889. Three of these divisions were deployed to southern Iraq and one to the north. Saddam would later say he regretted the rapid expansion of his "elite" units because they were not prepared militarily and in some cases their loyalty failed during the early days of the 1991 uprisings.

74. Harmony document folder ISGQ-2003-00046040.

75. Harmony media file ISGQ-2003-M0005889. Speaker is identified as LTG Ayyad Fateeh al-Rawi, commander of the Republican Guard (July 1987–March 1991).

76. Ibid. The Saudi Arabian port city of al-Mish'ab lies twenty kilometers south of al-Khafji.

77. Hamdani, "From the Golan to the Collapse of Baghdad," 157.

78. Ibid.

79. Ibid., 158.

80. Ibid. Hamdani was discounted at this conference for saying the Americans would take the indirect approach. In 2003, as a corps commander, he was discounted because he predicted that the Americans would take the direct approach, when the Iraqi senior leadership was convinced of the opposite.

81. Harmony document folder ISGQ-2003-M0004926. In Iraqi military documents, the term "mobilization" is generally used when describing movements on the ground or, in the case of the air force, repositioning aircraft from one hide-site to another.

82. Harmony document folder ISGP-2003-00031468.

83. Ibid.

84. Harmony document folder ISGP-2003-00030181.

85. Dhahran is the major administrative center for the Saudi Arabia oil industry. In August

1990, Dhahran, along with the nearby port of Dammam and the town of Khobar, became the hub of U.S. logistics activity supporting the military buildup.

86. Harmony document folder ISGP-2003-00033136. Iraqi document cited is correspondence number 137427, 9 August 1990.

87. Saddam seems to have identified pride, potential, and preservation as the key missions for his air arm. After the war, the commander of Coalition air forces, General Horner, explained that the Iraqis "had no idea what airpower is. We flew in one day as many sorties as [Saddam] faced in eight years of war with Iran. He had no air experience." Perry D. Jamieson, *Lucrative Targets—The U.S. Air Force in the Kuwait Theater of Operations* (Washington, DC: U.S. GPO, 2001), 171.

88. Harmony document folder ISGP-2003-00031468.

89. Ibid.

90. Iraq captured four U.S.–made I-HAWK missile batteries during the invasion. With the reluctant help of some Kuwaiti prisoners of war, the Iraqis got at least two into operating condition. The documents do not account for the remaining two.

91. Harmony document folder ISGP-2003-00031468; and Harmony document folder ISGQ-2003-00055358.

92. A copy of al-Ayyubi's memoir was serialized in eight parts in the Jordanian newspaper, *Al-Arab al-Yawm* (Arabic), on 25, 27, 29 October and 1, 3, 5, 10, and 12 November 1998. This public account of the Iraqi SSM force during 1991 is close to a copy of the original 1991 journal of events captured after the fall of the regime. See Harmony document folders ISGQ-2003-00046018 and ISGQ-2003-00046019.

93. Iraq's missile corps was organized primarily around five missile brigades with various supporting battalions and specialized units. The 223rd and 224th brigades were equipped with al-Husayn missiles (modified Scud-B with 650-kilometer range). The 225th and 226th missile brigades were equipped with various short-range missiles and rockets like the Ra'd missile (modified FROG-7 rocket with 70-kilometer range).

94. Hazim Abd al-Razzaq al-Ayyubi, "Forty-Three Missiles on the Zionist Entity," (Amman, Jordan: *Al-Arab al-Yawm*, in Arabic), 25 October 1998. The deployment of at least two missile brigades was complete by early April 1990.

95. According to al-Ayyubi, this was in response to a senior Israeli military officer's public statements threatening Iraq's weapons programs with a preemptive strike (reminiscent of the 1981 Israeli attack on Iraq's Osirak nuclear reactor and research site).

96. al-Ayyubi, "Forty-Three Missiles," 11. In his memoirs, al-Ayyubi indicates he was so convinced "the Zionist enemy" would use chemical weapons that he built a special "poison gas–proof chamber" in his home to protect his family.

97. Ibid.

98. Ibid. The description supports the supposition that Iraq's chemical arsenal was deployed and that some form of "doomsday" plan was in effect.

99. Ibid. These instructions came during a meeting with Saddam on 12 January.

100. Ibid.

101. Central Intelligence Agency, Directorate of Intelligence, "Prewar Status of Iraq's Weapons of Mass Destruction" (TOP SECRET), 15 January 1991, p. iii. (Declassified extract December 2002.) www.gwu.edu/~nsarchiv/NSAEBB/NSAEBB80/wmd04. pdf (accessed 15 December 2006). This estimate went on to note that Saddam's will-

ingness to use WMD "undoubtedly will be tempered if his opponents possess credible CW [chemical weapons] capabilities and appear willing to retaliate in kind."

102. In 1989, Iraq participated in two conferences on chemical weapon disarmament in the Middle East: the Paris Conference on the Prohibition of Chemical Weapons and the Government-Industry Conference against Chemical Weapons in Canberra, Australia. Both efforts did little more than provide a forum for Arab states, including Iraq, to defend their chemical weapons programs as "a poor man's equivalent of nuclear weapons." This, they explained, was justified in light of the perceived Israeli nuclear threat.

103. The "victory" Barzan is referring to here is the Iran-Iraq War. Harmony document folder ISGZ-2004-001472. In a memorandum commenting on Barzan's letter, the director of political affairs, Sab'awi Ibrahim al-Hasan, offers that "even in the event that the [Israeli-Palestinian] conflict has transformed from a military one to a conflict of civilization, the deterrence points [nuclear weapons] are still needed because neighboring countries and not Israel per se may achieve such technology before us."

104. Saddam Hussein, quoted in Amatzia Baram, "An Analysis of Iraqi WMD Strategy," *Nonproliferation Review*, vol. 8, no. 2 (Summer 2001): 30. According to postwar analysis, Saddam's threat in this speech to use binary chemical weapons was premature. Iraq's chemical missiles would not be ready until after August 1990. See Central Intelligence Agency, "Comprehensive Report of the Special Advisor to the DCI on Iraq's WMD," vol. 3 (Langley, VA: CIA, 30 September 2004), 9.

105. Warranted or not, in this view Saddam was launching a preemptive rhetorical strike in response to rising tensions. The other argument tends to discount the impact of the 1981 Israeli raid and views this statement as either a naked threat or a facet of Saddam's pan-Arab leadership appeal.

106. Harmony document folder ISGP-2003-00010140.

107. Harmony document folder ISGQ-2005-00031849.

108. Harmony media file ISGQ-2003-M0001716.

109. On 7 September 1990, the General Military Intelligence Directorate distributed to the corps commanders a report on the organization, armament, and doctrine of U.S. nuclear forces. Most of the information in this thirteen-page document was, at best, simplistic and outdated. It included descriptions of such weapons as the Sergeant Guided Missile (retired in 1977) along with 1950s-era Pentomic Army-like doctrinal statements such as "[American] nuclear use plans are set up the same in the corps, division, and the brigade" and "the preliminary nuclear bombardment starts twenty to thirty minutes before the main attack and it lasts for fifteen minutes." See Harmony document folder ISGP-2003-00033248.

110. Harmony document folder ISGQ-2003-00072723.

111. In 1991, the United States had a deterrent chemical weapons stockpile; however, it maintained a policy of "no first use." In 1993, the United States signed the Chemical Weapons Convention and all U.S. stockpiles and production capabilities were scheduled to be destroyed by 2007, but due to environmental and other concerns projections estimate it will be 2012 before this task is complete.

112. Harmony media file ISGQ-2003-M0005889. Other captured documents include the belief by some in the Iraqi military that the United States deployed nuclear-capable missile systems in support of Operation Desert Storm. In fact, by the fall of 1990, most

Pershing missiles (1a and II) were eliminated under INF (Intermediate-range Nuclear Forces Treaty (1987)) provisions. The last Pershing missile was destroyed in May 1991.

113. This discussion was part of a more general meeting that appears from the content to have taken place during the second week of January 1991. Central Intelligence Agency, "Comprehensive Report," 97–98. Aziz reportedly told the U.N. inspection teams after the war that Iraq destroyed its biological stocks in the fall of 1990 out of fear that a U.S. precision strike would unleash their effects on Iraq.

114. The question of "doomsday" or pre-designated launch orders was first raised during U.N. Special Commission interviews with Iraqi commanders in Baghdad during 1995 and 1996. Additional information on this issue was provided by Husayn Kamil during his short defection to Jordan after August 1995. See Baram, "Analysis of Iraqi, WMD Strategy," 25.

115. Central Intelligence Agency, "Comprehensive Report," 99.

116. Harmony document folder CMPC-2003-004325.

117. For a thoughtful analysis of the range of potential deterrence factors that most likely weighed on Saddam's decision, see Norman Cigar, "Chemical Weapons and the Gulf War: The Dog That Did Not Bark," *Studies in Conflict and Terrorism* 15, no. 2 (1992): 145–55.

118. Harmony media file ISGP-2003-10151751. This incident was a part of a seven-day gun battle between Palestinian factions across the globe. In addition to the Iraqi agent shot dead, one French policeman was killed and another wounded.

119. Levins, *Days of Fear*, 21–29. In the days following the invasion, Iraqi propaganda reported that the Iraqi military incursion into Kuwait was in response to an internal "republican" revolt of patriotic Kuwaiti military officers.

120. Harmony folder ISGP-2003-00026608. The memorandum noted that Ghassan al-Ali (the Abu Nidal Organization's Intelligence Directorate's Committee for Special Missions) was responsible for these operations, adding that "he is very bad." Judging from Ghassan's reported involvement in the 1985 massacres in the Vienna and Rome airports, the IIS had reason to be confident.

121. The Ba'ath government was secular while radical Islamist movements have generally declared such secular Arab governments apostates.

122. Abu Mus'ab al-Suri is the nom de guerre of Mustafa Abdul-Qadir Mustafa Hussein al-Sheikh Ahmed al-Mazeek al-Jakiri al-Rifa'ei. He was considered to be "the most prolific al-Qaeda ideologue and trainer alive" until his capture in 2006. See Murad al-Shishani, "Abu Mus'ab al-Suri and the Third Generation of Salafi-Jihadists," *Terrorism Monitor* 3, no. 16 (2005).

123. Abu-Mus'ab al-Suri, *The Call for Global Islamic Resistance*, Arabic version (widely available online as of 1 September 2006), CTC/OTA Translation and Analysis (October 2006), 1415, 1600.

124. Harmony folder ISGQ-2004-00257858.

125. Harmony folder ISGQ-2004-00257858.

126. Harmony folder ISGQ-2005-00116330.

127. Office of the Secretary of State, Office of the Coordinator for Counterterrorism, "Patterns of Global Terrorism: 1991: Middle East Overview," (Washington, DC), April 1991. For a detailed analysis of Saddam's terror threat during the Gulf War see W. Andrew

Terrill, "Saddam's Failed Counterstrike: Terrorism and the Gulf War," *Studies in Conflict and Terrorism* 16, no. 3 (1993): 219–32.

128. UNSC Resolution 678 "authorizes UN Member States to use all necessary means to uphold and implement resolution 660 and all subsequent relevant resolutions and to restore international peace and security in the area" to enforce the resolutions.

129. One 29 November, the UNSC passed Resolution 678 on a vote of 12-2 (China abstaining, Yemen and Cuba voting against). Iraq's RCC broadcast a statement on 30 November that described the resolution as "aggressive, illegal, and invalid." The RCC went on to vow it would "teach America's stooges an unparalleled lesson."

130. Paul Bracken, "Net Assessment: A Practical Guide," *Parameters* 36, no. 1 (2006): 95.

131. Upon the fall of the regime in April 2003, Izzat al-Duri went underground and has been reported to be supporting pro-Ba'ath insurgency groups. (Current as of November 2007)

132. The use of "heavy artillery" and "weapons we now make" in the same sentence in this context likely refers to binary chemical weapons.

133. Harmony media file ISGQ-2003-M0004609.

134. Harmony media file ISGQ-2003-M0001716.

135. Ibid.

136. Ibid.

137. Ibid.

138. Ibid.

139. Ibid.

140. Ibid.

141. Ibid.

142. Ibid.

143. Ibid.

144. The other side to this strategy is the "lose-by-not-winning" explanation of why larger powers don't easily "win" insurgencies.

145. Harmony media file ISGQ-2003-M0001716.

146. Ibid.

147. Ibid.

148. Ibid.

149. Ibid.

150. Ibid.

151. Ibid.

152. Ibid.

153. Ibid.

Chapter VIII

UM AL-MA'ARIK
(THE MOTHER OF ALL BATTLES)

But this is war, it's not just a regular problem and the results aren't
your everyday results.[1]

—TAHA RAMADAN

O n 26 December 1990, the GMID delivered a final military assessment
of the coming storm. The report noted there were more than 3,500
enemy tanks deployed in the Gulf region and an additional 634 tanks
along the Turkish front. It counted the number of American fighter aircraft in
the area around Iraq, including at sea, at 1,525, not counting support aircraft and
helicopters. Of these, more than 1,100 aircraft could conduct "air strikes against
strategic positions." All total the report estimated that these aircraft could sustain
approximately two hundred combat sorties per day.[2] In addition to the aircraft
totals, the Iraqi analysts noted the significant number of American ground-to-
ground missiles, like the Lance, Pershing, and cruise missiles in range of Iraq.
These missiles, combined with the "massive air threats, severely endanger the
[Iraq's] vital and strategic areas."[3]

This detailed intelligence assessment then offers three likely enemy courses
of action (COA):

Enemy COA One: "Launch intensive air and missile strikes against the
higher command posts; the next step will [then] be carried out depending on the results of the first attack and the reaction of our troops."

Enemy COA Two: "Launch intensive air and missile strikes against the
important strategic targets concentrating on the air force and air
defense resources, the command posts, radio and television stations . . .
communications centers, refineries, main warehouses, power stations,
scientific institutes, [and] military industrial establishments." In addition, the estimate continued, the enemy would concentrate on "bridges, field command posts, artillery posts, and weapons stockpiles." The
purpose of this course of action was to "isolate the operations zone"
and then "bombard our troops . . . when [they] launch their counter

attacks." The report concluded that "if the air strikes are effective as planned, the land forces will start a rapid advance to the depth of Iraqi territory."

Enemy COA Three: "Start simultaneously the air, missile, land, and naval operation."[4]

GMID analysts evaluated the enemy courses of action and determined that the first was the most likely to occur "if [the enemy] obtains definite information."[5] It is not clear to what information the author was referring, but one could reasonably assume he meant information necessary for a "decapitation" strike. If the required information for the first course of action was not available, then the Coalition would use the second course of action. The Directorate discounted the third course of action because "it will result in casualties to [American] troops."[6]

After all the preparations, the ministry of defense seemed just as concerned about what its own troops might do as what the Coalition was up to. On 6 January, the office of the chief of staff of the army sent out a top secret, personal, and immediate letter to all commanders reminding them that "the enemy

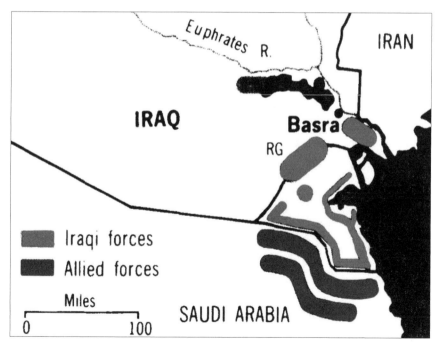

Figure 24. General disposition of forces. Before 17 January, most forces were concentrated on Kuwait. ("Central Command Briefing," *Military Review* 71, no. 9 (1991): 96. RG stands for Republican Guard.)

might perform a maneuver in order to try and draw our units [out of] their fortified defensive locations. We have to absolutely watch out for this issue."[7]

A follow-on series of letters from the chief of staff was disseminated on 9 January with even more specific guidance to the troops in Kuwait: "If the enemy achieves a penetration in the front, it is necessary that the commanders and others remain calm and do not react. Instead, we have to be cold-blooded and deal with the issue according to the leadership's calculations . . . to prevent the enemy from reaching its larger goals."[8]

The Iraqi troops in the Kuwaiti theater occupied themselves with last-minute preparations such as stockpiling required logistics, improving protective shelters, and updating themselves with lectures on the latest tactical intelligence. One of the lectures was meant to provide the latest intelligence on American armored forces. This lecture may help explain the generally poor quality of Iraqi tank gunnery when facing American forces.

On 3 January, all of the Iraqi armor officers in the Kuwaiti theater attended the presentation by a senior officer described only as "the tank commander." The lecturer was not identified by name, but was probably the commander of the prestigious Republican Guard Armor academy. The lecture addressed new methods of engaging enemy tanks and specifically emphasized issues such as how to avoid their range, noted as exceeding the T-72s by more than 800 meters, and how to deal with the new "armor-piercing rounds."[9] According to a senior commander's recollection of the lecture, the speaker had noted with confidence that "exercises were conducted on how to engage with American-made tanks which were captured from the Kuwait army. . . . The [Iraqi] armor directorate conducted and videotaped a number of experiments. . . . [American armor] weak points were identified. There was one obvious weak point in the American-made tank, it was the control panel found on top of the tank tower because the panel contained the laser range [finder] and the command and control system. *Therefore it was critical to inform all the soldiers of all ranks to aim at the control panel of the enemy tank*" [Emphasis added].[10]

On 11 January, the III Corps Commander held his final commanders' meeting before the beginning of hostilities. He emphasized staying in the shelters during the coming "air bombardment and hostile fire." However, once firing stopped, sounding like a Western front general in 1917, soldiers must "assume the firing positions." Above all, "we have to be calm during the execution." The commanders of the corps were reminded that they must

educate [their] soldiers about the enemy's psychological warfare. Iraq's soldiers must ignore the enemy's propaganda. We have to show perseverance and never retreat. Anyone who retreats [will] be handled as a hostile element. . . . We have to emphasize that the Iraqis will not be defeated by American female soldiers. The [coming] close combat with the enemy was a solid tactic because it will spare us the enemy's bombardment. . . . We have to increase our meetings with the soldiers to convince them that Kuwait is an Iraqi territory that we have to fight for, just like we would fight for al-Basra or Baghdad.[11]

In Baghdad, final staff preparations continued at a frenetic pace. Saddam's personal involvement in these last-minute machinations ran from the important to the trivial. During one such planning meeting with senior Iraqi commanders in early January 1991, Saddam discussed the status of overall preparations in view of the looming 15 January deadline to comply with the U.N. Security Council Resolution 678.[12] After they reviewed the status of various commands, the conversation became almost comical. Saddam and his staff appear lost in the time zones between New York and Baghdad:

Saddam: You know they have a time difference between us and them that works in our favor.

Unidentified Advisor: Yes sir. [The U.N. deadline] will be the 16th. We will be waiting for the night of the 16th!

Saddam: No. It will be the 15th here when it starts, one minute after midnight of the 14th towards the 15th. It will start with them at 8 o'clock in the morning. This could be used as a trick and they can say that they were within day 15 of the Iraqis and we attacked after midnight. Therefore our alert starts at 12 the night of the 14th onto the 15th which means from the end of light of the 14th.

Unidentified Advisor: Why don't we start the alert at least two days earlier or on the morning of the 14th?

Saddam: The morning of the 14th [so] be it and let us put our trust in Allah on the morning of the 14th . . . that is it.[13]

Saddam then asked his generals if it was prudent to allow the military to continue to take vacations, or whether they should recall all the soldiers and officers with the promise of vacation time at a later date. This question, no matter how odd it may appear on the eve of battle, in fact went to the heart of a critical issue for Saddam—military morale. Even during times of national crisis, like the Iran-Iraq War, the Iraqi military had upwards of 25 percent of its soldiers on leave at any given time. Time off with state-funded round-trip transportation was one of the few benefits in the Iraqi military. An unidentified officer told Saddam that since 1982 the army had been on full alert only once (during an unidentified missile test), but that if ordered was prepared to do so again. Saddam decided a full alert would go into affect on the morning of 14 January 1991.[14]

In this same discussion, Saddam sarcastically asked if the 15 January deadline was similar to the Iranian declaration during the Iran-Iraq War that 1987 would be "The Decisive Year." He wondered aloud if anything would happen "if the fifteenth passed and the Iranians, I mean the Americans," he laughed, didn't act. Saddam said:

> The Iranians assigned to that year [1987] as the year of resolution to mean that year they would bring the war to an end. We ourselves grabbed on to this term. This is because we wanted the war to come to an end and the issue to be resolved. We did not want the war to drag on for another thousand years! As a consequence I wrote a very harsh letter. [Someone says "One of the harshest letters."] Yes. It was a very harsh letter and it mentioned that we would drag the heads of the Iranians into the mud.... I said that we challenge you to make it the year of resolution![15]

Saddam reminded his staff that in 1987 the Iranians brought their "entire nation" to the fight but could not turn things around. Recalling the Iranian deadline, Saddam jokingly said, "the Gregorian calendar year came to an end and went and no resolution....We told them 'maybe you counted on the Islamic Hijri calendar . . . maybe the Persian calendar.'" Saddam reminded everyone that the Persians were planning on the "greater promise" of Allah but of course, according to Saddam "it was Allah who did it for us."[16] Saddam implied that, having worked once before, this same dynamic would work in the current crisis.

The rambling discussion then turned to the Iraqi Navy. One army officer pessimistically offered that "if we were to ask any unit of our navy to go out to sea to fight, then we should not expect it to come back."[17] Apparently their success during the invasion of Kuwait did not appreciably improve their reputation among their military peers. This lack of confidence in the Navy was not exclusively related to the relative strength of the Coalition armada but also to a generally low esteem within the defense ministry. One unidentified Republican Guard officer noted, "we should do the planning for the navy because they cannot be left on their own. I am also afraid for them during their exercises!"[18] Saddam acknowledged that Iraq's ships should remain in safe places lest Coalition air or naval attacks destroy them. He then suggested that they consider sending

Figure 25. Saddam coordinating the defense of Iraq, January 1991 (Harmony document folder ISGQ-2003-00049397)

some naval assets to Iranian harbors for temporary safe-keeping after which "we can return them here so that they can take action against the allied forces."[19] The naval officers present convinced Saddam that a dispersal plan within Iraqi waters, at least for the near term, would prove more effective. Saddam acknowledged that his naval forces were no match for the Coalition on the open sea and ordered them to "not take part in the coming battle."[20]

However, when it came to his air force, Saddam, as already noted, decided that evacuation was the only good option. In a decision he would later regret, Saddam sent some of Iraq's largest and hardest-to-protect aircraft (Soviet-made Ilyushin transports) to Iran in early January. Moreover, he ordered the remainder of the transport fleet hidden in the "hills and valleys."[21] Before the war was over, more than 120 frontline fighter aircraft would join the transports seeking shelter in Iran.

Continuing with the last-minute preparations, Saddam suggested an idea reminiscent of the U.S. Marine Corps' use of Navajo Indian radiomen to confound Japanese signals intelligence during WWII. In Saddam's version, Iraqi forces would use Kurdish in radio communications and then shift to Turkish,

Athuri (Assyrian), or one of several local dialects. Because the Saudis "only speak Arabic" the shifting language would confuse the Coalition and gain time for Iraqi forces. It is not clear if the Iraqis ever instituted this concept, but an officer present noted the difficulties Iraqi forces would encounter getting the correct linguists in place at each headquarters location.

Finally, Saddam offered advice to his senior commanders on preserving their headquarters, and by extension themselves.[22] In this area Saddam was speaking as a true expert. He emphasized his earlier guidance that all head-quarters be "covered, fortified, and kept secret." Commanders, Saddam noted, should also place additional emphasis on main and alternative headquarters. All commanders should keep moving between these sites in trucks, taxis, or other civilian transport—not staff cars. For security reasons, they should change cars often, and the cars should not attract attention. One officer suggested that com-manders all wear disdashas—the local one-piece menswear—instead of uni-forms. Saddam finally commented that with all of the security details, it would not be easy to hide. However, it was vitally important that commanders not do anything to attract attention to their positions.[23]

As the countdown to the U.N. deadline approached, Saddam spent time visiting units in the field, delivering motivational speeches to the Ba'ath party faithful, and peppering military staffs with questions and suggestions. On 13 January, he again reviewed the status of preparations for the coming battle. The discussion covered considerable ground and offers an insight into Saddam's mental agenda on the eve of battle.

Perhaps reflecting the ongoing concern about Coalition amphibious land-ings, the first issue discussed was the status of Iraqi naval mines. Saddam asked an unidentified naval officer for the status of the sea mine deployment. The officer explained that five of the minefields were already in place and a sixth and seventh minefield would be complete by the 15 January deadline.[24] Saddam asked the officer, "Can you cut about ahhh, two to three hundred mines loose and let them swim in the gulf?" The officer replied that while they could do as Saddam requested, the floating mines would be easily detected by Coalition helicopters in the daytime and destroyed. "However," this officer continued, "all these floating mines are very useful," because while vulnerable to counter-measures, "[the Coalition navies] will be occupied" dealing with them. Ano-ther officer, apparently familiar with operational dangers of such an idea and possibly the laws of war, pointed out that "these mines that we are going to release into the sea, I mean they would affect us as well, because of the tide . . . the mines could even reach Iran." Saddam reassured him that "we are not [mis] using the sea, just releasing a number of snakes and letting them go . . . toward our brothers."[25] After the war, the commander of the Iraqi Navy would justify the decision to release mines into the Gulf by saying that it was in response "to the enemy targeting civilian areas during their aggression."[26]

The second major issue discussed during the 13 January staff meeting was the contingency plans to destroy oil facilities in Kuwait—the Tariq Project. "Concerning the oil installations," an officer reported that "here is the order from your Excellency to blow up these . . . installations in case of a certain degree of danger, which we are waiting for an order from your Excellency. However, because al-Wafra [Southern Kuwait] is near the borders, your Excellency has given the local commander the authority to blow it up whenever he believes there is danger."[27]

The officer added that most of the naval aspects of the Tariq Project had the same command and control arrangements as did the ground components around al-Wafra. Authority was pre-delegated to the local commander so that the oil facilities under the navy's control would "not be spared." Saddam confirmed his order to destroy Kuwait's oil infrastructure "according to the situation . . . God willing."[28]

Unlike a discussion of naval mines or even destroying oil facilities, the third major issue on Saddam's agenda was not a military one, but it was nonetheless part of his strategy. In a move that could be seen as a cynical ploy to enlist Islam to his cause, Saddam placed the words Allah Akbar (God is Great) on Iraq's flag. The decision to break with both Ba'ath political doctrine and long-standing secular traditions was simple and direct:[29]

> Saddam: We want to place Allah Akbar on our flag. Abu Muthana, would you work on it?
>
> Abu Muthana: God willing.
>
> Saddam: Put it on the top corner of the flag. . . . Place it on the flag with precise measurements.
>
> Unidentified advisor: On the corner sir? . . . It should be between the stars, this way it would be seen when the flag is swirling.
>
> Saddam: It is not going to be visible anyway. . . . However, the important thing is to place it on the flag . . . because one would think of the flag as a rag but [with these] words on it . . . it cannot be disrespected.[30]

The final item on Saddam's meeting agenda, captured on this 13 January recording, was an update of the most recent intelligence concerning the Coalition. An unidentified intelligence officer noted in great detail the general shift in the American forces. He noted that large numbers of American units previously stationed along the Saudi coast were "heading toward Hafir al-Batin." The other Coalition activity of note was the accumulation of one hundred to eight hundred "large surface-to-surface missiles," also in the Hafir al-Batin vicinity.[31] All of this activity was along a limited set of road networks, several from the coast, but primarily one that ran along the border—the Tapline Road.[32]

Saddam asked the officer, "How far is the [Tapline] road from the [Iraqi] border?" The officer replied that the road was, at most, sixty to eighty kilometers distant. Saddam suggested they consider that "this road could be a target for our [Iraq's] helicopters. . . . [We] could strike [Coalition] vehicles and supplies."[33] The officers did not reply to Saddam's suggestion directly, but instead explained the significant difference between the American XVIII Airborne Corps and the VII Corps. Perhaps in this discreet way they made clear to Saddam the limited utility and potentially high cost of conducting helicopter raids against a heavy corps.[34]

After months of preparations, negotiations, accusations, and recriminations, Iraq was only days away from a fateful deadline. In a form of collective denial that would repeat itself in the run-up to the 2003 war, many senior Iraqis still did not believe war was a real possibility. As one officer recalled, "the president was mobilizing the nation. . . . He had visited the Iraqi armed forces on the southern operations theater on 15 January 1991; unfortunately, until that time many of our political and military leaders were 99.9 percent sure that the war would not start."[35]

The Air Campaign

17 JANUARY

Unknown to most of the Iraqi military, except to a thin line of Iraqi troops spread along the western desert, the war began at 0200 on 17 January. A flight of American AH-64 attack and MH-53 Pave Low helicopters crossed into Iraqi airspace to destroy a radar station guarding the approaches to Baghdad. The radio silence restrictions placed on Iraqi forces in the field all but ensured that the initial reports of this incursion did not make it to Baghdad or the air defense sector command. Even years after the war, many Iraqi officers questioned whether this operation actually took place as stated in "the diaries of Schwarzkopf."[36]

Brigadier General Hamdani spent the previous twenty-four hours on a final inspection tour of his battalions. In accordance with the directives of Saddam and the Republican Guard command, Hamdani had spread his three battalions and supporting troops carefully over one hundred square kilometers of southern Iraq. He was philosophical about their chances in the coming war. In his final prewar pep talk to the men of the 17th Brigade, he reminded them that even "if we fail [to] overcome the enemy's attack, they should remember that history always spoke favorably of those who died defending their homeland."[37] Their first opportunity to "die while trying" came a few hours later.

For Hamdani, the initial air attacks were heralded by one of his soldiers shouting "in a great panic" that "the planes are above us! The planes are above us!" Hamdami recalls:

> I ran out, finding my way with difficulty inside the simple shelter and heard the loud roar of hundreds of aircraft engines flying above us toward Iraq. At the time when our anti-aircraft batteries opened their fire, with an unnecessary generosity since all the planes were outside our firing range, I felt a strange feeling, "Oh, so it's the war. It was too easy to start and only God knows when it will end, and what will be the fate of our country and our people." I asked for a [flashlight] and looked at my watch; it was 0245 hours, just before dawn on 17 January 1991.[38]

The III Corps commander received a call at 0300 from the Army deputy chief of staff informing him that the IAF headquarters in Baghdad had just been struck. Within the hour, units across Kuwait began reporting enemy air activity. The beginning of the air campaign triggered two pre-planned operations in the III Corps. The first came in the form of coded orders at 0420 to the 8th Division and the 29th Division to begin sabotaging the oil fields at al-Wafrah and al-Burqun respectively. The second operation was to move the tactical missile batteries from their hidden locations and begin firing at al-Khafji and al-Mishab in Saudi Arabia. The first encouraging feedback on the effectiveness of the Iraqi missile strikes came in the afternoon of that first day.

At 1500, the III Corps commander recalled, they "dropped an enemy aircraft and captured the pilot." According to him, Iraqi intelligence "used information gleaned from the pilot through the interrogation process and the map found on him showing his mission [was] to engage land to land missiles."[39]

For Saddam, Coalition air attacks were unfolding just as he predicted. Early on the morning of 17 January, Saddam visited the air defense operations center in Baghdad to receive an update and provide guidance. His concern during those first few days was not what the Coalition was destroying, but that the air force and air defense forces not overreact. Saddam reminded them that their presence on the battlefield was more important than their military effectiveness in the greater scheme of his strategy for a long campaign.

Adaptation to the unfolding Coalition air campaign began almost immediately. Saddam directed his air force commanders to reposition the MiG-29s
to bases already struck by the Coalition. He suggested this would be safer since
he knew that over time "the enemy will try and focus on the bases which have
less damage." In addition, he noted that much of the air defense artillery around
Baghdad was firing in a continuous, intense, and apparently random fashion.
Saddam directed the commanders immediately to institute "disciplined shoot-
ing instructions because the enemy will try to force us to use our ammunition
continuously."[40]

The commander of Iraq's missile forces awoke on the morning of 17
January to the sound of anti-aircraft fire over Baghdad. In accordance with his
standing orders to strike the priority targets in Israel if the war started, General
al-Ayyubi immediately ordered the fueling and deployment of the al-Husayn
missiles at 0350.[41] At 1100 hours, a courier delivered a handwritten order from
Saddam with the simple order of the day: "Begin, with Allah's blessing, striking
targets inside the criminal Zionist entity with the heaviest fire possible, and
the need to be alert to the possibility of exposure. The strikes must be carried
out with 'ordinary' conventional ammunition for the missiles. The firing must
continue until further notice."[42]

Flight Staff Brig. Gen. Naji Khalifa Jasim al-A'Any had one of the most
important air defense commands in Iraq. His task was to protect Project 777, the
Iraqi nuclear weapons research facility, from enemy air attack. In a postwar discussion with Saddam, al-A'Any described how in the early days of the air campaign
the enemy "failed to achieve any of its objectives in terms of destroying the facilities due to the intensity of our fire and [our] passive protection methods."[43]
According to al-A'Any, his air defense unit actually fired the first shots of the
war. Moreover, they successfully "repelled" the Coalition's onslaught from 17
January until 3 February. According to his description, "when the enemy lost
hope on the F-16 fighter jets," they had to resort to F-117 Stealth fighters and
at 0830 on 3 February, the Coalition finally achieved its objectives. Saddam
congratulated him on the seventeen-day defense of this critical site and reminded him that despite the technology of modern war, the human mind augmented by concrete, were still the critical ingredients for success. Saddam noted that
the defense of the Iraqi nuclear site was a "lesson for the world and to the men
of air defenses worldwide to know that the Iraqis were well trained. Let them say:
It is possible that all these countries were flying sorties for seventeen days pound-
ing Iraq and they failed to precisely pinpoint and destroy a single target."[44]

At 1334 on 17 January, the minister of oil in coordination with the naval
headquarters gave the order to initiate the naval portions of the Tariq Project.

There were no written procedures as per Saddam's orders, and after some initial confusion, oil was successfully pumped into the waters of the Gulf. A short while later, the tankers also started to pump the first of what would become more than 8 million barrels of crude from their hulls into the Gulf. The Iraqi Navy commander later recalled that the spilled oil from Tariq Project "caused a loud echo" on the region's desalinization plants and the Coalition ships. The most immediate impact, however, was that "it forced the enemy troops to direct intense aviation strikes" against the oil facilities involved.[45]

18 JANUARY

After surveying some of the units and facilities of the missile corps, some already under direct Coalition air attack, General al-Ayyubi returned to his headquarters in Baghdad to monitor operations. At 0300 he received a radio message from the commander of the 224th Missile Brigade to confirm his strike orders. At 0310, the Iraqis launched eight missiles in quick succession at pre-designated targets in Tel Aviv and Haifa.[46] After this launch, the missile force quickly settled into a routine of confirming target guidance with Saddam, cycling launch vehicles through missile storage and fueling locations, establishing a secure firing position, and finally launching.

According to General al-Ayyubi, the limited number of mobile launch vehicles dictated a complex round-robin firing cycle.[47] The transporter-erector launchers (TELs) moved between launch locations in the western desert (when firing at Israel), through missile storage and loading units in ar-Ramadi and Baghdad to launch positions near ar-Rumayalah and Safwan (when firing at Riyadh), and finally to al-Amarah (when firing at Coalition forces on the Saudi Arabian coast). This cycle continued through the end of the war.

19 JANUARY

On 19 January, Saddam expressed concern about the effectiveness of enemy attacks on what he considered "vital targets." He directed his air defense forces to reposition anti-aircraft batteries away from the damaged areas and toward those "targets which [the enemy] had not [yet] destroyed."[48] Saddam was also clearly thinking ahead. In addition to shifting air defense assets away from targets already attacked, he suggested to the commander of the Iraqi Air Force that "we should also give priority to our ground units in the battlefront, because the enemy will focus his strikes on them after inflicting as much damage as he can on his targets in the deep center, and after making sure the deep center is exhausted. Then the enemy would be prepared for a counter ground operation, however if he [the enemy] engages in the ground operation, he would need to inflict a negative impact on our units through air strikes."[49]

Two days into the Coalition's air onslaught, Saddam was also concerned that the enemy's apparent ownership of the electronic spectrum was something his forces were completely unprepared for. On the 19th Saddam issued an order to address the challenge:

> In order to have a counter plan in place against the enemy, we must first understand the enemy's characteristics. . . . Among these characteristics, the enemy is advanced in the field of electronics and technology. . . . Therefore we must face him with counter procedures instead of trying to match his capabilities and attempt to become more advanced than him within a short period, which would not be possible at the present time. However . . . instead of facing the advanced complicated procedures, we should face him with simple methods . . . for example whenever the enemy is able to intercept our wire and wireless calls, the correct counter plan is not to buy code machines from the opposition country in the West [in order to] complicate the enemy's ability to understand our calls; rather, we should stop all our calls.[50]

Saddam went on to direct that wireless communications would not emanate from "a building that is more valuable than the communications equipment."[51] Additional steps included using personal letters for important communication, thereby preventing "a clerk or low-level employee in a department to view the same letters that are viewed by a member of the command, minister, and the high level cadre in the country and the party."[52] This last directive accounts for why much of the regime's most sensitive correspondence was handwritten and difficult to track through the otherwise exhaustive bureaucracy.

At 1800 on 19 January, Saddam met with General al-Ayyubi and told him he was concerned for the security of the missile forces. Saddam directed that additional personnel from GMID start escorting the missile convoys. As the Scud missile launches intensified, the Coalition directed intensive attacks on known or suspected missile locations. Later, the missile force commander noted that as of 19 January, more than 1,800 bombs had fallen near his units, with the loss of only one soldier and no significant equipment.[53] The operational pattern of firing, moving, confirming new targets, reloading, and firing again from a position five to ten kilometers from the previous one became more efficient with each launch. At 2145, the Iraqis fired the first two of what would eventually become more than forty missiles at Coalition forces in Saudi Arabia. Early the next morning the first of many reports of Coalition helicopters and special operations soldiers operating in the western desert began to filter into General al-Ayyubi.

20 JANUARY

An intelligence report dated 20 January updated the command on the effects of the first missile attacks on Israel. It said that "missiles hit in the area of the Defense Ministry and major communications stations in Tel-Aviv. The attack was effective. It caused a major panic. The state of emergency and readiness was declared in bases, airports, and hospitals. Israel has amassed its forces along the borders of Jordan and Syria."[54]

Offensive operations were not intended to be limited to the missile forces. On 20 January, the commander of III Corps received orders from Baghdad to "execute operations outside the borders and to destroy economic and military targets." In response, the corps staff developed plans "without delay" to conduct cross border raids into Saudi Arabia in order to "capture as many prisoners as they can."[55] The logic was explained by the III Corps commander: "We could not leave the element of surprise in the hands of our enemy. We had to identify the force that had the superiority against [the Coalition]. We had to learn that victory is not based on numbers but on faith."[56]

These initial attempts at ground offensive action were meant to "force the enemy to engage in a major ground battle [where we hope] that the enemy will suffer great losses." There was little, if any, effect from these "ambush patrols and raids" into Saudi Arabia, but the reports generated by them may have given confidence to those in Baghdad to try a much larger operation. As the III Corps commander recalled, they "considered the possibility of establishing control over [the] al-Khafji port in order to force the enemy to establish a position near our land forces [in order] to minimize his aerial activities against our strategic targets deep inside our territories."[57]

21 JANUARY

Less than a week into the war, the large-scale Coalition air attacks began to affect Saddam's confidence that Iraqi forces could engage the enemy *and* live to fight another day. On 21 January, based on "evidence showing that the enemy meant [to] destroy the infrastructure of Iraq," Saddam ordered the air defense staff to "cut down on everything . . . maintain the weapons and equipment and to cut down on the use of ammunition."[58] In his order to the air defense forces, Saddam explained that "the enemy is planning to shorten the battle, which we planned to prolong, the opposite of their expectation. Therefore, according to our calculations, the most important requirements of the long war are to conserve everything and execute the mission that is given to the men of the armed forces."[59]

The attacks on infrastructure were already having an impact near the front. Loss of bridges and supply trucks meant even the most basic supplies, while

Figure 26. Coalition damage to Iraqi airfield from a 1991 Iraq Air Force study
(Harmony folder ISGP-2003-00034642)

stockpiled at corps and division levels for a long battle, could not be regularly distributed below those levels. At least one Iraqi Army unit adopted a Bedouin solution to the loss from air strikes of its logistics vehicles: In late January, an order from the commander of the 25th Infantry Division directed that his soldiers round local camels up and assign them to those "with camel grazing experience." According to the commander, these replacement "vehicles" would not attract Coalition jets and could help deliver critical food and other provisions to the frontline units.[60]

In a postwar conference, this specific decision was noted as one of the reasons for a gradual collapse of Iraqi frontline morale. Not surprisingly, the Iraqi analyst making this observation was careful not to implicate the actual decision maker. He noted that troops received orders to not fire on aircraft out of range, but this "reduced [their] morale" and "caused a feeling of defeat" among the population because "the aircraft are seen by the eye and heard by the ear and the [troops] are able to see them, but cannot hit them. . . . Morale is weakened because we do not have the capability to fight them."[61]

Attending this same conference, Ali Hasan al-Majid added that the ammunition conservation policy actually increased Coalition airpower effectiveness.

He noted that a pilot who is not being shot at "finds himself in a safe position" and "his strikes will be certain and better than when [our] shots explode under him, even kilometers away."[62]

When the priority of air defense went from defense to survival, the air defense units confronted a new problem—a lack of mobility. According to one officer, the shortage of tow vehicles left many units exposed to the unrelenting Coalition attacks and under orders not to fire. Despite limitations on the number of trucks, the only thing that kept most of Iraq's air defense systems from destruction was repositioning. As one officer described to Saddam after the war, "Most of our equipment would have been destroyed because all the sites were open and photographed by the enemy. In fact, when we conducted our maneuver after the battle had already started Mr. President, the enemy attacked our former positions and bombarded empty buildings. Had it not been for our maneuver, our losses would have been catastrophic."[63]

On 22 January, Saddam ordered all ministries to "break down any device, [or] machine into vital parts . . . and move them outside [of] the sites that the enemy might recognize through air photography." Recognizing that what Iraq could not hide it could not preserve, Saddam admonished all of his ministers to disassemble whatever they could in order to "reassemble them intact once the war is over [and we are] crowned with a great victory."[64]

23 JANUARY

Just like their colleagues in Baghdad and Kuwait, the Republican Guard forces hunkered down in southern Iraq were feeling the impact of the unrelenting air attacks. The soldiers of Hamdani's 17th Brigade were enduring poundings from American B-52s, F-16s, and British Tornados. Hamdani recalled that "we resisted with all available weapons. . . . I lost both my anti-aircraft batteries within three weeks from the start of the war. I also lost many of my officers and soldiers in spite of my attempts to decrease the effects of the air bombing as much as possible by having one-third of my force change positions every day."[65]

As the war ended its first week, reports of Coalition forces moving west from Hafi al-Batin increased. The problem for the GMID, and one its analysts could not solve was—why? Notwithstanding the intelligence reports, Iraqi units in Kuwait remained focused on two primary enemy courses of action in late January. The Coalition was either going to move up the Wadi al-Batin, or it was going to execute a direct assault up the central axis to Kuwait City.[66]

In a preview of what would become a devastating case of operational paralysis in 2003, the Iraqi GMID in late January and early February 1991 struggled to reconcile the obvious amphibious threat in the east and the mysterious, but

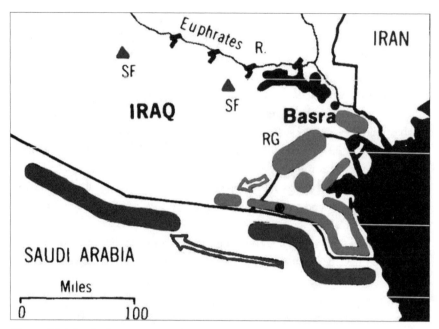

Figure 27. The Coalition moves to the west. "Once the air campaign started, he [Saddam] would be incapable of moving out to counter this move, even if he knew we made it." General Schwarzkopf ("Central Command Briefing," 96. RG stands for Republican Guard, SF is Special Forces.)

increasingly ominous shift of Coalition forces to the west.[67] Divining the form of the coming Coalition ground assault became increasingly difficult for the Iraqis as more and more information on the Coalition's deployments became available. The problem was not simply one of poor information management, although this clearly played a role, but more one of trying to make the situation fit preconceived notions.

In a report dated 23 January, the GMID Director described "a massive movement of hostile forces with helicopters going towards Rafha."[68] These forces reportedly included French units and tank transporters. The Director reflected on this information in light of information recently received from "one of our embassies abroad." The intelligence implied that the major elements of a Coalition plan "in case ground operations begin" were as follows:[69]

The Syrian and Egyptian forces would act as an "independent corps."
"The Americans were going to use an armored division to protect the left wing (the movement of the aforementioned columns in the direction of Rafha)."
Marine infantry with at least one heavy division will attack into the "coastal axis."

The United States will "preserve" the American VII Corps as a reserve.

Kuwaiti forces will constitute the frontline troops in any attack.

The Coalition will launch extensive "air raids to isolate Kuwait."

The "main ground assault" will be along the coast road.

Secondary assaults will occur all along "the combat front."

"Ground and sea attacks to hamper the counter-attacks by the Republican Guard," will be a major effort.

Seizing Kuwait City with "light American casualties" is the immediate objective.

The intelligence report concluded that a confrontation along the Wadi al-Batin was capable of causing "catastrophic casualties in the American Forces." Therefore, an attack along the "central axis" was the "best and most probable alternative" for the Coalition to execute.

The GMID Director's analysis of this unverifiable "enemy course of action" reinforces the long-standing assessment that the "central axis" was the most probable choice since it was "the closest of these approaches to Kuwait City." He went on to note that the Coalition would not make any final decisions until it could fully evaluate the effects of ongoing air operations. As for the movement of forces to the west of Hafir al-Batin, the director assessed that this "reinforces the likelihood of an attack against the [right] wing." Accordingly, the director recommended that increased protection to that sector and the "rear part of our forces is of utmost importance." Finally, he noted "it is possible that the American assessments [were] leaked with the objective of pushing us [so they can] find the wing and rear part of our forces."[70]

24–25 JANUARY

Around midday on the 24th, the Iraqi Air Force came close to completing its most daring and only significant strike mission of the war. The mission was to attack the huge oil export terminal center at Ras Tanura, Saudi Arabia.[71] The mission began with an order late on 22 January to immediately update plans and execute the previously proposed operation to destroy both the Ras Tanura facilities and the oil pumping and processing facility at al-Baqiq. For the Iraqi crews the challenge was Herculean if not suicidal.

During prewar planning, the mission was planned in detail. A target folder was prepared as early as 15 August. Assumptions about Coalition airpower and air defense reaction times were factored against what in hindsight were wildly optimistic assumptions about Iraqi air prowess. Even under these favorable circumstances, Iraqi planners noted that the "impossibility of using the element of surprise due to AWACS plane presence . . . and the competence of their air defense system . . . [will] result in more than 50 percent damages to our planes."[72] After a week of observing Coalition air power, the Iraqi Air Force staff officers updated their planning assumptions to include:

The enemy has achieved air superiority. "[Coalition] planes are freely present in all regions of Iraq."

The Iraqi Air Force lost the ability to move between bases. Transporting crews, parts, and even briefing officers to the dispersed fleet of aircraft was exceedingly difficult.

The airbases themselves were "busy repairing the tarmacs and runways and deactivating the bombs." Moving within the bases was becoming difficult.

The Coalition had an almost constant air patrol of F-14 and F-18 aircraft to the south and west of Kuwait. These aircraft were capable of detecting low altitude combat planes at a range of eighty to one hundred kilometers.

Notwithstanding the greatly reduced odds of success, the crews planned to depart Abu 'Ubaydi Airfield (near al-Kut) early on the 23rd. The mission profile had the Mirages fly south along the Iranian border, at extremely low altitude (thirty to fifty meters), and very high speed (940 kilometers per hour) to minimize the chances of detection. The biggest complication was the requirement to conduct an air-to-air refuel one hundred meters above the ground in increasingly hostile airspace. Coalition air raids on the Mirage base at 0930 on the 23rd delayed the mission and destroyed two of the aircraft planned for the mission. The aircraft were changed out and final preparations made when another Coalition air raid at 1625 destroyed another one of the "duty planes." Moreover, the air raids caused a base-wide power failure, trapping the second aircraft inside its hardened bunker. The mission was postponed again for just after sunrise on the 24th.

The mission was delayed yet again on the 24th. Ground crews were unable to clear the cluster bomb sub-munitions of the previous day's air raids from around the hangar doors. The Iraqi strike aircraft and their tankers finally got off the ground in the late morning. After completing a refueling operation along the Iranian border, the pair of Iraqi Mirage F-1s arrived "off our southern borders in the lands of Najad and Hijaz [Saudi Arabia]."[73]

A Coalition history of the Iraqi operation notes that, whether by plan or luck, the Iraqi Mirages flew along a control boundary between the U.S. Air Force and the U.S. Navy. The Iraqi jets made it to a point approximately seventy kilometers south of the Kuwaiti border, just off the Saudi coast, without being

Figure 28. Ras Tanura Oil Terminal, Saudi Arabia. Iraqi target folder photograph showing target areas for planned Mirage F-1 strikes. (Harmony document folder ISGP-2003-00037839)

challenged. At 0934, a Royal Saudi Air Force F-15C shot down both Iraqi jets with sidewinder missiles.[74] It is likely the Iraqi crews never saw the Saudi F-15Cs high above them. The Iraqi report on the mission concluded that, "after crossing this area [the Kuwaiti coastal waters], we did not get any information on our planes due to the low altitude and because it was outside the radar detection field of our equipment. Due to the many chances of intercepting our planes, it is possible that the enemy was able to down them."[75]

General al-Ayyubi's missile forces continued to launch missiles into Israel and Saudi Arabia even as the Coalition's "Scud-hunt" operations hit full stride. In the preceding days he received updated information on the "Israeli population" and the results of his earlier strikes and was able to adjust "the [targeting] of our missiles." The cat-and-mouse game with Coalition anti-missile operations became more complex. Added to the almost continuous reports of Coalition helicopters were the ever increasing road hazards to the convoys created by an increasing number of bomb craters. In the public version of his memoirs, General al-Ayyubi notes that at about this time "we began concealing launchers in the most unexpected places." In the captured version of the original document he revealed that, at least on the 24th, one of the creative launch sites was a refugee camp near mile marker 160 on the Baghdad-Amman Highway.[76] The 25th was the most successful launch day of the war for Iraq's missileers: they fired ten missiles at Coalition and Israeli targets.

During late January, a significant report caused new concerns about Iraq's southwestern border. On 25 January, in response to the growing threats, the I Corps headquarters received orders to move from Kirkuk to the vicinity of as-Samawah.[77] The move, coming after the beginning of the air campaign, occurred under almost continuous Coalition air attacks. By one estimate, the corps headquarters and at least one of its divisions were attacked by Coalition airpower more than 170 times before the start of ground operations.[78]

During a postwar review, Brig Gen. Ali Abbas Flyeh described the challenges faced by this headquarters. The I Corps sector ran from the boundary of the Iraqi VII Corps near the Kuwaiti border and extended west and north following the Iraqi border to the boundary of the V Corps near the Syrian-Jordanian border. To cover this 1,200-kilometer border, the corps commanded the 45th and 54th Infantry Divisions, the 3rd and 5th Border Guard Commands, and a reserve consisting of two special force brigades and a battalion of "special force tanks."[79] General Flyeh noted that, "[c]onsidering the shortage of available troops, only the most important [approaches] were held onto, and there were large gaps among the divisions, formations, and units."[80]

26 JANUARY

On 26 January, Saddam issued an order for the Iraqi Air Force to fly its surviving aircraft to Iran. A memorandum from the commander of the air force and air defense directed, as per Saddam's order, that eighteen Mirage, nine Sukhoi, and one Falcon-50 aircraft be "evacuated" to Iran.[81] Additional orders to the IAF followed steadily over the next three weeks. In a letter to his "courageous air falcons," Saddam explained that the decision to evacuate resulted from the enemy's now obvious air superiority and the limited impact of Iraqi planes during the current battle. "For safekeeping," Saddam told them "the planes were sent to Iran until the appropriate time comes to use them against the enemy."[82] It is not clear how much, if any, senior level coordination went on between Iraq and Iran before the first aircraft made the dash for safety. However, there are indications in Iraqi documents that there was at least some expectation of cooperation.

A notation in an Iraqi Air Force staff log from 13 February states that "the necessary actions to prepare the elements [that] will be departing for Iran for the purpose of extending the life of our aircraft" were complete and they would be ready to proceed by the 15th. A later entry in the same log notes they were going to "dispatch four [Su-25] pilots together with passports and photos for the purpose of completing their paperwork to proceed to Iran."[83] Regardless of expectations, and in light of the fact that Iran did not return the aircraft after the war, it appears that Saddam and the Iranian leadership did not have a common definition of "safekeeping."

According to Iraqi intelligence reports, a total of 137 Iraqi aircraft fled to Iran just before and during the war.[84] For their part, the Iranians only acknowledged 22 aircraft arriving at its airfields. According to Iraq intelligence reporting, Iran repainted the most advanced aircraft with Iranian colors almost as soon as they landed. A few months after the war, Iraqi intelligence reported that Iran was looking for nations to help train Iranian pilots in their newly acquired fleet of Soviet-built aircraft.[85]

27 JANUARY

Missile Brigade 224 reported to their commander that they captured five members of a Coalition Special Operations patrol and killed several more near the H2 airfield. The report further stated that an unknown number of soldiers escaped. A day later near ar-Ramadi, a member of the local Ba'ath security force captured a Coalition special operations soldier identified as being "Australian with British citizenship."[86] During the same week, General al-Ayyubi's log recorded that the 224 Missile Brigade "captured five infiltrators, two of them alive and some of them killed, one drowned in [the] river, one is injured with [a] sergeant rank, he was the commander of the patrol, one of them struggled, but he was killed and the other escaped."[87]

It was clear to General al-Ayyubi that his forces were being hunted by increasingly aggressive forces. The appropriate response to the Coalition threat in the western desert was a constant source of tension within the regime. A

TABLE 5. Iraqi Report of Aircraft Seeking Refuge in Iran
from 26 January to mid-February 1991

Aircraft Type	Number	Remarks
Sukhoi–20	4	3 destroyed
Sukhoi–22	40	5 destroyed
Sukhoi–24	24	2 destroyed
Sukhoi–25	7	
MiG–23	7	
MiG–23 (Variations)	4	1 destroyed
MiG–23 (Dual Seat)	1	
MiG–29	4	
Mirage F–1	24	
Ilyushin–76	15	
Jet Star	1	
Falcon–20	2	
Falcon–50	3	
Boeing 727 (Iranian)	1	
*Total	137	

*Source: Harmony document folder ISGP-2003-00030181. The report describes the destruction after crossing the border as the result of "bad weather." There is no explanation for the Fao-727 identified as Iranian in the report. It is possible that it was one of several Iranian aircraft that defected during the Iran-Iraq War.

memorandum from the Director of the Western Region Intelligence Directorate to his supervisor in Baghdad captures this tension. The 27 January document recounts various Coalition air attacks and commando raids, especially in the vicinity of ar-Ramadi during the previous week. Based on this information, the memorandum assessed that the Coalition intended to "conduct a wide airborne operation to take over our air force bases and create a direct threat to ar-Ramadi City and Baghdad in order to break up our defenses in Kuwait."[88]

To counteract this threat, the Director of the Western Region Intelligence Directorate proposed to shift Iraqi defenses to the western sector. The memorandum noted that its defenses "are weak and unable to counter a wide-range[ing] threat." He recommended that his command immediately be reinforced with mobile infantry units. A handwritten note at the bottom of the memorandum tersely acknowledged the higher headquarters receipt of the memorandum and added: "The counter[measure] procedures are the responsibility of the General

Staff. As for the regional intelligence directorates, their [only] duty is to convey intelligence information."[89]

Bagdad was not completely unsympathetic to the western region. Reports of helicopter insertions in the vicinity of the isolated towns of al-Qaim and ar-Rutbah, as well as near the highway landmark known as KM 160 received the highest priority.[90] The problem was not recognition but capability. Large units could no longer move across the open desert because of the Coalition's air dominance. In response to the threat, the GMID dispatched units of its commando force—Unit 999 (Deep Reconnaissance and Special Missions Battalion).[91] Unit 999 followed up on the reports, bolstered local defenses, and coordinated payment to local Bedouins for information on what they came across in the vast western wastelands.[92]

29 JANUARY

During the last week of January, Saddam focused on preserving as many assets as possible from the continued onslaught of Coalition aircraft. The remaining Iraqi aircraft consisted mostly of inoperable fixed wing and a fleet of army helicopters. To defeat Coalition targeting efforts, the helicopters were moved almost constantly for the rest of the war. The MIC established a committee to repair any air defense equipment that was repairable as soon as possible.[93]

Noting patterns in Coalition aircraft behavior, Saddam reportedly ordered his subordinates to establish "mobile" and "air intersection" ambushes in the area of the western desert and the central border with Iran. Given the limited number of missile systems available, mobility challenges, as well as the qualitative limitations of Iraqi air defense, this order had little if any effect on the Coalition's air campaign. One of Saddam's frustrations was the age of some of Iraq's best air defense systems. After the war, Saddam expressed significant frustration that "the Soviet Union had supplied Syria and Libya with a very advanced type of missile [and not Iraq]. The level of damage we could have inflicted on the enemy would have been much greater if we were to have had such systems." Saddam then rhetorically asked his air defense staff if they knew why they were denied such technology in this war: "because the Soviet Union would not give its quality weapons to those countries who really deserved them. That is the standard theory of the major powers. They give their weapons to parties who do not know how to use them."[94]

More than a week into the Coalition's air campaign, Iraqi naval leadership concluded that if any of their vessels were going to survive the war, they would have to make a run for safer waters. The closest refuge was the Iranian port of Bandar-e-Khomeini. During a postwar conference, one of the naval officers involved described the decision: "On the 29th of January, our command set up a quick plan to sail the ships to Iran in order to get them away from the influence of the enemy aerial bombardment. The pieces consisted of four missile boats, three landing barges, an artillery boat, and a medium minesweeper."[95]

Evacuating its ships to Iran would prove much more difficult than evacuating the air force. The commanders of the surviving flotilla would have to make the 230-kilometer journey under constant threat of Coalition aircraft, through coastal waters clogged with debris and recently released free-floating mines—all without the benefit of navigation radars or the use of radios.

Beginning at 2100 hours on 29 January, the nine Iraqi ships began to assemble from their hiding berths along the Khor Abdullah near the port of Umm Qasar. At 2345, three groups of three ships each departed at 20-minute intervals on their dangerous trek to Iran. At 0130 on 30 January, as the first three ships slowly weaved along the shallow coast, they were attacked by Coalition aircraft. The first aircraft "achieved a direct and influential hit which caused severe damages" on the command ship. Within fifteen minutes the other two ships in the lead group were sunk.[96] After witnessing the attacks, the second two groups of Iraqi ships changed course and continued toward Iran in deeper waters. Coalition aircraft reacquired the remaining six ships and attacked at 0730. After a series of strikes during the next hour, three more ships in the ill-fated flotilla were at the bottom of the Gulf.

Sometime after 1100, the three surviving Iraqi ships, "a missile boat, a landing barge, and an artillery boat," limped into the Port of Bandar-e-Khomeini.[97] The mission to "rescue our weapons from the assaults of the criminal enemies," was costly. In addition to the six sunken ships, the dash to Iran cost the Iraqi Navy "twenty martyrs: seven generals and thirteen other ranks," as well as sixty-eight prisoners. During a conference in 1993, an Iraqi naval officer lamented that, for some, the mission did not end on 30 January 1991: "The guests of Iran became prisoners after the involvement of the Iranian enemy in the page of betrayal and treason [the 1991 uprisings]. They were considered prisoners. Nine of them are still there. Two generals and several other individuals are still in prison in Iran, and it has been two and a half years."[98]

For their part, the Iranians appeared only too happy to add the remains of the Iraqi Navy to the growing number of Iraqi jets taking refuge from Coalition firepower. The change from 1988 could not have been more surreal.

Late on 29 January, the Iraqi III and IV Corps launched a major attack into the northeastern edge of Saudi Arabia. Elements of three divisions actually crossed the border, one along the coastal road and the other two farther inland near the al-Wafra Farms and a few kilometers farther west. The immediate tactical task of the operation was to capture the small city of al-Khafji. But as with all things, Saddam had a much larger purpose in mind. The details of the al-Khafji operation will not be repeated here (see Chapter 2 of this study—"The 'Victory' at al-Khafji") except to note that this operation, more than any other, fit within Saddam's aphorism, "the real chance is the one you use not the one you think about."[99] The introduction to an Iraqi top secret study of the al-Khafji Battle, frames the event in the uniquely Iraqi context:

> "after it became apparent that there was a determination that the [Coalition] did not want to face [Iraq] in a land battle because the [Coalition] aggressors were afraid of Iraqi determination due to their prior knowledge of the Iraqi fighter's strength and experience gained in the glorious war of Saddam's Qadisiyyah over the period of eight years."
>
> Based on all of the above and under the directives of the president and general commander of the armed forces (may Allah keep him), the command was given to the Iraqi armed forces to compel the enemy to enter into a land war, which the enemy was attempting to postpone its time and place after achieving the goal of destroying Iraqi forces and the anchors of their support through air power and missiles, thus, the plan was to enter into Saudi lands and occupy important locations that are the cornerstones of the mobilization and launching points of the allied forces for the purpose of destroying them and engaging them in a land battle at a time and place that suits our troops and not the enemy's.[100]

On 31 January, Iraq's first and only major ground offensive operation ended. Two Iraqi divisions suffered significant losses with little lasting operational or tactical gain to show for the effort. A postwar official military history recorded the principal operational lesson of the battle of al-Khafji somewhat tentatively as: "Battles are not won in the end except through the offensive and the al-Khafji battle represents the principle. [al-Khafji was the] prominent offensive battle our forces engaged in during Um al-Ma'arik, which proved the offensive capabilities of the Iraqi Army after 12 days since the start of the war."[101]

A few days after the engagement, Saddam's pronouncement of the strategic lesson that "the battle of al-Khafji had defamed the enemy, and it [is] considered a success," set the Ba'athist and therefore the official tone.[102]

Their defeated gathering[103]

FEBRUARY

In early February, a report from the GMID to the Army's chief of staff noted with alarm that reports were continuing to come in about "the presence of the [American] 82nd and 101st Airborne Divisions in addition to Saudi and French forces" in the vicinity of Ar'ar.[104] The chief of staff directed the undermanned I Corps to take necessary precautions. The staff in Baghdad further proposed that the corps quickly assign a division to "repel any enemy threats."[105]

For Saddam, it must have seemed that General al-Ayyubi's missile force was the only consistent bright spot in the reporting. Despite public statements of confidence and success, the Coalition's actions indicated an increased concern about the Scud launches or more specifically, its inability to stop them.[106] On 2 February, the commander of Saddam's missile forces gave him a detailed status report:

> From the beginning of the war until 28 January, Iraq fired fifty-two missiles: twenty missiles at Tel Aviv, eight at Haifa, thirteen at Riyadh, seven at Dhahran, two at Baqaq Oil Complex, one at al-Dammam, and one at al-Jubayl. The average was just more than four missiles per day.
> The launches concentrated on "three main centers" from eleven launch locations in five operational areas around Iraq.
> To date, losses to the missile force were one officer and five soldiers killed, seven officers and forty-one soldiers wounded, damage to nine of twenty-eight "launching bases," seventeen vehicles and three antiaircraft guns damaged. No launchers or missiles had been lost.

On 2 February, Saddam ordered a two-day break in the current launch schedule. Perhaps hoping to lengthen the campaign, Saddam ordered the missile firing average be cut in half to two missiles per day.

After the short break, General al-Ayyubi submitted a detailed inventory report to Saddam. Iraq started the war with 230 missiles and 75 "special warheads." So far they had fired 52 missiles. Thirty-four of the remaining missiles had maintenance problems. Moreover, there was only enough fuel for 118 missiles total, regardless of type or maintenance status. General al-Ayyubi asked Saddam to order the MIC to provide fuel for 60 more missiles, manufacture 15 new warheads (presumably conventional), repair 7 existing missiles, and manufacture 41 new missiles. This effort, plus the existing inventory would boost the useable inventory to 102 conventional missiles, 177 overall. In other words, without using any "special warheads," and based on the new firing schedule, Saddam's missileers reported that they could continue the fight until late March.[107]

5 FEBRUARY

A 5 February memorandum from the GMID Director to the presidential office demonstrated the growing tension at the highest levels between the assessed enemy course of action and the undeniable threat growing daily on Iraq's extreme right flank. Overcoming the leadership's fixation on the original enemy course of action proved difficult for several reasons. The first reason was purely pragmatic. The ongoing air campaign made any problem whose solution required major movements of Iraqi forces a non-starter. The second reason was that every time information concerning a western shift seemed irrefutable, new highly credible information arrived to refute it. For example, on 5 February an Iraqi military attaché passed information he obtained from a foreign intelligence source:[108]

> Most of the American armor was "assembling in the vicinity of Hafir al-Batin." "This force would conduct a diversionary operation in support of the amphibious landing planned for North of Kuwait City."
>
> The "primary operation" would be an amphibious operation north of Kuwait City. "An airborne operation might support the amphibious operation."
>
> In case the amphibious assaults were unsuccessful, "a direct assault by infantry into the teeth of the Iraqi defense south of Kuwait City near al-Wafra would occur."
>
> The Americans would work with the Turks to open a front in the north and "eliminate the Kurdish movement."

One GMID analysis of this information reflected the challenge they faced. The director warned that "they should deal cautiously with the intelligence . . . it could be used as a tool . . . it could be a part of hostile deception plans."[109] While being reasonably skeptical that the source might be part of such a plan, there was evidence to support this description of Coalition plans. For example, it was already clear the Americans had made significant preparations for an amphibious operation of some kind. On the other hand, the Iraqi intelligence services had reliable reports of the growing density of American armor west of Kuwait as well as increased enemy helicopter forces near Ar'ar (western limit of the Coalition's forces in Saudi Arabia). Media reporting also indicated a growing likelihood of a maneuver to the west.[110] By the end of the first week of February, the director appeared convinced that the previous focus on a Coalition amphibious operation and the American use of "naval infantry" as regular infantry in the center of the line was likely a deception. To him, a potentially high-risk amphibious operation did not make sense because the Americans would obviously "endure big losses" in any such operation.[111]

Iraqi missile operations continued. According to General al-Ayyubi's unpublished log, on 6 February, the presidential secretary forwarded new coordinates

Figure 29. Iraqi propaganda leaflet. This leaflet calls for the Arab members of the Coalition to join Iraq, so together they can crush America (Iraqi propaganda leaflet recovered in southern Kuwait by a members of the U.S. 3rd Armored Division on 3 March 1991)

for targets in Israel. The information, an evaluation of previous strikes dating back to 20 January, was developed by the PLO's Force 17 in support of the IIS.[112]

7 FEBRUARY

While the Iraqis attempted to determine if information they received was part of a Coalition deception, they simultaneously attempted a deception operation of their own. The GMID proposed a series of deception operations aimed at splitting the Coalition. Its aim was to convince the Arab forces assembled as part of the Coalition that the American forces were moving away from the main point of attack. In this way the United States could avoid casualties and force the Arabs to bear the brunt of the fighting.

The deception plan's key task was to broadcast messages through Baghdad radio, through Arab home fronts, and to use leaflets reading "American forces are moving away from the battlefield. American troops are afraid of our troops and they are abandoning [the] other allied forces." Moreover, the Iraqi deception planners explained that the Americans were not cut out for desert warfare because "they do not have enough shelters and are suffering from exposure."[113] In the meantime, perhaps to counter any potential of a real threat in the west, the IIS would leak through its agents that Iraq was prepared to conduct major cross-border operations in the vicinity of Rafha and Ar'ar. These operations would be supported by major operations of the Iraqi III and IV Corps in the vicinity of al-Kahfji and Hafir al-Batin. The Iraqi command, the leak would emphasize, expected that American forces would suffer major casualties.[114]

As in all wars, critical pieces of information exist that can have a major impact on events, but for reasons rarely discovered, fail to make it to the right decision maker at the right time. An Iraqi example of this phenomenon was a mid-January memorandum from the Iraqi military attaché in Amman to the Director of the GMID. The attaché relayed that according to a Palestinian laborer, the Americans had built large numbers of "tanks made of wood and iron" in the Hafir al-Batin area to deceive Iraqi forces.[115] At the time, the Iraqis considered Hafir al-Batin to be the western edge of the Coalition. The implication of this report should have raised alarm within the intelligence services. If this were true, the Americans were apparently trying to create the impression of large troop concentrations exactly where Iraqi intelligence said enemy troops were secretly concentrating.[116] It seems that the Iraqi planners should have asked themselves if the Americans were not massing at Hafir al-Batin then where were they? The conflicting data seem to have been lost in the process. The Iraqi propaganda messages that Coalition forces were moving to the west in order to avoid casualties ironically played into the Coalition deception effort. It is possible that Iraqi planners, on hearing reports of Coalition movements to the west of Hafir al-Batin, may have thought the Iraqi deception plan had been a success.

Notwithstanding the dueling deception operations, by the second week of February, new intelligence reports began to shake the confidence of Iraq's senior leadership on the direction of the coming attack. A "top secret and confidential" memorandum dated 12 February reminded the presidential secretary about a report on the 10th that the Turks had amassed 205,000 soldiers and more than 1,500 tanks along Iraq's northern border. Among other things, this high level report added:

"thousands of American and French Special Forces recently [arrived] in Turkey."
"Additional French forces were confirmed moving to Rafha" (Western limit of Coalition).
"Food rations and fuel [for] twenty thousand soldiers [was] in the area of Tarif . . . near the [Saudi] Jordan borders."
"[Since] 6 February a continuous movement of specialized vehicles was noticed and trucks loaded with equipment and carriers loaded with tanks and engineering equipment on the main road Qaysumah-Rafha-Ar'ar."

"A column of tank carriers loaded with sixty armored personnel carriers
. . . [was] moving towards an area [60 km South East of Rafha]."[117]

Moreover, this same report noted that an Iraqi "advanced reconnaissance
unit" (most likely GMID's Unit 999) observed more than one hundred helicopters within fifty kilometers of Rafha. The report went on to say, however,
that the aircraft were having "great difficulty landing." The GMID concluded
that the Coalition, based on all of the activity, had not completed its deployments and that the "air war of attrition will stay its course." However, it concluded, "our forces [should] be prepared for a confrontation and the likelihood
[that the Coalition] will accelerate the ground operation's timing."[118] The report
was still noncommittal on the actual point of the Coalition main effort.

Coalition air strikes on Iraqi forces inside Kuwait and along the southern
Iraqi border intensified during the second week of February. Brigadier General
Hamdani recalled that the Republican Guard positions in Southern Iraq were
hit "on average one air attack every two hours" during this time.[119] An officer
in the IV Corps recalled: "The enemy never stopped bothering us day and night
by all types of aircraft . . . high speed jets, slow flying jets, precision bombers, and
[other] combat jets. The weapons that really frustrated us and harmed us were
the slow-flying aircraft and the Marine types [A-6] and [A-10]. Sometimes they
spent the whole day suspended over our heads to the extent that our ears had
gotten used to their buzzing sounds."[120]

The biggest operational implication from the unrelenting air strikes was the
cumulative effect on morale. It is possible that Saddam was unaware how bad
morale had become in the Army by early February. The apparent size of the gap
between estimates of morale in Baghdad and actual morale at the front is a stunning example of bureaucratic self-deception on the part of the regime. A Coalition debrief of a deserter from the 20th Infantry Division in early February
1991 provides a useful data point:

> The morale of the 20th Division personnel is not different than the morale
> of the other divisions located in Kuwait. Everybody is suffering from very
> low morale. First, personnel do not believe in the cause for which they
> [were] placed in Kuwaiti lands. Second, the supply lines are cut off from
> them. The men get only one meal a day which does not exceed rice
> without meat. The water is scarce, each three men get 1.65 liters for drin-
> king water. . . . They are all thinking about surrendering to the Allied for-
> ces; however, fear is stopping them. Yet they see the best time to surrender
> is when the Allied forces start their ground attack.

The positions of the 20th division have been exposed to bombardment three times a day. . . . Equipment [has] not been replaced and the bodies of dead men remain in their position. The bombardment and not seeing any [Iraqi] resistance destroyed the morale of the men.[121]

9 FEBRUARY

Run-ins with Coalition special operations forces in the western desert were becoming more frequent and much more destructive by early February. Reports of mysterious helicopter operations and Bedouin sightings of small patrols only increased as February wore on.

One situation report noted that at 0200 on 9 February, "two American enemy groups attacked the al-Anbar Base for Space Research." The local defenders reported the incident in great detail. He described how the American commandos were thwarted in their attempt to enter the base and were trapped by the "brutal" counterattack of the Iraqi "emergency regiment." The Iraqis "defeated and drove off the attackers," who left behind one wounded man, inexplicably identified as British in the report, and a large amount of equipment. A subsequent interrogation of the wounded man confirmed that "their mission was to [find] and destroy Scud missile bases."[122]

10 FEBRUARY

By the second week of February, the Iraqi Air Force had reached the point where its sole function was to track its own losses to Coalition attacks. A sample of the entries from an Iraqi Air Force staff log recorded the often surprising and sometimes desperate conditions of Saddam's "courageous air falcons" between 10 and 16 February:[123]

"No aircraft have been sent away [flown to Iran] today due to hostile activity and the [fact that the] transfer of aircraft program has been postponed to an unannounced day." Notify the 24th Squadron to "disassemble [their aircraft] and deploy away from the base." (2/10)

"Confirm with Ali . . . with regard to increasing the amount of food for the enlisted personnel, [because] there is only enough food for the officers." (2/10)

"There is no need to send any MiG-23 pilots to Sa'ad Air Base, as there are no functional aircraft and that it is sufficient to send 5 MiG-21 pilots only." (2/10)

Base status: al-Huriyyah, Saddam, al-Baqr, and al-Rashid reported a "normal situation, runway functional." (2/10)

"The commander of the Air Academy proposed hiding MiG-23s by placing them in a trench and covering them with a tent." He pointed out

TABLE 6. **Iraqi Ground Order of Battle***

Area Headquarters	Regular Army (in KTO)	
Gulf Operations Command: Occupation	• II Corps •	• IV Corps •
Jihad Command: Counterattack	2nd Infantry	6th Armored
	51st Infantry	8th Infantry
Republican Guard	• III Corps •	10th Armored
1st Sub-Corps	1st Mechanized	17th Armored
Hammurabi Armored Division	3rd Armored	16th Infantry
Medina Armored Division	5th Mechanized	20th Infantry
Tawakalna Mechanized Division	7th Infantry	21st Infantry
Al-Faw Infantry Division	14th Infantry	34th Infantry
2nd Sub-Corps	18th Infantry	47th Infantry
Baghdad Mechanized Division	29th Infantry	52nd Armored
Nebuchadnezzar Infantry Division	27th Infantry	•VII Corps •
Adnan Infantry Division	28th Infantry	12th Armored
	31st Infantry	25th Infantry
Al-Abed Division	35th Infantry	26th Infantry
Al-Nida Division	49th Infantry	30th Infantry
Al-Quds Division	51st Infantry	45th Infantry
	• I Corps •	48th Infantry
Republican Guards Special Forces	54th Infantry	
Al-Mustafa Division		

*Note: Forces in Kuwait theater of operations (based on a June 2007 compilation of multiple sources).

that "the tent can then be covered with a layer of mud to match the surrounding area," however, care should be taken so that "the tent takes on a shape different from an aircraft." (2/11)

Report from the Ali base: "All MiG-23 aircraft have been evacuated except one of them which will be evacuated this evening. All Mirages have been evacuated" except for two because of damage to the bunker doors. (2/12)

A message to all bases: "Ensure that aircraft are placed outside the fence, one kilometer apart from each other . . . so that if an aircraft is hit, no other aircraft near by it will also be damaged." (2/16)

Scud missile launches against targets in Saudi Arabia and Israel continued, although as ordered at a reduced rate from previous weeks. On 13 February, Saddam ordered the missile forces to execute a "revenge" strike against U.S. forces in the vicinity of Hafir al-Batin for the civilian deaths at the al-Firdos bunker.[124] At 1145 on the 14th the missile brigades pooled their resources and fired six missiles simultaneously from northeast of Baghdad.[125]

14 FEBRUARY

As the air campaign wore on, reports of Coalition forces moving to the west continued to arrive at Iraqi intelligence headquarters.[126] One report dated 14 February noted that "continuous movement was recorded for [Coalition] troops, trucks full of equipment, tanks, transporters, and [other] equipment moving on the main road from Qaysumah [near Hafir al-Batin] and Su'ayrah to Ar'ar and Rafha [western deployment area for Coalition forces]."[127]

In yet another intelligence report from 14 February, the GMID noted the increase in Coalition activity. Specifically this report cited:

"Selective precision bombing" with an emphasis on logistics.
Operations to locate missile launchers and other "special equipment."
Attacks to destroy roads and bridges in Southern Iraq to "deny mobility."
Air strikes to destroy Iraqi minefields using "incendiary bombs" and other
      means including massive seven-ton bombs.

Based on the above, the analysts concluded that the time for "land operations was near." The GMID Director raised the warning of large-scale land operations to "imminent."[128]

15 FEBRUARY

Reports of an imminent Coalition ground offensive were now flooding Iraq's intelligence services. A report from the Iraqi Embassy in Jordan narrowed the start date for a ground offensive to the 18th. It indicated that Israel would participate in the assault with up to 260 combat aircraft and an airborne operation into the western desert to stop Iraqi missile attacks. The IIS judged this report as highly credible since it reportedly came from a sympathetic Western source.[129]

The 15th also brought a surprise announcement on Baghdad radio that the RCC was now prepared "to deal with Security Council Resolution 660, with the aim of reaching an honorable and acceptable solution, including withdrawal [from Kuwait]."[130] After an initial blush of optimism, it soon became clear that the 15 February announcement was only a slightly modified version of the

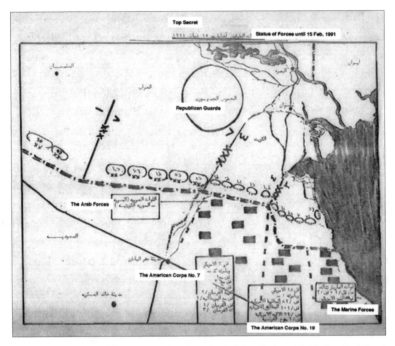

Figure 30. Status of forces, 15 February 1991. Map from a 1994 classified Iraqi history of the war. Curiously it does not include the Coalition buildup to the west (Harmony document folder ISGP-2003-00035810)

repudiated conditions for withdrawal previously presented by Iraqi officials. The Coalition air campaign continued unabated.

Despite the lack of progress on the diplomatic front, Iraq's offensive arm continued to report steady progress. The missile forces commander dispatched a letter to Saddam to report on the previous day's successful attacks executed "as vengeance for the innocent martyrs" of the al-Firdos bunker incident. The next entry in the log then noted that due to increasing threats from air strikes "our headquarters was changed to a school."[131] The missile forces received feedback on its attacks into Israel in the form of a report prepared by the PLO. According to the several days-old report, "The missiles hit one thousand Israelis, 14 were killed, 273 were injured, 818 were psychologically shocked, and 3,000 were evacuated from their houses. 1,000 houses were destroyed, and others were hit in Tel Aviv."[132]

16 FEBRUARY

A 16 February GMID memorandum, commenting on increasing reports of Coalition forces shifting to the western desert, noted that they were "correct and useful." The memorandum confirmed that "more than 1,000 tanks and vehicles, in addition to different types of weapons, missiles, and thousands of soldiers," were now in the vicinity of Ar'ar and Rafhah.[133] In its analysis of why the Coalition moved away from the center of the Iraq defense, the memorandum seemed to support both the Iraqi deception and the unshakable Iraqi view of the Coalition plan. Coalition forces might, the memorandum read, attack on "coaxial axes aiming to disperse the Iraqi forces [and] get them away from their [current] locations . . . forcing them into combat in unprepared locations . . . and dispersing them in the open."[134] Only a week before the beginning of the actual ground campaign and four weeks after the Coalition started shifting a massive force to the west of Iraq's defensive line, the Iraqi command system could not settle on an enemy course of action. This intellectual and bureaucratic inertia was about to change.

18 FEBRUARY

On 18 February a GMID intelligence report marked with Iraq's highest security classification (top secret, confidential, and urgent), was sent to the secretary of the president. The assessment contained a clear and generally accurate articulation of the Coalition's "left hook" plan, with the exception of the maneuver's ultimate objective. The GMID Director stated it now appeared that it was "the enemy's intention to make a main move from Ar'ar towards Karbala [to] al-Hilla and from there to Baghdad."[135] The ominous report continued: "the deployment of the American XVIII Airborne Corps and armor in the area of Rafha [and] Ar'ar . . . secures the possibility for the enemy to carry out massive airborne operations through the defenseless zones to get to the rear areas and threaten the main transportation lines . . . also to [make] a serious threat to the Southwest area and to advance the operations . . . in the direction of Karbala and as-Samawah."[136]

The director continued with the admission that "despite the obvious activities of the enemy, which aims at causing the maximum damage to our forces in the area of Kuwait" the large-scale deployment of Coalition forces in Ar'ar "does not give [us] a positive idea as to what their specific intentions are in view of their capability to move around fast."[137] Saddam's director of military intelligence then provides a pessimistic and ultimately accurate assessment: "we see that the dimensions of the conflict [are such] that we could not possibly overcome, as far as the Kuwaiti issue is concerned. We should prepare adequate forces in terms of reserves in Karbala-Samawah for fear of [the Coalition] carrying out massive strategic maneuvers, which aim at isolating our forces in the South and Southwest of the Euphrates River and hindering the movement of our forces and dealing with the [rest of] the situation through hostile airpower."[138]

It is unknown how the regime's senior leadership reacted to this seemingly dire assessment; however, it is likely that given the cost of repositioning forces on the battlefield under the Coalition air dominance, any option short of hoping the reports were wrong was probably ignored.

By the third week of February the cumulative effect of the Coalition's air attacks on the Iraqi military was moving well beyond the physical. By this point, even the ever-optimistic Republican Guard officers recognized the devastating impact on morale. The Republican Guard chief of staff related to Saddam in a May 1991 conference that

> during the aerial bombardment the role of the [Coalition] Air Force was very significant. . . . It significantly affected the weapons and equipment [of Iraq]. The enemy, when they bombed, focused their main bombing on certain central main targets . . . which were the VII Corps, . . . [the area around] al-Batin, Mutla [Pass] . . . the other central point was the III Corps. . . . This focus, plus the limited capabilities of our anti-aircraft weapons on the enemy airpower, had a very big psychological influence on the fighters, which led a large number to flee their corps and leave their defensive positions.[139]

The Ground Campaign

21 FEBRUARY

Most Iraqi military histories of the war record 21 February as the beginning of the ground war. While the number of cross-border reconnaissance missions and small-scale raids had steadily increased since 1 February, the Coalition's main effort was still almost three days away. Iraqi forces were increasingly isolated from their higher headquarters. In some units this isolation increased the effect of the Coalition's harassment. In other units, the Coalition's deceptions, feints, and raids caused them to execute pre-planned defensive orders in response to what they assumed were major attacks. From the Iraqi Regular Army's point of view, its defense of the forward lines between 21 and 23 February was a military success. Using a self-serving logic that would dominate the Iraqi perspective after the war, the regime decided that the U.S. objective as early as 21 February was to probe Iraqi defenses and only attack after locating an appropriate soft spot.

It is clear that the major Coalition deception operation worked as its planners had hoped. Despite warnings from the GMID and only hours before the ground assault, Iraq's senior leaders were still unsure of the Coalition's main point of attack. In addition to masking the main effort, Coalition deception

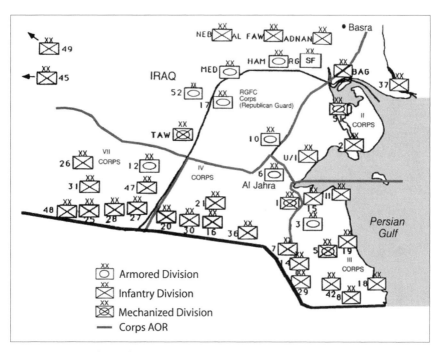

Figure 31. Map of Iraqi final deployments in Kuwait theater of operations on the eve of the ground war, 21 February 1991 (U.S. Department of Defense, "Iraqi Force Deployments in Kuwait Theater of Operations")

efforts also served to increase the confidence of some senior Iraqi military leaders. Saddam's narrow interpretation of the events at al-Khafji, that Coalition troops were timid and casualty adverse, was being validated with every "victory" over the probing attacks at the front.[140] As one senior Iraqi general recalled:

> On the 21st a group of enemy tanks . . . an estimated size of one battalion moved toward our covering troops in front of the battalion at the al-Manaqish region [center of Kuwait border] and attacked the covering troops using their [Coalition] artillery supported by missiles [and] armored vehicles . . . clashing with our troops . . . leading to heavy maneuvering and concluding [with] some of the enemy tanks and [armored vehicles] withdrawing. [At] 1500 [hours] the vehicles returned for the second time and tried to attack two different locations. . . . [The] enemy was unable to remove the covering troops because of our missiles [FROG and MRL] and our reserve armor retaliation. . . . The enemy was unable to defeat the covering troops and the [7th Division]. . . . The army commander called to present his appreciation to the soldiers for their resistance, and he gave a [commemorative] gun to each soldier.[141]

As Coalition ground activity along the front heated up, the missile forces narrowed their target lists in hopes of scoring a decisive psychological blow. Based on guidance from the GMID, the missile forces were directed to focus their efforts on the "enemy main base" at King Khalid Military City (KKMC) near Hafir al-Batin as well as the airbase in Bahrain. The record included the note that on 21 February, the commander of the missile forces allowed his fourth-grade son to press the launch button on one of the Scud missiles fired that day at KKMC.[142]

22 FEBRUARY

On 22 February, Iraqi commanders noted that attacks along the Kuwaiti border continued and even intensified despite the successful rebuff of Coalition forces the previous day.

> The enemy managed to move forward towards the 26th Division using heavy forces. The enemy tried to [defeat the division], but the enemy was forced to withdraw behind the border [with Saudi Arabia] . . . then the enemy returned with heavy armor toward the 14th Division. . . . At 1300 the enemy was forced to stop one kilometer in front of the [Iraqi] covering troops.
>
> On the same day, the enemy troops, using armor, managed to go forward toward the covering troops for the 29th Division. The enemy was forced to step backward after we launched twelve missiles. These missiles were successful in forcing half the enemy unit to withdraw and the other half to stop. The enemy's attacks and air raids became rapid on this day.[143]

As the intensity of the Coalition operations picked up, so too did Iraqi attempts to respond. One such response was the partial implementation of the Tariq Project. For the oil-as-a-weapon plan, the commanders of the III and IV Corps had the authority to initiate preliminary demolition without higher command concurrence. Not surprisingly, as smoke from oil fires began to darken the battlefield, the Coalition interpreted this defensive move as an attempt to preempt the invasion with a scorched earth withdrawal. On 22 February, a U.S. military spokesman in Saudi Arabia reported that Iraq had set fire to more than 140 oil wells and was igniting oil trenches along the Kuwait border.

Many Coalition analysts believed that local Iraqi commanders, even corps commanders, would only take action on clear orders from above. Ironically, an unintended consequence of the autonomy demonstrated by the initial oil field demolitions was that it made the last-minute cease-fire negotiations being hammered out in Moscow dead-on-arrival in Washington, D.C.[144] Actions in

Baghdad indicate that the regime was increasingly confident that a Soviet-brokered deal was in the offing and planned its actions accordingly.

Late on 22 February, after a suggestion from General al-Ayyubi, Saddam issued orders to plan an attack on Doha, Qatar "before the cease-fire" takes place. Qatar was an important target for two reasons. First, from a military perspective, the Doha airport "was a place of intensive grouping for aggressive forces from the USA and France." Second, the Persian Gulf States were going to need a practical reminder of Iraq's proximity and capability to influence the facts in the near future. Iraqi missile detachments needed at least forty-eight hours to re-supply for this mission. The major challenge was repositioning the few remaining long-range al-Hijarah missiles and associated equipment to a launch point southeast of al-Basra. The Iraqis completed planning and preparations late on the 24th for a scheduled launch sometime between 0200–0800 hours the next day.[145]

23 FEBRUARY

Border skirmishes continued unabated on the 23rd. The commanders along the Kuwait–Saudi Arabian border reported a significant increase in the number

Figure 32. Iraqi "Tariq Project" in action. Kuwaiti oil wells ablaze near al-Wafra Forest in southern Kuwait (U.S. Department of Defense, Oil wells burn out of control, Photograph ID: DFST9208042, Camera Operator: Tech. Sgt. Perry Heimer, taken 2 March 1991)

of clashes. In one case, III Corps reported that Coalition forces had surrounded and taken prisoner the entire 29th Division covering force (a battalion task force). Based on this and similar operations, the commander of the III Corps requested permission to pull his remaining covering troops back from the border, since it appeared "the enemy's intention is to surround our troop[s] one-by-one."[146] The army chief of staff agreed with this assessment of Coalition strategy, but ordered the corps to keep its covering troops in their locations. It seems the negative implications for cease-fire negotiations of even tactical withdrawal by Iraqi forces were still more dangerous than any local losses.

24 FEBRUARY

Reports of unusually heavy Coalition ground attacks began filtering into Baghdad a few hours before sunrise on the 24th. From some of the officers monitoring reports from the front, these new reports were either a continuation of the previous week's activity or an American ploy to pressure Iraq as a part of the ongoing diplomatic "negotiations" through the Soviet Union for a withdrawal. For a minority, it seemed possible that this might actually be the much-anticipated ground attack.

According to one of the early reports, troops of the Iraqi I Corps heard helicopters and tanks at approximately 0200 in the vicinity of the 45th Division.[147] This under-equipped infantry division had deployed in early February as part of the response to the reports of a Coalition buildup in the west. The I Corps commander's initial reports to Baghdad were calm. The situation in I Corps remained normal (compared to the previous day's activity), except for an increased presence of helicopters in his area, but overall "the situation was under control."[148]

As daylight broke the horizon, Iraqi commanders along the Kuwaiti border knew that these attacks were not the limited actions of the previous few days. Based on the intensity of Coalition fires, the corps commanders quickly assessed that "the enemy's attacks [since the 21st] were used to test our capability and attempts to remove our covering troops [in order to] gain access to the main [force] locations."[149] In the III Corps sector, the Coalition's attacks included heavy artillery attacks against the 7th and 14th Divisions beginning at 0515. "Heavy [Coalition] maneuvering" against the 14th Division then followed the artillery bombardment. This attack, the Iraqis later reported, was stopped by a battalion level armored counterattack.[150] As it was in many cases over the next three days, Iraqi units reported success at the beginning of an engagement—the end results were apparently assumed.

Just after sunrise, it was clear to Saddam's inner circle that the real ground war had begun. An extraordinary collection of captured audio preserved, in part,

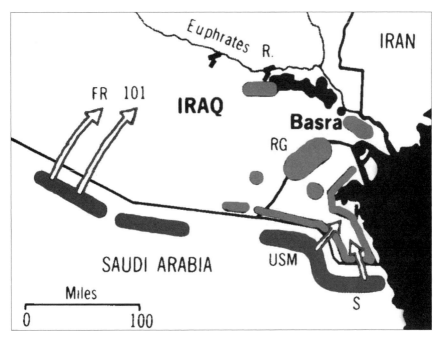

Figure 33. Opening assaults of Coalition ground operations. Coalition attacks were designed to continue to focus the Iraqis on Kuwait. Ground attacks were augmented by amphibious feints and naval gunfire ("Central Command Briefing," 98. RG stands for Repub-lican Guard, FR is French, 101 is the U.S. 101st Airborne Division, USM is U.S. Marine Corps, and S is Saudi Forces.)

the reaction of Saddam and his inner circle to the rapidly unfolding Coalition ground assault on 24 February.[151] The surprise and inevitable confusion of interpreting battlefield reporting is evident, as the discussion between Saddam and his senior advisers ranged from tactical details to diplomacy and back again.

Saddam, despite the flood of often-conflicting reports from the front, tried to remain focused on the strategic issues that, until that morning, appeared to be going Iraq's way. It is clear from Saddam's discussion of the diplomatic situation early on the morning of the 24th that the Iraqi leadership was stunned. The recordings of that morning capture the great frustration that last-minute negotiations through the Soviet Union over Kuwait's final status were not going to preclude the actual ground war.

Hamid (Saddam's personal secretary): The Soviet Union harmed us very greatly . . . it looks like they played a game with us . . . they tricked us . . . Gorbachev said in a meeting "Do not imagine that one day we will deceive you or trap you…or anything of that sort." . . . in any case saying is different than doing.

Saddam: We accepted everyone who tried to mediate between us and the enemy . . . this is what we did and even more.

Unidentified Male: In order to avoid the last phase of the conspiracy, we need to withdraw from the borders.

Saddam: On their fathers . . . in the name of God we will fight them from house to house.[152]

From Saddam's point of view the "mediations" under way by the Soviet Union were making great progress. After all, he had dispatched Tariq Aziz to Moscow several times since mid-February to finalize the concept originally proposed by President Gorbachev's envoy Primakov on the 12th. During the meeting in Moscow on the 18th, Gorbachev reportedly told Aziz to "ask Saddam to agree to Resolution 660 and to announce Iraq's willingness to withdraw from Kuwait and not to raise the issue of Palestine. Leave this issue to me. I will push for an international conference immediately after the end of this conflict. Leave it to me as my responsibility."[153]

Aziz agreed to take the message to his boss and return quickly to Moscow with the final answer. According to Aziz's recollection of Saddam's response, it seems clear that Saddam was negotiating and had reached a point where he was willing to back off on a key public position:

His Excellency said to me, "Alright, we agree to Resolution 660," and told me to go back to Moscow and meet Gorbachev; he said you must agree with him about the issue of withdrawal, and he [Saddam] told me about the details and timetable for withdrawal . . . taking into consideration our circumstances, because we have a large military force, etc. . . . He also said to me: "The last thing to tell Gorbachev is that Saddam Hussein tells you that the Palestinian issue has now become your [Gorbachev's] responsibility. . . . [Saddam] has done his part."[154]

Aziz announced in Moscow on the 22nd that Iraq would agree to an immediate cease-fire and Iraqi forces would withdraw from Kuwait over a three-week period if the international community would lift sanctions within forty-eight hours. From Saddam's point of view this was the final act of the war that began with international sanctions after the "liberation" of Kuwait and had continued under more than forty days of air attacks. All that remained were "technical details." This was likely the status of the war as Saddam saw it just as Coalition forces crossed the barriers into Kuwait and Iraq early on the 24th.

Across many time zones, translations, and perspectives, the interpretation of events in Washington was much different. To the United States, the 22 February announcement in Moscow constituted a list of conditions, not an acceptance of unconditional withdrawal. President Bush described, in his memoir of the period, the telephone conversation he had with President Gorbachev on the 22nd: "I want you [Gorbachev] to tell Aziz that the handwriting is on the wall. It is not just the United States: it is the rest of the Coalition, and we must accomplish it with our proposal now. He [Saddam] has not responded to [yours]. We have waited and waited. We've been patient. We need an answer now. . . . [Our] proposal is deadly serious."[155] The events of the 23rd did nothing to change either side's perceptions.

Amid the chaos of 24 February, possibly in an attempt to find the source of the confusion between Washington and Moscow, Saddam asked Hamid to read the recent exchange of letters with the Soviet Union out loud:

To the Soviet President Mr. Gorbachev,

We trusted you. We have placed Iraq's honor and the Iraqi Armed Forces' dignity in this trust; therefore we have agreed on your peace proposal, which you had provided to us in spite of all fiscal and mental severity that are facing the Iraqi fighter. This circumstance that we are facing is not easy, especially when the other side did not respond either way.

Even though we will keep our promise, Mr. President, we do know that the Americans especially their president have no honor and we do not trust them; therefore we are working only with your peace proposal. We agreed on it because of our strong trust only in you and the Soviet Union. The situation is now getting worse; the Americans send their threats and [are] planning to deceive Iraq. The way they [the Americans] presented their statements and threats; it seems like they have no respect for the Soviet Union's position. We do not hear your specific, clear response against their [the American] pathetic statements and threats. Our nation and army are confused; we are asking ourselves which one is more significant, the Soviet Union proposal or the American threats? Either way we need to [be] clear on this issue in order to prevent the Americans from deceiving our armed forces and our people, by your reply to this letter. We thank you for your response, greetings to you and to the people of the Soviet Union.

[Signed] Saddam Hussein.[156]

Hamid told Saddam that Iraq's Deputy Foreign Minister sent the letter through the Soviet Ambassador at 1900 on 23 February and requested a prompt reply. Reflecting the tension of those hours, Saddam noted that "now you can see why I was worried during the past two days. . . . This is what happened."[157]

Time was much shorter than Saddam's intuition let on. The Soviet president's reply to Saddam's letter arrived at the Ministry of Foreign Affairs at 0445 on 24 February. Again, Saddam asked Hamid to read this letter aloud:

Dear Mr. President Saddam Hussein,

We thank you for your personal letter concerning the situation that is getting bad....We are jointly to implement the procedures we have [agreed to]....We are working with you to implement a peaceful solution for the dispute. . . . Your decisions to agree on a peaceful solution were an extraordinarily important step and changes the entire situation.

After we received your letter indicating that you have approved the [peace] project that we had arranged with the Minister of Foreign Affairs, Tariq Aziz, here in Moscow, and it will be approved from the Iraqi government, therefore we quickly did the following steps, for the implementation of this mission; during the last twenty-four hours we made two long phone calls, the first one was with the American President George Bush, followed by the leaders of Britain, Germany, Italy, France, and Japan. . . .

This provides new analysis to the situation . . . to seek a fast solution for the mentioned peace proposal. We requested a special United Nations session to discuss the situation, which will include this case with other cases, including ceasefire and forces withdrawal. At this time, the United Nations members are meeting in New York discussing the situation. I should say that the reactions about this information are positive, and I presented my high respect for your effort to reach a peaceful solution to this situation.

At this same time, President Bush keeps pushing for the American request, and he is not willing to agree on our proposal. The American President claims he is doing this because he believes Iraq is planning to burn the Kuwait oil fields. Tariq Aziz played a good role in this situation, when he conducted a press conference condemning the Americans accusations against Iraq. . . .

If we can't convince it [the United States] through the United Nations to approve our peaceful solution, they [the Americans] will start land operations against the Iraqi forces in the Gulf.

We are taking tough procedures in order to avoid this turning point. At this time it is hard to say that these procedures are successful during this situation. It is very important that you withdraw your forces to the 1990 location before the war without delay, after this I believe that I can address a letter to President Bush requesting a fast solution to end this important situation without argument, it is very important for Iraq to support the proposal by actually withdrawing, and all of the other issues will be discussed in the UN session since many of the countries are suspicious about the twenty-one-day withdrawal period we had agreed on, these countries believe this delay is intentional, we suggest that you announce a different withdrawal period which can be nine or ten days. This statement will make a difference in our proposal and at the same time it will keep Iraq out of any problems.

I replied to your letter promptly because I know how important this time is, we are following the situation carefully in order to avoid any other alternatives, because from the beginning our goal is to protect lives and the honor of the Iraqis and the other Arab nations in the Gulf region.

Greetings, Mikhail Gorbachev (dated 24 February 1991)[158]

Hamid reminded Saddam that he (Saddam) had already sent a response to Gorbachev's reply letter that morning at 0700. Saddam corrected him, saying, "I wrote it at 0630. . . . At this time I hadn't received the news [of major ground attacks], therefore you need to go to the Russian ambassador and confirm with him the time and date of my letter and when it was sent to Moscow, to prove to them that this letter was written before I received the news . . . and this is what happened . . . so they would not say that this assurance came to us after the letter, hope to God everything will go well."[159]

Saddam appeared to have been anxious not to close down this lifeline through Moscow to the international community. He handed Hamid a copy of the letter, which he read for the benefit of the others present:

To Mr. President Gorbachev with respect,

I have received your response letter around 0600 on the 24th of February Baghdad time. I was very satisfied with its contents, and I would like to offer my special thanks for all your hard work in this matter, because any help you will offer us in this transaction period would make the withdrawal faster and we will use it to shorten not to expand it.

Mr. President Gorbachev we are confirming what we agreed on. President Bush's and his friends' concern is nothing but a matter of not trusting us, they do not believe that we will obey by what we say, and they are revealing their bad conscience, which is loaded with lies and deceptions. Bush's hands are loaded with the bloodshed and the killing of innocent people. . . . Finally, I wish you the luck with your agenda, because your agenda is to help the peace, which is the opposite of what Bush and his mercenaries [and] his friends are doing.

Peace upon you

Saddam Hussein—0630 Baghdad time[160]

Finding no obvious confusion between him and the Soviets in their under-standing of the state of negotiations over Kuwait's future, Saddam returned to the familiar comfort of the prewar grand conspiracy. He told Tariq Aziz, "I knew he [Gorbachev] would betray us, this liar." Saddam then asked Aziz, "Is it possible that their [Russian] intelligence did not know about it [the ground attack]?"[161] Saddam's longtime window to the international community was noncommittal:

> Yes it is possible, [however] they did not say they received such informa-tion. . . . We discussed the procedures that would be carried out by the Security Council and he informed me about the communications that were conducted by Gorbachev. When we were leaving, Primakov told me, "It has been shortened." . . . I told him "Look here Primakov, do not ask me for anything, you will be attending the Security Council meeting and if you wish to shorten the period by one, two, or three days that is up to you . . . that is to say, do not ask me."[162]

Aziz explained to Saddam that his final conversation with Gorbachev was cautiously optimistic. Aziz noted that after he thanked Gorbachev for his "firm stand against American aggression," the Soviet leader told him, "We will do what we can; now the political ground has changed, however, we will continue to stay on this new political ground."[163] On the way back to Baghdad through Amman, Aziz related how he watched the Russian Ambassador on the Cable News Network (CNN) describe the positive direction of events: "We [The Soviet Union] have our proposal and the Americans have their report therefore, we can find a . . . " Saddam, perhaps lamenting an apparently lost opportunity, finished Aziz's sentence with "compromise."[164]

The Iraqi acceptance of the Soviet cease-fire initiative appeared, to many of Saddam's inner circle on the morning of the 24th, to have rushed President Bush into a ground assault. "They were in a rush. . . . They did not expect us to agree. . . . They thought we would put forth other conditions," said one adviser, referring to the Moscow cease-fire agreement of the 22nd. Saddam concurred and noted that "they expected us to disagree with the Soviets and it would then become a conflict between the Soviets and us." Saddam added:

> When I saw that they [the Americans] were going to play around, I thought we must issue a statement, so that we do not give them the chance. . . . However, the most important thing to me is to make sure there would not be any confusion concerning the Soviet initiative and our agreement on it. [Someone in the room concurs "there was not any confusion"].

The last thing we did at [2300 hours] last night was issue a statement in the name of the revolutionary command council representative's director, attacking Bush, his devious methods, and his stands against the Soviets' initiative, and his persistence in the aggression.[165]

Saddam asked and was assured that in fact his statement went out at 2400 hours—before the ground assault began. The spokesmen added that in this same announcement he denied the American propaganda that Iraq was destroying the oil fields. Saddam, having authorized the Tariq Project, corrected him by noting that, if any oil fields were struck, they were "legitimate military targets, in order to cause diversions."[166]

Saddam and his advisers, perhaps hoping to salvage what they could from the stillborn Soviet initiative, began to discuss executing a hasty withdrawal. The conversation however, was a strange mix of unwarranted optimism, with Aziz boasting "it has been thirty-eight days since they began striking us, and they have not inflicted any losses upon us," and pragmatism in calculating the number of days required to withdraw from Kuwait.[167] Saddam presciently opined that they first consider "pulling back our units that are extended on the shoreline, because if they [the Coalition] cut off the roads [our units] would not have a way to return" home. Before the conversation could continue they were interrupted with the news from the Iraqi right flank that "the Americans and the French are attacking [in the west]."[168]

Aziz: The French are attacking?
    Unidentified Advisor 1: Yes, with them [the Americans].
    Saddam: Attacking? Or sitting in front of their division and crying?
    Aziz: The French?
    Saddam: Yes, they are asking for help and they have not even begun engaging yet [laughing].
    Unidentified Advisor 2: They are all the same.
    Aziz: This Mitterrand is a fox.
    Saddam: Mitterrand is very despicable.[169]

Reports received in Baghdad during that first morning indicated that a major tank assault against the 14th Infantry Division (the center of the Iraqi line) was under way. By 0900 the reports indicated that the division would likely be defeated. At the same time, III Corps reported heavy shelling on its positions on Faylakah Island. This activity was anticipated as the doctrinal precursor to an amphibious assault. To the west of the Kuwaiti border, the Iraqi VII

Corps was only reporting light activity consisting of "seven helicopters and a number of [infantry] carriers advancing from the east."[170]

Sometime that morning, Saddam rehearsed the text of a speech explaining the Coalition attack to the Iraqi people with his minister of information. Most of the text was prepared ahead of time, but for this impromptu rehearsal the military staff included some elements of the current situation report. As with many of his speeches, this one appears to reflect, in large measure, what Saddam believed or possibly hoped was actually happening:

> The deceiving enemy has carried out his evil assault in the battle against the following divisions 14th, 18th, 29th, 8th, 26th, 45th, against the Jihadist, 7th, 3rd, and 1st Army Corps, and against our brave naval infantry [on] Faylakah Island. . . . We are saying that the enemy continues to drown in his own blood and shame in front of our [frontline] units. . . . Despite all that took place, our faithful men were able to drive out the first surprise attack. . . . Generally, our units are in the best shape possible under this kind [of attack]. The enemy's attack has failed completely and the depraved enemies continue calling for help . . . the situation is under total control.[171]

As the reports picked up, an officer in Saddam's command center asked aloud, "Where are the French?" Another officer replied that they were moving toward an-Nasiriyah because they obviously "want to strike the right wing of the Republican Guard, or force the Republican Guard to come out in order to strike them with the air force and eliminate them." Saddam apparently thought that all these reports of a western attack were still part of a Coalition trick intended to draw his forces away from Kuwait. He awkwardly reminded his officers that "if it were not for their [the Coalition's] air forces, our Republican Guard units would have come out and slaughtered them."[172] To meet the still unclear Coalition force moving through Iraq's southwest, the Iraqi command ordered the 45th and 26th Infantry Divisions along with a collection of border guard and security units to "adjust" accordingly.

One officer pointed out that the Americans had yet to employ the 101st or 82nd Airborne Divisions. He recommended that they move an armored division to the vicinity of Karbala as well as reposition the Republican Guard "out of fear of this situation." The officer continued that this new Karbala-based reserve force should probably come down from the Iraqi defenses in the north so "we would not be forced to move an armored division from the Republican Guard or the VII Corps that are positioned in the Kuwait area and expose them to the enemy's air force."[173] Saddam seemed to think the assessment and recommendation were unwarranted based on the current information and again expressed optimism about any possible confrontation. "I say let us mislead them, let them come," Saddam told the officer, "if God is willing they will enter [Iraq] . . . so it will be their grave." Besides, Saddam continued, "I do not want to play with our reserves while we are on the verge of a war, which is why I will not agree to [your] suggestion."[174] Typical of these early exchanges, others in the room picked up on Saddam's tone and reflected back to him the soundness of his ideas:

> Saddam: Let them come, on the contrary let them come [all the way] to Karbala city, it will become their cemetery.
> Officer 1: By God, I think it would benefit us politically.
> Officer 2: It has a political benefit, I wish their attacks would underestimate Karbala . . . it is an Islamic city.
> Saddam: It is also militarized . . . if any soldier enters the city . . .
> Officer 1: They would not be able to bear it. [175]

It was still early in the ground war for the Iraqi senior leadership and, as the audio recordings of that day underline, confidence ebbed slowly. At approximately 1130 on 24 February, and perhaps reflecting on three days of ground assaults by the Coalition, Saddam agreed with his advisers that "our units remain excellent." Someone then reported to Saddam that the Coalition had announced, through the media, the capture of more than five hundred Iraqi prisoners of war since 0630 that day. According to another officer, reports in the international media noted that "whole sections of Iraqis [were] surrendering by the thousands." To Saddam and his inner circle this was an obvious "dirty" media trick. Saddam offered that "they would announce [such] things that they hope will occur or what they expect to occur." They all agreed with Saddam that the purpose of such transparently false announcements was to boost Coalition morale.[176]

Saddam was shown on a map where the French and American attacks along the Iraqi right wing were progressing. An unidentified officer repeated his earlier concern about the risk to the Republican Guard—if this attack succeeded. "Of course," he added "the Americans would have to cross the entire southern sector, so that they would be able to strike the Republican Guards and go on to Karbala." Another officer, recalling earlier prewar assessments of Coalition strategy, was less hopeful and noted that this move "would slow the [Republican Guard] and this means it would complicate the traffic and then they would conduct a Marine [assault] here [pointing to a map], north of Kuwait City.

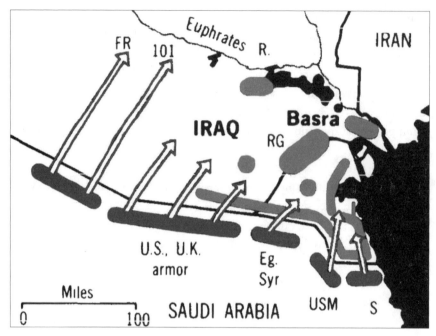

*Figure 34. Coalition progress late on 24 February. "If it had been our intention to des-
troy the country, if it had been our intention to overrun the country, we could have done
it unopposed, for all intents and purposes, from this position at that time. That was not
our intention; we have never said it was our intention." General Schwarzkopf* ("Central
Command Briefing," 99. RG stands for Republican Guard, FR is French, 101
is the U.S. 101st Airborne Division, Eg. is Egyptian, Syr is Syrian, USM is U.S.
Marine Corps, and

. . . [and] hold it." A group of officers recommended that Saddam quickly move
some troops from Kuwait (the Iraqi left wing) to face the threat coming from
the southwest (the Iraqi right wing) in order to "avoid being surrounded inside
[Kuwait]."[177] Saddam, perhaps relying on a kind of combat patience he learned
during the Iran-Iraq War, opted to wait "because whenever we reduce the force
on our wing, it will be weakened and [that] leads to an imbalance in our positions. . . . This subject is difficult for us, if you stay firmly or withdraw completely. As long as it remains fifty/fifty, we will stay there."[178]

Despite the earlier decision to keep the Iraqi Navy out of a direct confrontation during the war, they attempted at least two missions on the first day
of the ground war. The first was an aborted attempt to attack an American
"destroyer" operating near the Kuwaiti island of Qaruh. An Iraqi missile boat
departed the harbor at al-Shuaiba Kuwait at 1225 but was unable to acquire
the American ship due to "anti-electronic static" and aborted the mission. The
second mission of the day ended before it began. A Super Frelon helicopter

was dispatched to Kuwait "in order to initiate a suicidal attack against enemy ships." As recalled during a postwar conference, the helicopter "was exposed to an accident" before it could complete its mission.[179]

By mid-morning, the III Corps commander determined that Coalition forces were attacking the center of the Iraqi defense through the seam between the 8th and 29th Divisions. By 1400 Coalition forces had isolated and effectively surrounded an entire brigade of the 29th Division. After the war, the commander of the III Corps noted that, although the Coalition had some success in that morning's attacks, he was proud that "the enemy suffered many [casualties] which led them to lose control and [become] unsettled. . . . The enemy troops started to move around in the area organized because of [our] heavy firing from all locations."[180]

Despite the "heroic" defense put up by elements of the III Corps, Coalition forces continued to press their attacks. According to Iraqi accounts, in one instance local counterattacks by ten tanks stopped Coalition forces in front of the 29th Division's position. Several Iraqi generals reported that these initial attacks provided a detailed understanding of "the enemy's fighting methods." As the commander of the Iraqi III Corps recalled: "The enemy's fighting method was to enter the border suddenly and rapidly . . . supported first with air raids, then with the tanks and heavy [artillery] firing and then it advanced its troops. . . . When the enemy came close [to Iraqi troops] the enemy deployed behind the [Iraqi] location and surrounded the rear troops [thereby] avoiding the [Iraqi] troops."[181]

Saddam's reactions offer an interesting insight into his personal assessment of the Coalition plan. As his personal secretary described the stream of reports coming in from the various corps, Saddam became confused as to which unit was where and demanded his staff show him a detailed map. As the staff began reviewing the reports, this time on a map, Saddam told them, "When I point out the right wing, I mean the III Corps and when I say the II Corps, I mean the left wing and any other corps is the middle." The II and III Iraqi Corps were both on the Kuwaiti coast, the II Corps located north of Kuwait City while the III Corps was to the south. One can glean two related insights from Saddam's comments. First, his "eastern orientation" was not the same one generally used in the military and intelligence reports up to this point. The GMID, for example, framed most of its reports in terms of east (the III Corps sector) and west (the I Corps sector). Saddam either chose to reinterpret these reports or he was selectively ignoring information that did not fit within his preconceived concept. Second, Saddam's description of the right and left wing imply that, at least early on the 24th, he was still strongly oriented on an amphibious operation.[182]

Saddam continued to meet with his military and political advisers through-out the day. In a tape-recorded meeting sometime late in the day on the 24th, Saddam and his advisers discussed a wide range of topics as Coalition forces continued the attack into Kuwait and southern Iraq. One adviser, identified as Comrade Muhammad, implored Saddam to adopt a strategy for rallying the wider Arab Nation for the defense of Iraq. He suggested that they should "embarrass all the countries that sympathize with us" like Tunisia, Algeria, Mauritania, and Yemen into providing weapons and military equipment.[183] Comrade Muhammad added that they should "try to embarrass Iran from the Islamic side, to excite the religious individuals and in any way excite all the [Iranian] people, Parliament, religious individuals, organizations. We should try in any way so there will be sympathy from a religious side from all the Islamic countries, especially Iran."[184]

Comrade Muhammad stated that Iraq was in a fight for its national sur-vival. He recommended they "organize and arm [a] public army, organize the citizens and prepare them," as they did during the 1980s defense of al-Basra.[185] He continued that, given Iraq's extended border with Saudi Arabia, the enemy might even break through to an-Najaf and an-Nasiriyah. He advised Saddam to consider "arm[ing] the public and not just the trained individuals . . . [but] the ones who are trustful and capable of carrying a weapon . . . let it be a street war."[186] Comrade Muhammad enthusiastically recalled how Iraqi citizens had united after the opening night air strikes in January and stated that they only needed to inflict five thousand American casualties to win. Saddam calmly cor-rected him by saying the number was actually closer to five hundred or a ratio of four Iraqi casualties to every one American.[187]

As Saddam and his advisers calculated the potential cost of victory, trou-bling reports from the battlefield injected some reality into the discussions of Iraq's inevitable success. One of Saddam's advisers stated that the international media just reported that Coalition forces overran an entire Iraqi corps.

Saddam: This is lying.

Advisor: Everything is normal with [all] of our corps.

Saddam: We can say it blocked the attack, they were firing from far away and the corps blocked the attack. Our troops are there now and there is no possibility that it was taken by the enemy.

Advisor: There are a lot of news reports like [this] one sir.

Saddam: All of this news is wrong, but tell the news as it is. They [the enemy] tried to attack from different directions, but everything is under control, in a good way . . . [although] the sectors had some injuries because of the [artillery] fires.[188]

Being much closer to the fighting, the III Corps headquarters was not as out of touch with the situation as Baghdad. Nevertheless, its staff officers still failed to grasp the scale and scope of the Coalition offensive. As late as 2000 hours on 24 February, the III Corps commander described the situation in his sector as "settled."[189] The commander was apparently unaware that by this point in the battle the Coalition had already achieved a significant penetration of the 14th, 29th, and 8th Division's sectors. As a result, it had destroyed and captured, or penetrated four to five Iraqi brigades in the process. Moreover, a significant fight in the 18th Division's sector was continuing along the coastal road. The III Corps commander noted, almost reflexively, that during all of the fighting that day and "in spite of the enemy's huge penetration to many locations. . . . I made sure that the enemy's troops suffered the most casualties."[190]

According to the commander of the III Corps, his divisions did not remain entirely passive during the Coalition attacks against the 14th and 29th Divisions. The division commanders attempted to blunt Coalition attacks at the point of penetration, but could not "counterattack to restore their original positions" due to a shortage of infantry.[191] In one case, the III Corps reported that it was able to plug the gap between the 8th Division and the decimated 29th Division with a local counterattack. But by late in this first day, even the III Corps staff was beginning to understand that local counterattacks were insufficient. That evening, the III Corps commander began planning for "an ambitious multi-division counterattack for early the morning of the 25th." The objective of this attack was the al-Jaber Airbase and the purpose was to "retaliate against and destroy the enemy."[192]

The new III Corps' plan called for pincer movements from north and southeast of the Iraqi defensive line into the leading elements of the Coalition. Units from the north would include the 7th Division, whose task was to attack into the gap created by the near destruction of the 14th Division earlier in the day. The 7th Division would receive support from a mixed corps reserve unit comprised of members of the Iranian expatriate group known as the Mujahedin-e Khalq (MEK).[193] Meanwhile, the 5th Mechanized Division, of "victory at al-Khafji" fame, would attack with two brigades head-on into Coalition forces. While the counterattack was under way, the Iraqi 8th Infantry and the 3rd Armored Divisions would re-establish a defensive line running from the minefields in the east through al-Jaber and tie into the IV Corps to the west.[194]

Just before midnight, the III Corps commander met with Ali Hassan al-Majid to update Majid on the corps' status, brief him on the day's battle, and explain the just-completed counterattack plan. During the meeting, Majid reiterated the regime's order to destroy the Kuwaiti oil infrastructure, but also somewhat contradictorily "confirmed our stay in Kuwait and the *protection* of it"[195] [Emphasis added].

25 FEBRUARY

Early on the 25th, the Iraqi 5th Mechanized Division departed its assembly area to link up with elements of the 8th Division and begin the counterattack at first light. Between morning fog and the thick blanket of oil smoke, visibility was almost zero. Soldiers on foot slowly led Iraqi tanks to their attack positions. The slow pace worried the corps commander because he knew daylight would bring renewed Coalition air attacks.

At first light, the remains of the 5th Division completed a link-up with the 22nd Brigade of the 8th Division and moved toward the U.S. Marine Corps point of deepest penetration. Meanwhile, the 8th Brigade of the 3rd Armored Division linked up with a tank battalion from the 7th Division and also moved toward the American positions.[196] According to an Iraqi history, at 0710 the two arms of the pincer moved to initiate their attack on the lead American units. At around 0900, despite the fact that the engagement was fought in a minefield under conditions of near zero visibility, the corps reported that they destroyed a dozen American armored vehicles. The III Corps commander later recalled that the initial moments of the counterattack were a great success. "This action caused the enemy to withdraw from [the] battleground as our tanks were firing at the enemy tanks across the minefield while it was advancing to stop whatever was left of the penetration."[197]

By 1100, the Americans were forced to respond with "a heavy air raid on our troops" just to "retain their positions." Overall the commander described the battle on the morning of the 25th as "a heavy battle . . . [with] both sides suffering many casualties including armored vehicles and tanks."[198] In addition to the air attack, he recalled that his troops suffered attacks by "large numbers of anti-tank helicopters supported by columns of armor." It was "a fierce battle."[199] By 1300 and despite the efforts of his "brave soldiers," it was clear that the Americans had defeated the III Corps counterattack and "widened [their] area of penetration and continued to punch in deep."[200] In effect, the continuing American attack had split the III Corps right through the middle of its sector.

Despite the tactical losses, the III Corps commander later recalled one particularly bright spot on the 25th. As the Americans worked their way through the tangle of obstacles in the 18th Division's sector,

we downed an enemy helicopter that had two pilots. One of them died inside the chopper and the other one was brought [to us] at the airport. The surviving pilot was carrying on him the [American] plan of the attack.

There were five stages to the plan. [First] the enemy will attack our border posts and neutralized them. Second the enemy will maintain contact with his firepower until he neutralizes the obstacle formations. . . . Third, the enemy will advance in the direction of our Army's central command in the battlefield and will maintain contact with his firepower. Fourth, the enemy will take over the central command. Fifth, the enemy will push forward toward the airport of Kuwait and enter the city.[201]

According to the information he obtained from the downed aircraft, the III Corps commander determined that the Americans planned one day for each of their five steps. The American pilot, as well as the corps' analysis of his maps, were immediately sent to Baghdad. In his postwar comments, the III Corps commander seemed pleased that he alone "knew the American plan of action" even if he could do little to actually stop it.[202] He later asserted that since "according to the American plan" they were supposed to be in Kuwait City by the 25th, the III Corps had successfully delayed the enemy by one day. Once again using the military logic of the regime, a one-day delay was translated as "the enemy was defeated on the 25th."[203]

By the afternoon of the 25th, remnants of the III Corps fell back into Kuwait City and, according to its commander, "organized a plan to fight from the city's border and from inside the city in cooperation with the Gulf Operations Command." At this point in the battle for Kuwait, the III Corps commander reported to Baghdad that the 7th, 14th, and 29th Divisions were combat ineffective. He ordered his remaining divisions to re-establish a defensive line close to Kuwait City. However, before any significant movement occurred, the III Corps commander received a broken message that Saddam had ordered all remaining units to withdraw toward al-Basra "to cover the border [area] so we can distribute our divisions within the [Iraqi] cities."[204]

The End-of-the-Epic Duel

Notwithstanding the obvious incentive to craft a history that dovetails with Saddam's "truth," several official regime histories (both classified and unclassified) are generally consistent with many contemporary recordings and documents made during the war. One such history includes the Iraqi plan to withdraw and the perceived American reaction to it. More than any other set of circumstances, these events established the underlying logic of the "Iraq won the war" belief that still surprises most Western observers. As described by a senior general involved in the planning, the answer to the question of "why withdraw" was clear:

In order to answer such a question, we have to remember some major facts. The first fact is that the real goal of the Coalition forces was to destroy Iraq and not only to force Iraq to withdraw [its] forces from Kuwait. When the possible routes to occupy Iraq stretch [across the length of the southern border] . . . our duty required us to not keep the Iraqi troops [in Kuwait] or designate them to defend Kuwait City. . . . Otherwise, it would be easy for the Coalition countries to initiate an attack from any route they choose to take in order to isolate the greater part of the Iraqi Army in Kuwait and then attack Iraq in a situation where Iraq does not have any forces to protect its territories. The decision to withdraw was a smart one that came at the right time. *Defending Iraq from al-Basra instead of Kuwait caused the Coalition countries to miss out on two opportunities they craved for . . . the isolation and destruction of the Iraqi forces in Kuwait and then the destruction of Iraq. The decision to withdraw enabled Iraq to pull out [its] forces and their equipment so they could be successful defending Iraq.*[205] [Emphasis added]

"The plan to withdraw was set up in a hurry," according to Lt. Gen. Sultan Hasim, the deputy army chief of staff. Sometime during the day on 25 February, he gathered planning director Maj. Gen Khalid Hussein and director of movements Maj. Gen. Najib Awad, and "set up the plan." The minister of defense and the army chief of staff approved the plan soon after. Sultan wasted no time and tried to call the corps commanders to deliver a warning order even as the written orders were being prepared. With some difficulty he was able to talk to all of the corps headquarters with the exception of the Gulf Operations and III Corps, both in Kuwait City. To ensure they understood the orders, Sultan dispatched several senior officers with handwritten warning orders by road. After several attempts, the couriers reported back to Baghdad that they were unable to reach Kuwait City "because of the bombardment of the roads and the destruction of their vehicles."[206]

The plan, as Sultan described it, was a carefully timed series of movements designed to maximize traffic over the limited road networks heading north. According to the plan, on the night of 25/26 February the following units were to move in priority order:

"The troops of the headquarters of the Gulf Operations command, the popular forces, and the state workers" (located predominately in Kuwait City).

"The troops of III Corps."

The naval force. "Faylakah Island had permission [to begin] immediate withdrawal."[207]

On the night of 26–27 February, the second phase of the withdrawal was to proceed in the following priority:

The troops of IV Corps.

The troops of VI corps, "while maintaining continuous coordination with the IV Corps." "Communication must be constant between them."

The troops of II Corps, "while maintaining continuous coordination with the VI Corps." "Communication must be constant between them."

"The VII Corps is set to protect its troops by pulling back and breaking the wing to protect the troops of IV Corps during the withdrawal." VII Corps was directed to coordinate its movements with the troops of the Republican Guards to its north.[208]

The withdrawal plan required the Republican Guard to "keep the Tawakalna Ala Allah division in position until the last possible moment in order to protect the troops of the VII Corps and then the guard troops will be pulled out according to the plan to defend al-Basra."[209]

As transmitted, the order required the corps commanders to "destroy anything that could not be brought back." Furthermore, they were cautioned to "take care of the psychological situation of the fighters and to spare the morale as much as possible."[210] Apparently, the officers in Baghdad thought the "shame of withdrawal" was potentially the most significant morale problem in Kuwait at that moment.

According to the recollections of Iraq's former armed forces chief of staff, Lt. Gen. Husayn Rashid Muhammad, the "order" to withdraw began with a 2030 phone call on 25 February from Baghdad to his forward headquarters in al-Basra.

Mr. President called me in the evening and spoke with me. He told me "Husayn, I do not want our army to panic. Our soldiers do not like humiliation; they like to uphold their pride. Our goal is now to return our soldiers [to Iraq], but we want them to return with their heads up high [and] without humiliation." He told me many [other] things and I interpreted them as withdrawal.[211]

According to the later official Iraqi history of this exchange, Saddam provided the general detailed guidance on the phone that night:

"Start planning for the withdrawal immediately." The priority is "to protect the soldiers, morale, and the fighting spirit" of the force.

"Destroy all military equipment" that could not be brought out.

Establish a "protective line" running from as-Samawah, to an-Nasiriyah, to al-Qurna, and finally to al-Basra.

The rest of the divisions are to be arrayed "on a line of common patrol" outside Kuwait.

A written order will be delivered to the advanced command headquarters in al-Basra on the morning of the 26th with additional details.[212]

Husayn was perplexed. He knew any withdrawal was "not an easy decision to make" and "there was no room to make mistakes in understanding such a decision." He asked Saddam for clarification and was told that someone would be sent from Baghdad to Husayn's headquarters to provide further details. As Husayn later recalled, he felt that "a death sentence for me [would be] much easier than this order. This is a historical decision that would bring shame to Iraq [and] not only me."[213]

From Baghdad's perspective, the orders process went smoothly considering the circumstances. However, as military history often recounts, when one military organization plans an operation for another to execute, major errors and confusion are the best one can hope for. An example of the gap between plan and reality was the portion of the order that required III Corps to move several brigade-size units previously sent to reinforce the coastal defense, back to their parent units in western Kuwait before beginning movement.[214] It is not clear if these units actually tried to move under fire, perpendicular to the line of retreat or, if they did, if they ever made it.

Just because the order was going out to withdraw did not mean that Iraq was done fighting. Late on the 25th, General al-Ayyubi made the following journal entry about the Scud missile attack that would become the single deadliest strike against the Coalition during the war: "At 2035 hours, Dhahran was attacked with a very painful missile by Brigade 223. . . . I was very nervous at the beginning because, whenever I assigned them [223 Brigade] to attack with a group of missiles, they executed with [fewer] due to technical problems. When I heard about the U.S. losses and casualties, I stopped blaming them and I cheered up and encouraged them. Thank Allah for revenge."[215]

26 FEBRUARY

Early on the morning of 26 February, Baghdad Radio broadcast a speech in which Saddam explained to the Iraqi population, using logic he would employ for the next twelve years, how a withdrawal was a victory:

We start by saying that on this day, our valiant armed forces will complete their withdrawal from Kuwait. And on this day, our fight against aggression

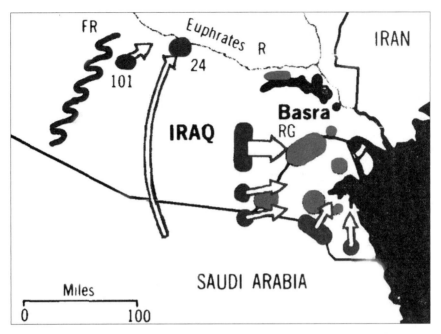

Figure 35. Coalition attacks, 25–26 February. "The 24th Infantry Division made an unbelievable move all the way across into the Tigris and Euphrates valley, and proceeded in blocking this avenue of egress out, which was the only avenue of egress left because we continued to make sure all the bridges stayed down." General Schwarzkopf ("Central Command Briefing," 99. RG stands for Republican Guard, FR is French, and 101 is the U.S. 101st Airborne Division.)

and the ranks of infidelity, joined in an ugly coalition comprising thirty countries, which officially enters war against us under the leadership of the United States of America—our fight against them will have lasted from the first month of this year, starting with the night of 16/17 January, until this moment in the current month, February. It was an epic duel . . . the harvest of the Mother of All Battles [has] succeeded.[216]

The sometimes less-than-subtle historical rewriting of the decision to withdraw began almost immediately after the combat ended. According to Ali Hasan al-Majid, sometime in late March 1991 Saddam determined that even the word "withdrawal" was an incorrect description for the maneuvers executed between 26 and 28 March. He decided that in order for Iraqi soldiers to learn the "most precise skills for conducting" such an operation in the future, the correct term should be "retreat battle."[217]

The late-night Baghdad radio announcement that Iraqi troops had been ordered to withdraw from Kuwait "in an organized way to positions they held prior to 1 August 1990" was the only withdrawal order many Iraqi troops in theater received. The Iraqi announcer said that "this [withdrawal] is regarded as practical compliance with UN Resolution 660. . . . Our armed forces, which have proven their ability to fight and stand fast, will confront any attempt to harm them while they are carrying out their orders."[218] It is possible that the Baghdad Radio message, coming before many of the military headquarters in Kuwait had an actual plan in hand, was intended to buy time. In actuality, the announcement contributed to the growing sense of panic against which Saddam had warned General Rashid a few days earlier.

Communications between forward headquarters in al-Basra and tactical headquarters in the Kuwait theater had nearly collapsed. Radio communication was either jammed or was not trusted. There was even talk about the Coalition using "fraud" to pass bogus orders over the radio, which added to the confusion.[219] Using the roads was unreliable and dangerous. Staff officers were left to deliver orders in person. Not only were they trying to drive against traffic, but there were constant air attacks, one of which resulted in the loss of several senior officers near the Mutla Ridge while they were trying to reach Kuwait City. Several staff officers later reported that even if they managed to make it to the tactical headquarters, they often found no commanding officers present. During a postwar conference, one senior Iraqi Army officer complained that "what was bad was the lack of commanders. When there is no commander how can a withdrawal take place? When there is no company commander or a regimental commander or a brigade commander, then how can you carry out a withdrawal?"[220]

One stunned corps commander, after being briefed on the order in person said that "he could not believe that this was really happening."[221] Other commanders found that even when they received and understood their orders, they confronted the extraordinarily difficult conditions of "being bombed and cars burning . . . continuous bombardment [plus] terrible rain and weather" in executing these orders.[222]

The problems associated with the withdrawal were not, as the minister of defense would later charge, a result of poor communications alone. One of the corps commanders in Kuwait understatedly described the whole situation as "abnormal":

"The truth is that the whole situation with the withdrawal was not a normal situation. It was not a situation we studied or prepared for in our exercises or under any circumstances. . . . [I]n the first place, there was no equality in this conflict. There was a very high level of difference, and it has never happened in history before, not even to a major superpower, where the whole world joins in against it, except for Germany [in World War II] . . . and Germany was not alone."[223]

A senior officer participating in a postwar discussion of the withdrawal noted, "Frankly, we had not planned for retreat, we had not given it a thought, therefore the majority of sectors were surprised to hear of the orders of withdrawal, even some of the leadership and commanders were surprised as well. Some of the commanders lost control of their units during the process of withdrawal. This was not due to—perhaps there was some negligence on their part—but this was caused by the large numbers of retreating sectors [simultaneously] piling onto the roads. I mean we could not identify our [own] fighters due to poor weather conditions at the time."[224]

Iraq's minister of defense later described the withdrawal as "one of the most dangerous, delicate, and most complicated phases of battle."[225] The larger issue of the withdrawal plan, beyond the inherent complexity of timing and sequencing of units moving on roads under constant air attack, was the simple question of: withdraw to where and for what purpose? The guidance from Baghdad included the directive that the withdrawing Iraq forces should be prepared to fight in the cities. Saddam ordered that each corps was to have a specific duty in the cities of the Euphrates region and that they would "cooperate with the popular organizations to defend [these] cities."[226] According to the army chief of staff:

"Mr. President—may God bless him—gave us directives to fight in the cities. A plan sent to us . . . [contained] instructions on how to fight in the cities and how we should be close to the cities. It listed instructions on how to mobilize the citizens . . . the armed forces were to enter the city and fight [in] an urban warfare style. So we envisioned a huge confrontation [against the Coalition] or [at least] a great challenge given our modest capabilities."[227]

The parallel nature of the Army and Republican Guard chains of command complicated the withdrawal and defensive reset. During a particularly lively postwar discussion, a senior Army officer complained that he and his staff never received information on the Republican Guard disposition around al-Basra as the Army made its way north out of Kuwait. Furthermore, this officer said, the information they did receive changed without warning. He suggested that perhaps there should have been a more open planning process and perhaps a joint plan for the defense of al-Basra. Saddam interjected to defend the actions

Figure 36. An common sight—Iraqi troops surrender to Coalition forces on 26 February 1991 (U.S. Department of Defense, Iraqi soldiers surrender to elements of the 1st Marine Division, Photograph ID: DMSN9302273, Camera Operator: Lance Cpl. R. Price, taken 26 February 1991)

of his Republican Guard: "It is not that we don't trust you [the Regular Army], but the commander of the guards has the right to do what he did. . . . This will remain the case and is not going to change. This means that I have to know every major matter, and it has to pass through me to the supervisor of the guards."[228]

As would be the case again in 2003, Saddam's apparent concern over a military-inspired coup remained more pressing than the external threat of a Western invasion.

Meanwhile, conditions in Kuwait on the morning of 26 February were changing at lightning speed. Chains of command were collapsing as headquarters were displaced and became exposed to Coalition attack from the air and ground. In some cases, because corps and division headquarters were displaced, orders were being passed to the tactical commands directly from the senior Ba'ath chain of command.[229]

At 0700 Saddam personally sent orders directly to the corps commanders to "evacuate all equipment and wounded." This countermanded the order issued only hours before to destroy what could not be moved.

At 1145 LTG Sultan adjusted the withdrawal plan based on feedback from his forward headquarters in al-Basra.

The IV, VI, and VII Corps are to withdraw with the support of the III Corps, the Jihad, and Republican Guard forces.

The II Corps, the Republican Guard forces headquarters, and the Jihad Corps headquarters are to withdraw beginning on the 27th.

At 1520 the Jihad Corps reported "very heavy bombing on the 42nd Brigade and 10th Division." It reported that it could not pull the brigade back toward the VII Corps as planned. A few minutes later the brigade "was reported to be in a heavy engagement and almost immediately communication was lost." The Jihad Corps also reported that enemy armor was approaching Jrishan (the far northern end of the Wadi al-Batin on the border between Kuwait and Iraq).

At 1610 LTG Sultan ordered the IV Corps to change its route-of-march from a northwestern exit [directly into Iraq] to one that instead required it to move through the II Corps area [far northeast Kuwait].

At 1740 a report came that the 42nd Brigade was back in radio contact with the Jihad Corps. What it initially reported as an enemy armor column, was in fact troops from the VII Corps withdrawing as originally ordered to the northwest.[230]

As this last report indicates, the same weather protecting many of the withdrawing troops from Coalition airpower was simultaneously rendering the Iraqi retreat a military disaster. The chaos and confusion of withdrawing under pressure resulted in many meeting engagements and a flood of misleading reports up through the Iraqi chain of command. One such engagement occurred late on 26 February between the U.S. 2nd Armored Cavalry Regiment and the Tawakalna Republican Guard Division. Coalition histories call this engagement the "Battle of 73 Easting" and count it as one of the most lopsided fights during the one hundred hours of ground combat.[231] But just as with the battle at al-Khafji, the Iraqi perspective of events—and more importantly their meaning—was entirely different. The commander of the Republican Guard described this battle in his official history, Republican Guard Battles, as a heroic outnumbered defense:

Once orders were issued to our army to withdraw from Kuwait, we were confronted with the other duty we had which was the defense of al-Basra and to secure the withdrawal of our armed forces from Kuwait. . . . We planned that if the enemy tried to interrupt our contact with al-Basra, the

Tawakalna 'Ala Allah Republican Guard force would come and participate in the defense of the city. But the enemy distracted the force during the withdrawal operation using three divisions, two of which were American and one British. The Tawakalna force . . . was able thanks to its good training and high spirits to engage in the battle with the enemy on the 26th of February and to inflict on him huge losses obliging him to interrupt his [attack] on al-Basra.[232]

The withdrawal continued throughout the night of the 26th. Specific orders were hastily being issued to tell units where to reassemble for the coming climactic defense of the regime.

27 FEBRUARY

The relentless Coalition pursuit of the Iraqi withdrawal continued. The lack of clear direction for Iraqi forces streaming into southern Iraq only made matters worse. To stabilize a rapidly deteriorating command situation, Saddam wrote a personal order (in the form of a letter) early on the 27th addressed to the "Advanced General Headquarters" in al-Basra to clarify the mission and restore some element of control:[233]

The Fellows, the Head and the members of the Advanced General Command in al-Basra Province,

It is a huge test . . . this is the test that God had wanted to increase the status of the believers and to expose those criminals from the infidels and traitors and show their true side in front of their people and in front of humanity. He also had increased their punishment and agony in this life and in the afterlife. According to us, the men's honor comes from their efficient faith and patience. The degrees of this honor had been lined up for those [who] deserve it from our people, our armed forces, and our struggler [Ba'ath] party.

According to these considerations, you will have your degree which is a high degree that we hope and wish for you and we are confident that you will get it. Because of the conditions of communications and transportation, the momentary influence of a decision, of gathering the political, popular, and partial field decision with the military field decision, setting up the abilities and energies of the people, the party, and the armed forces in one direction to be efficient at the moment of a common action and to increase the Jihad that God had wanted to keep us, our people, and our armed forces free. Because of all that, the formation of the advanced general command headquarters was decided in the Arabian Basra, the mother of all cities. We have to protect the safety, humanity, psychology, and the equipment of our armed forces. This should be the route taken to enter the battle and to prove the abilities of Jihad against the infidelity and the treason at this stage. This means we have to give up the idea of defending all territories, properties, and roads of Iraq for some time and to pick what we should defend from cities, territories, and properties. We have to accept the idea of not being able to make all the roads coming out of this city to another city open all the way. According to this brief analysis, the defense preparations that we thought to apply before the 27th of February are incorrect, because you are familiar with our available capabilities.[234] Right now, the goal is to ensure the best possible safety for the fighters and their weapons, to raise their morale, and to raise their fighting spirit in a similar manner to what happened after the battles of al-Shush, Dezfuz, al-Karun, al-Muhammara [Khorramshahr], and many other battles [battles during the Iran-Iraq War].

This requires our defense to line up along the edge of Basra city. Their effective part should be according to the method of defending the inside of Basra and not according to the old classical method of defending Basra as we stated before.[235] In general, what applies to Basra will apply to the rest of the cities in Iraq with some exceptions that we will decide according to the conditions and abilities.

According to that the defense should be in Basra. They should be around the edges of the city from the outside and around the inside based on a defense strategy that will protect the fighters and their weapons from the beasts and enables us to push them back, if they were to imagine that they could enter the city. These are the preparations that we need right now and the extra defense should be distributed in the other districts and municipalities north of Basra. We have to calculate the amount of troops and fighters that we need to keep the troops going in regard to food, supplies, weapons, and ammunition. It is no big deal to evacuate some of those people that we do not need from the city for some time if you find that necessary. You also have to calculate the negative results for such action on the people and the fighters. Do not take the details of this as an order, at the same time, do not pass [up on] the chore."

[Signed] God is great . . .

Saddam Hussein

27 February 1991

Saddam's letter resulted in a revised withdrawal order to "reset for the defense of our borders and cities according to the following points":

The Republican Guard's area of responsibility runs from al-Qurna, through al-Basra to the az-Zubair bridge. In addition, its forces were responsible for the internal defense of the city. The 10th Armored Division would be attached for the defense.

The VI Corps was responsible for the area just outside al-Basra to the south and southwest (Abu al-Kashib) tying in to the Republican Guard at the az-Zubair bridge. The VI Corps would control the 22nd, 23rd, 37th, and 56th Infantry Divisions.

The II Corps defense was to the west of al-Basra from the al-Basra airport and al-Shu'aiba base running along the highways westward for 5 km. The plan specified that the 17th Infantry Division would occupy the international airport while the 51st Division was to defend the area around the town of az-Zubair.

The III Corps was to defend the region around an-Nasiriyah.

The IV Corps was to defend the sector of as-Samawah with a command post at ad-Diwaniya.

The Gulf Operations Headquarters would concentrate its forces in al-Kut.

The al-Jihad Corps would assume responsibility for "internal security in the Southern Operation Zone (al-Ahwar)."

The I Corps would return to its prewar sector of Kirkuk after handing its responsibilities over to the VII Corps.[236]

At least that was the plan.

On the morning of the 27th, the commander of the Republican Guard contacted Baghdad and rendered the following reports and requests:

"The enemy is currently engaging the Nebuchadnezzar and Adnan Divisions." The Republican Guard commander reported that the 21st Brigade (Adnan Division) was collapsing. "The enemy is continuing [its] assault and there was a heavy bombardment by helicopters against the troops of the Nebuchadnezzar Division."

The Coalition was pushing forces onto Highway 8 and moving to the east.

The Republican Guard commander requested "an armored division be sent immediately to close the gap created by the near loss of the Tawakalna Ala Allah." This move would require the 17th and Medina Divisions to coordinate. At 1130 the 10th Division (II Corps) came under the command of the Republican Guard.

At 1240 the Republican Guard headquarters reported that the 2nd Armored and 14th Mechanized Brigades were moving into position "on the road to al-Busayyah. The 10th Division was still moving into position to control the road that ran east from al-Busayyah to the Oil Road which runs north-south along the Kuwait border. The Army chief of staff called the Republican Guard commander to "explain to him the potential danger of this direction." If the enemy gained control of this road network, the Army chief warned, they could cut off the escape route to al-Rumailaih, surround the Medina Division, and advance toward Safwan. The Army chief ordered that they "rush an artillery battalion into the fight to cut off the enemy attempts to sever the escape routes out of Kuwait."

In the early afternoon, the Republican Guard headquarters reported that the 10th Division reached its blocking position near the al-Rumailaih bridge. The 10th Division pushed the 17th Brigade forward toward the al-Busayyah–Oil Road to delay the enemy's advance.

Despite continuous engagements with the enemy and repeated "heavy helicopter assaults," "the status of the Nebuchadnezzar, Hammurabi, and Adnan [Divisions] was good." In addition, the Medina Division was "above the center, meaning at more than 50 percent strength."[237]

The tone of these final battlefield reports does not indicate, at least at the senior staff level, that the Iraqi military viewed itself as a defeated force. Considering the disparity between Iraqi and Coalition forces at this point in the ground campaign, this might seem difficult to believe. However, given Iraqi notions of what the Coalition's ultimate military objectives were, at least some in the regime saw reason for cautious optimism.

The Unilateral Cease-Fire

28 FEBRUARY

As the withdrawal continued, rumors of Coalition airborne operations against the rear areas ran rampant throughout the Iraqi forces on the morning of 28 February. Most of these rumors centered on al-Jalibah Airfield and Tallil Airbase. None ever proved true.

Other reports were coming into the headquarters in al-Basra that were much harder to believe than airborne drops in the Iraqi rear area. Reports from the Iraqi special forces brigade deployed to the south of Tallil Airbase confirmed that it was "engaging in battle with American forces. [They report] seeing armored units and artillery in this battle area."[238] Despite the earlier discussions about the threat to the Iraq rear area from the Coalition troops that moved to the western desert during the air campaign, this news came as a shock. With the sudden appearance of the U.S. Army's 24th Infantry Division and 101st Airborne Division, the battles in Kuwait were no longer distant from the relative safety of the headquarters in southern Iraq.

During a discussion recorded on 1 May 1991, Saddam offered his view of battlefield conditions immediately before the American announcement of a cease-fire: "After we established our position in al-Basra, [after] the withdrawal orders, every battalion had thirty-five tanks, which is the military standard. [We] considered the American strikes unsuccessful, regardless of their superiority. The morale and spirit of our people were the most critical issue, and it did not depend on just one situation, such as the number of damaged tanks, etc."[239]

Moreover, Saddam admitted that morale at the end of February was becoming a serious problem, saying that "the media played an important role in the Iraqis' morale as well, whenever you listened to the media, they [would] say, 'neither you nor your regime have any future.' The soldiers used to pray every day, it is true that he had thirty-five tanks in the battalion, yet he said, 'what is going to happen to us? It has been forty days.' That is exactly how he felt, as if he had no future."[240]

Yet despite all of the indicators of an impending collapse of morale, and with it his army, Saddam restated his belief that the morale of Iraqi troops was, in fact, the major factor in the nation's victory—the proof was the American declaration of a cease-fire.

The strongest and the wealthiest country in the world, with the most powerful media, harassed us . . . [yet] our battle was [only] on a medium level. . . . I am very sure the criminal Bush did not expedite the cease-fire until he realized that our armor was [resisting]. . . . He probably said to himself, "It is very apparent that he [Saddam] is going to cause us damage." He worried that the so-called victory would take an unfavorable turn; therefore he rushed alone, before the Security Council discussed the situation with him and decided on a cease-fire, in order for him to control the cease-fire situation.[241]

According to Lt. Gen. Sultan Hashim, "the cease-fire was [declared] because of an initiative from the United States and its allies." The proximate cause of this surprising event was obvious to the Iraqi generals managing the war: "This happened after they [the Coalition forces] were starting to report serious losses without them being able to accomplish their designed goals of

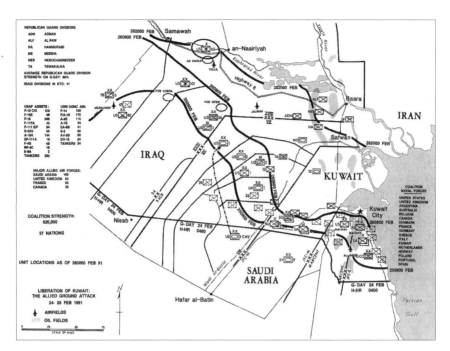

Figure 37. Collapse of the Iraqi defense. Coalition ground operations, 24–28 February 1991 (West Point Map, "Gulf War, Kuwaiti Liberation, 1991," www.dean.usma. edu/history/web03/atlases/conflicts%2058%20east/conflicts%20east%20%20 pages/wars%20conflicts%20east%20%20map%2056.htm (accessed 12 December 2006))

destroying the Iraqi forces, occupying Iraq, and dividing Iraq or to force a traitor regime on Iraq."[242]

In an official history of the Republican Guard's participation in the war, the authors succinctly capture the official Iraqi view of the cease-fire: "The adversary coalition forces, composed of twenty-eight armies at the head of which were U.S. forces, with the Republican Guard and the inability of these forces to infiltrate the defensive lines of the Republican Guard, the huge losses they incurred and their withdrawal from all the battles in the south of Iraq was an important factor which urged President George Bush to declare unilaterally the cease-fire."[243]

Yet another official history, with all the predictable hindsight of the regime's documents at this level, credited the cease-fire to Saddam's genius and President Bush's common sense:

From a practical point of view, Mr. President Leader Saddam Hussein was convinced that a ceasefire could only be achieved through confrontation. He believed that war must at some point become costly and subsequently

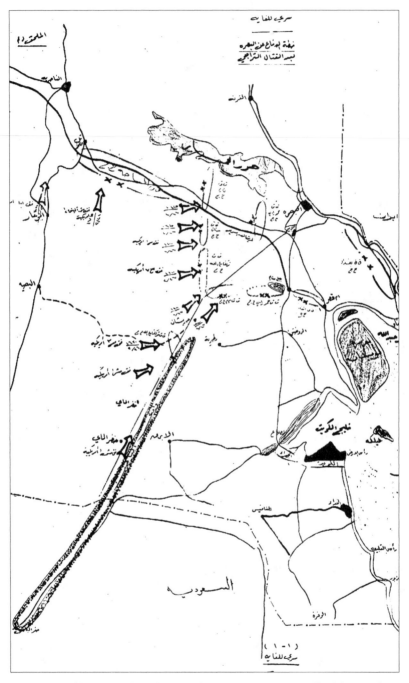

Figure 38. Republican Guard battles, 28 February 1991. An Iraqi official history showing the Republican Guard's "heroic" defense in southern Iraq (Harmony document folder IISP-2003-00026728)

a burden for the enemy. . . . Once the role of the technical advantage had been minimized by close-up and direct battles between Iraqi and enemy ground forces, the west began to suffer loses in lives and equipment exactly like Iraq and its leader Saddam Hussein had planned. That was why the American President George Bush understood before everyone else that it was not what he had thought, and he was beginning to fall into the trap and that [a] ceasefire was the only way out.[244]

Immediately after Baghdad accepted the cease-fire, Saddam ordered the various corps headquarters, most of whom were still moving into their defense-of-al-Basra positions, to return to what were essentially their prewar locations.[245] Just as these orders went out, the first of what would become a torrent of reports about a popular uprising arrived in Baghdad.

It is difficult to determine which events contributed most to the simultaneous chaos in Iraq's government, military, and large parts of its population. Causes close to the top of any list would certainly be the chaos created during the withdrawal, the vacuum created by fleeing and repositioning security forces inside Iraq, the lack of interior mobility due to destroyed bridges, and the unrelenting Coalition attacks on the Iraqi command and control system. The perception of omnipotent regime control and swift retribution for any infraction had, in the eyes of many inside Iraq and Washington, D.C., evaporated.

The unilateral declaration of a cease-fire did not end all fighting. On 2 March, units of the 17th Brigade, Hammurabi Division came into contact with the lead elements of the U.S. 24th Infantry Division at the southern end of the Hawr al-Hammar causeway just to the west of al-Basra. In the decidedly one-sided engagement, U.S. attack helicopters, mechanized infantry, and artillery destroyed more than six hundred Iraqi vehicles on an elevated dirt causeway. The chief of staff of the al-Abed Forces Command, Staff Brig. Gen. Ghazi Mohsen Marzouk, recalled that the Hammurabi commander reported the battle immediately to Republican Guard headquarters and asked for guidance.[246] The Republican Guard Headquarters replied that all previous movement orders were cancelled. An emergency order was issued for the immediate "return of all units to al-Basra because of the unusual conditions prevailing in the city."[247] The uprising had begun.

Saddam told his senior officers that the 2 March attack on the Hammurabi Division was clearly an act of revenge on the part of the Coalition. One officer present said this incident and other similar attacks along the so-called route of death showed that Iraq's enemies had "no compassion, no compassion."[248] Ironically, this opinion would change after the events of the March uprisings were examined. As an officer later explained to Saddam, if the Hammurabi Division had not run into the American force on the 2nd it would not have been available to return to al-Basra. At the time, al-Basra was a city about to fall into "the hands of the [rebels]." However, with the return of the surviving Brigades of the Hammurabi Division to al-Basra, "the [fighting] disappeared . . . [and] security prevailed." The officer added that at the time "we wanted to move the army to another place," but thanks to "Allah, Lord of the two worlds" it was refused by the Americans and returned to al-Basra.[249] Before the regime could turn its full attention to the rebellion, it needed to find a face-saving way to conclude the battle with the Coalition.

Late on the night of 2 March, the GMID Director, Lt. Gen. Sabir Abd al-Aziz, called Staff Lt. Gen. Sultan Hashim Ahmad Jabburi and told him that Saddam directed that he "head the team of negotiators who will sign the cease-fire agreement on behalf of Iraq."[250] The delegation was to consist of several officers, some chosen for their positions and others for their proximity to the negotiation site. In addition to General Sultan, the commander of the Iraqi III Corps, Lt. Gen. Salah Abbud Muhammad; the director of planning, Staff Maj. Gen. Khalid Husayn; and representatives from the Iraqi Navy and other commands in the southern region were part of the delegation. The Iraqis hastily assembled a briefing team including Lieutenant General Aziz; the army chief of staff; the defense minister; and a senior member of the foreign ministry to "brief me [Sultan] on the main points and the appropriate protocol and the manner of conducting business as an official delegation representing Iraq in these very difficult circumstances in which all forces of evil, betrayal, and treason [were] united against us."[251]

General Sultan experienced significant difficulty assembling his team and making the trip to the Safwan negotiation site. As he recalled, travel "was very difficult because the roads were blocked and al-Basra . . . was not yet completely cleared of all the disorderly elements." The delegation was fired at along the roads out of al-Basra by "traitors." In order to make it past rebel controlled areas, the delegation resorted to flanking each staff car with Republican Guard tanks for protection. Before the journey was over, one member of the delegation's security detail was wounded and had to be evacuated.

The complete delegation finally assembled near the Iraqi VII Corps head-quarters along the Safwan road. General Sultan briefed the team on the instructions he received from Baghdad and his personal expectations for their behavior. His bottom line was simple:

> "We are going to negotiate with the Americans. . . . Mr. President, the leader, has instructed me through LTG Sabir Abd al-Aziz to tell [this

delegation] 'to go with the feeling and spirit of the victorious, and to behave accordingly and not to shake hands with the infidels unless they held out their hand first.' I also told [the delegation] to respond to any insults from those they were about to meet . . . with a harsher insult. Say to them 'you [the Coalition] wouldn't be able to withstand 20 percent of what [we] resisted.'"[252]

According to one Western account of the meeting, Lieutenant General Sultan and the other members of Iraq's delegation looked stunned by the apparent scale of the Coalition operation.[253] For his part, Sultan recalled that "the Americans had prepared a military show to flex their muscle and display [their] arrogance. They had a force of more than a brigade, maybe close to a division deployed just to provide protection for the area. The soldiers were fit with large physiques, as if they were handpicked and brought there to impress us."[254]

Not surprisingly, the delegation's attitudes toward the cease-fire talks seemed to reflect Saddam's own view of the events of that day. As Saddam told his military staff on 3 March:

Let's suppose that they militarily won . . . let God and the people be the witness. See how big their shame is. See how worried they were before they began their attack . . . their attack on Baghdad. . . . There has been a reunion of the strongest powers existing in the world of the devils and the infidels. The strongest scientific, technological, and military powers [as well as] those with the highest financial and economic potentials [that] exist in the region and the world without any exception; they all got together against us and they did not succeed despite what happened. They did not dare attack Baghdad![255]

Lieutenant Sultan's recollection of the negotiations follows closely what was published in both General Schwarzkopf's and Saudi Arabia's General Khaled Bin Sultan's telling of the events. Discussions focused on the give and take over issues such as returning prisoners of war, status of weapons and mines in Kuwait, a one-kilometer buffer zone between forces, and the no-fly status of all Iraqi fixed-wing aircraft. The Iraqis requested and received permission to fly their helicopters so long as they did not go near any Coalition force.

Lieutenant General Sultan later described the atmosphere in the tent:

"We entered the meeting tent. Across from me was Schwarzkopf and across from Lieutenant General Salah (Iraqi III Corps) was Lieutenant General Khaled Bin Sultan al-Saud. Behind them sat one representative from each country that had participated in the hostilities including the Syrian, Egyptian, and Gulf states representatives. I swear, they were in [a] miserable state. Every one of them I tried to make eye contact with looked down in shame. They could not even look at us in the eye."[256]

Whether this description was reflective of his personal impression or only the regime's is unknown but telling nonetheless.

The Uprisings

Recounting the root causes, the diverse circumstances, and the specific events relating to the uprisings is beyond the scope of this study.[257] Research into the Iraqi archives indicates that the events immediately following the negotiations at Safwan would quickly overwhelm the regime, and in many ways brought it closer to collapse than had the war with Iran, or the just-completed "Mother of All Battles." What started in the south as a combination of a Shiite-based rebellion and localized military revolt, quickly spread to the Kurdish areas

Figure 39. Negotiations at Safwan, 3 March 1991. The Iraqi delegation (right) negotiates the terms of the cease-fire with Gen. H. Norman Schwarzkopf and HRH Khaled Bin Sultan Bin Abdul Aziz (U.S. Department of Defense, Negotiations at Safwan, Photograph ID: DAST9208032, Camera Operator: Sgt. Jose Trejo, taken 3 March 1991)

in the northern provinces and beyond. Before it was over less than a month later, the Ba'ath party would temporarily lose control of all but al-Anbar Province and it would require the most brutal methods the regime could muster to preserve itself.[258]

Trouble with Iraq's restive Shi'a majority, especially along the border areas with Iran, was nothing new for the regime. However, the events of 1991 went far beyond anything the regime had ever anticipated or experienced. Indicators of brewing trouble in Iraq's southern region emerged as early as 31 December 1990. Correspondence from the GMID to the senior leadership reads:

First: "Large groups of fugitives, traitors, and deported Iranians are under the command of the so-called Supreme Council for Islamic Revolution in Iraq and the so-called Iraq Islamic Liberation Army." They have opened centers in al-Ahwaz and Dezful [Southwestern Iran] where "they plan to attack Iraq when the war starts."

Second: "[The traitors] are expected to conduct extensive maneuvers in [the area] just east of the Iraq [border] where most of the Iranian troops will participate."

Third: It is concluded from the above that "Iran [is] profoundly concerned about events occurring in the region." These military groups and maneuvers "indicate Iranian bad intentions."[259]

The reporting continued in this vein until late February when the regime, not surprisingly, became singularly focused on its conventional fight with the Coalition. The "traitors" became the focus of attention once again just as Iraqi troops began streaming into al-Basra and the other cities in the south. The chaos engendered by Coalition air strikes on government facilities, bridges, and communications infrastructure combined with the broken pieces of an army in full-scale retreat mixing with a long-simmering insurgency created a perfect storm that soon engulfed the regime.[260] An Iraqi Army battalion commander captured by the Coalition described how the chaos in southern Iraq quickly turned retreating units against the regime: "If my division commander [had] ever ordered me to turn my guns against Saddam Hussein, I [would] do it. But who will be the officer to give this order? *I will never give this order, but I will follow the man who does*"[261] [Emphasis added].

For Saddam however, none of this was happenstance. In a discussion with senior military officers on 3 April 1991, Saddam explained how the uprisings (in the South and the North) were the actual purpose of the larger American plan:

"The Americans wanted to hurt Iraq by hurting its army. [Iraq's] army would get destroyed . . . [and] such an opportunity would be taken advantage of by all the greedy people or hateful ones or those who had beforehand [demonstrated] evil intentions against Iraq, whether they were from outside or inside Iraq. The entire siege that happened, the air bombardment until the land attack began, they were all methods used to create the appropriate environment for the operation [uprising] to take place. So the appropriate environment was created."[262]

The line of reasoning that the entire Coalition military campaign against Iraq was orchestrated in order to create the "appropriate environment" for an uprising resonated with the senior leadership's experiences. As grand conspiratorial theories often do, this one also had the advantage of explaining away the apparently inexplicable. The environment Saddam was describing was much more than just physical. In fact, previous explanations of "heroic" resistance by the Republican Guard in the closing days of the ground campaign proved that the Coalition was unable to complete the task through physical means alone. "The psychological factor was the most important factor," Saddam told his officers.[263] Moreover, according to Saddam, it was in the realm of the "psychological factor" that the Coalition had its greatest success, "meaning the feeling of defeat which spread to the government offices first, before the defeat happened in fact and became a physical and effective condition."[264] For many loyalists in the Iraqi military, this would become the "stabbed in the back" explanation to cover any failures on the battlefield. In this updated version of the German myth promulgated after World War I, the Iraqi Shi'a and their Persian co-religionists would ironically play the part of German Jews and Marxists.

In addition to the myths, Saddam provided a tactical reason why such a large segment of the population turned hostile. He emphasized that the public's negative "psychological factor" was brought on by the fact that many government ministries and offices were forced to "change locations" because of the war.[265] Saddam described how the Coalition's air strikes and the growing insurgent attacks

spread out to the point that the governors would [have to] change the location of his ministry and the [local] security director would change his location, and the police director would change his location and so on. . . . What happened was that the government was nonexistent. Well, the government was nonexistent. In such a way that whoever would say he was a Sultan, it was possible for him to become a Sultan. So, traitors showed up . . . supported by elements trained and specially prepared to play

Figure 40. Video capture of Ali Hassan al-Majid kicking a rebel suspect during an interrogation (Harmony media file IZSP-2003-10104084)

such a role by Iran. And they erupted in al-Basra and they erupted in other places . . . even in the north.[266]

Saddam's diagnosis of the specific pathology of the uprisings continued with descriptions that could easily have been pulled from Sir Aylmer L. Haldane's personal descriptions of the 1920 insurrection in Mesopotamia or any number of books about Iraq written after April 2003.[267] It is often overlooked in the operational analyses of the war that there were worse things for a regime like Saddam's than military "defeat" on a foreign [Kuwaiti] battlefield. As Saddam would later say, "The traitorous rebellion phase is now a thing of the past; but it was difficult and troublesome. . . . *The traitorous rebellion was more difficult than the phase which had been before it*"[268][Emphasis added].

In the end, the regime survived; however, for Saddam the war was far from over. From the beginning he viewed the 1991 war as a part of a larger historical narrative with chapters left to be written. Even Saddam's moniker for the war, Um Al-Ma'arik (Mother of all Battles), was meant to evoke a sense that the events of 1991 were but a subset of a long war. In an April 1991 discussion with his generals, Saddam reminded them that although this phase of the war was drawing to a close, there was much left to do before the beginning of the next:

Iraqi General: This was a harsh test through which the country went. No country in the world or in history went through such a test. No army, there is no army which went through this.

Saddam: What's important is to learn a lesson from it. . . .

Iraqi General: We will, sir.[269]

Notes

1. Harmony media file ISGQ-2003-M0004609.
2. This low estimate of the sortie rate Coalition air forces could generate was probably based on extrapolations of Iraqi capabilities and experience. The Coalition generated more than 2,700 sorties (all types) on the opening day and strikes averaged approximately 1,000 per day for the duration of the war.
3. Harmony document folder ISGP-2003-00033136. Iraqi document cited is correspondence number 22036, 26 December 1990. It appears that some of the American order of battle information in these Iraqi reports was a result of erroneous reporting and speculation in Western press reports. For example, a 24 August article in The Los Angles Times entitled "If Pentagon Gets a 'Go' It'll Be Massive Strike" reported that Lance missiles were being shipped to Saudi Arabia with other elements of the U.S. Army's III Corps artillery.
4. Ibid. Iraqi document cited is correspondence number 22036, 26 December 1990.
5. Ibid. The Iraqi document cited is correspondence number 22036, 26 December 1990.
6. Ibid. Iraqi document cited is correspondence number 22036, 26 December 1990.
7. Harmony document folder IST-A5053-002.
8. Ibid.
9. Harmony media file ISGQ-2003-M0003323.
10. Ibid. It is not clear how well this guidance was followed or how being told to aim at such a small target on the top of a moving tank, assuming it was in range at all, would improve the odds of destroying the much larger tank below it.
11. Ibid.
12. Harmony media file ISGQ-2003-M0006763.
13. Ibid.
14. There are numerous examples in the Iraqi after-action documents where, for unexplained reasons, the full-alert policy was either not enforced during the war or was actually relaxed after the opening day air strikes.
15. Harmony media file ISGQ-2003-M0006763.
16. Ibid.
17. Ibid.
18. Ibid.
19. Ibid.
20. Ibid.
21. The Iraqi Air Force had approximately thrity-eight Russian-built Ilyushin transport aircraft (Il-76 and Il-14) before 1991.
22. Harmony media file ISGQ-2003-M0006763.
23. Ibid.

24. The officer told Saddam that the remaining fields were going to consist of the 100 Russian and Italian mines still in the inventory.

25. Harmony media file ISGQ-2003-M0003916.

26. Harmony media file ISGQ-2003-M0006195.

27. Harmony media file ISGQ-2003-M0003916.

28. Ibid.

29. Clause 15 of the Ba'ath party's founding document (1947) states, "The national bond is the only bond existing in the Arab state, and it is this bond that promotes harmony among the citizens and their fusion in a single melting pot, while struggling against all other loyalties: religious, communal, tribal, racist, and regional." Cited in Bengio, *Saddam's Word*, 177. In an attempt to hold onto power after the end of the 1991 war, Saddam violated both the letter and spirit of all the rest of the tenants of this clause.

30. Harmony media file ISGQ-2003-M0003916. The public announcement about the change to the Iraqi flag was made on 14 January 1990.

31. Ibid.

32. The Tapline Road was the critical movement and supply route for the entire Coalition move to the west. Before the start of the ground campaign, more than 64,000 wheeled and tracked vehicles and 255,000 soldiers form the XVIII Airborne and VII Corps would pass over the Tapline Road as a part of "Schwarzkopf's Symphony." Scales, *Certain Victory*, 145.

33. Harmony media file ISGQ-2003-M0003916.

34. According to an Iraqi postwar awards memorandum, members of the GMID Unit 999 conducted "heroic" operations in the vicinity of the Tapline Road. These operations included raids on Saudi border stations, deep reconnaissance, and laying mines along roads in the vicinity of Ar'ar, Saudi Arabia. Harmony document folder ISGZ-2004-022906.

35. Hamdani, "From the Golan to the Collapse of Baghdad," 161.

36. Harmony media file ISGQ-2003-M0006247—Video of a conference discussing battles in 1991, 20 November 1995. One Iraqi officer went so far as to declare that they had no radars in operation in that area.

37. Hamdani, "From the Golan to the Collapse of Baghdad," 164.

38. Ibid.

39. Harmony media file ISGQ-2003-M0003323. While difficult to confirm, the aircraft "dropped" by the III Corps was probably a Kuwaiti A-4 Skyhawk shot down twenty-five kilometers south of Kuwait City. See Doris Cook et al., *Gulf War Air Power Survey*, Volume 5: *A Statistical Compendium and Chronology* (Washington, DC: U.S. Government Printing Office, 1993), 643.

40. Harmony document folder ISGP-2003-00031468.

41. al-Ayyubi, "Forty-Three Missiles, 11. According to al-Ayyubi, the first SSM shots were actually fired at 0845 from the Kuwait-based 225th Brigade (al-Ra'd missiles) against Coalition targets in the vicinity of al-Khafji.

42. Ibid.

43. Harmony media file ISGQ-2003-M0007641—Audiotape of a meeting between Saddam Hussein and members of the Iraqi Air Force and Air Defense forces, late 1991. According to this tape, the Iraqi nuclear site (Project 777) ended the war with 1,104

bomb craters "onsite." The Iraqi air defense unit assigned to defend the site reported 149 dead and 145 wounded.

44. Ibid.
45. Harmony media file ISGQ-2003-M0006201. One highly publicized Coalition air attack to stop the Tariq Project came on 27 January. Several U.S. Air Force F-111s used precision bombs to destroy the pumps at Mina al-Ahmadi Kuwait.
46. al-Ayyubi, "Forty-Three Missiles," 11.
47. Ibid.
48. Harmony document folder ISGP-2003-00031468.
49. Harmony folder ISGP-2003-00028432.
50. Ibid.
51. This directive makes it clear that Saddam believed that the Coalition could monitor and locate the regime's most secure communications. It also lends credence to the idea that the tragic Coalition attack on the al-Firdos air defense shelter (13 February) was, at least in part, a successful regime trap designed to generate civilian casualties. The prohibition on the use of wireless communications was lifted by Saddam's order on 2 March.
52. Harmony folder ISGP-2003-00028432.
53. al-Ayyubi, "Forty-Three Missiles," 13.
54. Harmony document folder ISGP-2003-00037278.
55. Harmony media file ISGQ-2003-M0003323.
56. Ibid.
57. Ibid.
58. Harmony document folder ISGP-2003-00031468.
59. Harmony folder ISGP-2003-00028432.
60. Harmony document folder ISGQ-2005-00026011—25th Infantry Division Camel Based Re-supply Plan, 28 January 1991. The 25th Infantry Division was a frontline unit just to the west of the Wadi al-Batin.
61. Harmony media file ISGQ-2003-M0006471.
62. Ibid.
63. Ibid.
64. Harmony document folder ISGQ-2003-00038432.
65. Hamdani, "From the Golan to the Collapse of Baghdad," 166.
66. Both enemy courses of action had variations of supporting airborne and/or amphibious landings in the vicinity of Kuwait City. See Harmony document folder FM8617.
67. See Woods et al, *Iraqi Perspectives Project*, 136–47.
68. Harmony document folder ISGP-2003-00033219. Rafha, Saudi Arabia is located almost three hundred kilometers to the west of Hafir al-Batin.
69. Ibid.
70. Ibid.
71. Ras Tanura was (and still is) the largest facility of its kind. A successful Iraqi strike (difficult but not impossible) on this facility would temporarily put at risk almost 7 million barrels of oil per day. To understand the impact of this, consider that when Kuwait's output of 1.5 million barrels per day stopped as a result of the Iraqi invasion, world oil prices more than doubled.
72. Harmony document folder ISGP-2003-00030181. AWACS stands for Airborne Warning and Control System.
73. Harmony document folder ISGP-2003-00030181.

74. For a good description of this event from the U.S. Navy's point of view see Edward J. Marolda and Robert J. Schneller Jr., *Shield and Sword—The United States Navy and the Persian Gulf War* (Washington, DC: U.S. GPO 1998), 205–06.

75. Harmony document folder ISGP-2003-00030181.

76. Harmony document folder ISGQ-2003-00046018. Also al-Ayyubi, "Forty-Three Missiles," 13.

77. Harmony media file ISGQ-2003-M0006167.

78. Ibid.

79. Ibid.

80. Ibid.

81. Harmony document folder ISGP-2003-00038432.

82. Harmony document folder ISGP-2003-00031468.

83. Harmony document folder ISGP-2003-00026182.

84. The number rises to 148 including those taken from Kuwait International Airport during the invasion. Harmony document folder ISGQ-2003-00023414.

85. Ibid.

86. Harmony document folder ISGQ-2003-00046018; Harmony document folder ISGZ-2005-000080; Harmony document folder ISGZ-2005-000080.

87. Harmony document folder ISGQ-2003-00046018. The capture reportedly took place between the airfield known as H2 and mile marker 180 on the Baghdad–Amman highway.

88. Harmony document folder ISGP-2003-00036959.

89. Ibid.

90. Harmony document folder ISGP-2003-00029963.

91. See Woods et al., *Iraqi Perspectives Project*, 131. Unit 999 was a commando organization and known as Iraq's "deep penetration unit." At one point it had battalions organized for operations in or against Iran, Saudi Arabia, Palestine, Turkey, sea-borne, and internal opposition. See Sean Boyne, "Inside Iraq's Security Network—Part Two," *Jane's Intelligence Review* 9, no. 8 (1997): 365.

92. Harmony document folder ISGP-2003-00029963. This same scenario repeated itself in March 2003 when the regime dispatched the same unit to check rumors of Coalition forces in the western desert.

93. Harmony document folder ISGP-2003-00031468.

94. Harmony media file ISGQ-2003-M0006471.

95. Harmony media file ISGQ-2003-M0006201.

96. Ibid. This engagement was described in a U.S. official history as the "Battle of Bubiyan Island" or the "Bubiyan Turkey Shoot." Over a period of thirteen hours, the Coalition reports noted twenty-one engagements, damaging or sinking seven missile boats, three amphibious ships, a minesweeper, and nine smaller vessels. See Department of Defense, "Final Report to Congress, Conduct of the Persian Gulf War," 195.

97. Ibid.

98. Ibid.

99. Harmony document folder IISP-2003-00045177.

100. Harmony media file ISGQ-2003-00054592.

101. Ibid.

102. Harmony document folder IISP-2003-00026728. Saddam reportedly made the comment on 5 February 1991.

103. From Saddam's speech on 10 February 1991. "Every hour and day that has passed since the beginning of the siege against the gathering of vanguard believers in Iraq is an hour and day of defeat for the gathering of atheism, oppression, and tyranny. The beginning of the first dark night of each new month is a mark of darkness for their lost hopes and a sign of frustration for their defeated gathering."

104. Harmony document folder ISGP-2003-00029963.

105. Ibid.

106. Saddam had come close to provoking Israel into the war by late January. On 28 January, a senior delegation of Israelis met with Secretary of Defense Cheney in Washington, D.C., and all but gave an ultimatum that if the United States did not put significant effort, including more ground forces, into the western deserts of Iraq, Israel would. See Atkinson, *Crusade*, 173–74.

107. Harmony document folder ISGQ-2003-00046018. Not surprisingly, the inventory numbers do not appear in the public version of General al-Ayyubi's journal.

108. Harmony document folder IZSP-2003-00300910.

109. Ibid.

110. Media reporting about a possible western flank option increased during late January. Some were very accurate in describing, for example, that the "heart of the plan is a sweeping flanking maneuver around Saddam's forces in Kuwait." It is difficult to know which Western news reports Iraqi leadership may or may not have read on any specific point. On the critical issue of a Coalition flanking attack, two of the more detailed examples available were Col. David H. Hackworth, "We'll Win But . . . ," *Newsweek* 117, no. 3 (1991): 26–31; and Barry J. Lane, "The Killing Ground," *Newsweek*, 117, no. 4 (1991): 28–31.

111. Harmony document folder IZSP-2003-00300910. It is not clear that the Iraqi military knew what to expect in case of an amphibious landing. The 15th Infantry Division, based in Kuwait City, had the mission to "defend in a death-defying manner" against any "hostile naval landing." But its orders include no special preparation for countering an over-the-shore assault. See Harmony document folder FM8621.

112. Harmony document folder ISGQ-2003-00046018. Force-17 was the Commando and Special Operations Unit of the PLO. It also served as Chairman Yasser Arafat's bodyguard force.

113. Harmony document folder IZSP-2003-00300910.

114. Ibid.

115. Harmony document folder ISGP-203-00029600.

116. The actual Coalition deception objective was to reinforce the belief that U.S. forces would conduct a frontal attack and not go west of the Wadi al-Batin. The deception depicted a two-corps attack into western Kuwait and a Marine attack along the coast.

117. Harmony document folder ISGP-2003-00033219.

118. Ibid.

119. Hamdani, "From the Golan to the Collapse of Baghdad," 169. According to the Coalition air plan, bombers and strike aircraft were scheduled "to hit the Republican Guard in the KTO every hour, twenty-four hours a day, until the end of the war." Cited in Jamieson, *Lucrative Targets*, 45.

120. Harmony media file ISGQ-2003-M0007641. The change in the Coalition targeting priorities shifted from strategic to interdiction targets with an objective of destroying 50 percent of Iraq's armor in the Kuwait theater of operations by the anticipated 21 February start of ground operations.

121. Harmony Document FM8607—20th Division defense plan, February 1991 (U). The document title is misleading. This document is actually a Coalition debrief of an Iraqi soldier taken in early February. The Iraqi soldier explained the Iraqi 20th Division defensive scheme and made extensive comments about the horrific conditions created by Coalition air strikes.

122. Harmony document folder IISP-2003-00029023.

123. Harmony document folder ISGP-2003-00026182.

124. What became known as "the al-Firdos bunker incident" began when Coalition signals intelligence detected emanations from the vicinity of the al-Firdos bunker in southwest Baghdad. Two F-117s attacked the bunker on the night of 13 February. It is estimated that 204 civilians, all of whom had sought shelter in the bunker, perished in the attack.

125. Harmony document folder ISGQ-2003-00046018 and Harmony document folder ISGQ-2003-00046019.

126. By mid-February the Coalition's XVIII Airborne Corps repositioned more than 115,000 soldiers, 21,000 wheeled and 4,300 tracked vehicles over 500 kilometers to the west of their initial deployment. At the same time, the Coalition's heavy VII Corps shifted 140,000 soldiers, 32,000 wheeled and 6,600 tracked vehicles more than 200 kilometers to the west. Scales, *Certain Victory*, 146.

127. Harmony document folder ISGP-2003-00031773.

128. Harmony document folder ISGP-2003-00036936. This analysis cites the two top secret memoranda (memo numbers 1611 and 1641) from GMID to the Iraqi leadership on 14 and 16 February 1991. Harmony document folder ISGP-2003-00033219 contains a copy of memorandum 1641.

129. Harmony document folder IZSP-2003-00300910—General Military Intelligence Directorate memorandum from Iraqi embassy, Amman, Jordan, 16 February 1991. The Iraqi document attributes the information to a retired French Admiral.

130. Freeman and Karsh, *Gulf Conflict (1990–1991)*, 378.

131. Harmony document folder ISGQ-2003-00046019.

132. Ibid. The journal noted that the report, though received on 15 February, was prepared on 10 February.

133. Harmony document folder ISGP-2003-00031773.

134. Ibid. This same report also notes the possibility of Israeli forces joining the Coalition in the western part of Iraq to "search for missile launching bases and opening a new front that needs big numbers of Iraqi forces."

135. Harmony document folder ISGP-2003-00033219.

136. Ibid.

137. Ibid.

138. Ibid. Apparently this estimate did not filter down to the front lines. Based on Iraqi prisoner-of-war interviews, in the days just before the ground assault, most frontline Iraqi commanders still expected the primary Coalition actions to be amphibious and through the Wadi al-Batin. See Jamieson, *Lucrative Targets*, 122–25.

139. Harmony media file ISGQ-2003-M0005371. This somewhat realistic recollection of

events on the part of senior military officers did not survive subsequent Iraqi "analyses" of the impact of Coalition airpower. The comments about the psychological impact of the air campaign dominated many Iraqi postwar discussions much more than did issues of equipment lost to air strikes. According to Coalition officers at the Joint Debriefing Center, by the start of the ground operation, some Iraqi divisions had lost 50 percent of their strength through desertions, "in some units the genuine foot race north really commenced when the bombs began to fall." Cited in Jamieson, *Lucrative Targets*, 72.

140. Coalition operations between 17 and 24 February included aggressive artillery raids and reconnaissance incursions into Iraq by elements of the U.S. VII Corps along the Wadi al-Batin. A Coalition deception operation known as Task Force Troy operated at the center of the Kuwaiti border along the I MEF and Joint Force (Arab) sectors. This 500-man mixed element simulated a division-size force through the use of deception and psychological operations. It also conducted aggressive raids and probes against Iraqi's forward positions in what became known as "drive-by shootings," since as their commander noted, his job was to "deceive the enemy, not amuse him." All of this activity was designed to focus Iraqi attention on the Kuwaiti frontier and away from the Coalition shift to the west and the specific U.S. Marine Corps attack zones to the east. Atkinson, *Crusade*, 334.

141. Harmony document folder ISGQ-2003-M0003959.

142. Harmony document folder ISGQ-2003-00046019. Whether this story was a sign of confidence or an embellishment of the record is unknown. According to another transcript, General al-Ayyubi's son launched two missiles that day, which he added to the one he launched as a first grader during the closing days of the Iran-Iraq War. See Harmony folder ISGQ-2003-M0006285.

143. Harmony document folder ISGQ-2003-M0003959. The Iraqi description of the location of the 26th Infantry Division in this review of the war does not match the Coalition's enemy order of battle graphic in Figure 31.

144. "News of the oil wells was taken to George Bush just as he was discussing with President Mitterrand the latter's call for a seventy-two hour delay [in the ground offensive]. The news concluded the discussion." Freeman and Karsh, *Gulf Conflict (1990–1991)*, 384. The timing of the oil well destruction was clearly seen as a purposeful negotiating tactic on Saddam's part, coming as it did just as the last-ditch efforts in Moscow and Paris were making progress. The purpose of the overall Project Tariq was part revenge and part military tactic, but the timing and circumstance of local execution was pure stupidity on the part of the Iraqis.

145. Harmony document folder ISGQ-2003-00046019.

146. Harmony document folder ISGQ-2003-M0003959.

147. Harmony media file ISGQ-2003-M0001722. It is unlikely that they heard tanks at this hour. Major ground forces did not cross into Iraq until 0400.

148. Ibid. Iraq agreed to a proposal by the Soviet Union for a conditional withdrawal on 22 February. The United States rejected the proposal on 23 February for failing to meet previously stated Coalition conditions.

149. Harmony document folder ISGQ-2003-M0003959. Iraqi reporting often ascribed success to any delay, repositioning, pause, or change in tactical approach in Coalition forces, regardless of the circumstance. This habit was also evident in Iraqi military reporting during OIF in 2003. See Woods et al., *Iraqi Perspectives Project*, 130–48.

150. Harmony media file ISGQ-2003-M0001722.

151. In most of the recording made on 24 February the only two participants identified by name or position are Saddam Hussein and his personal secretary, Abd Hamid Mahmud. For example see Harmony media file ISGQ-2003-M0001722.

152. Ibid.

153. Harmony document folder ISGQ-2003-00046032.

154. Ibid.

155. George Bush and Brent Scowcroft, *A World Transformed* (New York: Alfred A. Knopf, 1998), 476.

156. Harmony media file ISGQ-2003-M0001722.

157. Ibid.

158. Ibid.

159. Ibid.

160. Ibid.

161. Harmony media file ISGQ-2003-M0001720.

162. Ibid.

163. Ibid. It is not clear if this conversation took place before or after the "tense" eighty-three-minute discussion between President Bush and President Gorbachev on the morning of 23 February. This is the point where it became clear to Gorbachev that the Soviet initiative would fail to meet the Coalition's terms. For a clear description of the last-minute diplomacy between Moscow and Washington from a non-Iraqi perspective see Freeman and Karsh, *Gulf Conflict (1990–1991)*, 374–85.

164. Harmony media file ISGQ-2003-M0001720.

165. Ibid.

166. Ibid.

167. Ibid.

168. Ibid. Time is unclear.

169. Ibid. According to Coalition records, the French 6th Division along with the 2nd Brigade of the American 82nd Airborne Division crossed into Iraq at 0400 local time 24 February.

170. Harmony media file ISGQ-2003-M0001722.

171. Harmony media file ISGQ-2003-M0001720. It is not clear if this draft speech was ever made public by Saddam or his information minister. Saddam did give an uncharacteristically short radio address on the afternoon of 24 February, which focused on the "treachery" of the Coalition and tried to rally the Iraqi people to "fight them and show them no mercy," but it did not include any military details. FBIS-NEW-91-037—Saddam Hussein, speech on Baghdad Radio Service, in Arabic (0737 GMT 24 February 1991), 25 February 1991.

172. Harmony media file ISGQ-2003-M0001720.

173. Ibid. It is not clear how the force moving from the north of Iraq would be spared from Coalition air attack any more than a force moving from Kuwait.

174. Ibid.

175. Ibid. Karbala is one of the holiest cites in Shi'a Islam. During the Iran–Iraq War, Iran launched numerous attacks toward Karbala in the hope of stimulating a popular Shi'a uprising in Iraq. The city remained loyal to Saddam.

176. Ibid.

177. Ibid.

178. Ibid.

179. Harmony media file ISGQ-2003-M0006201. Several of the Iraqi Super Frelon helicopters were equipped to fire the French-made Exocet (AM-39) anti-ship missile. It is possible that what was remembered as a "suicide" mission may have been better described as a high-risk operation.

180. Harmony document folder ISGQ-2003-M0003943.

181. Ibid.

182. The threat of amphibious operations was a major portion of the Coalition's deception strategy. In addition to setting up the credibility of an attack from the sea through well-publicized exercises (Operation Imminent Thunder, 15–21 November, and a series of exercises called Sea Soldier), the Coalition ran two well-telegraphed amphibious demonstrations—one south and the other north of Kuwait City on 25 and 27 February. During a November 1991 review of the war with his senior ministers, Saddam's postwar recollection of events shifted dramatically, no doubt aided by hindsight. On the issue of an amphibious threat posed by the Coalition, Saddam stated, "We were correct even in discounting a beach invasion. We said that there is no way they would try a beach invasion and expose themselves and suffer losses. Are they ever ready to suffer such losses? Therefore they had to think of coming by land. And the beach invasion did not take place." See Harmony media file ISGQ-2003-M0005371.

183. Comrade Muhammad is not further identified in the tape. Judging from the context of the conversation, this is most likely Muhammad Hamzah Az-Zubaydi. Az-Zubaydi (a Shi'a) was a future prime minister and former deputy prime minister of Iraq. In March 1991 he became known in the West as Saddam's "Shi'a thug," for his enthusiastic participation in the suppression of the 1991 Shi'a uprisings. Harmony media file ISGQ-2003-M0001721.

184. Ibid.

185. Muhammad is referring to one of several battles for the city during the Iran-Iraq War.

186. Harmony media file ISGQ-2003-M0001721.

187. Ibid.

188. Ibid. The adviser is not identified on the tape.

189. Harmony document folder ISGQ-2003-M0003943.

190. Ibid.

191. Ibid. It is unstated in these conversations and many of the reports, but the term "shortage of infantry" was in effect a euphemism for units depleted by desertions and surrenders.

192. Harmony document folder ISGQ-2003-M0003959.

193. The MEK was a group of Iranian expatriates opposed to the Iranian Islamic revolution and the post-Shah regime. Saddam gave this group sanctuary, training, and weapons in its campaign to overthrow the regime in Tehran.

194. Harmony document folder ISGQ-2003-M0003959.

195. Ibid.

196. Harmony media file ISGQ-2003-M0006180.

197. Ibid.

198. Harmony document folder ISGQ-2003-M0003959.

199. Harmony media file ISGQ-2003-M0006180.

200. Harmony document folder ISGQ-2003-M0003959; and Harmony media file ISGQ-2003-M0006180.

201. Harmony media file ISGQ-2003-M0006180. The aircraft incorrectly referred to as a helicopter was probably a U.S. Marine OV-10A Bronco crewed by Maj. Joseph J. Small and Capt. David Spellacy. Spellacy was killed and Small was taken prisoner and severely beaten. When interrogated about this flight map, Small recalled that he told the Iraqis "the biggest grandest lie I think I've ever told in my entire life." See Joseph Hanneman, "Eye of the Storm," *Perspective* 3, no. 1 (2003): 6.

202. Harmony media file ISGQ-2003-M0006180. It is ironic that at the same time LTG Salah Aboud Mahmaud was reading the captured American "plan," one of his officers was giving the III Corps plan to the U.S. Marines. According to one account, just before the Iraqi counterattack on the morning of the 25th, the commander of the 22nd Brigade surrendered to the commander of Task Force Papa Bear and handed him the current Iraq III Corps map. Atkinson, *Crusade*, 411.

203. Harmony document folder ISGQ-2003-M0003959.

204. Ibid.

205. Harmony document folder ISGQ-2003-00046033.

206. Ibid.

207. Ibid.

208. Ibid.

209. Ibid.

210. Ibid.

211. Harmony media file ISGP-2003-10151507.

212. Harmony document folder ISGQ-2003-00046033.

213. Harmony media file ISGP-2003-10151507.

214. Harmony document folder ISGQ-2003-00046033. The order required the 78th, 123rd, and 246th brigades to return to the VI Corps while the 41st Armored Brigade and 676th Battalion were to return to the II Corps.

215. Harmony document folder ISGQ-2003-00046019. In this attack, twenty-nine U.S. soldiers were killed and ninety-nine were wounded.

216. FBIS-NES-90-038—"Saddam Hussein Speaks on Withdrawal from Kuwait 26 February 1991," broadcast, Baghdad Domestic Radio Service, in Arabic, (0824 GMT, 26 February 1991), 26 February 1991 (FOUO), cited in Bengio, Saddam Speaks, 207–12.

217. Harmony media file ISGQ-2003-M0006471. Judging from postwar after-action reviews and histories, and despite Saddam's apparent authorship, the term "retreat battle" did not catch on as the Iraqi doctrinal term.

218. Freeman and Karsh, *Gulf Conflict (1990–1991)*, 400.

219. Harmony document folder ISGQ-2003-M0003943.

220. Harmony document folder ISGQ-2003-M0004181. This officer recommended that the Iraq military should "concentrate on withdrawal and on more training for withdrawals."

221. Harmony document folder ISGQ-2003-M0003943.

222. Ibid.

223. Ibid.

224. Harmony media file ISGQ-2003-M0006273 (FOUO). Based on other comments, the speaker was probably the commander of the VI Corps during the 1991 war.

225. Harmony media file ISGQ-2003-M0006471.

226. Harmony document folder ISGQ-2003-00046033. Recollections are of Army Chief of Staff, LTG Husayn Rashid Muhammad. The "popular organizations" were probably the Popular Army, the Ba'ath party militias, as well as some tribal groups. Ironically, members of these same organizations were only days away from turning their guns on the regime that was planning to use them in its urban defense plan.

227. Harmony media file ISGP-2003-10151507.

228. Harmony document folder ISGQ-2003-M0004181.

229. Harmony document folder ISGQ-2003-00046033.

230. Ibid.

231. See Scales, Certain Victory, 261–63; and Atkinson, Crusade, 441–48.

232. Harmony document folder ISGQ-2003-00046040.

233. Harmony document folder ISGQ-2003-00046033. Saddam established the advanced general headquarters in al-Basra on 27 February to coordinate the defenses of the city and surrounding region. He placed his trusted deputy Ali Hasan al-Majid in command and gave him authority over all regime resources in the area. This ad hoc headquarters would become the model for the regional command and control scheme used during Operation Desert Fox and OIF.

234. A rare public admission of error on Saddam's part.

235. Saddam had earlier discussed a "people's defense," where the citizens would be armed to fight the invading army for every block. The method outlined for the defense of al-Basra, an outer and inner ring, is remarkably similar to the urban defense schemes Saddam applied during the regime's final defense in 2003. See Woods et al, Iraqi Perspectives Project, 80–83.

236. Harmony document folder ISGQ-2003-00046033.

237. Ibid.

238. Harmony document folder ISGQ-2003-M0005891. General Aayad Futayyih Khalifa. The Coalition unit being discussed here was probably the U.S. 24th Infantry Division (Mechanized).

239. Harmony media file ISGQ-2003-M0005373.

240. Ibid.

241. Ibid.

242. Harmony document folder ISGQ-2003-00046033. The Coalition commander's perspective could not have been any more different. General Schwarzkopf said in a 27 March interview, "We had them in a rout, and we could have continued to . . . wreak great destruction upon them. We could have completely closed the door and made it in fact a battle of annihilation." Cited in Jamieson, Lucrative Targets, 163.

243. Harmony document folder ISGQ-2003-00046040. In a later discussion with members of the air defense forces, Saddam opined that accumulation of experience engaging enemy aircraft between 17 January and 28 February started to scare the Coalition air forces and directly led to the cease-fire. Harmony media file ISGQ-2003-M0007641.

244. Harmony document folder ISGQ-2003-00046032.

245. I Corps to Kirkuk, II and III Corps in vicinity of al-Basra, IV Corps in al-Amara, the VI Corps to the Castle of Saleh (prewar sector), al-Jihad Corps in Karbala, the Gulf Operations Corps in al-Kut. Harmony document folder ISGQ-2003-00046033.

246. The al-Abed Forces Command (Republican Guard) was one of several corps-level

area commands established in late 1990 to facilitate the command and control of Iraq's defense.

247. Harmony document folder ISGQ-2003-00046040.

248. Harmony media file ISGQ-2003-M0003869. This event is described in Atkinson, *Crusade*, 481–84.

249. Harmony media file ISGQ-2003-M0006905.

250. Harmony document folder ISGQ-2003-00046032.

251. Ibid.

252. Ibid. At approximately the same time, General Schwarzkopf, when asked about his "negotiation plan," snapped, "This isn't a negotiation. . . . I don't plan to give them anything. I'm here to tell them exactly what we expect them to do." Schwarzkopf, *It Doesn't Take a Hero*, 483.

253. See Freeman and Karsh, *Gulf Conflict (1990–1991)*, 406–07.

254. Harmony document folder ISGQ-2003-00046032.

255. Harmony media file ISGQ-2003-M0003869.

256. Harmony document folder ISGQ-2003-00046032.

257. At this writing, detailed research into the regime's history of the 1991 uprisings is ongoing.

258. See Makiya, *Cruelty and Silence*, 1993, for a description of conditions in southern Iraq during this period.

259. Harmony document folder ISGP-2003-00033136. This warning could easily have been written in December 2002.

260. The destruction of bridges in 1991 had a significant impact on Saddam's ability to react to the rebellion and a surprisingly significant effect on his 2003 defense plan for Bagdad. In 1991, Coalition air planners identified fifty-four bridges that could carry vehicle traffic and targeted all of them. The result was that loyal military units could not move quickly to suppress the rebellions. In 2003, the Coalition did not target major bridges because they intended to cross many of them. Saddam, implementing a lesson from 1991, did not demolish the bridges so he would not be vulnerable to a repeat of the 1991 rebellion.

261. Vern Liebl, "The View from the Other Side of the Jebel (Hill)," *Command Magazine* no. 13 (1991): 33.

262. Harmony media file ISGQ-2003-M0006905.

263. Ibid.

264. Ibid.

265. This appears to be a euphemism for "evacuate" or "flee" in this context.

266. Harmony media file ISGQ-2003-M0006905.

267. See Lieutenant-General Sir Aylmer L. Haldane, *The Insurrection in Mesopotamia 1920*, 1922 ed. (Nashville: Battery Press, 2005). For more contemporary descriptions, see Ahmed S. Hashim, *Insurgency and Counterinsurgency in Iraq* (Ithaca, NY: Cornell University Press, 2006).

268. Harmony media file ISGQ-2003-M0003474.

269. Harmony media file ISGQ-2003-M0006905.

Chapter IX

IRAQI LESSONS LEARNED

The best minds are those that learn from the experiences of other people and other nations enough to help them in their dealings with life, knowledge, and war. The dumbest minds and the worst management are those that do not learn from the experiences of their people.[1]

—SADDAM HUSSEIN

I t is difficult to gauge from the record which insights the Iraqis recorded for the purpose of learning lessons and which they recorded for less altruistic reasons. The documents and tapes capture both. In one case, there were professional officers trying to extract useful insights from recent events. In others, the lessons-learned process was more political theater designed to re-establish Ba'ath party control over a historically suspect officer corps. Occasionally the conflicts between the two camps are obvious. In others it is an awkward mix with many of the participants moving effortlessly between real insights and political pabulum. Often the stark discontinuity between the political "truth" of the regime and the objective reason imposed on the battlefield is so large that whole topics are not discussed for fear of having to publicly reconcile the differences. Of course, none of this is unique to the 1991 war. Amatzia Baram described how a form of this tension seemed to exist within Saddam himself: "Saddam's learning curve is quite impressive when it comes to tactical lessons, but he seems to be unable to learn more profound lessons. His long term behavior is repetitive, even though his tactical decision-making process is improving constantly. . . . When it comes to his strategic outlook, or what might be defined as his vision of history and his role in it, he hasn't changed much since he became president in 1979."[2]

Nevertheless, the fact that extensive "lessons-learned" activities went on at all surprises many Western observers. Self-critical analysis was not an attribute one would normally assign to a regime like Saddam's, but in fact it was continuous, even if not always honest. The military analysis began with a Republican Guard lessons-learned conference concerning the Kuwait invasion in late

Figure 41. *Republican Guard lessons-learned conference*. (Harmony media file ISGQ-2003-M0006038)

August 1990.[3] Numerous other major lessons conferences and studies were commissioned covering the invasion of Kuwait but more often the 1991 war during 1991–95, with several studies continuing almost to the beginning of the regime's last war in 2003.

Based on the size of the effort, many parts of the regime seemed sincere in their effort to create a viable lessons-learned process. What is not always clear from reviewing tapes of Saddam's participation in these conferences is his personal motivation. It is possible he believed that by controlling the process he could control the lessons. Controlling perceptions was, after all, one of the keys to his regime's domestic survival. It is also likely that he was truly interested in correcting military deficiencies to the extent that he could. He considered himself still to be at war. In a November 1991 lessons-learned conference, Saddam gathered all the commanders from the war and personally facilitated a wide-ranging discussion of events.[4] He reminded his audience that "if we can't remember [events] like we should, let us not record it as facts, however, [we can] refer to it without final documentation. . . . This is the method we followed for the al-Qadisiya battle, which is not to wait for the field analysis to come, but to conduct a general analysis in the general command."[5]

Saddam's preferred process helps explain some of the often dramatic differences between the Iraqi "top-down" view of the 1991 war and the one that would likely emerge from the Iraqi soldiers in Kuwait. Once several of these senior level conferences were held at the top, it was unlikely that new "facts" would supplant the accepted narrative.

Before formulating lessons one must reach some conclusion as to what actually happened. In a 1993 recording, Saddam discussed his postwar view of the causes and effects of the 1991 war. The following selections of Saddam quotations are from a single conversation. (Some dialogue has been edited for space and readability.)

Why did the First Gulf War [the Iran-Iraq War] occur and what was its purpose? . . . It occurred from the opposite side for a primary reason which is our insistence on being Arabs, our beliefs, and our long-time heritage, which goes back a thousand years [which] interferes with [America's] malicious intentions.

Part of their [all Western nations including Israel] being does not want us Arabs to use such a deep heritage, spiritual, and Muslim. . . . When they confirmed [that] what they have been hearing about us was true, they started to conspire against us, which led to the [Second] Gulf War. [The conspiracy] started to progress and in it participated every malicious individual in the whole West, from journalist, to the television host, to the politician in the foreign ministry, to the soldier, to the general manager of a company, each one of them had a special duty. . . .

I am certain all of you remember America's first order, in February 1990, preceding the [Kuwait War] by six months[6] . . . the chain of attacks started, once with the giant howitzer,[7] and another time for the excuse of violating human rights when we executed a spy,[8] their [the United States] role in the region and in Kuwait became very clear. Since they [the United States] could not attack us with their army, they utilized their financial strength, in addition to Kuwait and its abilities. They used [our] Arabism as an excuse and a cover. . . .

Based on this situation we had to reply, especially because their [conspi-

Figure 42. Iraqi officers participating in a lessons-learned conference concerning the "Mother of all Battles" (Harmony media file ISGQ-2003-M0006471)

ratorial] intentions were moving to an implementation stage, utilizing their most advanced weapons. We had to reply with the same methods. We are incapable of financially destroying the Kuwaiti regime; however, we have an army. . . .

   We deeply believe that Kuwait is part of Iraq. We will not keep silent like the individuals before us, such as Abdul Karim Qasim.[9] He did not accomplish what we accomplished. However, he at least decided on returning Kuwait to Iraq and established all the needed facts. What we performed . . . will be recorded in history [with] a distinguished mark, and you must remind the Iraqis that despite all the denials—Kuwait is part of Iraq. . . . This war [1991], however, was beneficial for us. If you read the pages of the Um al-Ma'arik war, we must add pages for economy, politics, and military. It will contain pages on the first war in Kuwait [invasion], pages on the second war [defense and withdraw], and pages on the war between Iraq and Israel [Iraqi missiles fired at Israel during 1991]. The war between Iraq and Israel was the most recognized war, think about it! Who could ever launch missiles on Israel. . . . They stood around with their hands positioned on their heads and the missiles rained down on them. . . . The events of the first battle continued to be recorded up to the fourth war—the economic blockade on Iraq.[10]

Ever the strategic optimist, Saddam turned this narrative of events into the driving force behind Iraqi policy during the 1990s. The range of policy options, either initiated by Iraq or in response to the international community, starts from this narrative—not the one commonly held in the West.[11] For example, in 1992 Saddam explained to his senior military officers his assessment of future military threats based on the 1991 war:

> You quite realize that there is nothing to hinder our enemy from attacking us. The only question is whether he would succeed or not. From a technical point of view he would, but considering the financial issues and the competition the enemy faces in elections, these may constitute a barrier and that is not because the enemy's people support Iraq. . . .
>
> After their experiences with us, which did not achieve its ends regardless of the withdrawal from Kuwait, they might wonder how much force they need to deploy this time to achieve what they failed to do the last time.
>
> Some may think that the Iraqi Army is now weaker than it was on the nights of 16 and 17 [January 1991]; that is true, but the Iraqi Army is stronger than what it was like on the day of February 28th. With all its weapons, I see it [as] stronger.
>
> In consideration of the aforementioned, we see that the enemy needs to deploy a great deal of forces, we wonder how the enemy could finance [such a] deployment or the justifications the enemy would use this time; they justified the last war that Kuwait is an independent country with a royal government.[12]

As already noted, determining which lessons developed from honest insights and which resulted from purposeful myths under Saddam's regime is not an easy task. The contrast between the Coalition's historical narratives of Operation Desert Storm and the Iraqi version is often disorienting. Saddam appears to have had the same feelings when reviewing the histories of the Um Al-Ma'arik being published in the West. In a late 1992 discussion with senior officials, Saddam offered his critique of the view from the "other side of the hill":

> I've distributed two books to every military commander who was in charge of forces that fought the enemy during the war. The first book was authored by "Schwarzkopf" and the second book was written by the British commander [de la Billière]. I said to them; "Read the books; then obtain from them the way they narrated what had happened, because they [the enemy commanders] don't know how to write. They must have

learned how to write books only recently . . . and each one of you should try his best to recall the incidents and re-write them. Whenever you come across a lie or distorted facts, point them out, criticize them and state the authenticated and correct information, analysis and data, and direct your criticisms toward the two [Coalition] commanders. Their writings [are] full of propaganda and unfounded allegations."[13]

At the end of all the staff process, reviews, and internal debates it seems clear that a significant number of Iraq's strategic and tactical insights were never turned into lessons learned. The Iraqi staffs were not immune to the human and bureaucratic dynamic that makes any internal critique challenging; however, they also had to deal with Saddam's unique approach to these issues. He often correctly diagnosed a key element of a complex problem and then eliminated any explanation that may have reflected on his regime.

One example is evident in Saddam's statements made in the first few months after the war. In May 1991, Saddam lamented to a group of military advisers:

In the beginning, the Iraqis were very enthusiastic and said, "We will all go to the war and fight, including our women." They thought it would only last a short time. When the Americans observed the masses by land in front of them and observed our strength as well, they began to mobilize their troops and had plenty of time to utilize politics, diplomacy, the media, and economic methods in a combined fashion. They imposed a complete, true embargo and this operation lasted up to six months before we fired shots. . . All of those factors played an important role in weakening the spirit and morale of our soldiers.[14]

In another example, Saddam complained about the apparent lack of initiative on the part of his commanders. Saddam expressed his frustration at the inability or unwillingness of his corps and division commanders to react to unexpected enemy actions like "hostile airdrops." His search for an answer exposes much about the civil-military divide in Saddam's Iraq:

"A division commander, he has a whole division, but the Americans mount an airdrop with two Chinook helicopters nearby him and we see that he is incapable [of] dispatching ten soldiers to go and fire at those aircraft to defeat them. Oh my, what is this callousness? Is this caused by low morale? Is this caused by indifference? I feel that even stones are more flexible than them."[15]

Such ineptness was exacerbated, Saddam believed, because "there are a great percentage of army officers who [have] this type of rigid callous mentality." Saddam, reflecting on the reality of his recent "victory," worried about the effect of such a malady among his officers. He noted that even if troop morale were excellent, this callousness on the part of his officers was potentially disastrous since "we do not see anyone going out to engage the enemy."[16]

> No one counterattacks, our people are so rigid, it is like you give the soldier a plan, he follows the plan verbatim, he cannot deviate from the plan . . . they are so rigid. I see a large percentage of this type of folk who do not take the initiative in the Iraqi Army. . . . Find me the reasons for such practices find out what the causes of this phenomenon are; is it due to organization? Is it due to training? Is it due to the practice of whose responsibility it is? Is [it] due to legal requirements? Or [is it] all of the above? Find out for us! It is irrational, it is not right.[17]

It is not clear if Saddam ever received satisfactory answers to his questions. In his reflection on military initiative, he clearly identified one of the well-known weaknesses in totalitarian militaries. However, it seems inconceivable that he would have accepted any answer that reflected on the nature of his regime. The implications of such musings from Saddam likely gave rise to yet another military activity designed to change the method of reporting the symptoms and not curing the disease.

Selected Iraqi Military Lessons

In the end, the only strategic and operational lessons that mattered were those accepted by Saddam himself. This reality did not stop Saddam from encouraging a robust lessons-learned program nor did it inhibit military "intellectuals" from tackling the subject.[18] Some of the early lessons-learned discussions involving military staffs (normally without senior Ba'ath official attendance) captured the tensions at play. For example, in one surprisingly open lessons-learned conference, an unidentified Iraqi general commented,

> "We must have true lessons stated here. Um al Ma'arik [Mother of All Battles] also revealed a weakness in our military leadership . . . there are political leaders who clearly failed in their responsibility. . . . So I hope for us not to look at our troops and their distribution, but also to see the real lessons and . . . discuss within ourselves honestly, state our lessons if we

want to have a true and honest document . . . lessons learned affect the way true work in the future will be done, as if we were going into Kuwait today."[19]

One of the general's peers, also unidentified in this recording, offered a more realistic assessment of what they should do following the lessons-learned conference, noting,

"I discussed this issue with the chief of staff, because we will not have a chance other than this to look into every small and large matter *so that we can benefit from the positive lessons which the command may allow us*, for example, to teach in military institutes. And *if there are [any] negative points, then according to the permission of the political or military leadership we can also teach them*"[20] [Emphasis added].

This last quotation captures the reality of the political environment. Discussions were one thing, but the committing of "negative points" to paper required "permission." A good example of how this tension manifested itself is found in the GMID's contribution to a comprehensive lessons-learned project begun in the summer of 2001. At the end of an examination of the battle of al-Khafji, the authors placed all of their lessons learned in two categories: "The Enemy's Weak Points" and "Our Troops Points of Strength."[21] The obviously missing categories speak volumes.

Lessons from the Air Campaign

Iraq's inability to overcome the Coalition's asymmetric airpower capability was, ironically, a key component in Saddam's definition of victory. In another variation of the "win by not losing" theme already noted, the commander of the Republican Guard noted after the war that

"as we expected, the main air attacks objective was the destruction of the Republican Guard force. Thus, we remained subjected to the bombardment from this day [17 January 1991] until the cease-fire . . . and even two days after the official cease-fire. The arrangements we made were successful, and what a success, in standing up to the air attacks and reducing our losses to the minimum possible and to an extent which the enemy did not expect at all."[22]

THE IRAQI "GULF WAR AIRPOWER SURVEY"[23]
Saddam saw Iraq's performance in the face of the Coalition's unquestioned

air dominance as historic. When he expressed this belief, he was not referring to the normal metrics of airpower such as sorties generated, weapons dropped, targets destroyed, enemy aircraft shot down, etc. Saddam was projecting his "win-by-not-losing" concept onto the statistically driven assessments of his air staff. As early as 3 March 1991, Saddam was singing the praises of Iraq's performance in the face of the Coalition's air armada.

> How many were scared? I mean what kind of proportionality do we have for this attack? . . . Where is it written in the [history] books to have a preparatory bombardment for one month and a half? Which book is it? Was it ever recorded in a war? Let's begin from the time they used the sword to the time they resorted to the attacks . . . to the atomic attacks during World War II. I mean this attack could not be measured. . . . We should say in a decisive manner that [Iraq] is the master of the world, when it comes to faith . . . mental and nervous capabilities . . . and human tenacity because there has never been anything [like this attack] in history.[24]

Notwithstanding Saddam's definitive declarations, soon after the war the Iraqi minister of defense commissioned a detailed series of studies.[25] One extensive study was titled "Study on the Role of the Iraqi Air Force and Air Defense Command in Confronting the American Attack during Um Al-Ma'arik Battle." This detailed work accumulated the statistics of the air campaign and, as with most of the postwar studies of its kind, couched its lessons in careful terms.

> After examining what was mentioned in this study with regard to the enemy's confrontational air capabilities in all the aspects and the size of the air power [used] against our air forces during the phase of the aggression which lasted forty-two days, especially after achieving his air superiority (which gave him many advantages . . .) we could presume from a theoretical viewpoint that the losses in planes, personnel, equipment, and instruments of our air forces should be very large. But from a practical point of view and based on the table of losses of our air force were relatively few compared to what was available and the size, nature, and duration of the adversary air aggression.[26]

The major accomplishments of the Iraqi Air Force were measured in assets not lost. As the study noted "as a result of the competent measures our air force took to minimize the losses whether before or after the aggression, we were able to achieve the following":[27]

Seventy-five percent of all combat and specialized planes were "rescued." The report notes that this percent does not include "planes destroyed as a result of ground operations and riot." By comparison, the study continues, "the losses of the Arab forces in the 1967 War, on the Egyptian front, were approximately 70 percent of the operating forces" and the "Zionist airpower" then was much less than what Iraq faced in 1991.

The air force "rescued" 92 percent of all of the air weapons as a result of "concealment and dissemination." More than 98 percent of the "expensive guided weapons" were also saved.

Seventy-six percent of the "very expensive electronic war equipment" was preserved.

"The losses in personnel amounted to .096 percent and it is a small percentage."

In addition to the large-scale studies and conferences, the regime commissioned a series of studies to examine specific topics of interest. One of the early efforts—there were three total, and perhaps foreshadowing twelve more years of Coalition air operations—was assigned "to study and analyze the effects of smoke, dust, and dirt on [confusing] enemy missiles," as well as the Coalition Air Force operations against headquarters and other vital targets.[28] This early example of lessons covered a lot of ground.

In the category of "passive protection achieved through the defensive use of dust and smoke," the Iraqi committee found many innovations, but noted that overall the results remained "limited." Innovations such as generating obscurants by using jet engines to create local dust storms or burning substances designed to enhance smoke particles stood out to the committee "as promising." However, the committee noted that primary reasons for the limited success of these and other efforts was the near continuous Coalition air coverage over critical areas. This persistent presence caused the smoke teams to deplete their smoke generation supplies rapidly near crucial targets. In addition, the lack of early warning meant that frontline troops could not take full advantage of the obscurants before Coalition aircraft were releasing their weapons.[29]

This particular committee's assessment of the Coalition air campaign was specific and, perhaps owing to the early date of its analysis, largely unaffected by much of the political biases so prevalent in later studies. For the most part, the committee concluded that the Iraqi Air Force correctly anticipated the nature of the air campaign, even if it had not been able to blunt its impact. The study enumerated the eight characteristics of the Coalition's air concept as anticipated by Iraq's planners before the war, such as precision strikes, night operations,

TABLE 7. Iraqi Air Force Status, June 1991

Type of Plane/ Engine	TOTAL Single	TOTAL Dual	DESTROYED Single	DESTROYED Dual	DAMAGED Single	DAMAGED Dual	% Losses	IN IRAN Single	IN IRAN Dual	BALANCE Single	BALANCE Dual
Mirage F-1	76		23		6		40	24		23	
Mirage F-1 KU	8		2		2					4	
MiG-23BN	38		17				42	4		18	
Sukhoi-20	18		4		2		33	4		8	
Sukhoi-22R	10		1				29			9	
Sukhoi-M2	24		2		6			5		11	
Sukhoi-22 M3	16		7				43	9			
Sukhoi-22 M4	28		7				13	15		6	
Sukhoi-24	30		5				16	24		1	
Sukhoi-25	62	4	28	3	8		59	7		19	
Sukhoi-21 (RU, PRC)	174	62	56	9	32	14	46			86	29
MiG-23 ML	39		14		1		38	7		17	
MiG-23 MK	14		2		5		14			7	
MiG-23 MS	15		2		4		40			9	
MiG-25 R	9		3		3		34			3	
MiG-25 PD & PDS	19		13		1		73			5	
MiG-29	33	4	16	1	2	2	59	3	1	12	
MiG-23 Dual		21		8			66		1		
TU-16	3		3				100				
Bombardier B6D	4		4				100				
AN-(?)	5				3		80			2	
Ilyushin-76	19		3		1		21	15			
Falcon-20	2							2			
Falcon-50	3							3			
Jet Star	6		4				67	1			
MiG-25 Dual R+PD		7		3		2	71				
Sukhoi-22 Dual				3		1	16				
L-39	67				1		91			66	
Tucano	78		1		6		82			64	
Bravo	34		5		5		50			17	
Eloris	12						100			12	
Jet Proves	15						100			15	
BK	14		1		6		42			6	
Total	997		250		113			137		483	

Source: Appendix to Top Secret Iraqi Air Power Study Showing Losses from 1991 War (Harmony document folder ISGP-2003-00030181)

heavy use of cruise missiles, massive use of anti-radiation missiles, and electronic warfare to cripple air defense missile systems, all for the purpose of "end[ing] the air battle decisively and in the shortest period of time."[30]

The committee found that Iraqi estimates of the Coalition plan, drawn from a study of Western air doctrine and "captives' confessions," were accurate with the exception of three areas:

Most Coalition raids occurred at medium altitudes (especially after Iraq depleted its supply of air defense missiles and its radar system had collapsed in the first days of the war). The Iraqi prewar assumption had been that Coalition air raids would occur predominately at lower altitudes.

Coalition air attacks came "from several axes and continued throughout the entire period of the aggression." Iraqi prewar estimates had been that there would be a "couple of thousand [aircraft sorties], but in actuality it was tens of thousands."

The Iraqis clearly expected to retain some air force capability throughout the campaign. The report states "it was not taken into consideration that our interceptors would be neutralized in such a short period of time."[31]

The committee report summarized the Coalition air attacks that began on the morning of 17 January as operating "extensively at low and mid-range elevations."[32] Moreover, during the early days of the war, cruise missiles "were used extensively in order to lessen the loss of aircraft as well as [increase Iraqi] consumption of air defense resources, especially in the Baghdad area."[33] The report made special note of the losses of British Tornados during the first three days, resulting from their low-altitude attack profiles. However, the report then admitted that, while forcing Coalition aircraft to medium altitudes resulted in "a decrease in accuracy [of bombs]," the change also "intensified the raids on the same targets."[34]

In analyzing the effectiveness of Coalition air strikes, the committee constructed a representative target set consisting of locations the Coalition had actually bombed. This target set included an unspecified "special site,"[35] Project 777,[36] an Electric Plant, fifteen MIC factories, an Iraqi Air Force base, and a civilian airport. An analysis of the Coalition attacks (day, night, aircraft, and cruise missiles) on these facilities resulted in the following insights and statistics:

Percentage of the targets hit: 57 percent.[37]
Percentage of "guided projectiles" [precision munition]: 45 percent.

"The enemy did not apply the technique of comprehensive regional bombardment. Only the vital areas of the targets were bombed."

"The enemy succeeded in destroying most of the secured aircraft bunkers and command and control centers using guided aerial (1,000 kilogram) bombs, which proved the fragility of these bunkers." The report added, however that "the air defense command centers, which were designed as strike-proof entities, remained intact and unaffected."[38]

"The targets that efficiently applied smoke and dust were exposed to severe raids and bombing, more than necessary to destroy it."

"The principle of equipment dispersal emerged as effective, as it lessened the losses. [This] was particularly apparent when aircraft were dispersed outside their specified bunkers."[39]

The Iraqi analysis of losses to their own air defense forces indicates how effective the Coalition air defense suppression operations actually were. This same study notes that losses included 100 "interceptor" aircraft, 28 command and control centers, 200 warning and control radar systems (120 completely destroyed), 70 guided missile firing units, and 50 anti-aircraft artillery systems. By 23 January 1991, Coalition air attacks destroyed more than 65 percent of the SA-2 and SA-6 missiles as well as 26 percent of the SA-3s. The report described in detail how "the enemy continued to drain [our forces] until the end of the battle." According to this Iraqi analysis, by the end of the war the "destruction ratio" for the SA-2 was 98 percent, the SA-6 88 percent, and the SA-3 46 percent. The only positive notes were that Iraq's Roland missile systems survived the war largely intact (a loss of only 7 percent) and Coalition air attacks destroyed only one of the three operational I-HAWK air defense missile systems taken from Kuwait.[40]

In the Iraqi analysis of losses inflicted on the Coalition by the air defense, there are wide variances in the data. These early committees had to rely on the Coalition's announcements of average sorties per day because as one noted, "We could barely document the number of air sorties, which were extensive, [because] our communication was lost as well as our warning and control system [were] jammed by direct attacks from the enemy."[41]

The May 1991 report recognized three distinct sources of information. The first was the Iraqi air defense forces themselves, which downed an estimated "281 aircraft and a huge number of cruise missiles." The second was a census conducted of air defense units themselves where "overlapping statements that came from different units" were omitted. This estimate counted 150 aircraft and more than 200 cruise missiles downed. The final estimate was documented on "conclusive proof" consisting of aircraft wreckage, prisoner of war interrogations, pilots killed, and "press confessions" from the enemy's country. Based on these sources the estimate was 44 aircraft and 120 cruise missiles. The authors accounted for the differences in a number of ways including: the inability of Iraqi forces to locate downed aircraft wreckage; the propensity of some air defense units to report enemy aircraft use of chaff and flares as a hit; mistaking cruise missiles for aircraft; and counting launches as successful hits as in the case of some SA-2 and SA-3 crews. The bottom line evaluation of air defense performance was that because of "the enemy's extensive aerial threat with its developed advanced technologies, coupled with its [ability to operate] for long periods," the Iraqi Air Defense was "vastly outweighed."[42] The report noted three significant areas to explain the enemy's success.

> The first area that "explained the enemy's success" was in interceptor operations. "Despite forty-two intercept operations against enemy aircraft and the downing of six [enemy aircraft] during the first three days," the report noted that "the enemy effectively managed to cripple the interceptors' capabilities . . . and gain complete air superiority." This was achieved through destroying aircraft at their primary and secondary bases to include the use of time-delayed mines to obstruct aircraft taking off. Moreover, the "air was scanned by AWACS aircraft radars, which made the enemy command and control easier when intercepting our aircraft." Most surprisingly, the report noted that "after assessing that intercept operations were in vain, coupled with the expected losses, [the pilots] were not convinced and were afraid to carry out their missions (as many aircraft were destroyed moments after takeoff)."[43] Such honesty was rare in senior level reports and little of this kind of assessment appears in any lessons-learned documents dated after mid-1991.
>
> The second area was air defense missiles. Here the analyses noted that the force was highly trained and prepared. However, none of their systems "except for the [captured] HAWK, could deal simultaneously with more than one target at a time." Many of the SA-2 and SA-3 batteries were "easily bombed due to a lack of understanding the importance of maneuvering . . . the batteries that maneuvered were not hit but their previous locations were. The enemy conducted a high number of its missions at night thereby defeating optical and televised sighting devices." On the positive side, the study noted that the shoulder-fired SA-7 missiles proved effective against cruise missiles.[44]
>
> The final area that explained the Coalition's success was its ability to deal

with air defense warning and control radars. A large number of radars were kept inactive to avoid Coalition radar homing missiles, but even those radars fell victim to enemy targeting, because "they did not maneuver." The "extreme fear of attack" from anti-radar missiles impacted the adequate use of surviving radars. Critically, the report noted "the air defense switchboard was destroyed, which led to a break in communication between the Air Defense Sector Centers and the Air Defense Forces."[45]

In order to overcome these weaknesses and expand on areas where they found some success, the air defense study recommended that Iraq immediately:[46]

"Acquire more long-range missile systems capable of handling multiple targets."

"Upgrade training of radar and missile crews based on the experience of the war."

Study "innovative techniques for operating in the continuous presence of the AWACS and under air superiority."

"Secure night-vision apparatus and secure multiple communications nets between units."

"Improve passive protection for bases to include smoke generation techniques."

In a video of a 1995 military conference convened to discuss the performance of Army aviation and armored forces in the 1991 war, there is a banner in the background proclaiming that "the Faith is stronger than the Enemy's Weapons." The assembled generals discussed the effectiveness of various American aircraft and weapon systems as claimed in the "American Department of Defense report that was delivered to Congress." After several descriptions of B-52 strikes, A-10s, Maverick missiles, and Apache Helicopter tactics, one unidentified speaker challenged the conventional wisdom: "My opinion of the hostile aviation is that [it] had a limited effect on the ground forces in general, especially during the aerial assault that continued for more than forty days. With full control over the sky, and should they have had skilled, distinct, and experienced pilots like the Iraqi pilots, they would have taken half of the force out of the battle, but that didn't happen."[47]

In a 2001 classified Iraqi staff study on Coalition air losses, its author improves on the Iraqi analytical habit of restating the adversary's objectives and developing the data in such a way to prove it did not accomplish them. In the

case of the Iraqi air defense forces, he defined "success" as merely surviving the
Coalition's massive air attacks:

> "The main goal of the aggression at the beginning was to weaken and
> eliminate our air force and air defense in order to dominate the air and
> accomplish its goals. [However] they could not accomplish this to the last
> day of the first aggression and the evidence is demonstrated in the dow-
> ning of three fighter jets and three helicopters and capturing one pilot
> during the last two days of battle."[48]

Documenting the success of Iraq's air defense was a priority for the regime
during the war. On 18 January 1991, Saddam commissioned a committee to
document the downing of enemy aircraft since he believed the enemy would
try to conceal the truth by a "total media cover-up."[49] The 2001 study validated Saddam's earlier concerns by pointing out that soon after the campaign,
the Coalition announced losses of thirty-six aircraft, but that in the year 2000
these losses had been revised to seventy to eighty.[50] The report's author proudly
states that this proved Saddam's foresight, when he had noted that "the number
of announced or downed or hit aircraft is usually multiplied by four, especially
aircraft that attack ground forces because most of them are downed far away
from the [Iraqi] forces or inside enemy territory."[51]

During a 1991 conference, Saddam asked a senior member of the air
defense forces to asses how well their non-missile weapons performed.[52] The
officer responded that because these systems were old, manually operated, and
reliant on the human eye, they were only useful in daylight hours and their
results "weren't accurate.""Even if they were radar-directed," the officer continued, "the enemy managed to jam most of the hand-held radar units or blinded
them with hostile frequencies."[53] Saddam removed any doubt this officer might
have had about the proper assessment of these systems when he said "well, I
want to let you know that I am a fan of the non-radar conventional artillery
units." He continued:

> Very early on, as early as 1981, I requested that we should not depend
> solely on the missile systems because the Israeli enemy could jam them.
> When we were fighting Iran we used them. . . . We should not rely hea-
> vily on the radar-equipped guns only because that will make us more
> vulnerable . . . at least when they jam all the weapons, they won't be
> able to jam the non-radar artillery units. Hence the enemy would be
> forced to either attack in the old ways or to fire from a distance. We have

already seen their chances of hitting when they fire from afar. . . . We shouldn't depend on only one type of weapon in our air defense arsenal. . . . don't you think so?[54]

The officer answered, "Yes sir, that's right."[55]

During a 1995 military seminar, Saddam provided some insight into what he viewed as a key output of any airpower lessons-learned study: morale. The fact that he made his morale point using a statistical analysis of Coalition air-power also provides some insight into Saddam's conception of readiness.

After sitting through a review of airpower statistics, drawn primarily from the U.S. produced Conduct of the Persian Gulf War, Saddam told his staff to stop and consider both the numbers and, more importantly, the implications of the American claims.[56] He asked,

"Do we want to protect the fighters, or do we want to affect them in a negative way? We are to strengthen them. This is our duty. The fighter's rights are for us to protect him psychologically and to increase his morale to confront the enemy. If we do not do this then we are negligent. How can we do this and exaggerate? . . . I did not see presented or used numbers, except the number announced by the enemy. Where are our numbers?"[57]

Saddam then proceeded to provide an example of the kind of analysis he expected his staff to produce.

The enemy said about the Apache, that it conducted about 18,700 hours of operations. This is on page nine [of the Iraqi study]. [The Apache] num-bered 274 aircraft. Using simple calculations, if we take away 2700 hours from the 18,700 hours and said that the remaining 16,000 hours were all fight hours. And then we divide the 16,000 fight hours over 274 aircraft. The result is every two and a half days, during [the] one and a half months of bombardment, one fighting mission. . . . Based on the American numbers . . . each aircraft flies every two days. Does this show a high use? . . . How many fighting [sorties] would we have?[58]

Based on this analysis, Saddam noted that sixteen thousand hours would result in eight thousand "fighting missions." If you multiplied the number of missions by the weapons load of the aircraft, in this case sixteen Hellfire missiles, you would have 128,000 missiles. Finally, if the 128,000 missiles achieved the 72 percent success rate claimed by the Americans then they "would have hit

100,000 targets" during the battle. Saddam reminded them that his calculations were based on one kind of missile and one kind of aircraft: "how many will we come up with if we count the total load of an aircraft and of all missiles and all bombs." Finally, to make his point Saddam asked, "Did we have 100,000 hits in the front during the one and a half months?"[59]

When no one in the seminar took up Saddam's statistical challenge, he blasted their overall work by saying:

> "this is not a scientific study. . . . [Is] this how you conduct a scientific study? . . . That you opened the American booklets and records and gathered information from there. This is what happened. You are educating us according to the American booklets? OK, all of you fought and suffered, why did you waste so much blood?"[60]

Saddam then provided the "scientific method" he expected them to follow for any future analyses:

> Add all the airplanes and all the loads and all kinds of missiles and all kinds of bombs, and this way you can figure out the percentage of accuracy. This is a practical way. You are not talking about an army in Vietnam or an army in China. You are talking about your army. You know for sure how many vehicles, how many weapons, and how many tanks were hit. Take this into consideration along with the total airplanes and the payload and then divide . . . the result is how accurate the enemy is. I do not want you to forget anything.[61]

Finally, and in a very irritated tone, Saddam summarized his concepts for the role of both lessons and analyses.

> Mention the truth as is. Why do [you] give the enemy a free advertisement? Do we need this? We need to tell the fighter you were hit this much. This is your losses. And this case will not be repeated ever again. It will not be repeated. . . . I'm not saying the aggression will not be repeated. The aggressions might be repeated. However, an aggression such as this one that they fabricated against Iraq with all of this mobilization, finances, and military means will never happen again. When the fighter knows that the accuracy rate [of enemy aircraft] . . . was in their favor, then what would be the rate if things were not in their favor? Isn't this our duty toward the Iraqi fighter? It is the truth. It is not forged. Truth as is. When you show

the accuracy rate at 90 percent, then it is as if you wanted to harm your fighter psychologically. *I'm sure that you do not mean this. Correct the study.*[62] [Emphasis added]

After all, Saddam warned "you depicted all of this as if it is a bogyman . . . don't keep talking about it. This becomes an advertisement for the airplane. And this is what the Americans want."[63]

SENDING AIRCRAFT TO IRAN

It is apparent that Iraq never adequately planned how it was going to recover its combat aircraft from Iran's airfields after the war. This is somewhat surprising considering the air "evacuation" doctrine was not new to the 1991 war. In the early days of the Iran-Iraq War, Saddam evacuated a significant portion of his air force to "neutral" Arab states to protect them from Iranian air strikes. Given the deep distrust and animosity between Iran and most of its Arab neighbors in those years, Saddam had no trouble getting the aircraft back from their "neutral" locations. After the 1991 war, Iraq asked the United Nations to intervene on its behalf after Iran ignored its repeated requests to return the fighter aircraft. It is not surprising, given Iraq's international status after the war, that recovering its air force was wishful thinking at best.

Iraqi intelligence spent the summer and fall of 1991 closely following the fate of its nation's air force. Reports from 1991 include rumors that:

Israel demanded the aircraft be turned over to it as compensation for Iraqi missile strikes. According to Iraqi sources, Israel told the United States that failing to do so would result in air strikes to destroy the aircraft on the ground in Iran.

Iranian government representatives were finding buyers in Pakistan and China for the most advanced aircraft. There were even unconfirmed reports that Russia was attempting to "buy back" some of the aircraft.

Iran was "repainting all of the Iraqi fighter aircraft with Iranian flags."[64]

In the end, Iraq attempted to tie the fate of its aircraft to resolving issues such as the fate of Iran-Iraq War POWs and missing soldiers, but to no avail. The only aircraft returned were those Iraq initially seized during the Kuwait invasion and they went back to their original owner.

THE DISASSEMBLY DOCTRINE

After the war, in addition to the air evacuation doctrine, the Iraqi Air Force codified into its doctrine the practice of disassembling aircraft and hiding them away from air bases. A study by the commander of an Air Force "disassembly and repair unit," dated 1999, explained in detail the development of the doctrine beginning during the Iran-Iraq War and continuing through the 1991 war and beyond. In the 1980s, the problem was that the rapid buildup of the air fleet exceeded the number of hardened bunkers. In order to protect the large number of aircraft, Iraq moved the aircraft to "dirt bunkers" and launched a massive building program. The doctrine was revised in 1991:

> During the epic Mother of All Battles and exactly at the beginning of the battle, aircraft were moved to the fortified concrete bunkers to avoid all types of aerial strikes. . . . But the enemy was able to strike these bunkers, destroy them, and the aircraft inside them. While the battle was still going, orders were given to evacuate the [bunkers] of all of the aircraft to outside the airbase into the surrounding areas.[65]

The problem with moving the air force out of the base was the obvious fact that jet aircraft were not designed for that kind of environment. They got stuck in the mud, they were too large (even after partial disassembly) to move between buildings, and repair time was prohibitive. The study proposed developing or purchasing aircraft with the concealment mission built into the design. These new aircraft should be optimized for maneuvering between buildings, lightweight for moving across soft ground, and easily maneuvered by a wide variety of tow vehicles.[66]

In the end, the primary lessons of 1991 for the Iraqi Air Force and Air Defense Forces were ones of survival not employment. One officer captured these lessons after the war when he told Saddam that

> "we are proud and we can say that we economized with munitions and we have protected equipment and preparations and the Air Defense as well as the Air Force were saved till the end of the battle. [Furthermore] when we mention the loss of lives and equipment, casualties, they are not worth mentioning [because] they are light in comparison to the losses of the thirty aggressor countries."[67]

Lessons from the Ground Campaign

THE REPUBLICAN GUARD

Preparing for a lessons-learned conference scheduled for December 1995, members of the Republican Guard staff compiled a surprisingly candid assessment of the military aspects of Um Al-Ma'arik. It is impossible to know what impact this 250-page monograph had in a staff system that did not normally reward bad news or critical views. A review of some of the material actually discussed in the conference—attended by Saddam and the senior members of the RCC—indicates that this document was probably not shared outside the Republican Guard staff. In fact, in a 2003 interview one senior attendee of that December 1995 conference noted that it was at this point that Saddam's political truth of what occurred four years earlier overwhelmed whatever honesty was left in the military staffs.[68]

The lessons in this extraordinary staff document are recorded neutrally as "comments," but the authors leave little doubt about the lesson. This document covers events from buildup to invasion in July 1990 through the uprising in March 1991. The major comments on the "preparation and mobilization" (for the invasion of Kuwait) phase included:

"There was a failure to clarify the objective in an attempt to keep the matter classified."

"Mixing between the true nature of the mission and the information transmitted suggesting an exercise."

"The forces were fatigued by the implementation of training concepts for a strategy of a quick assault."

"Political advisory commissions were weak and there was a sense of fear and apprehension from speaking the truth or being frank in dealing with facts."

The planning and preparedness "anticipated the same scenario of the glorious al-Qadisiyah [Iran-Iraq War] battles."

There was a lack of intelligence about the enemy "because the mission was supposed to be an exercise."

"There was a failure to provide an adequate logistics supply."

The various commands were "delivering speeches with the assumption that [Iraq's] weapons were more advanced." "They were unrealistic and they failed to relate the facts."

"The ideas, plans, and doctrines were all based on the glorious al-Qadisiyah experience."[69]

The section titled "Phase of Entering Kuwait" reiterated many of the issues raised by Brigadier General Hamdani in his memoirs.

"Poor navigation and lack of sufficient resources [guides] familiar with the area. Failure to properly spread out the forces. Commanders were influenced by their experiences in the glorious al-Qadisiyah."

"The commanders did not take the operation seriously and some of them believed it was nothing more than a military deception."

"Some units deviated from their targets due to their failure to know the limits of the operation."

"There was a failure to clarify the ultimate objective to the forces."

"There was a failure to issue clear instructions on the manner of dealing with civilians, military bases, and facilities in a coordinated manner."

"A loss of command and control and a preoccupation of some soldiers with the booty of war."

"A failure to control the entrances and exits of cities."

"Some soldiers committed serious violations against the civilians due to the lack of a coordinated plan."

"Allowing civilians and businessman, etc., to enter and steal and plunder the property of the locals."

"Some senior officers and commanders were preoccupied with the booty of war, forgetting that was the property of the civilians, who were in fact Iraqis. This resulted in a feeling of resentment and hatred toward the military forces."

"The absence of plans for maintenance and recovery resulted in leaving [broken] equipment for a month or more."

"Some soldiers behaved in a manner that harmed the reputation of the forces."

"Lack of discipline in some units, where anyone who did not gain a share of the booty of war was considered a loser."

"Some senior officers and commanders displayed misconduct by collecting booty of war and in some cases they sent it to their families as their own personal property."

"There was a lack of sufficient information available about the enemy."

"Some units committed acts of plunder and destruction of equipment and against the institutions and businesses both intentionally and unintentionally."[70]

The next section is entitled "The Withdrawal from Kuwait." The bulk of the Republican Guard withdrew from Kuwait in September 1990. While this section appears to refer predominantly to this event, it also includes comments directed to the February 1991 withdrawal of the Iraqi Regular Army as well.

"Confusion and lack of good and clear plans of withdrawal in addition to a failure to specify positions for the forces to deploy to."

"A failure to cover a wide area during the redeployment of forces."

A failure to "concentrate supplies in the area of operations."

"Weak administration at all levels."

"Adoption of the same plans and the same counterattack tactics used in the glorious al-Qadisiyah."

"The responsibilities of the commands and the methods were vague and overwhelming."

"A lack of specific intelligence about the enemy."

"The leadership presented enemy weapons in an unrealistic manner."[71]

Lessons as Revelation

In a draft of an official presidential history of the 1991 war prepared in 1993, Saddam's decisions regarding "the main mobilization and the operational framework for commanding the military operations" were recorded in detail.[72] These decisions were examined in multiple venues as near sacred text and all significant lessons would obviously flow from these insights. The official history notes that the collection of Saddam's decisions dates to 5 February 1991. While one must assume a degree of revisionism in the text, it provides a useful starting point when looking at Saddam's strategic and operational perceptions before the ground campaign. An additional value of these statements is that one can read them as evidence of which lessons Saddam learned early in the campaign (the implication of a battle like al-Khafji for example). Some of the most significant of Saddam's thirty-five orders include:[73]

"If we were to react to the enemy's maneuvers, we would be trapped in the snare they set for us with their supremacy in the air. If you were to track the enemy's movement, that would only mean we were monitoring them and reacting to their repositioning of their troops and that would give them the chance to strike at the time of their choice."

"We have flexibility in terms of land outside the province of Kuwait; hence, we could trick the enemy forces and drag them to a certain depth in our territories and destroy them. But if we were to maneuver with our forces and reposition them in stationary defensive formation in front of the enemy's forces on [the] basis of what we used to do with the Iranian forces at a certain stage of the war, hence, that would only make it easier for the enemy to launch the strikes it wants."

"We should not be tempted into changing our current defensive positions in reaction to the hostile enemy movements because that requires being exposed on the surface of the ground and would force us into [suffering] a high-level [of] blood-shed until we manage to establish a new defensive position."

"The most important factor in breaking the enemy's morale and spirit is to inflict heavy losses on its forces to the extent [that] it would not be in a position to challenge [us] any further. Hence, any maneuver with our land forces which are entrenched into defensive positions in the province of Kuwait and its suburbs by bringing them out on the open land to combat the enemy's forces, that would be a fatal mistake and we shouldn't be dragged into it."

"Each one of you must forget the traditional way of doing things that you've been accustomed to, and which in turn have led to monotony and lack of creativity. You should create a genuine, nontraditional approach in your operations that would make the enemy believe that we are weak; hence use its forces unwisely. Techniques or tactics that we use—even if they proved to be a success—have to be changed to other methods before the enemy can get used to them."

"Beware of thinking in the traditional and monotonous way which was applied during our war with Iran. That method is impossible with our defensive strategy currently under consideration. We could spread our wing to cover all our shared borders with Saudi Arabia. When we feel that the enemy is capable of breaching our wing at the Jordanian borders, we would then spread our wing to cover our borders with Jordan."

"The enemy's vital targets are on the left wing [Kuwaiti coast]. When we spare the left wing and go for the target on the right, we would be helping the enemy realize what it was looking for. When we find ourselves in a position to adopt whatever newer tactics we want, hence, that would bleed the enemy and finish it; not by handling the targets on the right wing first."

"The armored forces and the mechanized infantry could get into the suburbs of the cities for hiding purposes. However, the soldiers should not be engaged in any conduct that might reflect negatively on our armed forces."

"When you consider withdrawal from any territories in the future, we should plan for it by tricking the enemy in the following way: We dispatch more forces with a message from the commander of the corps, and the withdrawal orders should be passed by word of mouth to the officer in charge."

"The battle of al-Khafji had defamed the enemy, and it was considered a success. But the lessons learned . . . that we [can] address and correct must be remembered in the future."

"We need to go into the minutest details and scrutinize things to the level of distribution of soldiers and weapons after occupying the target, and that was among the main factors for success. . . . Distribution of soldiers and weapons should have been put on paper, and shouldn't have been left for the junior commanders."

"Creativity is required of commanders and the enlisted."

"What we want is to have the enemy engage us in a land battle. In the current status quo you wouldn't be able to make the enemy suffer losses. The most important point is how to drag the enemy into striking us; hence we would be able to strike back."

"We should look for the enemy even by having agents from the intelligence on motorcycles that would go into deeper surveillances. We should also use our special forces and strike the enemy wherever [they] might be; we should not accept the idea of keeping everything safe until the enemy decides to get into land-warfare whenever it chooses."

"The brigade commander, the division commander, the brigade commandant, the intelligence officer, both party civilian and military officials should be prepared to fight the enemy, even if what we have at our disposal is light and medium weapons and nothing else. Even if the enemy is to get into our cities, we should continue fighting [him] relying on Allah to help us [provide] the enemy the defeat [he] deserves."

"We should plan wisely and not in reaction prior to getting into any battle. Even if we suffered twice the enemy losses or even three-fold we would still be winning."

According to BG Husayn Rashid Muhammad, Iraq's former armed forces chief of staff and a participant in the 1993 official history project:

[The] directives of Mr. President were not limited to the meeting of 5 February . . . but they date back as far as 2 August 1990 [and] the day of liberation of Kuwait. His directives were so many, and we used to record them in details, especially when I was in the position of operations deputy, and later as the joint-chiefs of staff. We used to execute his directives and follow-up their execution to the most junior levels, because we were in a race with time then. In every meeting Mr. President used to issue some directives in connection with the incidents in general and the battle in particular. Hence, we had a clear vision of the situation due to an accumulation of incidents and the directives related to the aggression and the probable routes.[74]

The Impact of Attack Helicopters

American attack helicopters had a profound effect on the psyche of many senior Iraqi ground commanders. It was not because they were specifically any more effective at destroying Iraqi armored vehicles than fixed-wing aircraft; the Iraqi statistics bear this out. The answer seems to have two components. First, was the helicopter's method of attack. Attack helicopters "sneak" up on armored formations from any direction and can bring to bear a high volume of aimed fire. The second reason was that, compared to fixed-wing aircraft, officers in the Iraqi Army felt they had at least a fighting chance against helicopters. By comparison, the reasoning went, fixed-wing attacks were like lightning strikes: one could minimize the chances of being struck, but one could not prevent it from striking.

According to BG Husayn Rashid Muhammad, Iraqi ground forces lost "1,772 tanks, 939 [Armored Personnel] Carriers, and 1,474 cannon."[75] Most of these losses were to air attacks of some sort. But during a ground forces lessons-learned conference, it was the AH-64 Apache that was the focus of attention:

> They didn't use the Apache during the aerial assault until after the start of the ground battle which started against the Republican Guards. There was a direct ground contact with American forces and they were able to occupy some of our sites [but] then we were able to drive them out of our area. They retreated to a distance that is out of effective range of our weapons. During this time, the Apache helicopters came and started to hassle our troops. The truth is that [they] caused damages that were not insignificant in the lines of the 2nd Armored Brigade. . . . Thus, it means, if we can get rid of its [the Apache's] effect, if we can have a direct battle with them [American ground forces], we will neutralize a lot of their weapons.[76]

It is not surprising then, given the presumption of some success in the tank-on-tank engagements, that many of Iraq's ground force lessons derived from dealing with Coalition airpower. An emphasis on countering the AH-64 Apache is a noticeable topic throughout many of the lesson learned studies during the decade after the war. In one example, officers in a 1995 conference discussed their surprise at American attack helicopters' ability to operate during limited visibility. One officer noted that during poor weather, Iraqi units "were hoping that these bad conditions [would] not let the enemy observe us." Another officer observed that despite the fact that the Iraqi military had studied the Apache since 1983, "we had no information about the effect of the Apache helicopter over and above six kilometers." Moreover, the officer continued, we were "not able to see or hear the sound of the helicopter when it attacks us."[77] Numerous suggestions were made about dealing with this threat to Iraqi armor, such as better camouflage, repositioning the force often, and changing the T-72 basic ammunition load to one containing almost 50 percent "self-detonating" shells for using against attack helicopters.

While the Iraqis never devised a technical solution for dealing with AH-64s, they did continue to address the challenge. In March 2003, AH-64s of the U.S. Army's V Corps were successfully ambushed as a result of an Iraqi doctrinal solution to their Apache problem. Rather than deal with the helicopters directly, the Iraqi forces organized anti-helicopter ambush teams and used an indirect or "swarming style" of attack. As the American helicopters settled into their battle positions according to U.S. attack helicopter doctrine (and validated on the battlefields in 1991), the Iraqi air defense ambush teams would swarm the area and "fire and forget" their weapons in the general direction of the aircraft. For the Iraqis, on this occasion at least, one of the insights of 1991 actually resulted in a lesson learned.[78]

The Lessons of al-Khafji

If one never understood the Iraqi context in which the al-Khafji battle took place, it would be difficult to comprehend some of Iraq's lessons. Even after reading and accepting at face value the Iraqi "official" version of events, it is still difficult to suspend one's disbelief long enough to accept that the Iraqis acted on these lessons. But as with all attempts to understand a battle from another's perspective, suspending disbelief is the price of admission.

The Iraqi view that al-Khafji was an Iraqi success story did not emerge slowly after months of reflection and self-serving hindsight. The implications and lessons of this "seminal" engagement during the Mother of All Battles were on the minds of Saddam and his senior military almost immediately. In one discussion, Saddam wondered what the impact would have been on the Coalition if his forces had "attacked . . . three days after the air attacks [began] or after the first bomb on Baghdad . . . we would have been able to disperse them [the Coalition]."[79] One of those present added that by the time the ground war started, the Iraqi forces had already lost "more than 60 to 70 percent of [our] fighting forces." However, he noted, if they had taken advantage of the opportunity presented at al-Khafji they "would have had a physical influence on the allies."[80] A colleague added that "the attack [at al-Khafji] should not have been limited but rather extensive . . . these were border police stations from which they would pull back . . . if we kept in contact with them, meaning that we went more in depth, we would have hurt them. We would have caused them great material damage. I believe this and this is the viewpoint of many persons, not only me, that we should have launched an extensive attack and not a limited one of a few raids."[81]

Saddam agreed. He added that, while "we never blame anyone" for the tactical decision made at the time, he regretted not attacking at al-Khafji with the Republican Guard. Saddam said, "After the operations at al-Khafji, some of the commanders came and said to me, 'Sir, we think there has been a mistake. It [looks as if] our assessment about the American army was wrong.' So imagine if we would have attacked them prior to that time and if we take into account the extent of the mistake—how the political situation would have changed. We will never know."[82]

A copy of the GMID review of its contributions to the battle of al-Khafji and subsequent lessons learned is interesting on several levels. First, the review committee completed the study in 2001. Although the intervening ten years afforded the authors opportunity to reflect, conduct additional research, and even examine external studies, they seemed determined to build on the accepted myth.

In the category of "The Enemy's Weak Points" observed during the battle of al-Khafji, the GMID study noted, without accompanying analysis or data, that:

"Coalition bombing was imprecise."
"Compared to our [Iraqi] tanks, the enemy's tanks were inefficient."
"The enemy did not use short-range anti-tank weapons during combat. They avoided direct or near-direct contact with our troops and were depending basically on their air force."
"The enemy's artillery was imprecise [and] had limited effect."[83]

In the category of "Our Points of Strength," the GMID study's authors provide a rather narrow set of observations about Iraqi troops in the battle of al-Khafji.

"Our armored forces, especially tanks, were efficient during close combat although there was no large-scale direct combat."
"Some detachments [anti-aircraft squads with SA-7 missiles] downed two helicopters and two fighters."
"Tanks of the 26th Armored Brigade fired on hostile aircraft using bursts [and] had a remarkable effect. . . . [They] compelled the helicopters to retreat and they never attacked again."[84]

Under the category of "Methods Adopted by the Enemy," the GMID observed that most of the Coalition troops who attacked al-Khafji were Saudi and Qatari, supported by Coalition air and artillery fires. Moreover, they observed that Coalition aircraft had the propensity to attack "from behind" and that this tactic "lessened the possibility of downing the aircraft and at the same time if an aircraft is hit it will fall in the sea or in the area controlled by the hostile [Coalition] forces."[85] One can assume that in the case of the first observation, the authors saw this as reinforcing Saddam's belief in the frail nature of Western troops. The second observation might help explain to the Iraqi leadership why so many Coalition aircraft were reportedly "shot down" by Iraqi troops and why they found so few crash sites later in Iraqi-held territory.[86]

An official history and lessons-learned study of the al-Khafji battle noted as a significant accomplishment that Iraq still had "offensive capabilities" twelve days after the start of the war. The study continues: "Had we been able to develop the al-Khafji operation to the middle and final stages then the main goal of the operation, which was to draw the enemy into a large scale desert battle, would have been fulfilled."[87]

In other words—if we had been successful . . . we would have been successful.

The Battle against the Zionists (Missile Strikes on Israel)

The Iraqi propensity to overstate its military effectiveness complicates any examination of Iraq's view of its campaign to launch Scud missiles against Israel and Saudi Arabia during Operation Desert Storm.[88] The constant drumbeat rhetoric about the "Zionist conspiracy," coupled with hard-learned experience on the battlefield created within the Iraqi military a mythical atmosphere about any military operations conducted against Israel. The Iraqis treated success, real or perceived, with a quixotic awe that placed lessons on this topic in a category all by themselves.[89]

Between 17 January and the end of the war, Iraq fired eighty-eight missiles.[90] The official Iraqi version of events noted that, after using all of its sources to determine the results, the following targets were "attacked and hit effectively":

"The ministry of defense and the army chief of staff's building in Tel Aviv."
"The main communications station in Tel Aviv."
"The al-Khudayrah Power Station."
"The industrial area of Tel Aviv."
"The gasoline refinery in Haifa."

"The technology institute in Haifa."
"The Haifa naval base."
"Haifa and Tel Aviv ports."
"Ben Gurion Airport."
"The Dimona [nuclear] reactor."[91]

If only a small portion of these claims had been true, Iraq would have indeed been able to claim some degree of militarily significant success.[92] According to many in Saddam's inner circle, the only reason the world did not appreciate Iraq's feat of arms was the "pervasive Zionist conspiracy" that worked to cover the truth.

The 2001 GMID roll-up of lessons learned included a section entitled "The General Military Intelligence Directorate role in Attacking Zionist targets with Ground-to-Ground Missiles." The section begins by establishing a set of "facts":

The Iraqi attack began on the second day of the Coalition aggression against it "thereby proving [Iraq's] defensive intent."
The Iraqi retaliation created a new regional "balance of power with Israel."
Iraqi actions fulfilled "the Iraqi president's vow that he would retaliate against Israel as revenge for their attack against the Iraqi reactor."[93]
Iraqi attacks hit the same classes of "vital targets" being struck by the Coalition in Iraq.
"Iraq was the first Arab country able to conduct effective offensive operations against the enemy [Israel]."[94]

The lessons of this campaign in part derived from the above "facts," but were, in most cases, referring to the myths of doing battle with the Zionists. The primary finding was the "Zionist war theory was proven wrong by [the] Iraqi missile attacks."[95] While a definition of the "Zionist war theory" was not part of the study, Iraqi authors suggested the evidence of its demise in the following terms:

The Iraqis gained the initiative and transferred the battlefield from outside to "inside the occupied land." Israel's "safe borders concept" was proven wrong as "all its vital targets became at the mercy of Iraqi missiles."
"Because of the frequent missile attacks, the enemy lost the ability to render a short or blitzkrieg war. On the contrary the situation converted into a costly war of attrition which exhausted the enemy."[96]
The failure of the American Patriot Missile system "forced the Israelis to develop the Arrow missile system." The implied victory was the great cost of missile development.

The Iraqi bombardment "convinced the Zionist military command of the
  Arab capability to inflict serious damage" and thereby "diminished the
  quality gap between them."

The success of the Iraqi missiles "forced the enemy to reconsider its military arrangement" and placed a huge financial burden on the "already
  exhausted Zionist economy."[97]

Finally, "the successful Iraqi bombardment surprised the Zionist community which [believed]—because of organized brainwashing performed
  by the intelligence services and the media—[that] the capabilities of
  Arab armies [were] not sufficient and therefore they would not risk
  conducting effective offensive operations."[98]

Sometime after the war, an obviously proud Saddam asked the Iraqi missile
forces commander to explain to the assembled military staffs "why the enemy
failed to hit any of the [launchers]." General al-Ayyubi, in keeping with such
occasions, gave all credit to Saddam's "practical guidance [and] clear combat
instructions."[99]

The steps taken to preserve Iraq's missile forces began before the invasion
of Kuwait. On 31 July 1990, firing units were deployed to the western areas and
were to be "ready to fire at Israel." According to al-Ayyubi, rehearsals during the
deployment allowed the missile crews to "reduce their firing time to four hours
from the time they received their orders." In addition to flushing the launch
systems, on 2 August 1990 Saddam ordered all missile maintenance and supply
warehouses emptied. Al-Ayyubi described this as a "big step in the war," because
it forced his missileers to discover that "simple tricks" and "natural covers" provided better protection than buildings and bunkers.[100]

After more than four months of field maneuvers, and just before the 15
January deadline, Saddam ordered Iraq's launchers withdrawn "to places near
Baghdad since it is safer and not empty . . . I mean the area is occupied." Saddam reminded the assembled officers that he in fact "wanted [the Coalition] to
watch when we withdrew" because it would force them to strike the missile
bases near the capital where the Iraqi air defense was better.[101]

Before redeploying Iraq's Scud and modified-Scud missiles to their designated hide and launch positions, al-Ayyubi ordered the creation of three missile deception units. The first was known as the "camouflage missile brigade."
It consisted of obsolete equipment "very similar to the Russian launchers" and
operated in the same way as the real missile units. The "first special camouflage
group" was the second unit. This second deception organization consisted of
Luna missile (FROG 7) launchers (some real and others decoy) deployed into

the western sector. The third unit, designated "the great special duty group," also consisted of Luna launchers (twenty-six launchers in total) deployed to southern Iraq. All three deception units used the exact tactics and procedures as the two brigades of real launchers. At one point in his discussion with Saddam, al-Ayyubi expressed amazement that with all the supposed capabilities of the enemy, they could not even find and hit the deception launchers.[102]

According to al-Ayyubi, one measure of the success of Saddam's "wisdom" was the fact that the postwar United Nations inspection teams insisted that Iraq "had at least two brigades in the Western area and two brigades in the Southern area." The inspectors were looking for twenty to one hundred launchers, not the fourteen that actually fired. Moreover, al-Ayyubi continued, the weapons inspectors "did not believe that we were on the move day and night. . . . We moved day and night even on the expressways, but [always] in small groups; we did not use a whole column like a parade or a unit presenting a show, but we took the combat component only and sent it to the site. We managed without a command location . . . without the administrative vehicle . . . we finished our survey[s] a long time ago."[103]

The success of Iraq's deception operations did not end with the cease-fire agreement at Safwan. As al-Ayyubi proudly told Saddam:

> So they hit the missile shelters . . . they hit the places we were not in . . . but they did not hit a place we were in during the war or close to it or a land communications faculty we were close to . . . they could not find [these places] either during the inspections that they performed since the resolution of the Security Council was enforced until this day. . . . They could not find any place where we hid our equipment because it is all natural covers and they enter near them. . . . They enter at about 100 or 200 meters, not to mention that we told them we complied. . . . But they did not go themselves to a place where we hid things, before or after the war . . . at all. This is regarding the al-Husayn missiles.[104]

Without a clear date, it is difficult to know which specific United Nations inspection General al-Ayyubi is describing. However, it is clear that despite the cost to the Iraqi people, Iraq's successful violation of UNSC Resolution 687 was a source of great pride to its leaders.

Notes

1. Harmony document folder FM8582.
2. Amatzia Baram, "Between Impediment and Advantage: Saddam's Iraq," United States Institute for Peace, *Special Report* no. 3 (June 1998).

3. Some of this analysis was recovered after the liberation of Kuwait and was published by the Kuwaiti government. See Hussain 'Isa Mal Allah, *The Iraqi War Criminals and their Crimes During the Iraqi Occupation of Kuwait.*

4. In addition to Saddam, participants in this conference included the assistant chief of staff (Lieutenant General Sultan), the Corps commanders, commander of the Air Force, the current and previous Ministers of Defense, the Deputy Minister of Defense (Hussein Kamel), and the Minister of the Interior.

5. Harmony media file ISGQ-2003-M0005371.

6. It is not entirely clear what specific events Saddam is referring with regard to "America's first order in February 1990." However, during that period the Bush administration and Congress had been in a year-long and often acrimonious debate about financial support to Iraq through the Export-Import bank. Public debate surrounding Iraq's past WMD use, Iraq's involvement in the growing Banca Nazionale del Lavoro scandal, and the Bush administration's controversial $1 billion agriculture loan guarantees was widespread. In addition, with the collapsing threat from the Soviet Union, U.S. CENTCOM revised its regional military plans for the Middle East. Public statements by the U.S. military commander in the region, General Schwarzkopf, that the United States needed to increase its presence and "Iraq has the capability to militarily coerce its neighbors," only added to the tensions.

7. On 22 March 1990, Gerald Bull, a Canadian ballistics expert, was murdered in Brussels. Public rumors circulated, especially in Iraq, that the Israeli intelligence service was responsible for the killing, because Bull was helping Iraq with a cannon system capable of hitting Israel.

8. On 15 March 1990, Iraq hanged the Iranian-born British journalist Farzad Bazoft for espionage. Britain recalled its ambassador to Baghdad the following day.

9. Abdul Karim Qasim was the Army officer who led the 1958 military coup that overthrew the ruling monarchy in Iraq. A populist, he served as the prime minister until ousted and murdered in a Ba'athist coup in 1963.

10. Harmony media file ISGQ-2003-M0005705.

11. The most obvious example was Saddam's attitude about the postwar UNSC Resolutions and related sanctions imposed on Iraq. The international community viewed these actions as an extension of Iraq's capitulation to international will resulting from an armed conflict. To Saddam, the resolutions were a naked extension of the same international conspiracy that existed before the war. Saddam's view seemed to be: how can your adversary dictate terms if the results of combat were not decisive? The "unbeaten" Saddam was looking for negotiation, the Coalition response was a dictation.

12. Harmony media file ISGQ-2003-M0006753.

13. Harmony media file ISGQ-2003-M0003474. Saddam's book reviews refer to Schwarzkopf's *It Doesn't Take a Hero*, and Peter de la Billière's, *Storm Command: A Personal Account of the Gulf War.*

14. Harmony media file ISGQ-2003-M0005373.

15. Harmony media file ISGQ-2003-M0004179.

16. Ibid.

17. Ibid.

18. It should be noted that regardless of how "honest" the various lessons-learned efforts were, the continuous nature of the studies does indicate that a degree of military profes-

sionalism survived the deleterious effects of Saddam's rule. The earliest al-Bakr Military University studies concerning the events of the war dated from May 1991 (CMPC-2004-001639) and the latest dates to September 2001 (ISGP-2003-00033136).

19. Harmony document folder ISGQ-2003-M0003943.
20. Ibid.
21. Harmony document folder ISGP-2003-00033136.
22. Harmony document folder ISGQ-2003-00046040.
23. The United States completed its five-volume *Gulf War Air Power Survey* in 1993. Eliot A. Cohen, ed., *Gulf War Air Power Survey*, vols. 1–5 (Washington, DC: U.S. Government Printing Office, 1993).
24. Harmony media file ISGQ-2003-M0003869.
25. This early lessons-learned committee was chartered on 16 May 1991. According to the former commander of the 17th Brigade of the Hammurabi Division, the Republican Guard Commander hosted an after-action review of the invasion on 23 August 1990 in al-Basra. Some of the documents resulting from these sessions were captured after the war and published in *The Iraqi War Criminals and Their Crimes during the Iraqi Occupation of Kuwait*, compiled by Hussain 'Isa Mal Allah.
26. Harmony document folder ISGP-2003-00030181.
27. Ibid.
28. Harmony document folder CMPC-2004-001639.
29. Ibid.
30. Ibid.
31. Ibid.
32. The Iraqi air defense officers determined that altitudes below 8 km (26,000 ft) were in the low–mid-range elevation.
33. Harmony document folder CMPC-2004-001639.
34. Ibid.
35. It is unclear how a "special site" is defined in this particular Iraqi study. In other documents, a "special site" alternatively referred to presidential sites, critical command and control facilities or, in some cases, a location associated with WMD activity.
36. Project 777 was part of Saddam's nuclear weapons research program located in a large research complex called Tuwaitha, a heavily defended site on the east bank of the Tigris River eighteen kilometers southeast of Baghdad.
37. The Iraq document notes that a "hit" is calculated as an impact point within a 100 m x 100 m box.
38. Coalition analysts reached the completely opposite conclusion about the survival of air defense command centers.
39. Harmony document folder CMPC-2004-001639.
40. Ibid. Other documents indicate only two of four captured I-HAWKs were ever operational.
41. Ibid.
42. Ibid. The U.S. *Gulf War Air Power Survey* counts thirty-eight Coalition losses. Cruise missiles lost are more difficult to determine. Of the more than 300 cruise missiles (conventional air-launched cruise missiles and Tomahawk land attack cruise missiles) launched, unclassified data indicates that ~90 percent made it to their intended target area.
43. Harmony document folder CMPC-2004-001639.

44. Ibid.

45. Ibid.

46. Ibid.

47. Harmony media file ISGQ-2003-M0006247.

48. Harmony document folder CMPC-2003-006876.

49. Ibid.

50. The *Gulf War Air Power Survey* noted thirty-eight combat losses during Desert Storm (17 January–28 February 1991). Many early histories of the war cited the number 36 from a CENTCOM briefing held 7 March 1991. It is not clear what "revision" the Iraqi author is referring to, but if one counts the total combat, non-combat, and helicopter losses the total is 75. See Cook et al., *Gulf War Air Power Survey*, vol. 5, 641; and the U.S. Department of Defense, "1991 Defense Almanac."

51. Harmony document folder CMPC-2003-006876.

52. Most of the non-missile air defense weapons in Iraq's arsenal in 1991 consisted of 23-mm, 37-mm, and 57-mm cannons.

53. Harmony media file ISGQ-2003-M0007641.

54. Ibid.

55. Ibid.

56. The discussion used statistics on AH-64 Attack Helicopter employment during Operation Desert Storm that matches those in U.S. Department of Defense, "Conduct of the Persian Gulf War," 670.

57. Harmony media file ISGQ-2003-M0004555.

58. Ibid.

59. Ibid.

60. Ibid.

61. Ibid.

62. Ibid.

63. Ibid. In this portion of his discussion Saddam was specifically referring to the U.S. Air Force A-10 Warthog.

64. Harmony document folder ISGQ-2003-00023414.

65. Harmony document folder ISGP-2003-00031842.

66. Ibid. During the Cold War, NATO aircraft (especially those like the A-10 and AV-8 Harrier) had contingency plans to use non-standard runways (autobahns, etc.) in order to stay in the fight and sustain an air campaign. The Iraqi variation of this concept seems to have little to do with actual fighting and everything to do with preservation.

67. Harmony media file ISGQ-2003-M0006028.

68. Woods et al., *Iraqi Perspectives Project*, 8–9.

69. Harmony document folder IISP-2003-00026728.

70. Ibid. The sheer number and variety of entries referring to plunder and criminal activity by Iraqi troops indicates the degree to which the chaos was pervasive.

71. Ibid.

72. This document is a draft (as indicated by editorial comments in the margins by the principles involved) official history. The document title is "A Session for Recalling the Humane and Heroic Stance of Mr. President the Leader." Apparently it was an ongoing project. The document records session number eight and was written on 20 November

1994. It is not clear from the documents reviewed if this project was completed. Harmony document folder ISGP-2003-00009833.

73. Ibid.

74. Ibid.

75. Harmony media file ISGQ-2003-M0006247. Coalition estimates of Iraqi equipment losses remain mired in controversy. The *Gulf War Air Power Survey* recorded destruction of Iraqi equipment as 2,633 tanks, 1,668 armored personnel carriers, and 2,192 artillery pieces. (These numbers include systems destroyed by air, ground combat or abandoned). See Murray, *Gulf War Air Power Survey*, vol. 2, 261.

76. Harmony media file ISGQ-2003-M0006247.

77. Harmony media file ISGQ-2003-M0004555.

78. For a description of how the Iraqi adaptation made its battlefield debut see Greg Fontenot, E. J. Gegen, and David Tohn, *On Point: The United States Army in Operation Iraqi Freedom* (Ft. Leavenworth: Combat Studies Institute Press, 2004), 179–89.

79. Harmony media file ISGQ-2003-M0003869.

80. Ibid. Speaker is identified only as Najd.

81. Ibid. Speaker is identified as Khalil.

82. Ibid.

83. Harmony document folder ISGP-2003-00033136.

84. Ibid.

85. Ibid.

86. For example, according to Iraqi battle analysis, their SA-7 teams downed two helicopters and two fighters. According to the *Gulf War Air Power Survey*, vol. 5, the only aircraft lost during the al-Khafji operation was an AC-130H over Southern Kuwait. The Coalition flew 267 sorties against Iraqi forces involved in the al-Khafji attack during the seventy-two-hour operation.

87. Harmony media file ISGQ-2003-00054592.

88. Iraq fired forty-two Scud missiles that reached Israel or nearby areas of Jordan beginning on 18 January 1991. Iraq launched these missiles from western Iraq against three general target areas: Tel Aviv, Haifa, and the Negev Desert in southern Israel, specifically, Dimona where Israel had a nuclear facility. Those hitting the West Bank presumably fell short of their intended targets in Israel proper. The Office of the Special Assistant to the Deputy Secretary of Defense for Gulf War Illnesses, "Information Paper on Iraq's Scud Ballistic Missiles" (released 25 July 2000). www.iraqwatch.org/government/US/Pentagon/dodscud.htm (accessed 30 August 2006).

89. Numerous Iraqi documents treat the missile strike against Israel as a distinct campaign executed during the larger war.

90. Murray, *Gulf War Air Power Survey*, 191.

91. Harmony document folder ISGP-2003-00033136. The attacks did have a considerable political impact on diverting sorties to the anti-Scud hunt. But they hit none of these targets.

92. The *Gulf War Air Power Survey* found that although the direct effects of the Scuds were almost nonexistent, the indirect effects made them one of Iraq's most effective weapons. The Scud Hunt drew large numbers of aircraft away from more productive operations. See Cook et al., *Gulf War Air Power Survey*, vol. 5, 190.

93. On 7 June 1981, the Israeli Air Force struck the Iraqi nuclear reactor Osirak out of concern that it was part of a nuclear weapons development program.

94. Harmony document folder ISGP-2003-00033136. Quoted and paraphrased material used.

95. Ibid.

96. In this case, the report seems to conflate Israel's response to the missiles with the Coalition's action. The missiles affected the allocation of certain airpower assets in the Coalition's execution of Operation Desert Storm, but the 100-hour ground war could hardly be considered a "war of attrition."

97. The "financial burden" is an apparent reference to the cost to Israel of developing the Arrow Anti-ballistic missile system.

98. Harmony document folder ISGP-2003-00033136. Quoted and paraphrased material used.

99. Harmony folder ISGQ-2003-M0006285.

100. Ibid.

101. Ibid.

102. Ibid. Assuming each deception unit was about the same size (twenty-six launchers), the Iraqis successfully hid their fourteen real launchers among seventy-eight fake ones.

103. Ibid.

104. Ibid. UNSC Resolution 687, paragraph 7 (b) required "the destruction, removal, or rendering harmless all . . . ballistic missiles with a range greater than 150 kilometers."

Chapter X
SADDAM'S STRATEGIC LESSONS OF THE WAR

All the world is now saying "Man, why are we afraid so much? Bush fell and Iraq lasted!"[1]

—SADDAM HUSSEIN, 1993

n a 1992 discussion with senior officers, Saddam succinctly articulated the strategic lesson he took from the 1991 war, which became the lens through which he would view the coming decade:

"Through the last war the countries of the world realized a lot about America and what they discovered [comports] with our former analyses in February 1990.[2] Long before the Kuwait war, we expected America to stand alone in power in the world. We expected America to behave unwisely when it seize[d] power and our expectations came true. This change astonished the people of the world, that no one dared stand against America, but Iraq, this small country with all its circumstances as a third world country, resisted America."[3]

He reminded the assembled military men that "in light of the aforementioned, that we are sure war is inevitable; nothing will stop it save they realize that they [cannot] accomplish their goals."[4] Continuing to describe his strategic lesson at the same meeting, Saddam said that "the decisive factor is Iraq, without [depending] on the Arabic role. [W]e know the potential of the Arab countries and we cannot ask for more. We, as leaders of Jihad, cannot ask for help but we should proceed on training and morale preparation. [A]s you know, everything already in the Iraqi border is a main factor for victory, [and] what is outside Iraq are only secondary factors, we have previous experience in that."[5]

It appears that in Saddam's reading of recent history, the Arabs would no longer be considered reliable partners in creating the long-dreamed-of pan-Arab state. Saddam had led Iraq into two wars to rally the Arabs to their historic destiny and both time they failed him. It seems possible that, given Iraq's heroic performance, Saddam's long-held vision of unifying the Arab Nation as a precursor to dealing with Israel was no longer required, because it was not possible. In 1993 Saddam noted that "Israel is more concerned and anxious regarding the power of our army, than when the war started because they could not believe that [our] troops fought thirty-three countries in a month and a half and [are] still in good spirits."[6]

Continuing, Saddam was incredulous at the reaction of the international community in general and the United States more specifically to the military results of the war. In his view:

> [T]he [Republican] guards played a very important role, and we thank Allah, in the history when they write about Napoleon's guard, they will arrange them next to the Republican Guard of Iraq . . . after all the conspiracies and attacks that occurred, which lasted a month and a half [and] the betrayal that occurred inside Iraq. . . . I believe that all the American and French officers, if they were honest, they would be ashamed of their history, because where is the courage, when you measure it and compare it to weapons between the sword fighter and the show-off?[7]

Saddam's conception of how an external power might react militarily to his actions seems bounded by his own personal experiences. However, the distinction between his rational analysis and self-deception in such matters is difficult to discern even after reviewing hundreds of hours of the dictator's conversations. In the case of the 1991 war, Saddam appears to have drawn lessons that significantly influenced his assessments during the months leading up to the 2003 war.

In a recording of a meeting in 1991 between Saddam and his senior military advisers, he provided his assessment as "the chief of the general command," saying, "If we would have attacked them [the Coalition], after they launched the first bomb on Baghdad, if we would have attacked immediately, we would have taken our revenge in a better way. . . . I cannot say that the picture would have changed. No. But we would have hurt them more . . . we did not hurt them in a significant manner directly and physically."[8]

Saddam went on to predict a long confrontation with the United States. He told his generals to

> be assured that we will and you will see it in your lifetime, God willing. America was over when the first bomb was launched on Baghdad. It came to an end spiritually and everything they are willing to do cannot protect

them. I know they are masters of the world. . . . But they arrived to the summit in circumstances filled with despicable and corrupted intentions. . . . Although America and the thirty countries want to celebrate their victory over Iraq, the latter will wear them away from the inside because of what they did to Iraq. [W]ith each passing day more scandals are disclosed and more signs of weakness come to light.[9]

He offered an example of the strategic shifts taking place as a result of the just-concluded battle:

An educational operation took place and nothing [like this] ever happen-ed before. It took them [the United States] a long time before having the courage to launch the first bomb and attack Baghdad. This education will not be worthless. This education will play a role in the mind of the observer to pressure the United States and show it how to behave. Now the entire world is convinced. France is convinced. China is convinced. Now, even France, China, and the Soviet Union are convinced that Amer-ica came to dominate the world by attacking Iraq. It did not . . . come to defend the values of international law. This will begin corroding all their policies, and everybody will begin fearing America. And the fear has begun. . . . This fear will push towards the formation of a political coalition. You will see, even those who were the enemies of Iraq, they will come not before long and say, "We are sorry . . . forgive us for what happened. We were not thinking right."[10]

A popular pastime in the months following the war among Saddam and his advisers was to discuss the inevitable and in some cases impending collapse of the United States. In December 1991, Saddam provided his own take on Paul Kennedy's theory of imperial over-reach:[11]

America now, now faces difficulties as a result of expansion of its influence namely, it is incapable of satisfying its obligations, I mean, America has promised countries of Eastern Europe and have not satisfied its promise. It has promised the Soviet Union and has not satisf[ied] its promise. Now third world countries have all become Americans . . . they say "we are now Americans, make [us] happy." Well America does not have the means to make them happy and prosperous . . . we are all convinced that if it was not for Arab land and Arab money, this [the 1991 war] would not have happened.[12]

Taha Ramadan wholeheartedly agreed with Saddam's assessments and added, "If someone from the outside is looking into this picture, he would regard our analysis as unrealistic, but we view it as realistic . . . which makes me think about what has been happening in the last few months, [that it] has had more positive than negative effects."[13]

Following his aborted military threat against Kuwait in October 1994, Saddam explained the unfolding of events and the implication for the future in terms of his strategic lessons from 1991.[14] He noted:

> What happened on August 2nd showed the near and far [enemies] to think twice about pressuring Iraq. However . . . the Gulf people . . . especially the Saudis and the Kuwaitis, imagined that they were able to destroy and bring down, through their military, political, and economic alliances, and sanctions, in order to bring down Iraq just as they planned.
>
> Suddenly they realized what was going on, just as Israel realized when they were hit with the [Iraqi] missiles. Israel's security was relying on their expansion in the Arab land. . . . Israel realized after they were hit with the Iraqi missiles during the Mother of All Battles that they cannot play their games with us.[15]

In Saddam's analysis, he even took credit for something he normally reviled Arab leaders for doing, negotiating over the long-term solution in Palestine:

> [The Iraqi missile strikes on Israel in 1991] . . . forced the Americans to negotiate with the Syrians, Jordanians, and the Palestinians. If these countries were capable of negotiating and standing together, they could have benefited far more than they have. However, if it [were] not for the missile strikes against Israel, the strength and firm stance of Iraq against the thirty-three enemies, they would have achieved nothing. . . . During that period, they thought they could ensure peace through their methods. That is to say, their security is to humiliate and disarm Iraq of [its] capability. [These] last events, disregarding the details . . . suddenly, the Americans, the West, and the world realized there was no luck or hope in the course that they were taking.[16]

Saddam's interaction with the world between the invasion of Kuwait and the international reaction to his saber-rattling in October 1994 taught him that the international community was taking the wrong course. Saddam felt empowered by his understanding of unfolding events. The power was not only manifest in his ability to manipulate the course of events in the region, but because it provided yet another venue to rally the Arab "nation" to his cause:

[The Americans] force the Iraqi people to rise and have an impact on events. [The Iraqis] are noble and capable of having an impact on the events and their military capability is far better than what they thought. ...That is to say, when only two units form, our great army moved from north to south, it was real chaos and fear. The Kuwaitis ran for the borders and the Saudis closed their borders to them. [The Kuwaitis] were sleeping in the desert and so on. Meanwhile the Saudi family was shaking in fear and calling for foreigners to come to their lands.

Saddam went on to hint at lessons the Iranians might have been learning from their old foes the Iraqis. He declared that "the Iranians are our friends in fighting, that is to say we have fought each other for eight years, [and] we know them. Nevertheless, they are saying, 'What is this? These people [the Iraqis] are still alive, posing a threat, able to move army units, and the world is scared of them.'"[17]

Saddam continued discussing postwar lessons by noting that other Arab leaders like Libyan president Muammar al-Qaddafi were "jealous" of Iraq. Gaddafi could not explain to the Libyan people Iraq's apparent power despite its limited military capability. Saddam opined that the Libyan people, being noble Arabs, were hurt and wanted to know what their leaders were doing to reach Iraq's level of strength. Despite all of the setbacks and challenges, for Saddam, this kind of feedback was at last a sign of success in his long struggle to lead the Arab people. Optimistically, he believed Iraq was entering the "last stage of the conflict," and that soon "Iraq [would] be in an appropriate position in the world and the Arab world, just as Iraq wishes."[18]

Finally, Saddam realized that regional power meant nothing if Iraq could not exercise that power free from international restrictions. In much the same way he manipulated Arab and Islamic issues within the Middle East, Saddam believed he could manipulate nationalism and economic competition among the world powers:

There is no use of military action without a political motive . . . at the appropriate time. The big political issue is that Russia was sleeping [during 1991] but felt a deep sense of respect for Iraq. Now they are thinking about how to build relations with Iraq, in order to have an effect on the region. In the end, this effect will support their existence as a major country. This is what they discovered and Iraq started helping Russia on their role, to gain their role back, not for Russia, but for the Arabs, Iraq, the region, and for humanity. This brief description calls for us to be calm and relaxed. . . . If they [the United States] try to instigate here or there . . . we should not get excited, we should monitor events. Moreover, we should increase our ability and know God is going to help us. Now our people have more confidence in themselves [because] they are watching the end of the sanctions.[19]

Saddam's Analysis of His Adversary

Understanding the American political system was not one of Saddam's strong points. To be fair, with one exception, members of Iraq's RCC were no better informed of the workings of the American political processes than most of the U.S. government was on Iraq's system, though it was considerably more opaque. Setting aside the regime's lack of understanding, the conversations after the war about the war's political impact on the United States say a great deal about the regime's perspective on the world at large.

In a conversation recorded in early December 1992, Saddam and his senior advisers analyzed the impact of the 1991 war on the American political scene and the implications for rapprochement with the incoming administration. Tariq Aziz, perhaps reflecting a more sophisticated understanding of the dynamics in Washington, D.C., began the conversation with two cautions. First, that Iraq "shouldn't take a formal stand [in] what occurred in the American elections."[20] Aziz acknowledged that such a statement could only harden the position of the incoming administration. Second was that as the Iraqis considered what policies the new U.S. president might follow, they should remember that the politics of the election campaign are one thing "but the politics [as] practiced are something else."[21] The rest of Saddam's advisers were decidedly more provincial in their comments.

Iraqi Vice President Taha Ramadan did not believe Bush lost the 1992 election because the Americans did not "like the Iraq War." Bush lost, according to Ramadan, because he failed to deliver on the promise that the war "was going to bring economic power to America." Moreover, according to the vice president, Bush "didn't succeed in this war because he didn't succeed in removing Saddam Hussein. Now he [Bush] is removed and Saddam Hussein [still] exists."[22] Another adviser joined in with the opinion that, while Clinton won the election inside America, it was Saddam who won the election "on the level of the world."[23]

Another participant, identified only as Badar, offered the assessment that "Bush's fall is a victory to us from two angles." The first was that Bush had personalized the dispute with Iraq and as a result his actions "involved spite." This personal "project" to overthrow Saddam Hussein failed in the worst possible way. In this analysis, instead of removing Saddam, Bush was "overthrown ... and Saddam Hussein lasted." According to Badar, the second angle was even more significant. Bush failed to win the election not only because he failed to deliver the economic benefit of a war with Iraq, but because his use of postwar sanctions was actually "violating the Security Council Resolution."[24]

Saddam's political analysis of the American presidential election was produced by a mix of factors, some of which changed depending on the time and audience. The most consistent perhaps reflected Saddam's beliefs about leadership and what makes a historically successful leader. In response to Ramadan and Badar, Saddam rhetorically commented, "Doesn't Bush's fall include a [piece] of Iraq's role in his fall? In other words, wasn't the Mother of All Battles a basic reason for overthrowing Bush?"[25]

Saddam observed that there were many reasons for Bush's failure to win the election and they were not all due to "Clinton's characteristics ... nor ... the American internal situation."[26] While one could not accurately estimate Iraq's role, Saddam was sure that Bush's failure to "save the West from the regime in Iraq" was significant.[27] Saddam then noted that Bush failed because he "could not achieve success" after both having said he would save the West from Saddam and then declaring victory after having failed to do so. For Saddam, this conclusion was not much of an intellectual stretch, given that "declaring victory after having failed to do so" was something with which he was familiar.

Notes

1. Harmony folder ISGQ-2003-M0007446.
2. This is likely in reference to Saddam's 24 February 1990 speech at the opening of the fourth summit of the ACC in Amman, Jordan. Saddam's analysis of the changing international balance of power noted that the United States would soon be unbounded by the competition of the Cold War and its "undisciplined and irresponsible behavior will engender hostility and grudges." He urged his fellow Arab leaders to unite and confront this looming menace. FBIS-NES-90-039, 27 February 1990.
3. Harmony media file ISGQ-2003-M0006753. Saddam points to the American "dominion over oil" as its strategic focus.
4. Ibid.
5. Ibid.
6. Harmony media file ISGQ-2003-M0005705.
7. Ibid.
8. Harmony media file ISGQ-2003-M0003869.

9. Ibid.

10. Ibid.

11. See Paul Kennedy, *The Rise and Fall of Great Powers* (New York: Random House, 1987). As already noted, this same theory animates many Salafi Jihadist strategists in their confrontation with the United States. See Jarret M. Brachman and William F. McCants, "Stealing Al Qaeda's Playbook," *Studies in Conflict and Terrorism*, 29, no. 4 (February 2006), 309–21.

12. Harmony media file ISGQ-2003-M0004615.

13. Harmony media file ISGQ-2003-M0004615. Ramadan's analysis included the prediction that no one would see the collapse of America coming. It would occur with less than twelve to twenty-four hours notice.

14. During the first week of October 1994, Iraq moved the Hammurabi and al-Nida Republican Guard Divisions from northern Iraq to the vicinity of al-Basra. By 9 October, the Iraqis had massed more than 80,000 troops within twelve miles of the Kuwaiti border. The United States responded with a rapid deployment of significant ground, air, and naval forces to the region in an operation known as Operation Vigilant Warrior. By 16 October, Iraqi troops had begun to withdraw and return to garrison locations.

15. Harmony media file ISGQ-2003-M0005002.

16. Ibid.

17. Ibid.

18. Ibid.

19. Ibid. For more on the methods used to act on this "lesson" see Woods et al., *Iraqi Perspectives Project*, 25–32; Central Intelligence Agency, "Comprehensive Report on Iraq's WMD," 2004; and Independent Inquiry Committee into the United Nations Oil-for-Food Programme, "Manipulation of the Oil-For-Food Programme by the Iraqi Regime," also known as the Volcker Report (27 October 2005), www.iic-offp.org (accessed 1 June 2005).

20. Harmony folder ISGQ-2003-M0007446.

21. Ibid.

22. Ibid.

23. Ibid. Speaker is identified in the tape by Saddam as Dr. Elyas.

24. Ibid. The "economic benefits" were not specified nor were the UNSC Resolution violations.

25. Ibid.

26. Ibid.

27. Ibid.

Epilogue
INSIGHTS FROM THE IRAQI PERSPECTIVE

> Ignorance, especially the ignorance of educated men, can be a
> more powerful force than knowledge. Ethnocentrism in histori-
> cal studies, whatever its advantages in scholarly training, is likely
> to feed parochialism in the societies which those historians serve;
> and such parochialism can have pretty disastrous results.[1]
>
> —SIR MICHAEL HOWARD

Adversaries often think differently. The larger the gap between the adversaries' cultures, histories, and languages, the more dramatic the differences in how each side views the strategic situation as well as the
other side. History suggests that these dramatic differences are not always apparent. Saddam saw Iraq, the region, the world, and the structures binding them
together very differently than did the leaders of the various coalitions that had
confronted him over the years.

A British diplomat once described Soviet dictator Joseph Stalin's Welt-
anschauung (worldview) as "a curious mixture of shrewdness and nonsense."[2]
The same observation, and for many of the same reasons, is appropriate to Saddam Hussein. The seemingly insurmountable challenge that confronted many
of the dictator's adversaries over the years was in knowing which ingredient in
this "curious mix" would dominate at any given time. Because the only worldview inside Iraq that mattered between 1979 and 2003 was Saddam's, the failure
to understand his rationality made encounters with Iraq problematic. Given the
cognitive and philosophic limitations associated with judging someone's rationality, one could ask if it is worth the effort. Why stand on the "other side of the
hill," if much of what one can see from that vantage point is not useful?

The purpose of standing on the enemy's side of the hill is not an altruistic
one. It concerns making the effort to map an alternative worldview in order to
defeat one's adversary. Such a map can provide a degree of understanding or, at
the least, the context within which one can judge an adversary's decisions and
anticipate his future actions. One can argue that understanding an adversary
is an essential—if not the essential—ingredient in defeating him. For policy

makers, seeing the world through an adversary's eyes can optimize strategic choices. For military planners, such understanding is equally important and goes well beyond the traditional order of battle and doctrinal assessments. Short of a military strategy of annihilation, one's adversary normally decides when the war has ended. Trying to create the conditions under which an adversary comes to that decision quickly, and at the least cost, has for better or worse been a holy grail for U.S. military planners since World War II.

Although events following the 2003 overthrow of Saddam Hussein's regime have recently focused attention on the limits that constrained American understanding of the Iraqi context, one should remember that war is a two-sided struggle. The events surrounding the 1991 war were the first of a long series of engagements, where understanding was in short supply on both sides. At the strategic level, Saddam's ignorance of the international system in general and the United States in particular was in a class by itself. Often ignoring the advice of his advisers, Saddam Hussein viewed the international community through a unique set of "Tikriti-colored glasses." This often led to a process shaped by a thuggish instinct and an unshakeable belief in grand conspiracy theories.

For many reasons, the specific insights illuminated in this study are unique to Saddam and the regime he created. Given this unique mapping, or modeling, using the behavior of Saddam's regime as a template to understand other totalitarian regimes would be of limited value. Moreover, such a template could cloud understanding a non-Saddam perspective even more.

However, there are insights arising from this study that are applicable when applied to the issue of confronting contemporary totalitarian states. Some could also describe previous totalitarian regimes. To the extent that is true, this study merely represents a new addition to the literature. Some of the insights from this study are indirect. Indirect insights result from Americans looking into a mirror at their assumptions, presumptions, reactions, and actions when dealing with this regime.

The contemporary nature of the material covered in this and related studies, the residual effects of removing Saddam Hussein's regime in 2003, and the opportunity to update a new generation on the adversary's perspective makes some insights worth repeating:

> Do not assume a common understanding of events with your adversary. The cause-and-effect of recent, much less centuries-old, historical events can lead to significant differences in rational choices. In addition to the usual American-Zionist conspiracies, Saddam was convinced the

United States was actively supporting efforts to destroy Iraq during the decade leading up to the 1990 crisis.

Victory is in the eye of the beholder. Saddam defined "victory" as not "losing" in the face of overwhelming odds. His claims of success after 1991 mirror those following the end of the Iran-Iraq War in 1988. Not surprisingly, Saddam defined losing in simple and personal terms—being removed from power. Using Saddam's framework of understanding, he did not lose the 1991 confrontation.

Do not assume a gap between public rhetoric and private beliefs. While many of the public pronouncements of Saddam's regime concerning both the Kuwait issue and subsequent military operations were couched in ambiguous language, they reflected the regime's private positions. Saddam took great pride in saying in public what he intended and using subsequent events to validate his historic role.

Military innovation and adaptation does occur in totalitarian states. While in general it holds true that tactical or operations brilliance cannot make up for poor strategy, it is also true that necessity is the mother of invention. The Iraqi military surprised many observers in its conduct of the initial invasion of Kuwait. Moreover, Iraqi attempts to survive the Coalition's air dominance, while not successful, set in motion a significant program of adaptation designed to conduct military operations despite Western airpower.

In war, Clausewitz noted, "facts are seldom fully known and the underlying motive even less so," because they may have been "intentionally concealed by those in command, or, if they happen to be transitory and accidental, history may not have recorded them at all."[3] Through the study of heretofore inaccessible information, many of the facts that are "seldom known" may now come to light to contribute the long-absent adversary context. In that sense, this study, notwithstanding its limitations, has succeeded. The documents, audiotapes, and videotapes used to produce this work were, for the most part, secreted away in a closed society. It is only through the extraordinary circumstances of OIF that they are ours to examine.[4] It would be a shame not to use them.

Notes

1. Howard, *Lessons of History*, 16.
2. Christopher Andrew and Julie Elkner, "Stalin and Foreign Intelligence," *Totalitarian Movements and Political Religions* 4, no. 1 (2003): 77.
3. Clausewitz, *On War*, 181.

4. A fascinating historical parallel is the exploitation of the records of the Nazi regime in the decades following WWII. Among the uses of this material was support to war crimes tribunals, historical research (Army "Green Book" series), doctrinal development, and intelligence operations. See Kevin Soutor, "To Stem the Red Tide: The German Report Series and its Effects on American Defense Doctrine, 1948–1954," *Journal of Military History* 57, no. 4 (1993): 653–88.

Appendix A: Timeline

Year	Date	Event
1963	8 Feb	Iraqi Prime Minister Qasim is ousted in a coup led by the Arab Ba'ath Socialist Party.
	18 Nov	The Ba'ath government is overthrown by a group of military officers.
1968	17 Jul	A Ba'ath-led coup ousts Prime Minister Arif. Gen. Ahmad Hasan al-Bakr becomes president. Saddam Hussein, relative of Bakr, becomes vice president.
1978	17 Sep	The Camp David Peace Accords are signed between Israel and Egypt.
		Arab League meeting in Baghdad condemns Camp David Accords.
1979	16 Jan	Islamic Revolution ousts the Shah of Iran. Ayatollah Khomeini arrives in Tehran in February.
	16 Jul	President Al-Bakr resigns and is succeeded by Vice President Saddam Hussein. Within days, Saddam executes at least twenty potential rivals, members of the Ba'ath party, and military.
1980	4 Sep	Iran shells Iraqi border towns. On 17 September, Iraq abrogates the 1975 treaty with Iran. An eight-year war between Iraq and Iran begins.
1981	7 Jun	Israel attacks an Iraqi nuclear research center at Tuwaythah near Baghdad.
1988	16 Mar	Iraq attacks the Kurdish town of Halabjah with a mix of poison gas and nerve agents, killing 5,000 people.
	20 Aug	The Iran-Iraq War ends in a stalemate—an estimated one million soldiers are killed in eight years of fighting.
1990	15 Feb	Voice of America suggests that the overthrow of Romania's dictator might be a model for the Middle East.
	19 Feb	Saddam Hussein demands that U.S. warships depart the Persian Gulf.

1990	21 Feb	U.S. State Department publishes a report outlining human rights abuses in Iraq.
	15 Mar	A British journalist is hanged in Iraq for espionage.
	2 Apr	Saddam says Iraq has binary weapons and will "make fire eat half of Israel if it tries anything against Iraq."
	30 May	At an Arab League Summit, Saddam calls for Arabs to liberate Jerusalem and demands $27 billion from Kuwait for its oil overproduction.
	15 Jul	Tariq Aziz accuses Kuwait of stealing Iraqi oil from the Rumaila oil field.
	17 Jul	Saddam threatens action if Kuwait (and the United Arab Emirates) fail to comply with new oil quotas designed to raise oil prices.
	20 Jul	Kuwait rebuts Iraqi demands and says it is about getting them to forgive Iraq's war debt.
	22 Jul	Egypt's Hosni Mubarak offers to mediate and says he has Saddam's assurances that Iraq will not move against Kuwait.
	24 Jul	Iraqi troops deploy to the Kuwaiti border.
		The United States begins naval exercise with the United Arab Emirates.
	25 Jul	Saddam meets with the U.S. ambassador.
		Saddam sends a message to President Bush saying he desires to resolve the crisis peacefully.
	31 Jul	Talks between Iraq and Kuwait open in Jeddah, Saudi Arabia.
	1 Aug	Iraq walks out on Jeddah talks.
	2 Aug	Iraq invades Kuwait.
		UNSC Resolution 660 calls for a full withdrawal.
		Soviet Union suspends delivery of military equipment to Iraq.
		Iraq warns other countries not to interfere or "we will make Kuwait a graveyard for those who launch any aggression."
		British Airways Flight 149 (378 passenger and crew) is trapped at Kuwait International Airport after making a fuel stop just as the invasion began.
		Arab League convenes an emergency meeting in Cairo.
	3 Aug	Limited resistance continues inside Kuwait.

1990		United States and Soviet Union issue a joint statement condemning the invasion and calling for an immediate withdrawal.
		Soviet Union suspends all arms sales to Iraq.
		Arab League members condemn the invasion of Kuwait (five nations vote against the condemnation or abstain).
		Gulf Cooperation Council emergency ministerial meeting in Cairo demands immediate withdrawal of Iraqi forces.
	4 Aug	Iraq announces a new government has formed in Kuwait.
	5 Aug	Baghdad radio announces the formation of eleven new Iraqi army divisions.
	6 Aug	UNSC Resolution 661 imposes economic sanctions on Iraq.
		Saudi King Fahd agrees to permit U.S. troops on Saudi soil.
		Saddam Hussein announces that the seizure of Kuwait is irreversible.
	7 Aug	15,000 U.S. troops begin moving into Saudi Arabia.
	8 Aug	President Bush declares that "a line has been drawn in the sand."
		Iraq announces the formal annexation of Kuwait.
		UNSC Resolution 662 declares the Iraqi annexation of Kuwait "null and void."
		King Hussein of Jordan calls for an Arab solution to the crisis.
	9 Aug	Saddam sends a message to President Bush saying he has no aggressive plans toward Saudi Arabia.
		Iraq orders all embassies in Kuwait closed by 24 August.
	10 Aug	An emergency Arab summit votes twelve to eight to send a pan-Arab force to join American troops.
		Saddam announces a "peace-plan" based on Israeli withdrawal from occupied territories.
		Saddam calls for a Jihad to defend Mecca from the Americans and Zionists. He calls on Arabs to rebel against the "Emirs of Oil."
	11 Aug	First Egyptian troops arrive in Saudi Arabia to establish pan-Arab force.

1990	12 Aug	Iraqi Parliament calls for attacks on hostile targets anywhere in the world if Iraq is attacked.
		Saddam announces conditions for an Iraqi withdrawal including Israel's withdrawal from Palestinian territories, Syrian troops out of Lebanon, and U.S. troops out of the region. The details of the withdrawal from Kuwait would be "consistent with Iraq's historic rights."
		Iranian President Rafsanjani condemns U.S. and foreign presence in the Gulf.
	13 Aug	King Hussein of Jordan holds talks in Baghdad with Saddam.
	15 Aug	Saddam agrees to all of Iran's remaining demands in a final peace treaty dating from the end of the Iran-Iraq War.
	18 Aug	UNSC Resolution 664 demands Iraq free all hostages immediately.
	19 Aug	United States calls up reserves for the first time since the Vietnam War.
	20 Aug	Iraq announces that Western hostages will be moved to vital military installations to deter attack.
	24 Aug	U.S. State Department criticizes Soviet Union for keeping military advisers in Iraq.
	25 Aug	UNSC Resolution 665 authorizes force to halt ships violating the economic blockage on Iraq.
	28 Aug	Saddam Hussein announces that all women and children being detained in Iraq and Kuwait will be released.
	5 Sep	Saddam Hussein calls for an Islamic holy war against U.S. forces and calls for the overthrow of Saudi Arabia's King Fahd.
	9 Sep	President Bush and Soviet President Gorbachev declare unconditional support for sanctions against Iraq.
	10 Sep	Iran and Iraq renew full diplomatic relations.
		Iraq offers free oil to countries willing to break the blockade.
	11 Sep	President Bush addresses joint session of Congress.
	13 Sep	UNSC Resolution 666 permits humanitarian food shipments to Iraq.
		Syria agrees to send 10,000 troops to Saudi Arabia.
		Iraqi troops storm French and Belgian ambassadors' quarters in Kuwait.

1990	16 Sep	UNSC Resolution 667 condemns Iraq's aggressive actions against embassies in Kuwait.
	17 Sep	USAF Chief of Staff Michael J. Dugan is relieved for discussing planning of air operations against Iraq.
	21 Sep	Saddam Hussein promises "mother of all battles" if Coalition forces attack.
		UNSC Resolution 670 imposes an air embargo on Iraq.
	1 Oct	U.S. Congress passes a joint resolution supporting President Bush's efforts to "deter aggression."
	2 Oct	French troops arrive in Saudi Arabia.
	18 Oct	U.S. deployments reach 209,000.
	20 Oct	Anti-war marches staged across the U.S.
	23 Oct	Iraq announces all French hostages can leave.
	29 Oct	UNSC Resolution 674 calls for the release of the hostages and holds Iraq responsible for damages to Kuwait.
	1 Nov	Iraq announces that family members of hostages can visit for Christmas.
	5 Nov	President Turgut Ozal of Turkey rules out a northern front against Iraq.
	7 Nov	British Prime Minister Margaret Thatcher says, "Either he gets out of Kuwait soon, or we and our allies will remove him by force."
	8 Nov	President Bush announces he will double the size of U.S. forces in the region. A second U.S. Corps is ordered deployed to Iraq.
	15 Nov	U.S. Amphibious Exercise *Imminent Thunder* begins in Persian Gulf.
	16 Nov	U.S. rejects a Soviet suggestion that the Kuwait crisis be linked to the Israeli-Palestinian conflict.
	19 Nov	Iraq announces it will send 250,000 additional troops to Kuwait and calls up reserves.
	22 Nov	President Bush visits U.S. troops in Saudi Arabia.
	25 Nov	Soviet President Gorbachev tells Tariq Aziz that Iraq must comply with international demands or "the U.N. resolution will be adopted—a tough one."
	27 Nov	Saudi Arabia offers the USSR a $1 billion loan.
	28 Nov	UNSC Resolution 677 condemns Iraq for attempting to drive out Kuwaitis and repopulate their country.

1990	29 Nov	UNSC Resolution 678 gives Iraq until 15 January to comply with all previous resolutions. After that date, Coalition forces are authorized "to use all necessary means" to force compliance.
	2 Dec	Iraq test fires Scud missile within Iraq.
	6 Dec	Saddam announces he will release all hostages, citing a changing U.S. position.
	14 Dec	Last American hostages depart Iraq.
	20 Dec	Soviet Foreign Minister Shevardnadze resigns.
	26 Dec	Iraq test fires Scud missile within Iraq.
		U.S. deployments reach 300,000.
	29 Dec	U.S. Congressional Democrats threaten to cut off funds for Operation Desert Shield unless the President seeks Congressional approval before attacking Iraq.
1991	1 Jan	Saddam Hussein visits Iraqi troops in the Kuwait theater of operations.
	6 Jan	Saddam Hussein declares, "The results of this battle will be great, and all the world and future generations will talk about it."
	7 Jan	The Gulf War begins with Coalition forces aerial bombing Iraq—Operation Desert Storm.
	9 Jan	U.S. Secretary of State Baker meets with Tariq Aziz in Geneva. Iraq vows to attack Israel if war begins. Aziz refuses to accept a letter from President Bush to Saddam Hussein.
	11 Jan	U.S. State Department warns that Iraqi terrorists are planning attacks throughout the Gulf region.
	12 Jan	U.S. Congress authorizes the use of forces necessary to fulfill U.N. commitments.
		U.S. closes embassy in Baghdad.
		U.S. expels Iraqi diplomats.
	14 Jan	Iraqi National Assembly votes to support Saddam Hussein's policy in Kuwait.
	15 Jan	U.N. deadline for withdrawal passes.
		A White House official says, "It's no longer a question of whether, but when." Coalition forces attack.
	17 Jan	President Bush announces, "The liberation of Kuwait has begun. . . . We will not fail." (1830 Washington, D.C., 16 Jan)

1991	17 Jan	Operation Desert Storm begins at 0230 in Baghdad with air and missile attacks.
		Saddam declares, "The great showdown has begun! The Mother of All Battles is under way. . . . Iraq will never surrender."
		Iraq launches Scud missiles at Israel and Saudi Arabia.
	18 Jan	Coalition aircraft drop 2,500 tons of ordnance in the first 24 hours.
	19 Jan	U.S. deploys Patriot missile batteries in Israel to defeat Iraqi Scud attacks.
		U.S. deployments reach 460,000 troops.
	20 Jan	Iraqi television broadcast pictures of captured Coalition air force personnel.
	21 Jan	Iraq announces it will use Coalition prisoners as human shields.
	22 Jan	Soviet President Gorbachev calls for a peaceful solution to the Gulf War.
	23 Jan	President Bush urges that Saddam Hussein be brought to "justice."
	23 Jan	U.S. Chairman of the Joint Chiefs of Staff says, "Our strategy for dealing with this army is very simple. First we're going to cut it off, then we are going to kill it."
	24 Jan	Saudi officials report oil slicks. Iraq claims they were caused by Coalition bombing.
		Iraqi forces fire rockets at U.S. Marine positions near al-Khafji, Saudi Arabia.
	25 Jan	Two Iraqi Mirage F-1s are shot down by a Saudi F-15 pilot.
	26 Jan	Oil spills threaten Saudi desalinization plants.
		Iraq begins flying its air force to Iran for safety.
	28 Jan	Saddam says Iraqi troops will "win the admiration of the world with their fighting prowess."
	29 Jan	Iraq launches a multi-division operation into Saudi Arabia to seize al-Khafji and disrupt the Coalition.
	13 Feb	Heavy civilian casualties result after the Coalition air attack on a bunker in central Baghdad.
	24 Feb	Coalition ground operation begins.
	27 Feb	Kuwait is liberated by Coalition forces.

| 1991 | 3 Mar | Iraq accepts the terms of a cease-fire. The primary cease-fire resolution is UNSC Resolution 687 (April 3) requiring Iraq to end its WMD programs, recognize Kuwait, account for missing Kuwaitis, return Kuwaiti property, and stop supporting international terrorism. Iraq is required to stop repressing its citizens. |

Appendix B: Key Personalities

The list below is intended to clarify the narrative in this study, not to be comprehensive. Biographical entries are limited to the context in this study.

IRAQI	
Saddam Hussein	President of Iraq, commander in chief Iraqi Armed Forces
Tariq Aziz	Foreign Minister (1983–91) and Deputy Prime Minister (1979–2003) of Iraq
Taha Ramadan	Member of the Revolutionary Command Council
Izzat Ibrahim al-Duri	Member of the Revolutionary Command Council
Hussein Kamel Hassan al-Majid	Head, Military Industrial Commission and Saddam's son-in-law
Ali Hassan al-Majid, aka "Chemical Ali"	Governor of Kuwait, Aug–Nov 1990
Latif Nayyif Jasim	Minister of Information
Barzan Ibrahim al-Tikriti	Former Head of Iraqi Intelligence 1979–83, Ambassador to U.N. in Geneva 1988–97, Saddam's half brother
Sabawi Ibrahim Hasan al-Tikriti	Director, Iraqi Intelligence Service in Kuwait, Saddam's half brother
Lt. Gen. Husayn Rashid Muhammed	Chief of Staff, Iraqi Armed Forces
Lt. Gen. Nazir Khazraji	Chief of Staff, Iraqi Armed Forces (relieved Oct 1990)
Col. Abid Hamid Mahmud al-Tikriti	Saddam's personal secretary, senior bodyguard, and member of his inner circle
Staff Lieutenant General al-Janabi	Staff Officer, Iraqi Armed Forces

Lt. Gen. Aayad Futayyih Khalifa al-Rawi	Commander, Republican Guard
Maj. Gen. Muzahim Sa'b Hasan al-Tikriti	Commander, Iraqi Air and Air Defense Forces
Maj. Gen. Kamil Sajit Aziz	Commander, Gulf Operations Command
Maj. Gen. Mahmud Fayzi Muhammad al-Hazza	Commander, Jihad Operations Command
Maj. Gen. Ibrahim Isma'il Muhammad	Commander, I Corps
Maj. Gen. Ibrahim 'Abd al-Sattar Muhammad	Commander, II Corps
Maj. Gen. Salah Aboud Mahmaud	Commander, III Corps
Maj. Gen. Iyad Khalil Zaki	Commander, IV Corps
Maj. Gen. Ali Muhammad Shallal	Commander, V Corps
Maj. Gen. 'Abd al-Wahid Shinan al-Ribat	Commander, VI Corps
Maj. Gen. Ahmad Ibrahim Hammash	Commander, VII Corps
Maj. Gen. Qais Abd al-Razaq	Commander, Hammurabi Division
Brig. Gen. Ra'ad Hamdani	Commander, 17th Brigade, Hammurabi Republican Guard Division
Lt. Gen. Sabir 'Abd al'Aziz Hussein al-Duri	Director, General Military Intelligence Directorate, 1991
Lt. Gen. Zuhayr Talib Abd al-Satter al-Naqi	Director, General Military Intelligence Directorate, 2003
Sabah Talat Kadrat	Deputy Ambassador to U.N. in New York
Staff Brig. Gen. Ghazi Mohsen Marzouk	Chief of Staff, al-Abed Forces Command
Lt. Gen. Hazim Abd al-Razzaq al-Ayyubi	Commander, Surface-to-Surface Missile Forces
Maj. Gen. Ghalib Muhammad Hassun	Commander, Naval and Coastal Defense Forces
Lt. Gen. A'mir Mohammad Rasheed	Director, Military Manufacturing and the Oil Ministry
Col. Hasan Sawadi	Commander, 440 Naval Infantry Brigade

Lt. Col. Saed Jalio	Naval Task Force commander during Kuwait invasion
Naval colonel Muzahim Mustafa	Naval Task Force commander during Kuwait invasion
Comrade Tahir (Tahir Jalil Habbush al-Tikriti)	Director, Iraqi Intelligence Service
Sa'dun Hammadi	Prime Minister of Iraq, Mar–Sept 1991
Flight Staff Brig. Gen. Naji Khalifa Jasim al-A'Any	Commander, Project 777 Air Defense on 17 Jan 1991
Gen. Sa'di Tuma Abbas al-Jabburi	Minister of Defense, Nov 1990–Apr 1991
Staff Maj. Gen. Khalid Husayn	Director of Planning, General Staff
Staff Lt. Gen. Sultan Hashim Ahmad Jabburi	Deputy Chief of Staff, Army
Abdul Karim Qasim	Prime Minister of Iraq, July 1958–Feb 1963
MIDDLE EASTERN	
Gaafar Muhammad an-Nimeiry	President of Sudan, 1971–85
Field Marshal Mohammed Anwar Al Sadat	President of Egypt 1970–81, signed Camp David Peace accords with Israel in 1978
Menachem Begin	Prime Minister of Israel, negotiated Camp David Accords with President Sadat of Egypt in 1978
Gamal Abdel Nasser	President of Egypt, 1954–70
Houari Boumédienne	President of Algeria, 1965–78
Grand Ayatollah Ruhollah Musavi Khomeini	Supreme Leader of Iran, 1979–89
Akbar Hashemi Rafsanjani	President of Iran, 1989–97
Abu Righal	Character from the Quran who showed an invading army the way to Mecca in 571 CE
Fahad bin Abdul Aziz al-Saud	King and Prime Minister of Saudi Arabia and leader of the House of Saud 1982–2005
Jaber III al-Ahmad al-Jaber al-Sabah	Emir of Kuwait, 1977–2006
Crown Prince Sheikh Saad al Abdullah as Salim	Prime Minister of Kuwait, 1978–2003
Yasser Arafat	Chairman, Palestine Liberation Organization, 1969–2004

Hosni Mubarak	President of Egypt, 1981–present
Field Marshal Ali Abdullah Saleh	President of the Yemen Arab Republic (North Yemen), 1978–90, President of Yemen 1990–present
Muammar Abu Minyar al-Qaddafi	Leader of Libya, 1969–present
Crown Prince Abdullah	Second in line for the Saudi throne
General Khaled bin Sultan	Saudi Arabian General, Commander, Joint Forces during Operations Desert Shield and Desert Storm
INTERNATIONAL	
Gen. Colin Powell	U.S. Chairman of the Joint Chiefs of Staff, 1989–93
Richard Cheney	U.S. Secretary of Defense, 1989–93
George H. W. Bush	41st President of the United States, 1989–93
April Glaspie	U.S. Ambassador to Iraq, 1989–91
Joseph C. Wilson	Deputy Chief of Mission at the U.S. Embassy in Baghdad, Iraq, 1988–91
François Mittérrand	President of the French Republic, 1981–95
Margaret Thatcher	Prime Minister of the United Kingdom, 1979–90
Gen. H. Norman Schwarzkopf	Commander, U.S. Central Command, 1988–91
Edward Shevardnadze	Foreign Minister of the Soviet Union, 1985–91
Yevgeny Primakov	Member of Soviet Presidential Council, 1990–91, Mikhail Gorbachev's special envoy to Iraq, 1991
Mikhail Gorbachev	President and General Secretary of the Communist Party of the Soviet Union, 1985–91
Gen. Peter de la Billiére	Commander in Chief of the British forces, 1990–91

Acronyms and Abbreviations

ACC	Arab Cooperation Council
BG	Brigadier General
CE	Common Era
CENTCOM	U.S. Central Command
CIA	Central Intelligence Agency
CNN	Cable News Network
COA	courses of action
DoD	U.S. Department of Defense
FBIS	Foreign Broadcast Information Service
FOUO	For Official Use Only
FROG	Free Rocket Over Ground
GMID	General Military Intelligence Directorate
HAWK	"Homing All the Way Killer" missile
IAF	Iraqi Air Force
IDA	Institute for Defense Analyses
IIS	Iraqi Intelligence Service
INF	Intermediate-Range Nuclear Forces
IPP	Iraqi Perspectives Project
JAWP	Joint Advanced Warfighting Program
JCOA	Joint Center for Operational Analysis
JFCOM	U.S. Joint Forces Command
KKMC	King Khalid Military City
LTC	Lieutenant Colonel
LTG	Lieutenant General
MBT	Main Battle Tanks
MEF	Marine Expeditionary Force
MEK	Mujahedin-e Khalq, Iranian expatriate group
MG	Major General
MIC	Military Industrial Commission
NATO	North Atlantic Treaty Organization
OIF	Operation Iraqi Freedom

ONW	Operation Northern Watch
OPEC	Organization of Petroleum-Exporting Countries
OSW	Operation Southern Watch
PLO	Palestinian Liberation Organization
RCC	Iraqi Revolutionary Command Council
SEAL	member of the U.S. Navy specially trained in "Sea, Air, Land" combat
SLAR	Side-Looking Airborne Radar
SSM	surface-to-surface missile
TEL	transporter-erector launcher
UAR	United Arab Republic
UAV	unmanned aerial vehicle
U.N.	United Nations
UNSC	United Nations Security Council
U.S.	United States
USA	U.S. Army
USAF	U.S. Air Force
WMD	weapons of mass destruction
WWII	World War II

References

Note: In many instances, the Harmony document folders comprise more than one item—for example, a collection of memoranda, related documents, or a mix of reports and memos. Each Harmony document folder has its own unique document number; individual items within the folder do not. Consequently, the reader may see the same number with different titles and/or media types. All material derived from Harmony documents and media files in this study have been cleared for unlimited public distribution by the study's U.S. government sponsor. This clearance, however, does not apply to the original Harmony documents and media files, which retain their original handling instructions and caveats [For Official Use Only (FOUO)] as noted.

Books, Periodicals, Reports, Web Sites

al-Ayyubi, Hazim Abd al-Razzaq. "Forty-Three Missiles on the Zionist Entity." *Al-Arab al-Yawm (Arabic)*, Amman, Jordan 25, 27, 29 October; 1, 3, 5, 10, and 12 November 1998

Allen, Charles E. "Warning and Iraq's Invasion of Kuwait: A Retrospective Look." *Defense Intelligence Journal* 7, no. 2 (1998): 33–44.

al-Naqi, LTG Zuhayr Talib Abd al-Satter. Author's interview. Baghdad, Iraq, 14 November 2003.

al-Suri, Abu-Mus'ab. The Call for Global Islamic Resistance. Arabic version widely available on the Internet as of 1 January 2007.

American Embassy Baghdad to Secretary of State, cable, 6 August 1990. Subject: "Main Points of Charge's Meeting with President Saddam Hussein." Declassified 11 August 1999. www.margaretthatcher.org/archive/displaydocument.asp?docid=110715 (accessed 22 August 2006).

Andrew, Christopher, and Julie Elkner. "Stalin and Foreign Intelligence." *Totalitarian Movements & Political Religions* 4, no. 1 (2003).

Arkin, William M. "Baghdad: The Urban Sanctuary in Desert Storm." *Airpower Journal* no. 11 (1997): 4–20.

Atkinson, Rick. *Crusade: The Untold Story of the Persian Gulf War.* New York: Houghton Mifflin Co., 1993.

Baram, Amatzia. "An Analysis of Iraqi WMD Strategy." *Nonproliferation Review* (Summer 2001).

———. "Between Impediment and Advantage: Saddam's Iraq." United States Institute for Peace, *Special Report* no. 3 (1998).

———. "The Invasion of Kuwait: Decision-making in Baghdad." *Iraq's Road to War,* ed. Amatzia Baram and Barry Rubin. New York: St. Martin's Press, 1993.

Bengio, Ofra. *Saddam's Word: Political Discourse in Iraq.* New York: Oxford University Press, 1998.

———. *Saddam Speaks on the Gulf Crisis: A Collection of Documents.* Tel Aviv: Tel Aviv University, 1992.

Bergquist, Ronald E. *The Role of Airpower in the Iran-Iraq War.* Washington, DC: U.S. Government Printing Office, 1988.

Biddle, Stephen. "Victory Misunderstood: What the Gulf War Tells Us about the Future of Conflict." *International Security* 21, no. 2 (1996): 139-79.

bin Sultan, General Khaled. *Desert Warrior: A Personal View of the Gulf War by the Joint Forces Commander.* New York: Harper Collins, 1995.

Boyne, Sean. "Inside Iraq's Security Network—Part Two." *Jane's Intelligence Review* 9, no. 8 (1997).

Brachman, Jarret M., and William F. McCants. "Stealing Al Qaeda's Playbook." *Studies in Conflict and Terrorism* (February 2006).

Bracken, Paul. "Net Assessment: A Practical Guide." *Parameters* 36, no. 1 (2006).

Bush, George, and Brent Scowcroft. *A World Transformed.* New York: Alfred A. Knopf, 1998.

Bush, President George H.W. "Remarks by the President to the Joint Session of Congress." 11 September 1990. http://bushlibrary.tamu.edu/research/papers/ 1990/90091101.html (accessed 1 December 2006).

"Central Command Briefing." *Military Review.* 71, no. 9 (1991).

Chadwick, Frank. *Gulf War Fact Book.* Bloomington, IN: GDW Inc., 1991.

Church, George J. "The Gulf: Saddam's Strategies." *Time,* 1 October 1990. www.time.com/time/printout/0,8816,971282,00.html (accessed 6 March 2007).

Cigar, Norman. "Chemical Weapons and the Gulf War: The Dog that Did Not Bark." *Studies in Conflict and Terrorism* 15, no. 2 (1992): 145-55.

Cohen, Eliot A., ed. *Gulf War Air Power Survey Summary Report.* Washington, DC: U.S. Government Printing Office, 1993.

Cole, Hugh M. "Writing Contemporary Military History." *Military Affairs* 12, no. 3 (1948).

Cooley, John K. "Pre-war Gulf Diplomacy." *Survival* 33, no. 2 (1991).

Cook, Doris, Maj. Lewis D. Hill, and Dr. Aron Pinker. *Gulf War Air Power Survey,*

Volume 5: A Statistical Compendium and Chronology. Washington, DC: U.S. Government Printing Office, 1993.

Cordesman, Anthony H. and Khalid R. Al-Rodhan. "The Gulf Military Forces in an Era of Asymmetric War: Iraq." *Center for Strategic and International Studies*, 28 June 2006.

Corgan, Michael T. "Clausewitz on War and the Gulf War." *Eagle in the Desert: Looking Back on U.S. Involvement in the Persian Gulf War*, ed. William Head and Earl H. Tilford Jr. Westport, CT: Praeger, 1996.

Cureton, Charles H. *U.S. Marines in the Persian Gulf, 1990–1991: With the 1st Marine Division in Desert Shield and Desert Storm*. Washington, DC: U.S. GPO, 1993.

de la Billière, Peter. *Storm Command: A Personal Account of the Gulf War*. London: Harper Collins, 1993 paperback ed.

Defense Science Board Task Force. "The Role and Status of DoD Red Teaming Activities." September 2003.

Finlan, Alastair. *The Gulf War 1991*. Oxford: Osprey Publishing, 2003.

Fontenot, Greg, E. J. Gegen, and David Tohn. *On Point: The United States Army in Operation Iraqi Freedom*. Ft. Leavenworth: Combat Studies Institute Press, 2004.

Freeman, Lawrence and Efraim Karsh. *The Gulf Conflict (1990–1991): Diplomacy and War in the New World Order*. Princeton, NJ: Princeton University Press, 1993.

Freeman, Robert, ed. *The Middle East After Iraq's Invasion of Kuwait*. Gainesville: University Press of Florida, 1993.

Friedrish, Otto. "He Gives Us Hope." *Time*, 27 August 1990.

Gordon, Michael R. and Bernard E. Trainor. *The Generals' War*. New York: Little Brown and Company, 1995.

Grant, Rebecca. "The Epic Little Battle of Khafji." *Air Force Magazine* 81, no. 2 (1998).

Haldane, Lieutenant-General Sir Aylmer L. *The Insurrection in Mesopotamia 1920*. 1922 reprint. Nashville: The Battery Press, 2005.

Hamdani, LTG Ra'ad. Author's interview. Baghdad, Iraq, 10 November 2003.

———. "From the Golan to the Collapse of Baghdad: Six Wars in Thirty Years." Unpublished Memoirs. January 2004.

Hanneman, Joseph. "Eye of the Storm." Perspective 3, no. 1 (2003).

Hart Jr., LTC Fred L. "The Iraqi Invasion of Kuwait: An Eyewitness Account." Carlisle Barracks, PA: U.S. Army War College, 1 May 1998.

Hart, B. H. Liddel. *The Other Side of the Hill*. London: Cassell and Co., 1948.

Haselkorn, Avigdor. *The Continuing Storm—Poisonous Weapons and Deterrence*. New Haven: Yale University Press, 1999.

Hashim, Ahmed S. "Saddam Husayn and Civil-Military Relations in Iraq: The Quest for Legitimacy and Power." *Middle East Journal* 57, no. 1 (2003).

———. *Insurgency and Counterinsurgency in Iraq*. Ithaca, NY: Cornell University Press, 2006.

Head, William and Earl H. Tilford. *The Eagle in the Desert: Looking Back on US Involvement in the Persian Gulf War*. Westport: Praeger Publishers, 1996.

Heydemann, Steven. *War, Institutions, and Social Change in the Middle East*. Berkeley: University of California Press, 2000.

Hiro, Dilip. *The Longest War*. New York: Routledge, 1991.

Hoagland, Jim. "Outgoing Officers." *Washington Post*, 13 September 1990.

Hopwood, Derek, Habib Ishow, and Thomas Koszinowski. *Iraq: Power and Society*. Oxford: Ithaca Press, 1993.

Howard, Michael. *The Lessons of History*. New Haven: Yale University Press, 1991.

Hussein, Saddam. "Victory Day." Message read by announcer on Baghdad Radio, 7 August 1990. FBIS-NES-90-153, 8 August 1990.

———. Speech, Baghdad Radio Service, in Arabic, 0737 GMT, 24 February 1991. FBIS-NEW-91-037, 25 February 1991.

Independent Inquiry Committee into the United Nations Oil-for-Food Programme. "Manipulation of the Oil-For-Food Programme by the Iraqi Regime." Also known as the Volcker Report, 27 October 2005. www.iic-offp.org (accessed 1 June 2005).

International Institute for Strategic Studies. *The Military Balance: 1988–1989*. London: Brassey's, 1988.

———. *The Military Balance: 1989–1990*. London: Brassey's, 1989.

———. *The Military Balance: 1990–1991*. London: Brassey's, 1990.

Jamieson, Perry D. *Lucrative Targets—The U.S. Air Force in the Kuwait Theater of Operations*. Washington, DC: U.S. GPO, 2001.

Kadhim, Abbas. "Civil-Military Relations in Iraq (1921–2006): An Introductory Survey." *Strategic Insights* 5, no. 5 (2006).

Kazemi, Ali Asghar, "Peace through Deception: The Iran Iraq Correspondence," in Farhang Rajaee, ed. *Iranian Perspectives on the Iran-Iraq War*. Gainesville: University Press of Florida, 1997.

Keegan, John. *The Battle for History: Re-fighting World War II*. New York: Random House, 1995.

Kennedy, Paul. *The Rise and Fall of Great Powers*. New York: Random House, 1987.

Lane, Barry J. "The Killing Ground." *Newsweek*, 28 January 1991.

Laqueur, Walter, and Barry Rubin, eds. *The Israel Arab Reader: A Documentary History of the Middle East Conflict*. New York: Penguin Books, 2001.

Lauterpacht, E., et al., eds. *The Kuwait Crisis: Basic Documents.* Cambridge: Grotius Publications Ltd., 1991.

Levins, John. *Days of Fear: The Inside Story of the Iraqi Invasion of Kuwait.* Dubai: Motivate Publishing, 1997.

Lewis, Bernard. *The Political Language of Islam.* Chicago: University of Chicago Press, 1988.

Liebl, Vern. "The View from the Other Side of the Jebel (Hill)." *Command Magazine* no. 13 (1991).

Lukitz, Liora. *A Quest in the Middle East: Gertrude Bell and the Making of Modern Iraq.* New York: St. Martin's Press, 2006.

Luttwak, Edward N. *Strategy: The Logic of War and Peace.* Cambridge, MA: Harvard University Press, 1987.

Makiya, Kanan. *Cruelty and Silence, War, Tyranny, Uprising, and the Arab World.* New York: W.W. Norton & Company, 1993.

Mal Allah, Hussain 'Isa. *The Iraqi War Criminals and Their Crimes during the Iraqi Occupation of Kuwait.* Kuwait: Center for Research and Studies on Kuwait, 1998.

Marolda, Edward J. and Robert J. Schneller Jr. *Shield and Sword—The United States Navy and the Persian Gulf War.* Washington, DC: U.S. GPO, 1998.

Marr, Phebe. *The Modern History of Iraq.* Cambridge: Westview Press, 2004.

Melton, Gary P. "XVIII Airborne Corps Desert Deception." *Military Intelligence Professional Bulletin* 17, no. 4 (1991).

Middle East Research and Information Project. "Baghdad Summit: 'The Palestinian Question Is the Essence of the Conflict.'" MERIP Report no. 73, December 1978.

Morris, David J. *Storm on the Horizon: Khafji—The Battle That Changed the Course of the Gulf War.* New York: Free Press, 2004.

Murray, Williamson. *Gulf War Airpower Survey,* Volume 2: *Operations/Effects and Effectiveness.* Washington, DC: U.S. GPO, 1993.

Neff, Donald. "The U.S., Israel, and Iran: Backdrop to War." *Journal of Palestinian Studies* 20, no. 4 (1991).

Neustadt, Richard E., and Ernest R. May. *Thinking in Time: The Uses of History for Decision Makers.* New York: The Free Press, 1986.

Ni'mat, Salamah. Interview with Staff General Nizar al-Khazraji, al-Hayah (Arabic) London, 16 April 1996. (Open Source Center, FTS19960416000591)

Oberdorfer, Don. "Glaspie Says Saddam Is Guilty of Deception." *Washington Post,* 21 March 1991.

O'Loughlin, John, Tom Mayer, and Edward S. Greenberg. *War and its Consequences: Lessons from the Persian Gulf Conflict.* New York: Harper Collins, 1994.

Pagonis, LTG William G. *Moving Mountains: Lessons in Leadership and Logistics from the Gulf War*. Boston: Harvard Business School Press, 1992.

PBS Frontline. "The Gulf War." www.pbs.org/wgbh/pages/frontline/gulf/oral/aziz/1.html (accessed 1 September 2006).

Pitman, Sarah, and George J. Walker. *Desert Shield/Desert Storm: Evaluation of Public Domain Battle Plans*, Volume II. SAIC study prepared for U.S. Central Command, 31 May 1991. Includes *Los Angles Times* article "If Pentagon Gets a 'Go' It'll Be Massive Strike," 24 August 1990.

Pokrant, Marvin. *Desert Shield at Sea—What the Navy Really Did*. Westport, CT: Greenwood Press, 1999.

Pollack, Kenneth M. *Arabs at War: Military Effectiveness, 1948–1991*. Lincoln: University of Nebraska Press, 2002.

Powell, Colin with Joseph E. Persico. *My American Journey*. New York: Random House, 1995.

Russell, Sharon Stanton, and Muhammad Ali al-Ramadham. "Kuwait's Migration Policy since the Gulf War." *International Journal of Middle Eastern Studies* 26, no. 4 (1994).

"Saad al-Bazzaz: An Insider's view of Iraq." *Middle East Quarterly*, 2, no. 4, (1995).

Scales, Robert. *Certain Victory*. Washington, DC: Brassey's, 1994.

Schwarzkopf, H. Norman, with Peter Petre. *It Doesn't Take a Hero*. New York: Bantam, 1992.

Segal, David. "The Iran-Iraq War: A Military Analysis." *Foreign Affairs* 88, no. 5 (1988): 946-63.

Shulman, Milton. *Defeat in the West*. 1947 reprint. London: Cassell Publishing, 2003.

Sifry, Micah L., and Christopher Cerf, eds. *The Gulf War Reader*. New York: Times Books, 1991.

Soutor, Kevin. "To Stem the Red Tide: The German Report Series and its Effects on American Defense Doctrine, 1948–1954." *Journal of Military History* 57, no. 4 (1993): 653-88.

Stanton, Martin. *Road to Baghdad—Behind Enemy Lines: The Adventures of an American Soldier in the Gulf War*. New York: Ballantine Books, 2003.

Stein, Janice Gross. "Deterrence and Compellence in the Gulf, 1990–1991: A Failed or Impossible Task?" *International Security* 17, no. 2 (1992).

Swain, Richard M. *Lucky War—Third Army in Desert Storm*. Ft. Leavenworth: U.S. Army Command and General Staff College Press, 1994.

Telhami, Shibley. "Arab Public Opinion and the Gulf War." *Political Science Quarterly* 108, no. 3 (1993).

Titus, James. "The Battle of Khafji: An Overview and Preliminary Analysis." Monograph. Maxwell AFB, AL: Airpower Research Institute, Air University, September 1996.

Tzu, Sun. *The Art of War.* Trans. Thomas Cleary. Boston: Shambhala Publications, 1988.

U.S. News and World Report. Triumph without Victory: The Unreported History of the Gulf War. New York: Three Rivers Press, 1993.

von Clausewitz, Carl. *On War.* Ed. and trans. Michael Howard and Peter Paret. New York: Alfred A. Knopf, 1993.

Watson, Bruce W. et al. *Military Lessons of the Gulf War.* London: Greenhill Books, 1991.

Woods, Kevin et al. *Iraqi Perspectives Project: A View of Operation Iraqi Freedom from Saddam's Senior Leadership.* Washington, DC: U.S. GPO, 2006.

Yetiv, Steve A. *Persian Gulf Crisis.* Westport, CT: Greenwood Publishing Group, 1997.

Yost, David S. "France and the Gulf War of 1990–1991: Political-Military Lessons Learned." *Journal of Strategic Studies* 16, no. 3 (1993): 339–74.

U.S. Government Publications

Central Intelligence Agency. "Comprehensive Report of the Special Advisor to the DCI on Iraq's WMD." Volumes 1–3. Langley, VA: CIA, 30 September 2004.

———. "Putting Noncombatants at Risk: Saddam's Use of 'Human Shields." Washington, DC: CIA, January 2003.

Central Intelligence Agency, Directorate of Intelligence. "Prewar Status of Iraq's Weapons of Mass Destruction." (TOP SECRET) 15 January 1991. Declassified extract December 2002. www.gwu.edu/~nsarchiv/NSAEBB/ NSAEBB80/ wmd04.pdf (accessed 15 December 2006).

Office of the Secretary of State, Office of the Coordinator for Counterterrorism. "Patterns of Global Terrorism: 1991: Middle East Overview." Washington, DC, April 1991.

Office of the Special Assistant to the Deputy Secretary of Defense for Gulf War Illnesses. Information Paper on Iraq's Scud Ballistic Missiles. Released 25 July 2000. www.iraqwatch.org/government/US/Pentagon/dodscud.htm (accessed 30 August 2006).

Prados, Alfred B. "Iraq: Post-War Challenges and U.S. Responses, 1991-1998." Congressional Research Service, Report for Congress 98-386-F (updated 31 March 1999).

———. "Iraq: Former and Recent Military Confrontations with the United

States." Congressional Research Service, Issue Brief for Congress, IB94049 (updated 6 September 2002).

U.S. Department of Defense. "Final Report to Congress: Conduct of the Persian Gulf War." Washington, DC: U.S. GPO, April 1992.

The White House. National Security Directive 26, Subject: U.S. Policy toward the Persian Gulf, 2 October 1989. (SECRET / declassified 26 May 1999). http://bushlibrary.tamu.edu/research/directives.html (accessed 1 December 2006).

————. National Security Directive 45, Subject: U.S. Policy in Response to the Iraqi Invasion of Kuwait, 20 August 1990. (SECRET / declassified 22 November 1996). http://bushlibrary.tamu.edu/research/directives.html (accessed 1 December 2006).

————. National Security Directive 54, Subject: Responding to Iraqi Aggression in the Gulf, 15 January 1991. (TOP SECRET / declassified on 5 June 1997). http://bushlibrary.tamu.edu/research/directives.html (accessed 1 December 2006).

Harmony Media Files

Video

Harmony media file ISGQ-2003-M0003323—Iraqi III Corps commander discusses the Gulf War, undated. (FOUO)

Harmony media file ISGQ-2003-M0003326—Seminar on the 5th Division in Al-Khafji combat during the First Gulf War, date unknown. (FOUO)

Harmony media file ISGQ-2003-M0005872—A conference of Republican Guards, special forces, air force, and air defense leaders discussing the invasion of Kuwait, date unknown. (FOUO)

Harmony media file ISGQ-2003-M0005879—Videotape of minister of defense Ali Hasan al-Majid and armed forces chief of staff General Ayad Futayyih Khalifa al-Rawi discussing the invasion of Kuwait, ca. 1993. (FOUO)

Harmony media file ISGQ-2003-M0005889—Videotape of Republican Guard officers discussing 1991 war, 1993. (FOUO)

Harmony media file ISGQ-2003-M0006027—Military seminar discussing Republican Guard actions on 2 August 1990, ca. 1993. (FOUO)

Harmony media file ISGQ-2003-M0006028—Videotape of Saddam meeting with officers concerning the 1991 Gulf War, ca. 1992. (FOUO)

Harmony media file ISGQ-2003-M0006038—Military Seminar on the Republican Guard during the Invasion of Kuwait, ca. 1993. (FOUO)

Harmony media file ISGQ-2003-M0006048—Saddam Hussein Meeting with Yasser Arafat, 19 April 1990. (FOUO)

Harmony media file ISGQ-2003-M0006167—Video of Ali Hasan al-Majid and several senior officers discussing the 1991 war, 11 May 1993. (FOUO)

Harmony media file ISGQ-2003-M0006168—IV Corps Commander and senior staff discuss operations during 1991 war, ca. 1993. (FOUO)

Harmony media file ISGQ-2003-M0006180—III Corps Commander discusses events of the Gulf War, 10 May 1992. (FOUO)

Harmony media file ISGQ-2003-M0006181—Iraqi high-ranking personnel analyzing the Battle of al-Khafji, ca. 1993. (FOUO)

Harmony media file ISGQ-2003-M0006183—Iraqi commanders discuss Battle of al-Khafji, ca. 1993. (FOUO)

Harmony media file ISGQ-2003-M0006195—Recording of Staff RADM Gha'ib Hasan giving a post war lecture to the officers of the Iraqi Naval Forces Command, ca. 1993. (FOUO)

Harmony media file ISGQ-2003-M0006198—Videotape of the 5th Scientific Seminar on the Strategic Role of Um al-Ma'arik Battle, Al-Bakr University for Military Studies, 15 May 1992. (FOUO)

Harmony media file ISGQ-2003-M0006201—Video of a Meeting of the Naval Forces Leadership, ca. 1993. (FOUO)

Harmony media file ISGQ-2003-M0006247—Video of a conference discussing battles in 1991, 20 November 1995. (FOUO)

Harmony media file ISGQ-2003-M0006248—Video of meeting between Saddam Hussein and Yasser Arafat, 19 April 1990. (FOUO)

Harmony media file ISGQ-2003-M0006273—Videotape of an Iraqi lesson learned conference discussing IV and VI Corps Operations in 1991, ca. 1992. (FOUO)

Harmony media file ISGQ-2003-M0006471—Minister of Defense Ali Hasan al-Majid discussion with senior officers, ca. 1991. (FOUO)

Harmony media file IZSP-2003-10103729—Meeting between military, scientific, and academic leaders on defeating cruise missiles, late November 1990. (FOUO)

Audio

Harmony media file ISGP-2003-10151507—Audiotape of LTG Husayn Rashid Muhammad discussing 1991 Gulf War, 11 April 1995. (FOUO)

Harmony media file ISGP-2003-10151576—Saddam Hussein discussing the historical right of Iraqi in Kuwait, ca. November 1990. (FOUO)

Harmony media file ISGP-2003-10151704—Saddam and staff discuss Camp David, ca. 1978. (FOUO)

Harmony media file ISGP-2003-10151751—Audio file of Vice President Saddam Hussein discussing the Palestinian situation, 8 September 1978. (FOUO)

Harmony media file ISGP-2003-10151758—Revolutionary Command Council (RCC) Meeting held shortly after 1979 Baghdad conference, ca. 1979. (FOUO)

Harmony media file ISGQ-2003-M0001716—State Command and Revolutionary Command Council meeting, November 1990. (FOUO)

Harmony media file ISGQ-2003-M0001720—Recording of an Iraqi command meeting on 24 February 1991. (FOUO)

Harmony media file ISGQ-2003-M0001721—Audio recording of Taha Ramadan discussing world events with Saddam on 24 February 1991. (FOUO)

Harmony media file ISGQ-2003-M0001722—Recording of an Iraqi command meeting on 24 February 1991. (FOUO)

Harmony media file ISGQ-2003-M0003473—Saddam Hussein in a national command meeting discussing the impact of the Gulf War on the Arab world, ca. 1993. (FOUO)

Harmony media file ISGQ-2003-M0003474—Saddam Hussein meeting with the national command, 1992. (FOUO)

Harmony media file ISGQ-2003-M0003629—Audiotape of a meeting of the Iraqi Revolutionary Command Council on 20 September 1990. (FOUO)

Harmony media file ISGQ-2003-M0003677—Saddam Hussein and senior official discuss preparations for Baghdad conference (February 1990). (FOUO)

Harmony media file ISGQ-2003-M0003811—Saddam discussing regional situation, 1 January 1980. (FOUO)

Harmony media file ISGQ-2003-M0003852—Audio recording of Saddam meeting with his Ministerial Council on 4 August 1990. (FOUO)

Harmony media file ISGQ-2003-M0003853—Recording of a meeting between Saddam and Iraqi officials regarding Kuwait invasion, late August 1990. (FOUO)

Harmony media file ISGQ-2003-M0003869—Saddam meeting with his senior military commanders after the withdrawal from Kuwait, 3 March 1991. (FOUO)

Harmony media file ISGQ-2003-M0003916—Saddam Hussein meeting with senior commanders, 13 January 1991. (FOUO)

Harmony media file ISGQ-2003-M0003943—Iraqi lessons-learned conference, ca. 1993. (FOUO)

Harmony media file ISGQ-2003-M0003958—Military Seminar on the Um Al-Ma'arik, 10 May 1993. (FOUO)

Harmony media file ISGQ-2003-M0003959—Saddam discusses Gulf War with military leaders, ca. 1993. (FOUO)

Harmony media file ISGQ-2003-M0004179—Audio recording of Saddam's evaluation of events after invasion of Kuwait, date uncertain. (FOUO)

Harmony media file ISGQ-2003-M0004181—Audio recording of Saddam Hussein and senior officers discussing the Gulf War, ca. 1993. (FOUO)

Harmony media file ISGQ-2003-M0004189—Audio recording of a letter from President Rafsanjani being read to Saddam Hussein discussing the occupation of Kuwait, 8 August 1990. (FOUO)

Harmony media file ISGQ-2003-M0004353—Saddam meeting with senior official prior to Arab League Conference in Tunisia, ca. November 1979. (FOUO)

Harmony media file ISGQ-2003-M0004555—Audio recording of Saddam Hussein attending a military seminar, 27 November 1995. (FOUO)

Harmony media file ISGQ-2003-M0004608—Audio recording of a Revolutionary Command Council meeting on 1 November 1990. (FOUO)

Harmony media file ISGQ-2003-M0004609—Audio recording of a Revolutionary Command Council meeting on 2 November 1990. (FOUO)

Harmony media file ISGQ-2003-M0004615—Saddam speaks about the war against the Coalition, 21 December 1991. (FOUO)

Harmony media file ISGQ-2003-M0004926—Third day of a joint military seminar, 22 November 1995. (FOUO)

Harmony media file ISGQ-2003-M0005002—Saddam Hussein meeting with Iraqi officials concerning post–Gulf War Iraq, ca. late 1994/early 1995. (FOUO)

Harmony media file ISGQ-2003-M0005309—Audiotape of Saddam meeting with senior leaders, 30 September 1990. (FOUO)

Harmony media file ISGQ-2003-M0005325—Meeting with Saddam Hussein on Kuwaiti policies, 20 September 1990. (FOUO)

Harmony media file ISGQ-2003-M0005346—Saddam Hussein meeting with his ministerial council, 1982. (FOUO)

Harmony media file ISGQ-2003-M0005371—Saddam discussing military matters with senior Ba'ath officials, 17 November 1991. (FOUO)

Harmony media file ISGQ-2003-M0005373—Saddam meeting with senior army commanders on 1 May 1991. (FOUO)

Harmony media file ISGQ-2003-M0005705—Meeting chaired by Saddam Hussein discussing events following the end of the 1991 war, ca. 1993. (FOUO)

Harmony media file ISGP-2003-M0006183—Iraqi commanders discuss Battle of al-Khafji, ca. 1993. (FOUO)

Harmony media file ISGQ-2003-M0006285— Videotape of Saddam and senior officers reviewing lessons from the 1991 war, ca. 1993. (FOUO)

Harmony media file ISGQ-2003-M0006753—Saddam and his commanders discuss the retreat from Kuwait, ca. 1992. (FOUO)

Harmony media file ISGQ-2003-M0006763—Saddam discussing 15 January 1991 deadline with his military commanders in early January 1991. (FOUO)

Harmony media file ISGQ-2003-M0006905—Audio recording of a meeting between Saddam Hussein and senior military officers on 3 April 1991. (FOUO)

Harmony media file ISGQ-2003-M0006909—Saddam discussing post-invasion Arab policy with high-ranking officials, early August 1990. (FOUO)

Harmony media file ISGQ-2003-M0007111—Saddam Hussein's letter to President Rafsanjani, 17 August 1990. (FOUO)

Harmony media file ISGQ-2003-M0007446—Audiotape of meeting between Saddam and Ba'ath party members discussing the 1992 U.S. presidential election, January 1993. (FOUO)

Harmony media file ISGQ-2003-M0007540—Audio recording of a meeting between Saddam and military commanders, ca. 1983. (FOUO)

Harmony media file ISGQ-2003-M0007641—Audiotape of a meeting between Saddam Hussein and members of the Iraqi air force and air defense forces, late 1991. (FOUO)

Harmony Document Folders

Harmony document folder CMPC-2003-004325—Memorandum to Defense Diwan from Ministry of Industry (Ref no. 2/1/35/9/160), Subject: "Munitions Receiving, 31 December 1990" and Subject: "Minutes of Special Warheads," 11 January 1991. (FOUO)

Harmony document folder ISGQ-2003-M0005891—Iraqi military officials meeting to discuss 1991 Gulf War, ca. 1993. (FOUO)

Harmony document folder CMPC-2003-006876—Iraqi report on Gulf War air losses, ca. 2001. (FOUO)

Harmony document folder CMPC-2004-001639—Report on strategies and damages of enemy air strikes, ca. May 1991. (FOUO)

Harmony document folder FM8556—Artillery operations order no. 2, III Corps Artillery, 24 September 1990. (FOUO)

Harmony document folder FM8582—Iraqi Air Force flight information guide, ca. 1995. (FOUO)

Harmony document folder FM8607—20th Division defense plan, February 1991. (FOUO)

Harmony document folder FM8617—8th Mechanized Brigade (3rd Armored

Division), battle group order no. 4, 21 January 1991. (FOUO)

Harmony document folder FM8621—15th Division counterattack plan no. 1, 8 January 1991. (FOUO)

Harmony document folder FM8615—15th Division counter–sea landing plan, no. 1, 8 January 1991. (FOUO)

Harmony document folder FM8625—3rd Armored Division maneuver plan no. 3, 29 November 1990. (FOUO)

Harmony document folder FM9108—5th Mechanized Infantry Division Command maneuver plan no. 1, 31 August 1990. (FOUO)

Harmony document folder FM9108—Directives, 20th Mechanized Infantry Brigade, 5th Mechanized Division, 26 November. This document related the contents of a III Corps (Iraqi top secret and personal) letter 8224, 24 November. (FOUO)

Harmony document folder IISP-2003-00026728—Iraqi study on the 1991 Gulf War in Kuwait, 1 August 1995. (FOUO)

Harmony document folder IISP-2003-00029023—Memorandum from general staff of the Army (Intelligence) to General Military Intelligence Directorate, Subject: Detailed Report, Sequence Number: 1/19/24/1762, 25 February 1991. (FOUO)

Harmony document folder IISP-2003-00036124—Correspondence among military intelligence directorates on security conditions in Kuwait, various dates between 26 August and 25 October 1990. (FOUO)

Harmony document folder IISP-2003-00043745—Research about the Iraqi Popular Army, 1988.

Harmony document folder IISP-2003-00045177—Ba'ath party collection of Saddam's aphorisms, 23 January 2003. (FOUO)

Harmony document folder ISGP-2003-00009833—A draft transcript of interviews compiled for an official Iraqi history of events, ca. 1995. (FOUO)

Harmony document folder ISGP-2003-00010140—Vice President Saddam Hussein speech to Al-Bakr University, entitled "The Role of the Iraqi Armed Forces in the Arabic—Zionist Conflict," 6 March 1978. (FOUO)

Harmony document folder ISGP-2003-00026182—Iraqi Air Force operations center log, dates 10–17 February 1991. (FOUO)

Harmony document folder ISGP-2003-00026600—Memorandum from Deputy Director, General Military Intelligence Directorate, Subject: "Requirements for Satellite Photographs," 18 October 1990. (FOUO)

Harmony document folder ISGP-2003-00026600—Correspondence of General Military Intelligence Directorate, 22 October 1990. (FOUO)

Harmony document folder ISGP-2003-00026608—Memorandum from the

IIS Operations Department to the Head of the Security Committee, no. A/90/106, Reference: External Operations, 2 September 1990. (FOUO)

Harmony document folder ISGP-2003-00026610—Memorandum from III Corps Commander to the General Military Intelligence Directorate (Office 1/Division 19), 3 October 1990. (FOUO)

Harmony document folder ISGP-2003-00028432—Circulation from the presidency council, no. 1/4/62, signed by Ahmad Husain, 19 January 1991. (FOUO)

Harmony document folder ISGP-2003-00028432—Letter from Saddam Hussein to men of the Air Defense, 21 January 1990. (FOUO)

Harmony document folder ISGP-2003-00028432—Memorandum from Saddam Hussein to commander of the Iraqi Air Force, 19 January 1991. (FOUO)

Harmony document folder ISGP-2003-00029600—Memorandum from General Military Intelligence Directorate to presidential secretariat (no. D1.S3/D2), 7 August 1990. (FOUO)

Harmony document folder ISGP-2003-00029600—Memorandum from General Military Intelligence Directorate (Southern Zone Intelligence Branch) to the Secretary, President's Office, 4 August 1990. (FOUO)

Harmony document folder ISGP-2003-00029600—Memorandum from General Military Intelligence Directorate (Southern Zone Intelligence Branch) to the Secretary, President's Office, 4 August 1990. (FOUO)

Harmony document folder ISGP-2003-00029963—Memoranda from Commander Unit 999 to Director General Military Intelligence Directorate, 3 and 4 February 1991. (FOUO)

Harmony document folder ISGP-2003-00029963—Memorandum from air force and air defense command (D1/District 3) to General Military Intelligence Directorate, 2 February 1991. (FOUO)

Harmony document folder ISGP-2003-00029963—Memorandum from General Military Intelligence Directorate to army chief of staff (S1/Dpt/19/18), 3 February 1991. (FOUO)

Harmony document folder ISGP-2003-00030181—Study on the Role of the Iraqi Air Force and Air Defense Command in Confronting the American Attack (classified Iraqi top secret and personal), 1991. (FOUO)

Harmony document folder ISGP-2003-00031468—Study entitled "Role of the Air Force and Air Defense in the Mother of All Battles," 5 October 1991. (FOUO)

Harmony document folder ISGP-2003-00031515—Intelligence reports regarding Coalition movements, November 1990. (FOUO)

Harmony document folder ISGP-2003-00031773—General Military Intelligence Directorate memorandum from 1st Directorate to 19th Section, 14 February 1991. (FOUO)

Harmony document folder ISGP-2003-00031773—Memorandum from 19th Section to Section director General Military Intelligence Directorate, 16 February 1991. (FOUO)

Harmony document folder ISGP-2003-00031842—Study on Evacuation and Concealing Disassembled Aircraft, 5 August 1999. (FOUO)

Harmony document folder ISGP-2003-00032772—Iraqi map showing location of Coalition forces, 25 November 1990. (FOUO)

Harmony document folder ISGP-2003-00033136—Role of the General Military Intelligence Directorate in Um Al-Ma'arik Battle and in controlling riots (Iraqi top secret), 15 July 2001. (FOUO)

Harmony document folder ISGP-2003-00033219—Intelligence Report from General Military Intelligence Directorate (D1/Section 19/8) to presidential secretary, 23 January 1991. (FOUO)

Harmony document folder ISGP-2003-00033219—Intelligence report from General Military Intelligence Directorate to presidential secretary (Directorate 1 Section 19/1584), 12 February 1991. (FOUO)

Harmony document folder ISGP-2003-00033219—Intelligence Report from General Military Intelligence Directorate to Presidential Secretary (Directorate 1/1641), 18 February 1991. (FOUO)

Harmony document folder ISGP-2003-00033219—Memorandum no. 128441 from Director General Military Intelligence Directorate to Secretary, President's Office, 29 August 1990. (FOUO)

Harmony document folder ISGP-2003-00033219 contains a copy of memorandum 1641. (FOUO)

Harmony document folder ISGP-2003-00033248—"Telegrams, Memorandum, and Reports of Intelligence Information by Various Sources," August and September 1990. (FOUO)

Harmony document folder ISGP-2003-00033248—Memorandum from Director General Military Intelligence Directorate to presidential secretary, Subject: An American-Israeli Plan (140/D/3/1/3/2606), 7 August 1990. (FOUO)

Harmony document folder ISGP-2003-00033248—Memorandum from Director of the Intelligence Center (General Military Intelligence Directorate) to the presidential secretary (AS Center/1555798) and attachment, 7 September 1990. (FOUO)

Harmony document folder ISGP-2003-00033248—Memorandum from Director General Military Intelligence Directorate to presidential secretary,

Subject: "Organization and Armament of the Nuclear Units in the American Armed Forces (Intelligence Center/157091)," 9 September 1990. (FOUO)

Harmony document folder ISGP-2003-00033503—General Military Intelligence Directorate correspondence with III Corps Headquarters, 20 August 1990. (FOUO)

Harmony document folder ISGP-2003-00033524—General Military Intelligence Directorate and III Corps correspondence on al-Khafji, 24 January 1991. (FOUO)

Harmony document folder ISGP-2003-00033524—Iraqi III Corps Intelligence Staff Intelligence Report on Al-Khafji region and South Rajiyah Station, 24 January 1991. (FOUO)

Harmony document folder ISGP-2003-00035810—Intelligence estimates in the case of a war with Kuwait, ca. 1994. (FOUO)

Harmony document folder ISGP-2003-00036936—General Military Intelligence Directorate Mother of all Battles analysis, 11 June 1991. (FOUO)

Harmony document folder ISGP-2003-00036959—Director of the Western Region Intelligence Directorate (Section 1/Division 5/31/531) to General Military Intelligence Directorate, 27 January 1990. (FOUO)

Harmony document folder ISGP-2003-00037278—Collection of Intelligence Reports, 1 March 1991. (FOUO)

Harmony document folder ISGP-2003-00037981—Aerial Photograph of Saudi Arabian Naval Base, July 1990. (FOUO)

Harmony document folder ISGP-2003-00038232—Aerial Photograph of Kuwait City, July 1990. (FOUO)

Harmony document folder ISGP-2003-00038233—Iraqi Air Force reconnaissance imagery of Kuwait City, 11 July 1990. (FOUO)

Harmony document folder ISGP-2003-00038256—An intelligence report by the Iraq Air Intelligence Directorate about the Kuwait International Airport, 11 July 1990. (FOUO)

Harmony document folder ISGP-2003-00038432—Memorandum from air force and air defense commander to the presidency of the republic, Subject "Dispersion Measures," no. Center/3, 26 January 1991. (FOUO)

Harmony document folder ISGP-2003-00038521—Aerial Photo of Raas al-Khafji Town, 18 August 1990. (FOUO)

Harmony document folder ISGP-2003-00038524—Aerial Photograph of Kuwaiti Desalinization Plant, July 1990. (FOUO)

Harmony document folder ISGP-203-00029600—Intelligence reports on the war against Kuwait, 15 January 1991. (FOUO)

Harmony document folder ISGQ-2003-00023414—Collection of General Military Intelligence Directorate and Foreign Affairs memoranda on Iraqi aircraft in Iran between April and November 1991. (FOUO)

Harmony document folder ISGQ-2003-00038432—Order from Saddam to all ministers concerning preserving equipment, 22 January 1991. (FOUO)

Harmony document folder ISGQ-2003-00044897—Transcript of a meeting between Saddam and the Yemeni president, 4 August 1990. (FOUO)

Harmony document folder ISGQ-2003-00045740—Iraqi transcript of a meeting between Saddam Hussein and the Soviet delegation, 6 October 1990. (FOUO)

Harmony document folder ISGQ-2003-00046018—"Partial Daily Journal of the Commander of Iraqi Missile Forces"—part 1, ca. 1991. (FOUO)

Harmony document folder ISGQ-2003-00046019—"Partial Daily Journal of the Commander of Iraqi Missile Forces"—part 2, ca. 1991. (FOUO)

Harmony document folder ISGQ-2003-00046032—A Report of the Gulf War cease-fire situation, ca. 1994. (FOUO)

Harmony document folder ISGQ-2003-00046033—Portion of official Iraqi history of 1991 war, ca. 1995. (FOUO)

Harmony document folder ISGQ-2003-00046040—History of Republican Guard Battles, undated. (FOUO)

Harmony document folder ISGQ-2003-00049397—Documentation on the events of the 1990 Iraqi Invasion of Kuwait, 25 September 1992. (FOUO)

Harmony media file ISGQ-2003-00054592 – al-Khafji battle in the III Corps Sector, ca. 1999. (FOUO)

Harmony document folder ISGQ-2003-00055154—al-Bakr University, "concept sketch for al-Khafji," undated. (FOUO)

Harmony document folder ISGQ-2003-00055358—Air Defense Command Attack Report 8 April 2003 (0600-1600) (Memorandum #191), 8 April 2003. (FOUO)

Harmony document folder ISGQ-2003-00072723—Correspondence Concerning Emergency Evacuation Plan in Case of Nuclear Attack, 29 December 1990. (FOUO)

Harmony document folder ISGQ-2003-00300189—Memorandum from Director Iraqi Intelligence Service to the Secretary of the Office of the President (Iraqi top secret-personal), no. 425/k, 18 January 1993. (FOUO)

Harmony document folder ISGQ-2004-00257858—Memorandum from Director, General Military Intelligence Directorate to Deputy Chief of the Revolutionary Command Council, Reference 689, 5 November 1990. (FOUO)

Harmony document folder ISGQ-2005-00026011—25th Infantry Division Camel Based Re-supply Plan, 28 January 1991. (FOUO)

Harmony document folder ISGQ-2005-00031849—IIS Memoranda on a Proposal by Pakistani Scientist Dr. Abd al-Qadir Khan, 6 October 1990. (FOUO)

Harmony document folder ISGQ-2005-00116330—Ministry of Defense Memorandum, no. 41184, Subject: "Arab Volunteer Section Participation," 29 September 1990. (FOUO)

Harmony document folder ISGZ-2004-00028216—Correspondence between IIS and Organization of Friendship, Peace, and Solidarity on Iraqi delegations, 18 February 2003. (FOUO)

Harmony document folder ISGZ-2004-001472—Letter from Barzan Ibrahim al-Tikriti to Saddam Hussein, 4 September 1989. (FOUO)

Harmony document folder ISGZ-2004-022906—Heroic Acts by Members of Unit 999, August 1991. (FOUO)

Harmony document folder ISGZ-2004-026434—Collection of Photographs of Saddam Hussein on Different Occasions, between 1987 and 2002. (FOUO)

Harmony document folder ISGZ-2005-000080—Directorate of General Security, Evaluation of Participation in Um al-Ma'arik, Colonel Muhhammad, ca. 1991. (FOUO)

Harmony document folder ISGZ-2005-000080—Report of the Capture of a Coalition Soldier near ar-Ramadi, ca. 1991. (FOUO)

Harmony document folder ISGZ-2005-601477—Collection of photos of Saddam Hussein, ca. 1991. (FOUO)

Harmony document folder IST-A5053-002—General Command of the Armed Forces, "Orders and Instructions" log, reference letter no. 1029, 15 October 1990. (FOUO)

Harmony document folder IST-A5053-002—General Command of the Armed Forces, "Orders and Instructions" log, reference letter no. 6033, 10 November 1990. (FOUO)

Harmony document folder IST-A5053-002—General Command of the Armed Forces, "Orders and Instructions" log, reference letter no. 184, 6 January 1991. (FOUO)

Harmony document folder IST-A5053-002—General Command of the Armed Forces, "Orders and Instructions" log, reference letter no. 315, 9 January 1991. (FOUO)

Harmony document folder IZSP-2003-00300910—General Military Intelligence Directorate memorandum from Iraqi Embassy, Amman, Jordan, 16 February 1991. (FOUO)

Harmony document folder IZSP-2003-00300910—Memorandum from Director General Military Intelligence Directorate to presidential office, 5 February 1991. (FOUO)

Harmony document folder IZSP-2003-00300910—Memorandum from Director General Military Intelligence Directorate to presidential office, Subject: "Pakistan Intelligence Stand," 5 February 1991. (FOUO)

Harmony document folder IZSP-2003-00300910—Memorandum from director General Military Intelligence Directorate to president, Subject: "Summary of the Suggested Deception Plan," 5 February 1991. (FOUO)

Harmony document folder NGIC-96-0404—Lecture: The Preemptive Attack and the Spoiling Attack, 20 July 1985. (FOUO)

Harmony document folder NGIC-96-0528—Kadhima Forces Command Operations Order no. 4, 24 November 1990. (FOUO)

INDEX

aircraft carriers, 146–47

Al Capone theory of international relations, 53–54

Algeria, 104, 224

ammunition conservation policy, 186–87

amphibious operations, 134–36, 178, 199, 223

Arab Cooperation Council (ACC), 42

Arab fighter program, 156–59

Arab League, 32–33, 103

Arab nation: defense of Iraq by, 224; illegitimate leaders, 33; Iranian threat to unity of, 37–38; Kuwait invasion and unity of, 54–57, 93–95, 104–5; Kuwait invasion reactions, 103–5; unity goal of Saddam, 32–36, 104–5; as unreliable partners, 299–300; warfighting experience of, 36

Arafat, Yasser, 50–52

Ayyubi, Hazim Abd al-Razzaq al-, 149–51, 182, 183, 184, 192, 193, 198, 211, 230, 292–93

Aziz, Tariq: Bagdad Summit resolutions, 32–33; international reaction to invasion, 108–12; U.S. conspiracy against Iraq, 48; U.S. political system, analysis of, 304–5; U.S. reaction to invasion, 114–15; U.S. thinking, assessment of, 162–63; withdrawal negotiations, 214, 218

Ba'ath party, 33, 247, 262

Begin, Menacham, 32

bin Sultan, Khaled, 14

biological weapons. *See* weapons of mass destruction (WMD)

Bush, George H. W.: cease-fire declaration, 241, 243; declaration of end of war, 9; election loss by, 304–5; hostage situation, 106; Kuwait liberation from Iraqi invasion, 1; message from Saddam following Kuwait invasion, 95–96; reaction to Kuwait invasion, 108; withdrawal negotiations, 215

Camp David Peace Accords, 32, 34

chemical weapons. *See* weapons of mass destruction (WMD)

Coalition forces: activity of, goal of, 247–49, 276–77; activity of, prewar, 179–80; activity of, speculation about, 172–73, 187–89, 198–99, 206–8; air attacks of, defense against, 130, 132–34; air attacks of, impact of, 186–87, 287–88; aircraft carriers, 146–47; amphibious operations, 134–36, 178, 199, 223; anti-missile operations, 192; assessment of threat of, 126–30, 131; at al-Khafji, 14, 16, 22, 23–24, 25, 26, 290; at al-Khafji, determination of, 18, 197; losses of, 26, 274–75, 277; plans of, capture of, 226–27; ships, attacks against, 222–23

communications, radio, 177–78, 231–32

conspiracy theories, 42, 43, 47–52, 53, 63, 218, 247–48, 290, 291, 308
critical analysis, xxi

Decisive Year declaration, 176
Duri, Izzat Ibrahim al-, 53, 112, 117–18, 158, 159–60

Egypt, 2, 32, 34, 104, 158
elephant, year of the, 40–41
Europe, 41–42

Fahd, King, 47
Faylakah Island, 73, 74, 75, 77, 78, 219
fedayeen operations, 151, 156–59
Fedayeen Saddam, 151
Firdos command post bunker, al-, 4, 205, 206
France: Gulf War operations, 219, 220; hostage situation, 107, 108; policies toward Iraq, 41; reaction to Kuwait invasion, 111–13; support for campaign against Iraq, 2

Germany, 3
Glaspie, April, 49
Gorbachev, Mikhail, 109, 111, 213–18
Great Britain, 2
Gulf War. *See* Persian Gulf War

Hamdani, Ra'ad: air campaign effects on, 187, 202; ground defense plans, 144; Kuwait invasion operations, 82–88; Kuwait invasion planning, 61–65, 66–67, 69–70; Kuwait occupation, chaos during, 101–2; Kuwait occupation, Kuwaitis exodus during, 99–100; Kuwait occupation, lawlessness during, 100–101; preparations for war, 180–81

Hasan, Gha'ib, 72–73
history and historical perspective, xix–xxiii, 307–9
hostage situation, 106–8
Hussein, Saddam: air campaign, 4, 181–82, 183–84, 185; air campaign analysis, 277–80; air campaign, defense against, 130, 132; air campaign defense plans, 133–34; aircraft evacuation to Iran, 192–93; Arab unity goal of, 32–36, 104–5; Arab unity goal of, Iranian threat to, 37–38; assassination threat to, 42–43; Coalition activity, speculation about, 223; confidence of, 94–96, 302–3; conspiracy against by U.S., 48–52; coup concerns of, 233–34; decision-making style of, 53, 262; disdain for U.S., 108; ground campaign analysis, 284–86; ground campaign reaction, 212–13; ground defense plans, 140; hostage situation, 107–8; Israeli policy toward Iraq, 39–40; al-Khafji battle, 14, 17–18, 27; al-Khafji battle lessons, 288–89; Kuwait defense plan, 125–26, 129; Kuwait invasion decision, 53–54; Kuwait invasion planning, 62, 63; Kuwait invasion reactions, 93–96; Kuwait occupation, looting during, 98–99, 102–3; Kuwait policy, 38–39; Kuwait withdrawal, 5–6, 7, 229–31, 236–38; Kuwait withdrawal negotiations, 213–19; lessons learned conference participation, 263–64; lessons learned from Gulf War, 299–304; message to Bush following Kuwait invasion, 95–96; military officers, lack of initiative of, 267–68; military

strategy abilities of, 15, 27; military threats, assessment of, 266; missile systems, 195; morale of Iraqis, 240; as pen of history, 31; performance of Iraqi forces, 220–21, 224, 270; postwar view, 264–68; preparations for war, 175–80; speech explaining Coalition attack, 220; success of Gulf War, 11; Um Al-Ma'arik, 249; uprisings, explanation of, 247–49; U.S. collapse, prediction of, 301–2; U.S. confrontation, prediction of, 300–301; U.S. political system, analysis of, 304–5; vision of history and his role, 31, 262; warfighting experience of Arabs, 36; win-by-not-losing strategy, 162; WMD use, 152, 154–55; worldview of, 307–9; year of the elephant, 40–41; Zionist enemy, 34–35, 36

Iran: Arab unity goal, threat to, 37–38; Decisive Year declaration, 176; Iranian revolution, 36–37; Iraq, animosity toward, 36–37; Iraq, relationship with, 105–6; Iraqi Air Force evacuation to, 192–93, 194, 280; Iraqi Navy evacuation to, 195–96; reaction to Kuwait invasion, 105–6; Saddam's analysis of, 303; WMD use against, 153

Iran-Iraq War: damage to Iraq from, 41, 60; Decisive Year declaration, 176; events leading to, 36–39; Iraqi Air Force evacuation, 280; lessons learned from, 66; prisoners from, 105; Qadissiya, al-, battle, 17

Iraq: Arab unity role of, 33, 36; citizens, arming of, 224; civil defense preparations, 163; conspiracies against, 42,

43, 47–52, 53, 63, 218, 247–48, 290, 291, 308; flag, changes to, 179; Gulf War, assessment prior to start of, 159–63; Gulf War, damage from, 4, 9, 247; history of, Saddam as pen of, 31; Iran, relationship with, 36–37, 105–6; Iran-Iraq War, damage from, 41, 60; Israeli policy toward, 39–40; Israeli threat to, 71–72; negotiations with Kuwait and oil prices, 52–53; negotiations with Kuwait, failure of, 69–70; nuclear facility, air raid on, 70, 71; regional enemies vs. far enemy, 161, 162; as regional power, 302–4; uprisings, 9, 246–49; U.S. threat to, 42–43; wartime debts, 41, 47, 53; WMD threat to, 153–54; WMD use against, 151

Iraqi Air Force (IAF): air defense plans, 144–49; aircraft evacuation to Iran, 192–93, 194, 280; disassembly doctrine, 280–81; Kuwait invasion operations, 71–72, 78–80; losses during Gulf War, 203–4, 270–71, 272, 274; losses during Iran-Iraq War, 70; performance of, xxiii, 177, 269–80; Ras Tanura terminal mission, 189–91; reconnaissance missions, 71; repositioning equipment, 187; reputation of, 70; strength of, 61, 70

Iraqi forces: ammunition conservation policy, 186–87; army aviation, 80–81, 87; buildup of, 125–26; fight-in-the-cities directive, 233; ground order of battle, 204; military officers, lack of initiative of, 267–68; morale of, 21, 26–27, 175–76, 185–86, 202–3, 208, 240, 267, 268; performance of, 7, 173–75; preparations for war, 173–80; as prisoners, 221;

radio communications, 177–78, 231–32; reputation after Kuwait occupation, 87–88; strength of, 61; success of Gulf War, 11, 227–28, 239; surrender of, 221; vacation schedules, 175–76; withdrawal of, 3, 5–6, 7–8, 227–39, 283–84. *See also* Iraqi Air Force (IAF); Iraqi Navy; Popular Army, Iraqi; Regular Army, Iraqi; Republican Guard, Iraqi; surface-to-surface missile corps, Iraqi

Iraqi Navy: evacuation to Iran, 195–96; Gulf War operations, 222–23; Kuwait defense plan, 134–36; Kuwait invasion operations, 73–78; Kuwait invasion planning, 72–73; mines, 134, 135, 178–79; performance of, 176–77; strength of, 61

Israel: air raid on Iraqi nuclear facility, 70, 71; attack threat from Iraq, 160–61; Camp David Peace Accords, 32, 34; destruction of as Saddam's goal, 32, 34–35; Iraq policy, 39–40; missile attacks on, 185, 192, 199–200, 205, 206; missile attacks on, lessons from, 290–92; missile targets in, 149, 150, 290–91; reaction to Kuwait invasion, 95; Saddam's analysis of, 300, 302; strengthening of, 41; threat to Iraq from, 71–72; war against, 34–35, 36; warfighting experience of, 36; withdrawal from Palestinian territory, 104, 109, 214, 302; WMD threat to, 151, 152, 155; as Zionist enemy, 34–35, 36; Zionist war theory, 291–92

Jalio, Saed, 75, 77
Jasim, Latif Nayyif, 37, 39, 118
Jordan, 104, 302

Kamil, Husayn, 93, 154–55
Kari system, 4
Khafji, al-: attack by Iraqis, 5, 20–23; capture by Iraqis, 5, 23–25, 196–97; Coalition air attacks, 22, 23–24, 25, 26; Coalition forces, determination of, 18, 197; Coalition forces in, 14, 16; duration of operations, 24, 25; evacuation of, 5, 14; lessons learned from, 197, 269, 288–90; losses during, 22, 24, 26, 197; mission of battle, 16; morale of Iraqis, 21, 26–27; planning for battle, 14–20; strategic significance, 27; success of Iraqi forces, 14–15, 26–27, 197; withdrawal from, 25–26

Kuwait: air bases in, 66, 71; Iranian policy toward, 39; Iraqi policy toward, 38–39; islands off of, 73, 74, 77–78, 219; liberation of, 9; naval bases, 73, 74, 76–77, 78; negotiations with Iraq and oil prices, 52–53; negotiations with Iraq, failure of, 69–70; oil facilities, 225–26; policies toward Iraq, 47; as traitor, 32

Kuwait, invasion of: air operations, 78–81; decision to invade, 53–57; defense plan against Iraq, 82; ground operations, 81–88; hostage situation, 106–8; intelligence about, 64–65, 66–67, 71; as internal affair, 93; naval operations, 73–78; planning for, 60–70, 72–73; reaction to, 1–3, 93–96, 103–18, 124–26; as unity achieved, 93–95; as unity goal, 54–57, 104–5

Kuwait, occupation and defense of: air defense, 144–49; chaos during, 99–102; Coalition air attacks, defense against, 130, 132–34; Coalition military reactions, assessment of threat of, 126–30, 131; counterinsurgency techniques, 97–98; fedayeen operations, 151, 156–59; ground defense, 137–44; Kuwaiti exodus during, 99–100, 102; Kuwaiti resistance activities, 96–97, 98, 101; lawlessness during, 87–88, 100–101; looting during, 98–99, 102–3; naval defense, 134–37; "special weapons", 150, 151–56; surface-to-surface missile forces, 149–51; withdrawal from, 3, 5–6, 7–8, 227–39, 283–84; withdrawal from, conditions for, 205–6; withdrawal negotiations, 213–19

Kuwait Air Force, 71, 78–80, 81, 82

Kuwait City: drive to liberate, 6; intelligence about, 66–67; invasion of, 83–88; invasion planning, 65; urban defense operations, 137

Kuwait ground forces, 82–83, 86–87

Kuwait Navy, 73–78

Lebanon, 52, 104

lessons learned by Iraqis: air campaign, 269–81; conferences to analyze and gather lessons, 262–64; ground campaign, 281–88; al-Khafji battle, 197, 269, 288–90; lack of development of, 267; military leadership weaknesses, 268–69; negative points, documentation of, 269; Saddam's view of, 299–304

Libya, 38, 104, 195, 303

Mahmaud, Salah Aboud, 17–18, 21, 22, 25

Majid, Ali Hassan al- (Chemical Ali): ammunition conservation policy,

186–87; helicopter losses during Kuwait invasion, 81; IAF performance during Kuwait invasion, 80; Kuwaiti oil facilities, 225–26; Kuwaiti resistance activities, 96–97; operations in Kuwait following invasion, 93; recommendations about Kuwait, 96–97; retreat battles, 231

Mauritania, 104, 224

mines, naval, 134, 135, 178–79

missile forces. See surface-to-surface missile corps, Iraqi

Mubarak, Hosni, 52, 55

Muhammed, Husayn Rashid, 16, 129–30, 229–30, 286, 287

Mustafa, Muzahim, 73, 75–76, 77, 78

Nasser, Gamal Abdel, 34, 36, 39, 55

Nimeiry, Muhammad Gaafur al-, 33

nuclear facilities, 70, 71, 182

nuclear weapons, 152–54

oil: burning to obscure targets, 132; facilities for, 74, 225–26; price of, 52–53; smoke from, effects of, 271; as weapon (Project Tariq), 136–37, 179, 182–83, 210, 211, 219

Operation Desert Storm (Gulf War). See Persian Gulf War

Palestine: fedayeen operations, 158; fratricidal warfare, 156; Iraqi support for, 51, 157; long-term solution for, 302; withdrawal of Israel from, 104, 109, 214, 302

Palestinian Liberation Organization (PLO), 38, 104, 126, 206

Persian Gulf States, 37, 104

Persian Gulf War: air campaign, 3–5, 180–97; air campaign, analysis of,

269–80; assessment by Iraq prior to start of, 159–63; cease-fire declaration and negotiations, 239–46; civil defense preparations prior to, 163; civilian losses, 4, 205, 206; Coalition activity, speculation about, 172–73, 187–89, 198–99, 206–8, 223; Coalition plan, capture of, 226–27; deception plans, 199, 200, 208–9; denial of war possibility, 162–63, 180; events leading to, 1–3; goal of, 247–49, 276–77; ground campaign, 5–9, 208–27; ground campaign analysis, 281–88; ground campaign preparations, 205, 206–7; history of, Coalition vs. Iraqi, 266–67; losses during, 26, 203–4, 224, 270–71, 272, 274–75, 277; missile attacks, 184–85, 198, 199–200, 205, 206, 210; perspectives on, 9, 11; postwar view, 264–68; preparations for, 173–80; suicide attacks, 222–23; withdrawal negotiations, 210–11, 213–19; withdrawal of Iraqi forces, 3, 5–6, 7–8, 227–39. *See also* Khafji, al-; lessons learned by Iraqis

Popular Army, Iraqi, 100, 102, 125

Powell, Colin, 1, 3

Primakov, Yevgeny, 109, 110, 112, 214, 218

Project 17, 63, 72

Qaddafi, Muammar al-, 104, 303

Qadissiya, al-, battle, 17

Qatar, 211

radio communications, 177–78, 231–32

Ramadan, Taha: assessment of war prior to start, 160, 161; Bush's election

loss, 304; international reaction to invasion, 111, 113; looting of Kuwait, 99; Security Council resolutions, 113; U.S. collapse, prediction of, 302; U.S. political system, analysis of, 304; U.S. reaction to invasion, 115–16

Rawi, Aayad Futayyih Khalifa al-, 60, 88, 133, 154

red teaming, xxii–xxiii

Regular Army, Iraqi: army aviation, 80–81, 87, 276; buildup of, 125, 126; Coalition drive against, 6; destruction of, 9; ground defense plans, 141–42; ground order of battle, 204; strength of, 61; withdrawal of, 7–8, 233–34, 283–84

Republican Guard, Iraqi: Adnan Division, 66; air campaign effects on, 187, 269; attack of by Kuwait Air Force, 78; Baghdad Division, 66, 87; buildup of, 125, 126; cease-fire, view of, 241; Coalition drive against, 6; coordination between IAF and, 80; defensive position of, 125; destruction of, 7–8; ground defense plans, 142–44; ground order of battle, 204; Hammurabi Division, 62–65, 81–86, 87; Kuwait invasion operations, 81–88; Kuwait invasion planning, 62–70; lessons learned conference, 262–63, 281–84; Medina Armored Division, 66, 86; morale of, 208; Nebuchadnezzar Division, 86; performance of, 220–21, 300; reputation after Kuwait occupation, 87–88; sanctuary for, 9; Seventy-Three Easting, Battle of, 8, 235–36; strength of, 61; Tawakalna Division, 7, 8, 65–

66, 235–36; withdrawal of, 7, 229, 233–34, 238–39, 283–84

Revolutionary Command Council (RCC), 52–53, 205–6

Ruq'I, al-, 18

Sadat, Anwar, 32, 33, 34

Saudi Arabia: Arab unity role of, 33; Iraqi attack plans for, 16; maps of, 127; missile attacks on, 192, 205; missile targets in, 150, 290–91; pact with Iraq, 47; reaction to Kuwait invasion, 95, 104; staging ground for campaign against Iraq, 2–3; as traitor, 32

Sawadi, Hasan, 73

Schwarzkopf, H. Norman: advance against Iraqi defenses, 7; book written by, 266–67; cease-fire negotiations, 245–46; al-Khafji battle, 14, 27; Kuwait liberation from Iraqi invasion, 3

Seventy-Three Easting, Battle of, 8, 235–36

smoke and dust, effects of, 271

Soviet Union: reaction to Kuwait invasion, 108–11, 112; threat to Iraq from, 42; weakened position of, 41, 52; withdrawal negotiations, 210–11, 213–19

Sudan, 104, 158

suicide attacks, 222–23

suicide volunteers, 158

surface-to-surface missile corps, Iraqi, 149–51, 184–85, 195, 198, 199–200, 205, 206, 210, 290–93

Syria: Arab unity role of, 33; fedayeen operations, 158; missile technology, 195; reaction to Kuwait invasion, 104; support for campaign against Iraq, 2; as unreliable partners, 38; U.S. negotiations with, 302; withdrawal from Lebanon, 104

Tariq Project, 136–37, 179, 182–83, 210, 211, 219

Thatcher, Margaret, 1

Tikriti, Barzan Ibrahim al-, 41–43, 152

Tikriti, Sabawi Ibrahim Hasan al-, 86–87, 93, 97–98

totalitarian states, xxii, 268, 308–9

Tunisia, 104, 224

Um Al-Ma'arik, 249

United Nations (UN): postwar inspection teams, 293; sanctions following Iraqi invasion of Kuwait, 3; Security Council resolutions, 106, 113; Security Council resolution 598, 105; Security Council resolution 660, 103–4, 113, 205–6, 232; Security Council resolution 678, 113, 159, 162, 163; Security Council resolution 687, 293; Security Council resolution to crush U.S. forces, 163; U.S. control of, 108

United States: assessment of thinking of prior to war, 162–63; collapse of, prediction of, 301–2; confrontation with, prediction of, 300–301; conspiracy against Iraq, 47–52; control of UN by, 108; political system of, analysis of, 304–5; reaction to Kuwait invasion, 95–96, 114–18; regional strength, gain of, 41; removal of from Arab region, 35; threat to Iraq from, 42–43; WMD threat from, 153–54 uprisings, 9, 246–49

Wafra, al-, 21, 22, 24
weapons of mass destruction (WMD):
dispersal of, 155–56; failure to use,
156; Iraqi-Israeli verbal battle over,
72; "special weapons", 150, 151–56;
threat of U.S. use of, 153–54; threat
to Israel from, 151, 152, 155; use
against Iran, 151, 153

win-by-not-losing strategy, 162, 269,
309
worldview of adversaries, 307–9

year of the elephant, 40–41
Yemen, 104, 163, 224

Zionist enemy. *See* Israel
Zionist war theory, 291–92

ABOUT THE AUTHOR

Kevin M. Woods is an analyst with the Institute for Defense Analyses. He previously served as an officer in the U.S. Army in numerous worldwide operational assignments, retiring as a lieutenant colonel in 2004. A resident of Northern Virginia, he is also the coauthor of a companion volume on the 2003 Gulf War.